PEARSON

ALWAYS LEARNING

Intercultural Relations

Communication, Identity, and Conflict

Gary Weaver, Ph.D.
Professor and Executive Director of the Intercultural
Management Institute
School of International Service
American University
Washington, DC

Cover Art: *Courtesy of Pearson Learning Solutions.*

Copyright © 2014, 2013, 2001 by Pearson Learning Solutions
All rights reserved.

This copyright covers material written expressly for this volume by the editor/s as well as
the compilation itself. It does not cover the individual selections herein that first appeared
elsewhere. Permission to reprint these has been obtained by Pearson Learning Solutions for
this edition only. Further reproduction by any means, electronic or mechanical, including
photocopying and recording, or by any information storage or retrieval system, must be
arranged with the individual copyright holders noted.

All trademarks, service marks, registered trademarks, and registered service marks are the
property of their respective owners and are used herein for identification purposes only.

Pearson Learning Solutions, 501 Boylston Street, Suite 900, Boston, MA 02116
A Pearson Education Company
www.pearsoned.com

Printed in the United States of America

10   16

000200010271788838

EEB/SK

ISBN 10: 1-269-61617-X
ISBN 13: 978-1-269-61617-1

Table of Contents

SECTION IV: CROSS-CULTURAL ADAPTATION 135

Acknowledgments

For over a decade the most recent version of the anthology *Culture, Communication and Conflict: Readings in Intercultural Relations* was used in courses at over 35 universities and read by professionals in the field of intercultural management, education, and training. However, some of the 69 articles were outdated and many were available over the Internet. The book was an intercultural relations handbook or encyclopedia of sorts but modern information technology and a rapidly changing world overtook its usefulness. It was time for a new book.

Frankly, the price for the anthology had ratcheted up so much that it was too expensive for many students and practitioners. This is true of many textbooks today. There was a need for a book that was up-to-date, conceptually rich, and yet affordable. It had to be academically sound but also written in everyday language in a way to make it useful for scholars and people engaged in the practice of intercultural communication.

This book was a result of years of discussion and collaboration among faculty and students at American University (AU). It is impossible to list everyone who spent endless hours suggesting revisions, editing rough drafts, sending me articles to review, and encouraging me as this book evolved. In addition, friends in this field from around the world gave me vital information to help me to be as thorough and accurate as possible. Many have been in this field since it first began.

My colleagues who teach cross-cultural communications in the School of International Service (SIS) and hundreds of current and former students gave invaluable advice as to what concepts ought to be included and reviewed rough drafts. Some faculty spent days reading rough drafts. With the great advice I have received from so many people who are very knowledgeable about this field, any errors or omissions are completely my fault.

There are some individuals who were essential to the publication of this book and continually encouraged me over the years. Jerry Higgins at Pearson Publishing has remained absolutely steadfast in his support even when it was not his responsibility. He has become a great friend and never gave up even when I missed deadlines and was ready to let go of this project.

Dan Deming started out as a teaching assistant who first nagged me about coming out with a new book. He became editor of the *Intercultural Management Quarterly* and director of the Intercultural Management Institute (IMI) before moving on to the Department of State. He is a gifted editor and without him this book would never have moved beyond a few incoherent pages.

I have had some extraordinarily loyal and talented faculty colleagues, teaching assistants, and former students who put in all the hard work of digging up articles, checking citations and facts, and reading through numerous revisions. Robert Kelley, Ryan Dalton, and Marc Hedman read every word and sacrificed their work and personal lives to help me meet deadlines. I am deeply grateful for their careful editing and writing. I am especially indebted to Ryan Dalton at American University for his endless patience and superb editing skills in producing this newest version. Ryan was my graduate assistant and served as the managing editor of the *Intercultural Management Quarterly*. We were joined by Maryvel Firda and Ellen Browne at Pearson. This revision team made corrections, improved the format and illustrations, and selected a new cover design that is more appropriate to this text. Many thanks for the vast improvements that were made.

I'm sure I've omitted some colleagues and friends who helped out. I hope they'll forgive me if their names do not appear in these acknowledgements.

Lastly this book would not have been possible without the unending patience and encouragement of my wife Marte and daughter Alia as they gently pushed me along to complete the manuscript.

SECTION I
WHAT IS CULTURE?

Anthropologist Edward Hall, the "grandfather" of intercultural relations studies, defined culture as communication in his 1958 award-winning book, *The Silent Language*. He found that how we communicate without using words is determined by our culture and we unconsciously learn this "silent language" simply by growing up in a particular culture. We are unaware that the greatest misunderstandings and the primary source of conflict between people of different cultures is often a matter of different meanings given to nonverbal messages that are specific to each culture.

With modern global communications and transportation and the international nature of politics and commerce, almost every organization requires executives and managers who can deal with people of all cultural backgrounds. This is also true within countries due to the steady flow of people across national borders and the domestic growth of multicultural workforces. Understanding other cultures and developing skills for more effective cross-cultural communication is increasingly more important in the culturally interdependent world of today and tomorrow.

This also means that to be well-educated requires cultural and intercultural competence in all academic disciplines and for all professions. Intercultural relations is an applied area of knowledge and skills that is found in diplomacy, political science, medicine, communications, business, and counseling. Almost every diplomat, soldier, law enforcement officer, lawyer, business person, psychologist, teacher, nurse, and medical doctor understands the need to be able to communicate effectively with people of various cultural backgrounds and to understand their values, beliefs, ways of thinking, and worldviews.

Only a few decades ago, few people even used the word "culture" in their everyday discourse. Today, it seems that almost everything is related to culture and cultural differences. There are hundreds of books available with the words "cross-cultural" or "intercultural" in their titles, there are at least a half dozen major journals in this field, hundreds of dissertations have been written about some aspect of intercultural relations, and most universities and colleges have courses in intercultural relations.

With globalization, the increased flow of people across national borders, modern international telecommunications and travel, and the rapidly increasing diversity in all communities, intercultural relations continues to grow as an academic area. There is now a vast and growing amount of research to support practitioners. Anyone who intends to work with people from other cultures is expected to be educated and equipped with the skills to effectively interact with others and to be able to analyze and overcome barriers to cross-cultural communication, adjustment, and conflict.

The first segment of this book begins with an overview of the field of intercultural relations—its evolution as an area of applied academic inquiry, the terminology which is often misused and misunderstood, and consideration of some of the major concepts and scholars. This is a fairly new academic area that is growing very rapidly and thus it is important to realize that definitions are continually changing and new concepts are constantly being introduced. Furthermore, there is a healthy disagreement among scholars and practitioners regarding the nature of the field and many of the issues that are explored by interculturalists.

At the end of each section in this book are a handful of seminal pieces written by scholars and practitioners. In no way are these pieces comprehensive or exhaustive. Hundreds of articles and chapters from books were considered for inclusion and are available in libraries or electronically. These pieces were selected because they illustrate or highlight concepts covered in each section of this book.

WHAT IS CULTURE?

The word "culture" was seldom heard in casual conversation less than two decades ago and it had various confusing meanings. Some thought of culture as "good taste," for others it was art or music, and for many it was something that people in exotic foreign lands had.

Today everyone seems to be talking about culture. Many would even argue that the term is overused and misused to describe any behavior that is shared by a group of people. We now refer to generational cultures, gender cultures, sports cultures, organization cultures, and tech cultures. The term is now routinely used to describe everything from a civilization that extends over thousands of years and includes hundreds of cultures to a small group of people working together in an office.

Among academics in the United States culture was originally an anthropological term used to describe the behavior and customs of people in a particular society—usually one outside the so-called Western world. But because of its recent widespread and informal use, it has nearly lost its academic and professional meaning and many anthropologists no longer write about culture. In the United States, although it is viewed primarily within the purview of social sciences such as anthropology, sociology, linguistics and international relations, the concept of culture is found in almost every field within the curriculum of major universities including the humanities—art, music, history, literature, and so on.

In some languages, culture means art, music, and literature. But a more anthropological definition would find that these are the external manifestations of internal culture. Over time, they become the relics or artifacts of a particular people. We might examine these external aspects of culture to discover the unique system of values, beliefs, and worldviews shared by people within a society. They are the results of culture and certainly give us great insights into the internal culture of any group of people.

Fortunately a common meaning for culture is emerging, and most experts would agree on its basic characteristics. Culture is simply *the way of life of a group of people passed down from one generation to the next through learning*. Culture is not inherited, but instead learned unconsciously during our formative years simply by growing up in a particular family. Most of us will tend to raise our children with the same cultural values conveyed to our parents by our grandparents.

Let us consider three words that are sometimes confused and misused. Although they are often used interchangeably and even as synonyms, they actually describe very different phenomena. The process of acquiring our underlying, native or *primary culture* is termed *enculturation*. We learn this culture informally and tacitly through our interactions with others, who are usually family members, during our first four or five years of life. Learning or adapting to another or *secondary culture* is referred to as *acculturation*. This acquisition of another culture within or outside our own society tends to be more conscious and explicit and can take place at any time. For example, we learn the practices of our religious faith at our church, synagogue, or mosque and go through some ceremony, such as confirmation or a bar mitzvah, that certifies to everyone in the community that we have fully learned the customs, practices, values, and beliefs of our faith and have been accepted as members of this community or secondary culture.

Some individuals grow up overseas in a culture that is different than that of their parents. Until they leave home, they are primarily influenced by the culture of their parents. But as they go to school and interact with local people they acquire the local culture. They may even move from one primary culture to another during their childhood. Thus, they may have multiple primary cultural identities that may even be in conflict with each other. They are bicultural or multicultural.

The primary culture supersedes secondary cultures, which often overlap and are ranked in some sort of hierarchy that continually changes. We are a mixture of many different secondary cultural identities that vary in importance during our lifetime, but the primary culture underlies all others. You might grow up as a member of the Maasai tribe in rural Kenya but later you study at a large university in Philadelphia. Added to your primary culture (Kenyan Maasai) is the university student culture (Temple University student and alumnus) and perhaps an urban, American culture (Philadelphian). However, the values, beliefs, and ways of thinking that you learned in Kenya tend to stay with you the rest of your life.

Assimilation means to be accepted into a culture as a fully participating member of equal status with everyone else.[1] It is granted by the mainstream culture. One may enculturate or acculturate, but the power to assimilate rests in the hands of the dominant culture. In the 1950s, a black American in the deep South might learn all the cultural values and rules of the dominant culture and might behave as any average American in Mississippi or Alabama. Nevertheless, because of discrimination based on racism, he or she might not be treated as equal to everyone else in the society. A white immigrant from Germany could change his name from Schmidt to Smith, change his religious faith from Catholic to Protestant, and gradually eliminate his German accent, and he becomes an "American." The black American may be a third or fourth generation American but is still not as fully assimilated as a first generation immigrant from Germany.[2]

The phrase "way of life" can mean many different things, just as culture means many different things, depending upon your vantage point. We often speak of the "traditional Mexican way of life," "the nomadic way of life," "the Jewish way of life," or "the soldier's way of life." These expressions reflect the idea that people within groups share common courses of conduct, customs, beliefs, perceptions, ways of thinking and solving problems, and values. Our membership in some groups is very long, broad, and deep, such as civilizations or national cultures, while others are short-lived and easily lose their immediate importance, such as being a part of a specific university culture. Our secondary cultures overlap with our primary culture throughout life, and the relative importance or ranking of particular secondary cultures is constantly changing.

We informally or tacitly acquire our primary culture well before adolescence during our formative years as our basic personality is taking shape. The concept of culture has always had a somewhat psychoanalytic meaning, with a heavy emphasis on the importance of its hidden or unconscious aspects. Sigmund Freud would argue that our basic personality is determined during our childhood years as we socialize with family members. Because it is unconsciously learned so early in life, we are usually unaware of its existence and take our own culture for granted until we are surrounded by people who are different.

When we go to other countries to work or live we do not lose our culture by adapting to another culture. At that time, we contrast and compare our own culture with theirs and thereby become more consciously aware of our own. Similar to the psychoanalytic phenomenon of realizing how we are embedded or trapped in traumatic childhood experiences that were long forgotten or "repressed" in the unconscious mind, when we enter another culture we also raise our internal culture to conscious awareness. The irony is that the way to find your culture is to leave it and interact with people from another culture.[3] Of course, you need not go overseas to experience this self-awareness. In many countries there are numerous ethnic, racial, and religious neighborhoods or regions. Unfortunately, very often people avoid interacting with people from other cultures, even within their own country.

Culture is an abstraction—a concept or idea. It is not something concrete or tangible. We can't see it or touch it, but we know it exists because people from the same society have roughly the same customs or behavior, basic beliefs and values, and ways of viewing the world. Culture causes this to happen. As with any abstraction, there are many ways of describing and explaining the concept.

We know of the existence of culture through deductive logic and inference. The same is true for another abstract concept: personality. We can't see a personality or touch it, yet we know it exists and that it describes the characteristic behavior of a person. Culture and personality are social constructs. This is why scientific, inductive, quantitative, and positivistic kinds of research are inappropriate when we are doing cross-cultural research. There is nothing tangible to look at or observe that can be directly measured. The same may be true when we are doing research on personality. We infer it exists based upon observed behavior and interaction with another person. We might say that he or she is "outgoing" or very "humble." Not only does that abstract generalization help us to describe and explain behavior, it also allows us to make some tentative predictions as to how the person might act and react in certain social situations.

Just as we cannot explain an individual's behavior without understanding his or her personality, it is virtually impossible to explain the social, economic, or political behavior of a people or a society without first understanding their culture. With this knowledge, we can explain the society's behavior and public policies. We may also be able to anticipate how people in that society would perceive certain situations or respond to certain messages. We can better predict how they will react to what we say or do.

Of course, each of us has a distinct and unique personality that is a result of genetics and our experiences—both nature *and* nurture. One of the significant differences between culture and personality is that culture is entirely a consequence of nurture. No one is born with a culture. We usually acquire it so early in life that it almost seems as if culture is part of our DNA, but it really is learned.

We acquire our culture by growing up in a human community. It is a product of socialization that begins with the family. The social structures and physical environment also play a part. Nomadic and rural people around the globe probably share some similar cultural characteristics. And a person from urban Paris may have more in common with someone from New York City than with a villager in a remote rural area of France.

When we describe someone as an extrovert, we must generalize. We know that there are times and situations when the person may be a bit withdrawn or introverted. But his or her characteristic behavior is that of an extrovert. This generalization allows us to explain and predict an individual's behavior in various social situations.

Personality and culture are inside our heads and both are abstractions, generalizations, and social constructs whose existence is based upon inference.[4] They are not "real" in the sense that mountains or buildings are real. We assume they exist based upon what we can observe. Children's folk stories and the themes of popular literature, art, and music reveal shared values, ways of thinking, beliefs, and worldviews that are characteristic of a particular culture. Although it is very difficult to determine a person's personality, we agree that someone is an "extrovert" because he or she is very outgoing and enjoys interacting with others.

No one would argue that a person is born with a culture. However, it is almost impossible to imagine a human being without some kind of culture. Because it is acquired so early in life and is primarily unconscious, it appears that it is almost biological. For example, scholars of *kinesics*, or body movement, find that we develop a rhythm of moving shortly after birth which is shared with others in our society. This includes how we walk, gesture, and even the cadence of our speech.[5] A playground filled with children running about may appear to be totally chaotic. However, if we film them and slow down the film, we find that their movements are synchronized. As one child jumps up and down on one side of the playground, another does the same dance nearby.[6]

People from New York City find that Caribbean people move very slowly and their speech is almost melodic. On the other hand, people from the Bahamas find that New Yorkers seem to be in a rush and their voices are loud, shrill, and abrasive. The culture of the Bahamas is much more homogeneous than New York City and thus the rhythm is more obvious than in the Big Apple. People who are born and grow up in New York enjoy the rhythm of the city and are quite comfortable with the pace of life.

What is the relationship between biology and learning when it comes to the development of personality? Is personality mostly a matter of biology and genes or is it matter of socialization? Although physiological psychologists would probably emphasize the importance of the brain, genes, and heredity, cognitive psychologists stress the importance of experience. Today, this nature/nurture debate still goes on, but most would agree that it is a matter of both biology and learning.

The culture we acquire during childhood tends to stay with us throughout our life. We humans are born with few, if any, instincts. We literally have to learn to be human and we learn this from our primary culture. We do know of humans who did not grow up in a human culture and therefore took on none of the characteristics we would call "human." Probably the most famous example is Victor, a 12-year-old child found apparently wild in rural France in 1799. He was seen around wolves and acted like an animal. He couldn't speak and he ran on all fours. It was assumed that he had been raised by wolves and he was referred to as the "wolf boy" or "feral child." However, there's no solid evidence that he was ever raised by a wolf. Instead, he was probably abandoned at a very early age by his parents, survived outside a human culture, and consequently never took on the characteristics we would call human.[7]

A vital part of our cultural programming is being socialized to feel that we are not alone, but rather belong to a group. This begins with family and friends with whom we share a common identity and ways of perceiving reality. As we go through life we also become members of a hierarchy of *secondary cultures*. We have a sense of belonging with people within these cultures and we identify with them and share their ways of looking at the world. Although the primary culture becomes the *leitmotif* for our lives, these other cultures are ranked according to their importance at particular times throughout our lifetimes.

In almost every country there is a variety of local or regional cultures. There is also usually a culture that is commonly shared throughout the nation, and this is usually referred to as the "mainstream" or "dominant" culture. There are many ethnic and racial groups in the United States; there are different customs in the rural south and the urban north; and there are certainly regional dialects of English. Nevertheless, English is still the dominant language, and there are many basic values, beliefs, and worldviews that almost all Americans share regardless of their regional or ethnic differences.

Although culture is a generalization, it should never become a stereotype. Culture is a very useful framework for explaining and predicting the characteristic behavior of a group of people, as long as we realize that our descriptions are generalizations. *They can never apply to everyone in every situation all of the time.* As with all generalizations, there are numerous exceptions and if the generalization becomes too sweeping or when there are too many exceptions, we simply discard the generalization. We know that there are many individual differences between people within the same group or society just as each tree in the forest is unique. Nevertheless, we can discuss categories of trees such as maples, oaks, and pines and still acknowledge the singular nature of each individual tree in the forest.

To add to this complexity, no two people belong to exactly the same secondary cultures at exactly the same time, and therefore we are all "culturally unique."[8] We belong to various generational and occupational cultures, different organizational cultures, and even cultural identity groups such as ethnic, religious, or sexual orientation cultures.

A twenty-five year old Bedouin from Saudi Arabia who studied at a university in London might join an American corporation. His primary cultural identity includes being a Bedouin Arab, male, and Muslim. His secondary cultural identities are: graduate of a British university who studied finance and works for an American corporation. He will never lose his primary cultural identity and yet the ranking of his secondary cultural identities change throughout his lifetime. At a corporation meeting, he might explain his point of view on an issue by prefacing his remarks with the phrase, "As a Bedouin Muslim with a British education in corporate finance, I see it this way." This young man has a very unique way of thinking and perceiving reality which he brings to every corporate meeting.

When we are trying to explain why a person from another society behaves as he or she does, we ought to *begin* with the question, "Could this be a matter of culture?" This is a reasonable first guess. It allows us to simplify and focus our search for explanations of behavior. Behavior is not always a matter of culture. Someone's obnoxious, abrasive, and offensive behavior might be peculiar to that individual. There may indeed be a wide array of idiosyncratic reasons for a person's behavior, such as personal background, health, economic stress, and so on. Again, when our cultural generalization is obviously inaccurate or untrue for most people within a group, it is no longer useful for explaining the behavior of an individual and therefore must be discarded.

To illustrate, consider the following true incident. A group of university students were crossing into Canada from the United States during the 1970s. During the routine inspection of their papers and automobile, Canadian immigration officers notified the students that they found a problem with the vehicle's muffler. It was coming loose from the automobile and making too much noise. Nevertheless, after this brief holdup, they were allowed to proceed into Canada.

Immediately after leaving the border crossing, the students engaged in a lively discussion about how they were held up by the white Canadian officials because some of them were black. The officers were deemed racist for harassing the group about the muffler to intentionally delay and perhaps provoke them. There was nothing wrong with their automobile. However, about 20 minutes after driving into Canada, their car's muffler fell off.

When we explain behavior as cultural, we are making a *trait attribution*—it's typical of "those people." This is especially true of negative behavior. However, when "we" engage in the same behavior, we make a *situation attribution*—the circumstances caused the bad behavior. This is what is often referred to as the *fundamental attribution error*. Rather than make a trait or cultural attribution, the cause of the behavior may be situational.

There is an enormous difference between a reasonable and well-founded cultural generalization and a stereotype. When we stereotype people from a culture, we force everyone to fit our characterization or category. There is no room for individual variation or alternative explanations for behavior. Cultural stereotypes are often a result of once accurate generalizations that have become outdated. Furthermore, both positive and negative cultural stereotypes are almost always false or misleading and thus are not useful for understanding others.

Stereotypes are ultimately counterproductive when it comes to interacting with people from other cultures. They amount to inaccurate, and usually negative "rules of thumb." Although they seem to be useful, they actually limit cross-cultural understanding and perpetuate prejudice. We might label an entire group of people as "angry" when, in fact, they tend to avoid smiling at strangers and they might view us as "superficial" or "deceptive" because we smile at everyone. Or based upon meeting one or two people from a particular country, we conclude that everyone in that country is loud and boisterous. The few people we met may have shouted simply because we met them at a noisy party.

It is impossible to discuss culture without generalizing because all behavior then becomes idiosyncratic. We end up denying the very existence of culture. We should continually ask ourselves if our generalizations are reasonable, accurate, and useful. If not, they are stereotypes and must be avoided.

Culture is a social system with many parts and links between the parts. In any social or physical system, if we add, subtract, or change one part, and if we add, subtract, or change one link, we alter the entire system. We can predict the impact of the change produced by the intervention if we know the nature of the system and the balance between the parts and links, the nature of the new change, and how the change is introduced.

An atom is a physical system of electrons, protons, and neutrons in electrical balance. If we insert another electron, we may destroy the atom because it becomes unstable. However, it could simply absorb the new electron and produce a new atom. Or the new electron might be rejected and have no impact whatsoever. If we know the make-up of the atom, the nature of the new electron, and how it is introduced, we can predict what will happen.

In the 1950s, there was great debate in academic circles as to the impact of introducing technology from one culture to another. Some would argue that new technology coming from the developed world would benefit developing countries while others believed the technology would destroy the indigenous cultures. Anthropologist Margaret Mead was commissioned by UNESCO to produce a report to the UN to resolve this disagreement. In her research of various cultures, she found that it all depends upon the nature of the technology, the make-up of the social system, and how the technology is introduced.[9]

In a small village in Australia, an Aborigine family may have one ax to chop wood for the fireplace or for cooking. There are three sons and each must ask the father to use the family ax. What happens if we give every son an ax? It may undermine the authority of the father who, in this society, is the guardian of the ax. Whenever a son requests to use the ax, he communicates respect to his father and acknowledges his role. If we know the symbolic importance of controlling the ax, we can predict that giving an ax to each son will disrupt the social system. Imagine in the United States if three adolescent sons all have keys to the family automobile. If we understand the role of father, sons, and authority in the family, we can anticipate the result of introducing new elements.

MODELS FOR ANALYZING CULTURE

There are various ways of examining culture. For example, we can discuss each culture in terms of its components. We might begin with what we can observe—how people behave or what type of art and literature is most common. People in all cultures eat food and raise their children. However, the types of food they prefer and how the food is prepared and eaten may depend on their culture—the majority of Americans eat hamburgers with their hands. And the ways in which people raise their children tend to be different in each culture.

This examination also allows us to explore *why* people of different cultures behave as they do. The dominant attitudes, values, and beliefs shape or motivate behavior. In some cultures, food is an important aspect of social life—who is invited to one's home to share a meal with the family may depend upon the person's age, gender, or social class. Appropriate table manners are a way of showing respect for others. The underlying explanation for explicit behavior or *external culture* shared by people in a particular culture requires a more in-depth understanding of their common values, beliefs, and worldviews—their *internal culture*. With this knowledge we can explain their behavior. It allows us to answer the question, "Why?" *Why* do they have those customs? *Why* do they view the situation this way?

We can also contrast and compare these hidden aspects of cultures such as their unspoken and implicit traditional or mainstream attitudes, values, beliefs, ways of perceiving reality, types of discourse or interaction, and so forth. One culture may emphasize individualism and independence while another values collectivism and interdependence. In turn, we have a system for analyzing and interpreting their explicit behavior.

When people from different cultures come together there is often misunderstanding and conflict caused by these differences. We can often explain why people from other cultures behave as they do if we have a more comprehensive understanding of their culture. And we can often understand why we behave as we do if we are consciously aware of our own culture. More importantly, we can anticipate where misunderstandings and conflict will take place when we interact with those who are culturally different if we understand the process of intercultural communication.

All social sciences use models to sort through an endless array of data and variables that could explain behavior. In the physical sciences, we can more easily restrict the number of variables we want to consider in study and our theories might be based upon quantifiable data such as mathematical models. However, human behavior is much more complex than a laboratory chemistry experiment and there are thousands of variables that shape behavior. The social sciences are much more subjective and thus we can't even agree on definitions for pride, honor, fear, or aggression and yet we agree that they often lead nations into war.

To simplify our search for the cause of human behavior, we use models which are maps that contain information that we think is useful while eliminating the clutter of data that might not be relevant to our understanding. Thus, models are always incomplete distortions and simplifications of a very complicated reality. If we keep this in mind, we realize the limitations of social science models. Nevertheless, they are essential for understanding human behavior.

We use models and maps every day. Which map we use depends upon what we are trying to understand or accomplish. In New York, to move from one part of the city to another, a subway map might be more useful than a surface map. The above ground data is too complex and filled with simply unnecessary information for getting from point A to point B. If the purpose of the map is just to move around the city easily, the subway map is perfectly appropriate. If the purpose of the map is to help us find each museum or landmark, the surface map may be more useful. Moreover, it is quite probable that we would want to have both maps. Of course, we could always use some kind of GPS instrument in today's world.

When we consider culture, there are various "maps" we can use—linguistics and communications, shared values or ways of thinking, traditions, national identity, and so on. We also could extrapolate from a study of one village to many similar villages around the world. These ethnographic studies are highly deductive rather than inductive and qualitative rather than quantitative. This would be typical of cultural anthropology. They provide great depth of analysis and allow us to put behavior into the context of various aspects of a culture. The scope of the inquiry is very open and we aren't quite sure where the data will lead us.

A more sociological approach would tend to be inductive and qualitative and a matter of gathering together as much data as possible, selecting out the facts that are relevant, and reaching a conclusion. Rather than extrapolating from an in-depth study of a few villages, we would gather specific facts from hundreds of villages and then look for patterns. This is more systematic and the research design limits the kinds of data we can include, but it gives us greater breadth of analysis.

Or we could combine quantitative and qualitative research to explain a person's behavior. A public opinion poll might tell us what percentage of people support a particular public policy but only in-depth interviews with individuals can explain why they hold their views.

Economic behavior may be a result of behaviors that were either rewarded or not rewarded. Through the studies of hundreds of societies, we may find those with the greatest progress are also in which individual entrepreneurial behavior is highly rewarded with financial success.[10] A psychoanalytic study of a handful of individuals and their childhood experiences might help us explain why people who have had similar experiences behave as they do. This is an underlying explanation for why some societies are more "authoritarian" than others. The typical father figure in these cultures is often a disciplinarian who raises his male children to respect his authority.[11]

It is important to remember that models are social constructs of reality which never give us a complete understanding of a social phenomenon. They are always limited. They are either useful or not useful for explaining and even predicting behavior. In addition, the factors that help us understand an individual's behavior might not be useful for explaining the behavior or an entire society. An individual might be "paranoid," but can an entire nation be described as paranoid? If a nation has been invaded by numerous enemies over hundreds of years during which they lost millions of people fighting those wars, are their leaders likely to be irrationally fearful of threats from other countries?

Making comparisons between individual identity, personality development, and behavior with national identity, political or economic, and international behavior is always a stretch because a person and a nation are so very different. Still, this comparison may give us great insight because of its simplicity. We are not overwhelmed by a plethora of variables.

Analogies should not be taken literally and yet they give us great understanding of a complex reality. They serve as heuristic devices. When we say that "an individual is like a nation," we are using the individual as an analogy for a nation and yet we know that there are vast differences. There are indeed many parallels between the evolution of the national political identity of a people and the way in which its citizens perceive their nation's role in the world ("national image") and the evolution of an individual's identity and his or her role in the overall society. For the individual, the childhood or formative years are often the most important for shaping identity, attitudes, and perception of oneself and others.[12] The same may be true for the evolution of a national identity.

There are also many differences between an individual and a nation. For example, this is especially true when it comes to moral or ethical behavior. An individual could die for his or her ethics but should a leader sacrifice his or her nation's existence to maintain ethical behavior? This is the major theme Reinhold Niebuhr's famous book *Moral Man and Immoral Society*.[13]

If we bear in mind the qualifications that we must make when using models or analogies, they allow us to better understand the behavior of groups of people and how they share common values, ways of perceiving the world, and ways of solving problems. In fact, it is almost impossible to discuss national identity or national culture without using models and analogies.

THE ICEBERG ANALOGY OR MODEL

Sigmund Freud believed that our personality is like an iceberg. Most of it is hidden under the water level of awareness, submerged in the unconscious mind. Our personalities are largely shaped during childhood and control much of our conscious behavior throughout our lives. To truly understand the behavior of another person, we must begin by examining his or her formative years when his or her personality was being developed. The same is true for culture. If we want to understand the behavior within a society (external culture) we should begin by examining its history or formative years. The basic values, thought patterns, beliefs, and worldviews of a people (internal culture) were shaped in the past and have been handed down from one generation to another through learning.

Children learn their internal culture in childhood just as they acquire their primary personality during their formative years. It is learned implicitly or informally through interpersonal interaction with other people from the culture. If we are acculturating or learning another culture, knowledge of the internal culture is best acquired experientially and on a very personal level by participation within the culture. We learn this larger and more significant part of culture on a gut level when we actually live in that culture.

An iceberg analogy has also been used by various cultural anthropologists to explain external and internal, or overt and covert culture.[14] However, cultures are perhaps more complex than an iceberg with an overt or tip above the water level of awareness (conscious mind) and the larger implicit or hidden part below the water level of awareness (unconscious). But this simple analogy certainly emphasizes the importance of internal or hidden culture.

Indeed, we can identify various layers to the "iceberg" such as beliefs, values, thought patterns, and perceptions, and, just as the unconscious shapes the conscious mind in Freudian theory, the hidden or internal parts shape the external aspects of culture.[15] Some aspects of culture are both conscious and unconscious such as religious, political, or economic beliefs. Hall never considered values, beliefs, or thought patterns in his writings.

This iceberg analogy of culture is useful because it is also a cybernetics or systems model of culture.[16] The parts are interrelated and must be understood in terms of their relationship. Although the tip of the iceberg is overt, it provides insight into what lies beneath the water level of awareness. When we learn a language, we also learn a great deal about the beliefs and values of people who speak the language, how they think, and how they perceive reality. The preparation and presentation of food might reveal the importance of hospitality or gender roles. The art and music is filled with stories of tragedy or melodrama, the history of the people, and the dreams they hold.

When we draw a graphic representation of this iceberg analogy or model, the tip of the iceberg is external culture and can be learned explicitly. It includes behaviors, habits, language, food, dress, and so on. We can observe this part of another culture and learn it without necessarily participating in the culture. For example, we can formally learn the meanings they give to specific words or phrases in their verbal communication. But this is only *information* about a culture or people—it is not *understanding*. By focusing on the tip of the iceberg, we may know *what* people do but we cannot know *why* they behave as they do unless we go beneath the water level of awareness. To truly understand why people behave as they do, you have to go beneath the water level of awareness into the area of internal culture which includes values and patterns of thought.

As with any cybernetics model, we can see the relationships between the parts of the system and also the links between the parts. Many capitalists would argue that the only way you can change the tip of the iceberg (productivity) is to change the base of the iceberg (such values as individualism and hard work). This is the fundamental position of people such as David McClelland in his book *The Achieving Society* or Lawrence Harrison in his books *Culture*

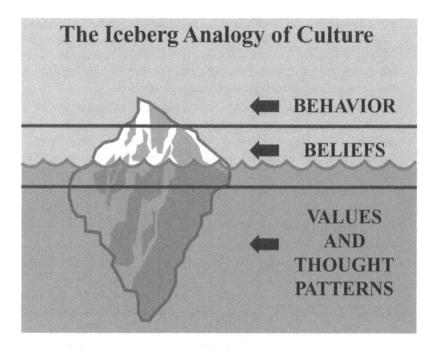

Matters or *The Central Liberal Truth*.[17] On the other hand, others such as Leon Festinger or even many Marxists would argue that if we change the tip of the iceberg—the behaviors of people—in turn, we will change their beliefs and perhaps their values. This is the basic tenet of Festinger's theory of cognitive dissonance.[18] When behaviors do not agree or are dissonant with our beliefs, we cannot deny the reality of the behavior. We must change our beliefs to create consonance. Marxists would argue that if we change the means of production, we will change the very nature of the society including their overall quality of life.

When we enter another culture, we usually only see the tips of the iceberg or external culture. People speak different languages, eat different food, and worship in different ways. When we live in another culture, we very soon learn the basics of the language, become accustomed to the food, and even participate in religious or family rituals. This is the easiest part of a culture to learn because it is explicit. When sojourners go through pre-departure programs to prepare them for working or living overseas, they often only concentrate on this small part of culture.

Sojourners are often unduly concerned about making a mistake when it comes to local language or customs. Although no one wants to behave foolishly or to violate local customs, it is almost inevitable that this will happen. An offense at this tip-of-the-iceberg level is usually accepted by local people who expect "foreigners" to say words incorrectly or to have difficulty eating local food. Sojourners often use this as an excuse for avoiding interaction with local people: "I don't want to go to their home because I'll say the wrong word or use the wrong gesture." Most Americans have ancestors who could not speak English and there have even been presidents who had difficulty with syntax and grammar. When a visitor confuses or mispronounces a word, the worst that usually happens is that Americans laugh.

In the middle of the iceberg—slightly above and slightly below the water level—are beliefs. Some religious, political, or economic beliefs are consciously held while others may be very unconscious. A Saudi child might formally or consciously learn his or her fundamental religious beliefs by studying Islam with a religious teacher. The child also knows of the existence of God by the time he or she can speak Arabic, long before entering religious schools, because many of the everyday phrases in Arabic have the word God in them: "I'll see you at noon, *In shallah* (God willing)" or, "I scored a goal in football, *Alhamdulillah*."

Beliefs are not necessarily congruent. We can hold contradictory beliefs. An average American believes in individual freedom, but also agrees that there is a need for a social and civil order. At times it may be necessary to give up some individual freedom for the good of the overall society. The two beliefs can be contradictory and in opposition.

An offense at this middle level is certainly more serious than using the wrong gesture. Local people do not laugh when a visitor insults or belittles their religious beliefs. Those with conservative political beliefs do not find it amusing when liberals mock their views.

By far the largest, most important and totally hidden part of culture is at the base. This part of culture is almost entirely learned unconsciously and its most significant components include basic values, ways of thinking, and worldviews. We can certainly add other parts to this level such as attitudes, the meanings given to nonverbal messages or context, and systems of logic. If we compare the concept of personality with culture, this level of culture is similar to *basic* personality in that it is unconsciously acquired very early in life and changes very little throughout one's lifetime.

A common mistake we often make is when we assume that if a person behaves as we do, he thinks as we do and shares our values—he is "one of us" and shares our culture. For example, I might have a co-worker in Egypt who speaks fluent English, dresses like an average young adult American male, enjoys popular American music, and even joins all the Americans after work for a few beers. As an American, I begin to think that my friend Abdul is really an American. However, if I get into a conflict with Abdul, I discover that he really is a very typical Egyptian in terms of his values, worldviews, and ways of viewing our conflict. In other words, though we can change on the outside (external culture), it does not necessarily mean we have changed inside (internal culture).

When people from different cultures come together and interact, most of the confusion, misunderstanding, and conflict occurs at this third and hidden level of internal culture. As you can see with the illustration below, when the icebergs collide it occurs well beneath the water level of awareness, at their bases. When this happens, we suddenly realize that people in the other culture do not think as we do, nor do they necessarily share our values and worldviews. We become lost and disoriented. But this is when we are really learning about another culture because we are forced to ask the question, "Why?" "Why do they do and say what they do?" "Why do they see things the way they do?" And to answer these questions you have got to get inside their heads.

More importantly however, from a cross-cultural point of view, when the icebergs collide, you are forced to ask yourself the question, "Why am I reacting the way I am reacting?" It is ironic, but the truth is that the best way to find one's own culture is to leave it. But not just

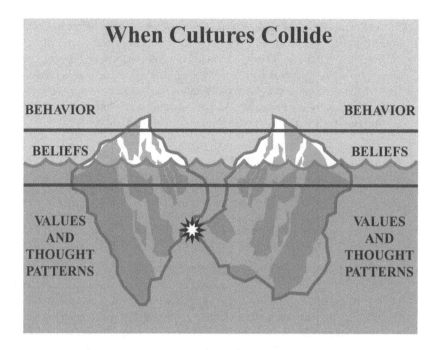

When Cultures Collide

BEHAVIOR   BEHAVIOR

BELIEFS   BELIEFS

VALUES   VALUES
AND   AND
THOUGHT   THOUGHT
PATTERNS   PATTERNS

leave it—to interact with those who are culturally different. This is where you gain greater insight about yourself, when you are inescapably confronted with the other. This also means that as we interact with people from other cultures both internationally and domestically, the cultural differences will not disappear. Rather, we will become more aware of the differences and usually our own culture becomes even more important to us.

Much has been made about the leveling or culturally homogenizing impact of globalization. But this often occurs at the tip of the cultural iceberg. Just because young people in Milwaukee eat tacos, enjoy mariachi music, and speak Spanish does not mean that they are Mexican. On the other hand, it is probably true that the pervasiveness of American television and movies must have some effect on most cultures around the globe.

The technology of modern communications, in and of itself, must have some globalizing impact. In a small nonwestern village, the primary ways families socialize might be by visiting each other's homes, community events such as weddings or religious ceremonies, and even meeting other families in the early evenings on weekends at the local public park. Children learn their social customs and ways of interacting in these communal encounters. However, when the internet is introduced to this society, children no longer need to go to the park to be entertained or informed and they may fail to learn their face-to-face social interactive skills, and especially the meanings given to such nonverbal messages as gestures or tone of voice. In turn, as these children grow up, they no longer go to the park on Sunday evening to meet other families and the local coffee shop closes down.

THEORIES OF INTERCULTURAL RELATIONS

Whenever we consider the impact of culture on the interaction of people, we are entering the field of study that today is usually referred to as "intercultural relations." This area of inquiry ranges from interpersonal communication to relations between states, it includes both domestic and international interactions between different peoples and even explores the impact of modern communication technologies on societies around the globe. Under this umbrella, we would also find cross-cultural, intercultural, and international communications. Concepts from the field of intercultural relations are commonly found in such applied fields of study as law, business, medicine, and international relations as well as various social science courses taught on university campuses around the world.

The first theories of intercultural relations date back to Ibn Khaldun (1332–1406), the father of historical sociology. In his *Introduction to History,* he theorized that as tribal people move to cities their social structures change as do the ways in which they interact.[19] A century before Machiavelli wrote *The Prince,* Ibn Khaldun wrote of power, community, and social cohesion in the Islamic world. Six hundred years before the development of contemporary theories of communication and development, he wrote of the social, political, and economic growth and disintegration of societies.

Ibn Khaldun was concerned with the nature of human interaction within and between cultures. He believed that as people move from nomadic tribes or traditional rural villages to complex urban societies there is a disruption in human interaction and cohesion. This disruption creates enormous psychological stress and produces what we today would term a "counter-cultural" reaction. After they have moved into the complex, urban environment, people long for simplicity, cohesion, and a sense of belonging that cannot easily be found in a city.

Nearly five hundred years later, the German sociologist Ferdinand Tönnies (1855–1936) theorized that as people move from a socially and religiously homogeneous rural community (*Gemeinschaft*) to a heterogeneous urban society (*Gesellschaft*), the relationships between people change.[20] A merchant class will arise, an externalized system of law-and-order will develop to ensure predictability of human behavior, and the consequent dehumanization or alienation will cause people to long for the social order and sense of belonging provided by the village. While Ibn Khaldun believed that the tension between the worlds of the rural and urban would be passed down from one generation to another over hundreds of years, Tönnies thought it would create a counter-cultural reaction within only one or two generations.

Ibn Khaldun saw this as a conflict between polar opposites—the rural village or tribe versus the urban city—and he thought that eventually all people would move back to the purity and psychological security of the rural community. Tönnies was much less polar in his approach. Most cultures fall somewhere along a continuum between a *Gesellschaft* and a *Gemeinschaft*—it is all a matter of degree. For example, today urbanized northern European cultures tend to be typical of *Gesellschafts*, while rural, African cultures tend to be more typical of *Gemeinschafts*. Moreover, Tönnies was a dialectical thinker. Out of the conflict between rural community and urban society emerges some sort of thesis that is better than either extreme.

Ibn Khaldun and Ferdinand Tönnies were interdisciplinary scholars who drew from history and theology as well as fields of inquiry that were not even considered academic disciplines in their days such as politics, economics, cultural anthropology, and psychology. Both are considered seminal scholars in the discipline we now know as sociology. Their multidisciplinary approach helped them to develop their theories of culture and communication, the impact of social change on the individual, and the dynamic nature of culture. Ibn Khaldun and Tönnies not only contrasted and compared social and cultural groups and their interactions with each other, but also described how modern technology and social change in an urban society produced psychological stress for the individual and a desire to return to the stability, harmony, and balance of the traditional community.

Their *comparative* approach assumed that one social system or culture could be contrasted with another. Ibn Khaldun's ideal was the rural nomadic homogeneous community and he believed that the trauma of living in an urban environment would cause people to long for the purity and simplicity of their previous rural life. Tönnies tended to view the urban heterogeneous *Gesellschaft* society as less discriminatory and oppressive than a homogenous rural *Gemeinschaft* community, although his ideal culture was a blend of a *Gemeinschaft* and a *Gesellschaft*.

The primary difficulty of these comparative approaches was the assumption that there is a hierarchy of cultures and there exists a standard or ideal culture with which other cultures may be contrasted. Those lower in the cultural hierarchy were often viewed as somewhat pathological versions of the exemplar. In more contemporary political and development theory, this can be found in the view that "developing" countries[21] which adapt Western or American economic and political practices and values will grow faster economically and become more democratic.[22]

The success of the U.S. economic and political experiment was seen by some as *prima facie* evidence that Americans hold special values that lead to a more prosperous and democratic society. These values were firmly rooted in the soil of utopian Calvinism and Puritanism. With chauvinistic enthusiasm many believers in American Exceptionalism sought to share their way of life with others. If you discovered the cure for cancer, wouldn't you share it with others? This concern for others was often unrequited and even perceived as American cultural imperialism.[23]

As early as the late 1890s, anthropologist Franz Boas questioned the then popular comparative approach and developed an approach that today is known as "cultural relativism," "contextualism," or "post-modern relativity."[24] Margaret Mead and Ruth Benedict, students of Franz Boas, shared his view that human behavior can only be understood in the context of, and relative to, each particular culture. It did not condone all behavior nor imply that all behavior is acceptable.

Today there seems to be some confusion between *cultural relativism* and *ethical relativism*. Ethical relativism is a catch phrase meaning that the practices in every culture are acceptable. In effect, there are no ethics. It is highly unlikely that anyone actually holds this view and it is thus somewhat of a straw man position. It may be a spin-off of the comparative approach with an unspoken assumption that those who are "civilized" have some kind of universal ethical system and those who don't share that system are therefore "uncivilized."

Cultural relativism simply rejects the hierarchical ethnocentrism of extreme versions of the comparative approach. If there is great discrimination against women in a particular culture, this is abhorrent to most anthropologists. However to understand why that practice exists in particular culture, one would need to know the internal culture or values and worldviews that undergird the behavior.

On the other hand, it is possible to identity *patterns of behavior* that are shared by cultures. Cultures can be compared as long as we don't go to the extreme of arguing that one culture is superior to all others. We can reject the evaluative and ethnocentric nature of the comparative approach and yet acknowledge that people in rural villages all over the world share certain values and worldviews. People living in heterogeneous urban centers often share practices that are typical of big cities.

The extreme version of cultural relativism argues that each culture has its own characteristic cluster of values, beliefs, and behaviors that cannot be compared with other cultures. This *particularism* carried too far can even end up with the claim that "we're all individuals," thereby negating the very existence of culture.

Each approach can be useful for understanding behavior as long as we don't see it as exclusive. We can prefer one approach over another and even determine that one approach is more nuanced and useful than others. But we need not ignore the other approaches. We are individuals but all humans also belong to a culture and there are similarities and differences between cultures. If not carried to their extremes, these approaches can actually complement each other and create a synergistic understanding of human behavior.

Another difficulty with these early studies of culture and change is that they did not consider the interaction between people of different cultures. Their studies contrasted and compared cultures and therefore were cross-cultural but not really intercultural in nature. Many of the early studies of culture ignored communication or viewed it as very monological and unidirectional rather than dialogical and multidirectional. Messages flowed from the so-called Western world to the non-Western world and feedback or reactions to those messages were taken into account to be sure that the messages were received as they were intended. This type of monological communication was usually purposive with the intent to persuade. In many ways, culture was viewed as an obstacle to overcome as the Western world helped the non-West to become more Westernized. Very little research considered communication between people of non-Western cultures or the impact of the non-West on the West.

Anthropologist and sociolinguist Edward Hall is often considered the first scholar to link communication and culture and thus is often called the "grandfather" of intercultural studies. In his earliest books, *The Silent Language* (1959) and *The Hidden Dimension* (1966), he defined culture as "communication." He was not referring simply to language but rather to the ways in which people communicate without the use of words. The ways in which we nonverbally communicate and the meanings we give to those messages are learned unconsciously simply by growing up in a culture. To a large extent, their meanings and usage are not explicitly taught but are learned tacitly and are understood at a subconscious level. This includes social distance, eye contact, touch, movement, gestures, synchrony, and even the use of time.

In the U.S., children learn that they should stand about an arm's length away from another person when conversing. To stand closer invades the other person's personal space and communicates "pushiness." It is perhaps only ten to twelve inches for a Bedouin Arab. In the U.S., avoiding eye contact when someone is speaking to you means that you really don't care what they have to say, yet in Puerto Rico if an adult is reprimanding a child, the child is expected to look down and away from the adult to acknowledge the reprimand. Americans seldom use touch to communicate, especially between individuals of the same sex and yet in Mexico people often greet others with a big hug or *un abrazo*.

We unconsciously learn these ways of communicating and the meanings we give to nonverbal cues are hidden or internal and specific to each culture. Tone of voice or body movements can only be truly understood when placed within the context of each individual culture. Among mainstream white Americans, a loud voice and waving of arms might indicate anger while in an ethnic Italian community it could mean sincerity. The message "loud voice and waving of arms" communicates completely different meanings. Hall describes *high-context* cultures as those in which people are more likely to use nonverbal ways of interacting and where they prefer face-to-face communication because it allows them to use face, posture, tone of voice, and gestures to send messages.

In high-context cultures, even verbal messages might not be clearly understood unless you know the culture because the connotative and denotative meanings of words may be very different. Words can mean different things depending upon context. For example, ten or twenty years ago, an American adolescent inner-city black male might tell you that you have a "bad car." But this could also mean that you have a "good car." If you are from his culture, you know exactly what he means by the word "bad" and it all depends upon his tone of voice, facial expression, and even your relationship with him.

Certainly language is an important aspect of any culture, and when we learn a language we also gain great insights into the values, worldviews, beliefs, and ways of thinking of a people. Nevertheless, language is mostly an external part of culture and the same language may be shared by people in very different cultures. One could learn a language without necessarily living with the people who speak that language. This is especially true for what Edward Hall refers to as a *low-context* culture where words are the primary way of communicating and the denotative and connotative meanings of words are roughly the same.

Ethnographer Clifford Geertz further linked culture and communication in his 1973 book *The Interpretation of Cultures*.[25] He took a cognitive or linguistic approach and viewed culture in terms of shared meanings. When a people in a society agree on the meanings given to words or things they then create some sort of culture. When we communicate, we send messages, not meanings. The meanings are inside our heads, and if we come from the same culture, messages will elicit similar or parallel meanings. If we come from different cultures, the same message may have very different meanings or perhaps no meaning at all.

Other linguists claim that language limits, or even determines, perception and thought. Consequently, when we learn a new language we also acquire a new way of perceiving the world. This is often referred to as the linguistic relativity principle, or the Sapir-Whorf Hypothesis.[26] Eskimos may have numerous words to describe snow that do not exist in other languages—new snow, wet snow, dry snow, blowing snow, fluffy snow, and so on. They perceive and conceive of various kinds of snow. On the other hand, although we may not have a word for each kind of snow, we may still be able to perceive these differences. For a dressmaker, the distinction between the colors "magenta" and "pink" may be important. If we are dressmakers, we may not know what these words mean but we can recognize the subtle differences in shades of a similar color.

It is reasonable then to conclude that language, perception, and thought are all interconnected and people in the same culture who share the same language do indeed tend to share perceptions and thought patterns. When we learn their language we also learn a new way of perceiving reality. In the new language, words may exist to differentiate subtle differences that they perceive because they are significant in their society. In turn, we learn a new way of thinking about those differences.

Perception and cognition go together. What information gets into our heads and how we organize the information to deal with the world is culturally determined. Marshall Singer emphasized perception and believed that how we perceive reality is determined by our culture; those in the same primary or secondary culture tend to view the world in a similar way. An example of this would be when we say, "As Catholics, we see the problem this way." What we are really saying is, "*As members of a group called Roman Catholics, we share a common way of viewing this situation.*" Culture then is a matter of shared perceptions as well as shared meanings. What information gets into our heads and how we organize that information to solve problems is to a large extent determined by our culture.

We come into this world a bit like un-programmed computers, and culture is our software.[27] When we program a computer, we decide what information ought to be included or excluded. At a very early age, our culture determines how we perceive reality or what information we pay attention to. For example, in many Western or low-context cultures, people learn to pay more attention to words than nonverbal communication. In addition, computers are programmed to organize information in certain ways to solve problems. People think and solve problems in ways that are similar to others in their culture. In some cultures, people connect things in a rather poetic matter. They are high-context or associative thinkers. In other cultures, people disconnect things in rather linear or quantitative ways.

Culture shapes how we perceive reality and determines what information gets into our heads and how we use that information to solve problems. Just as the way in which information is organized and the capacity a computer has for processing that information is the most important part of programming the computer, the same is true of individuals. The way we solve problems, the logic we normally use to deal with the world, and the way in which we think are probably the most important parts of our cultural programming.

INPUT PROGRAM OUTPUT

Perception and   Ways of solving problems,   Behavior
Information   Logic, and Thought Patterns

People in more traditional non-Western cultures tend to be Dionysian, deductive, or qualitative thinkers while people in more urban and Western culture tend to be Apollonian, inductive, or quantitative thinkers. Although many earlier German philosophers used these terms, Friedrich Nietzsche is often credited with being the first to describe ancient Greek tragedy as the result of the juxtaposition of these two dichotomous ways of thinking in his book *The Birth of Tragedy*.[28] Dionysus represents passion, chaos, and experience while the god Apollo strives for order, logic, perfection, and contemplation. A theme in many Greek tragedies was the eternal conflict between these two ways of thinking often found in the same person or the same society.

In the mid-20th century, anthropologists such as Ruth Benedict and Margaret Mead used these terms to characterize cultures that value excess, displays of emotion, impulsiveness, and disorder (Dionysian) contrasted with those that value restraint, modesty, inductive logic, and control (Apollonian).[29] Dionysian deductive logic and research would be highly qualitative, experiential, and incomplete. Without knowing where the exploration would lead, he or she would intuitively relate a few observations to lead to great insight and understanding. An Apollonian researcher would begin with a well-developed design that would explain the approach and methodology to be used in the exploration after which he or she would gather together a great quantity of facts and then select those which are relevant to solving problems.

These are two very different ways of solving problems. The Dionysian thinker would be typical of Sigmund Freud who came up with a broad theory of personality based on his experience in Vienna with a handful of neurotic patients. The Apollonian researcher is exemplified by B.F. Skinner who observed the behavior of thousands of rats and pigeons in controlled laboratory experiments and concluded that human behavior is simply a matter of scheduled reinforcement of rewards and punishments. The ethnographic study of an anthropologist who examines behavior in the context of a culture is Dionysian and a sociologist who amasses thousands of pieces of data, tends to be much more of an Apollonian. There's a tension between these two ways of thinking, but Nietzsche may have been correct in concluding that reality is tragedy and it is found by the juxtaposition of these two culturally-shaped ways of thinking.

Most of culture is internal—the base of the cultural iceberg. To this extent, culture is indeed synonymous with "mind" as Edward Hall defines it in his book *Beyond Culture* or "the software of the mind" as Geert Hofstede views it. We do indeed begin life somewhat like unprogrammed computers. This cultural "program" subsequently determines our behavior. To understand someone's behavior (output) it is necessary to first understand how the person experiences or perceives the world (input) and how that person has learned to organize and utilize that information to solve problems (program).

Years ago when computers could handle only a limited amount of information or when they solved simple problems, they were often "overloaded" and crashed when given too much information or when the problems were too complex. At this point, programmers enlarged the information capacity or made the program more sophisticated. Human beings are similar. When we are forced to consider more information or solve more complex problems, we become overloaded and break down. At that time, we reprogram ourselves to pay attention to a broader array of information and to develop more problem-solving systems.

Early studies of culture described it as monolithic, static, and external, whereas most recent studies see it as multifaceted and diverse even within nation-states or regions, continually changing, and mostly internal. It is important to realize that although external culture (behaviors or customs) changes fairly easily with modern technology, internal culture changes much more slowly. The underlying values, beliefs, worldviews, and thought patterns often remain relatively stable across many generations. This is especially true for the so-called "mainstream" or "dominant" culture that is shared by most people within a state or region.

In the 1950s and 1960s, there were many comparative ethnographic studies where culture was viewed as mostly a matter of external differences. Non-Western cultures were viewed as almost the opposite of Western cultures. This dualistic or Manichaean way of viewing culture failed to see the subtleties and nuances of internal cultures and, even more importantly, it did not present characteristics of culture ranging along some sort of continuum.[30] And this approach often failed to consider the similarities between cultures.

In the middle of the 1960s, Hall and other authors were often misunderstood as being rigidly dualistic. They were accused of dividing the world into oppositional categories such as the East versus the West or the developed versus underdeveloped or developing world. Perhaps this was part of a Cold War dichotomous view of the Communist versus Free World. Few scholars of cross-cultural or intercultural communication actually viewed culture in these bi-polar categories. For example, Hall always saw cultures along a continuum of high- and low-context cultures with various combinations along the continuum. Many critiques presented Hall as a dualistic thinker and they cleverly deconstructed a construct he never created. This straw manning of Hall was often annoying and intellectually dishonest, but was nevertheless rather entertaining.[31] Most importantly, it failed to see the most important contribution that Hall made, which was a movement from contrasting and comparing cultures to considering communication between people of different cultures.

CROSS-CULTURAL AND INTERCULTURAL COMMUNICATION

While it is not necessary to agree on the definition of phrases commonly used in the broad area of intercultural relations, it may be useful to consider some of the differences between such terms as cross-cultural, intercultural, and international communication. "Cultural competency" is being replaced by "intercultural competency," and intercultural negotiation has become a required skill for international business people, the military, and all agencies of a government engaged in international relations.

Today, the terms *cross-cultural* and *intercultural* communication are often used interchangeably, yet they are somewhat different in terms of area of inquiry, depth of analysis, and scope. *Cross-cultural* studies began as a field of inquiry that contrasted and compared aspects of different cultures. Ethnography was a basic research tool. For example, anthropologists explored how people in one society educated their children compared and contrasted with the childhood raising practices in another society. People in all cultures have headaches, but the way they treat the pain may differ. In Asia one might rub a salve on one's temples, in France it is common to use suppositories, and in the United States people usually take pills.

Early *cross-cultural communication* scholars examined the impact of technology and mass communication on cultures and the interaction between so-called "developed" and "developing" nations. Cultural anthropologist Margaret Mead's *Cultural Patterns and Technical Change* used a systems theory approach to investigate the impact of technological change on a variety of traditional non-Western cultures. To predict the consequences of inserting a new technology into a social system, one must understand the make-up of the society and the communication links between people, the nature of the technological input, and the way in which it is introduced. In other words, a great deal depends upon the culture. There is no reason to expect that technological change will necessarily "destroy" another culture.

Cross-cultural communication studies were rather vertical and tended to concentrate on such external cultural aspects as customs, practices, and language. Experts were concerned with the relationships between elements of the cultural and social system. Religious practices, the social make-up of the society, and personal, social, economic, and political behavior of people are different in each culture. Of course, there are also some similarities with other cultures. Americans and the British speak English, but these are two different cultures.

Intercultural communication was an expansion of cross-cultural communication studies as scholars considered what happens when people of different cultures interact on a more interpersonal level, not only between but also within nations. This approach was much more concerned with "internal" rather than "external" culture. Although the values may be unconscious and internal they impact the more overt and external part of culture such as behavior and customs. We can compare cultures horizontally and consider what happens when values, thought patterns, and ways of perceiving reality collide. Of course, the fields of cross-cultural and intercultural communication overlap and actually blend together but the focus is a bit different.

Propaganda studies during and after World War II assumed that messages are sent by radio or print which persuade people to see things in a particular way. However, with intercultural communication research we discovered that people are not simply passive receivers of messages. People in each culture pay attention to some messages more than others and the meanings they give to those messages depend upon their cultural, social, and personal background. Belief systems and image theory, motivation theory, national and ethnic identity, power relations between subcultures and the dominant culture—all of these areas became a part of intercultural communication studies.

International communications emerged with the evolution of international relations as a field of study within the realm of social sciences and especially international relations. Until World War II, international relations studies were often considered one of the humanities such as foreign affairs or diplomatic history. However, with the evolution of systems theory and sociology, international relations became a social science in the United States with ties to political science, economics, sociology, psychology, anthropology, and communications theory. Cold War studies of the political and economic development of nations, modern telecommunications policies and practices, and the creation of foreign policies took culture and communication into account. Just as international communications had from the very beginning grown out of (and was embedded in) international relations research and theory, cross-cultural communication studies were part of international communications.

Many of the early theories of communication and political and economic development in the late 1950s and early 1960s were actually cross-cultural in nature because they compared development in the West with so called Third World countries. According to these theorists, such as Daniel Lerner, Wilbur Shramm, and Lucian Pye,[32] newly emerging nations would evolve in the same way as the industrialized and urbanized West. Modern communication and transportation grids would allow for a growing national economy and a national civic culture with increased citizen participation, and these nations would mimic the growth patterns of the Western world and move from one stage of development to the other in a rather lockstep way. Implicit in these theories was an assumption that this would lead to a more capitalistic economy with greater economic growth and, concurrently, a democratic political system—based upon such democratic values as equality of all, individual freedom, free elections, and so on.

More recently, many scholars have begun to use the term *intercultural relations* to include cross-cultural and intercultural studies, interpersonal and mass communication, and both the theoretical and applied aspects of this scholarly field. It includes a wide variety of approaches and theories, including linguistics, sociology, communications, psychology, economics, political science, and international relations. Research methodologies could range from Dionysian and qualitative case studies to Apollonian quantitative empiricism or ideally any number of combinations.

This broader area of inquiry includes both international and domestic studies of culture and communication and it is more than simply research or theory. Today we could consider intercultural relations as an applied field that includes education and training to understand the dynamics of intercultural communication as well as to prepare people to be more effective in their interactions with people from other cultures.

As the world becomes smaller and interactions between people from different cultures increase, this field has also become applied. Businesses want their employees to be more effective in other cultures both domestically and internationally, negotiations between diplomats require an understanding of other cultures, and military success overseas may depend upon the knowledge members of the armed forces have of local people.

It is very unlikely that any American could get hired for a managerial position today who could only deal effectively with people from his or her own culture. This is also true of many other countries where ethnic, racial, and national diversity is increasing and companies are becoming more global. No longer do we assume that negotiation is simply a matter of applying certain universal communication skills to all encounters. How and what people negotiate depends upon their cultural values, beliefs, and worldviews. In some cultures, drinking a few cups of tea and developing trust and personal relationships must precede any discussion on the matters at hand. The United States military has learned from its experiences in Vietnam and the Middle East that winning the support of local people is essential to the success of any overseas mission and understanding the cultures of local people will ultimately save lives.

Increasing the knowledge people may have of other cultures is often referred to as *cultural competency*. Often this was a matter of understanding a particular region of the world and was included in various kinds of so-called "area studies." However, *competency* implied more than just knowledge or understanding of a culture. It meant that one has communication skills and knows something about how to interact with people in a local country.

Recently, the phrase *intercultural competency* is used to describe not only an understanding of one's own culture and other cultures, but also the ability to communicate with people from various cultural backgrounds and the ability to analyze and interpret what happens when there is a conflict between people of different cultures. Negotiation and mediation between people of different cultures are all part of this area of knowledge and this collection of skills.

DIFFERENCES <u>AND</u> SIMILARITIES

Cross-cultural communication often was highlighted by studies that contrasted and compared one culture with another. Most of these comparisons involved differences. What are the differences in puberty rituals around the world? What are the differences between Roman Catholic and Protestant countries in Europe? How are child-raising practices different in Germany and

Iran? Very few scholars today would view culture as simply a matter of differences. Although we might begin with differences, we also must consider similarities by using a contrast and comparison approach similar to Tönnies, where both differences and similarities are identified.

The greater danger, however, is assuming *perceived similarities*, and thereby trying to explain another culture in terms of one's own. This can have the effect of actually denying the existence of different cultures as we strive to find all of the ways in which we are alike. Very often, this approach marginalizes and minimizes the legitimacy and significance of other cultural identities. These pitfalls and dangers are reduced if we first move from a study of differences to one of similarities. The reverse sequence is, frankly, often counterproductive because we then tend to ignore differences and focus only on similarities. It is difficult to see differences when we are blinded by similarities.

It is true that peoples in all cultures love their children, believe in some kind of divine being, and want to live in peace with each other. Perhaps 90% of the humans around the globe share these values and aspirations. The problem is the 10% of differences in the way they apply their values and fulfill their aspirations. In the U.S., children are expected to leave home to go to school or work when they reach the age of 19 or 20 years. Love means "letting go" of children to allow them to be self-reliant and independent. This might be perceived as cruel and unloving in many Asian cultures where sons, and especially daughters, are supposed to stay at home as long as possible. Many wars have been fought because of differing religious beliefs and practices rather than rational decision-making. In some cultures, peace means containing expanding hegemony from others and deterring aggression by building up military forces. In another country, this could be seen as offensive rather than defensive, encirclement rather than containment, and might lead to a pre-emptive military strike rather than peace.

Interculturalists are often accused of overemphasizing differences. "You people keep talking about differences all the time. Why don't you talk about similarities? Aren't we all human?"[33] Of course there are indeed similarities between cultures. It is all a matter of sequencing. Once we acknowledge the differences, then we can talk about the similarities. If you do not deal with the differences, and instead only focus on the similarities, you are essentially denying *the other* and that which makes his or her culture unique. The great danger is that when you begin by talking about similarities you often fail to acknowledge and value the genuine differences that exist.

It is not unlike a family. In the United States, teenagers seem to go through a stage in life when they assert their given right to be unique and distinct individuals. They want to be similar to other teenagers, but they also definitely want to be *different* than their parents. This is adolescent rebellion. A teenage girl has an earring in her eyebrow, all of her clothing is black, and her hair is four shades of pink. She is indeed very different! Each day she may assert her right to be different but her parents keep assuring her that she's just like them. Finally, one evening, in exasperation, her father says, "Okay, you're different. You've got an earring in your eyebrow." Now the conversation can move onto a discussion of how she is also similar in some ways to her parents. If we continue to deny differences, we cannot talk about the similarities because they cannot be heard over the rejection of the differences.

When we acknowledge differences and accept the reality that there is *diversion* we can move on and come together to some kind of *conversion*. Differences are good. It is not a matter of overcoming the differences, but what you do with these differences. For example, in the United States during the 70s and 80s, there was a dramatic increase in the number of women entering the workforce and the percentage promoted to managerial and supervisory positions.[34] Training programs were invented by human resource offices and universities to help these women succeed. The programs were called "Assertiveness Training." The idea was that women must be trained to be as *assertive* and aggressive as men. You see, the only thing wrong with women was that they acted like women—if they acted like men, they would be perfectly competent human beings. Women were considered to be underdeveloped men or pathological versions of men.

When faced with a problem, why would any organization want women who think like men sitting around the table? Most companies today want a wide variety of perspectives brought to the table to enhance creative problem-solving. Everyone looks forward to going to work if they can bring their cultures with them and find that these differences in ways of thinking, values, and beliefs are actually welcomed and valued. We were not "valuing diversity" or providing "diversity training." This was simply social cloning.

The issue is no longer how to get rid of differences, but rather how to manage diversity to increase creativity and productivity. Government-enforced "affirmative action" programs are seldom necessary today because almost all organizations want to recruit qualified employees from different backgrounds. As the society becomes more diverse, it is obviously essential to have employees and managers who reflect that diversity in the workplace. These differences are not an obstacle but instead an opportunity.

Differences provide an opportunity for more imaginative thinking. For example, if we gave every person in a room a personality test and divided them up according to the results, we might place extroverts in one group, introverts in another, and have a third mixed group of extroverts and introverts. Then, ask everyone to solve a problem. Chances are that the group of introverts would solve the problem quickly because they all think the same. In fact, because they are introverts, they may feel compelled to agree with each other. So, they may suffer from groupthink.[35] The extroverts also solve the problem very quickly because they all think the same. The mixed group is a nightmare. They cannot decide when to stop the chit-chat and get down to business or how to pick a leader. However, the research is abundantly clear that if you can manage this group effectively it will come up with a longer and more creative list of solutions. That is the value of diversity.

Now, implement the solutions. The introverts and extroverts will quickly implement their solutions because they think the same. But members of the mixed group may engage in end-less debate regarding ranking the solutions or the best way to apply the solutions. This is the problem with diversity. While it allows for creative brainstorming and innovative problem-solving, it can interfere with implementation.

The psychological approach assumes similarity and often denies the existence of dif-ferences. That is the weakness of many of these psychological approaches when it comes to understanding conflict between people from different cultures. We ought to question many of the psychological assumptions and findings by looking at them from a cultural point-of-view, and asking, "Does this apply to every culture?" "Is everyone in the world motivated by the same rewards or punishments?" "How do people from different societies view this problem?" "Do all people solve problems in the same way?"

The field of intercultural relations is completely interdisciplinary and we need to bring together all viewpoints to better understand the dynamics of cross-cultural communication. It is never the anthropological versus the psychological approach but rather some combination of findings from various disciplines such as international relations, political science, anthropology, psychology, economics, communications, and so on. Any single discipline alone would be inadequate.

CONTRAST CULTURE CONTINUUM

We can also consider horizontal models that allow us to contrast and compare cultures according to such characteristics as social structure, philosophic outlook, basic values, and/ or ways of interacting. These contrasts are oversimplifications and generalizations, but they allow us to consider the differences and similarities between cultures.

Cultures might be placed along a continuum ranging from the abstractive, low-context, and urban to the associative, high-context, and rural. Most cultures tend to fall on one side of the continuum or the other. However, no single culture falls completely within any one category. Differences between cultures are a matter of degree. For example, people in one culture may be more abstractive or low-context than people in another culture.

The terms abstractive and associative refer to cognitive patterns or problem-solving approaches. Abstractive thought is quantitative and inductive and found in physical scientific research. It is also typical of sociological studies. We gather a vast array of data or facts and then select out (abstract) those which are relevant to solving a problem. Associative thought is qualitative and deductive. We tie together selected facts to reach a conclusion. This is typical of a more case-study approach found in ethnographic studies of anthropology.

Scholars such as Edmund Glenn believed that abstractive thought was typical of Western urban cultures whereas associative thought was commonly found in non-Western and rural cultures.[36] B.F. Skinner, who is often credited with being the primary seminal scholar in the behavioral school of psychology, conducted perhaps tens of thousands of experiments with laboratory rats and pigeons to reach his conclusions that most of human behavior is a result of some kind of schedule of rewards and punishments. If a behavior is rewarded, it tends to be repeated whereas when a behavior is not rewarded or is punished, it tends to cease. From Skinner's research we can explain much of human behavior such as gambling or the causes of phobias.

A classic example of associative thought is found in fiction. Sherlock Holmes often solves a problem with limited information. He finds a shard of glass, a drop of blood, and perhaps a strand of hair, and then associates or relates these few bits of information to solve a crime. Dr. Watson, his assistant, then exclaims, "Brilliant deduction!" Sherlock Holmes is not a scientist; he is a poet. Poetry, by definition, is highly associative. For example, when we say the phrase, "the babbling brook," we are using a poetic expression in American English because the phrase sets off a series of associations in our minds—perhaps it reminds us of our first romance. In many non-Western cultures, everyone is a poet. You ask a question and another person responds with a metaphor or a story.

Low-context and high-context are terms used by Edward Hall to describe types of communication found in different cultures.[37] In many Western cultures the most common type of communication involves words, especially written communication, where the connotative and denotative meanings are congruent. You do not need to understand the culture to understand the meaning of a message because it is highly factual and direct. In many non-Western cultures, the meaning of a message can only be understood in the context of the culture and the connotative and denotative meanings may be very different. Moreover, the primary form of communication is spoken face-to-face communication where the nonverbal aspects of communication are vital to understanding the true meaning of a message.

A legal contract is vital to conducting business in many Western countries and it must be unambiguous to all parties. Much of the business negotiation may be done with email and memos. In many small villages in rural Latin American countries, one's word accompanied by a smile and a handshake is sufficient to conduct everyday business. It might be almost an insult to insist that a legal document is necessary to finalize an agreement.

Theoretically, we could place the Swiss-German, urban American, urban Greek or Egyptian, and rural Bedouin Arab cultures along this continuum as follows:

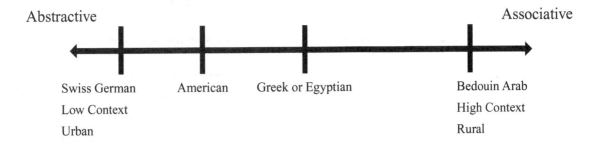

Abstractive   Associative

Swiss German   American Greek or Egyptian   Bedouin Arab
Low Context   High Context
Urban   Rural

As with all typologies, these descriptions never apply to everyone in a particular culture at all times. For example, rural Americans from the South may fall on the right hand side of this continuum. Also, people from some cultures may be a combination of types. Greeks, Italians, Turks, Egyptians, and other Mediterranean peoples could be described as both Western and Eastern or Dionysian and Apollonian. They may fall in the middle of the continuum.

While most people come from cultures that lean toward one end of the continuum, some are more bicultural or multicultural. For example, an American may have lived in a small, Southern rural town during his or her formative years and later adapted to the culture of Manhattan in New York City. Initially, there was a clash of values when this person arrived in Manhattan, but after years of acculturation, he or she can move easily and authentically between the two contrasting cultures.

Cultures might include gender or ethnic and racial groups within a particular society. Some authors would place Anglo-American males on the abstractive, low-context end of this continuum, while Anglo-American women and African Americans might be placed on the associative or high-context end.

The following chart is simply a heuristic device that can help us sort out the various contrasts and comparisons used by authors throughout the literature. This list is neither totally inclusive nor comprehensive. We could add many other terms and categories. And there is overlap between categories—social structure affects basic values and vice versa. In a society where the typical family is the nuclear family composed of the husband, wife, and children and there is great physical and social mobility, independence and self-reliance may be significant values. These values, in turn, encourage people to be mobile and perhaps restrict the size of their family.

It is important to continually remind ourselves that this type of chart is actually a *continuum* and no culture or person falls neatly into one side of the chart or the other. There are various gradations between the extremes. Some cultures fall into the middle of the chart because they are a mixture of the contrasting characterizations. And some individuals fall into the center because they are bicultural or multicultural.

Culture Contrast Continuum

CHARACTERISTIC CULTURE	
Abstractive	Associative[38]
Gesellschaft	*Gemeinschaft*[39]
Society	Community
Urban	Rural
Apollonian	Dionysian[40]
Heterogeneous	Homogeneous
SOCIAL STRUCTURE	
Individualistic	Collective[41]
Small or nuclear family	Extended family
Overt social rules	Implicit social rules
Loose in-group/out-group distinction	Rigid in-group/out-group distinction
Achieved or earned status	Ascribed status[42]
Flexible roles	Rigid roles
Loosely integrated	Highly integrated
Class	Caste
Social and physical mobility	Little social or physical mobility
Low-power distance	High-power distance[43]

PHILOSOPHIC OUTLOOK	
Mastery or control over nature	Harmony with or subjugation to nature[44]
Melodramatic/escapist	Tragic/realistic[45]
Humane/inhuman	Human/inhumane
Objective	Subjective
Quantitative	Qualitative
Alloplastic	Autoplastic[46]
Mind/body dichotomy	Union of mind and body
PSYCHOLOGICAL ORIENTATION	
Psychology of abundance	Psychology of scarcity[47]
Schizoid or fragmented	Comprehensive or holistic[48]
Need for achievement	Need for affiliation[49]
Abstractive and logical	Anthropomorphic and complexive[50]
Masculine	Feminine[51]
Direct responsibility	Indirect responsibility
Great use of extensions	Little use of extensions
Extension transference	No extension transference[52]
Steep pleasure gradient	Flat pleasure gradient[53]
Weak uncertainty avoidance	Strong uncertainty avoidance[54]
Guilt-internal	Shame-external
THOUGHT PATTERNS	
Analytic	Relational[55]
Theoretical learning and knowledge	Experiential or kinesthetic learning and knowledge
Dichotomous/divisions	Holistic/joining together
Linear-separations	Nonlinear-comprehensive
Abstractions/prose	Imagery/poetry
BASIC VALUES	
Doing	Being[56]
Change/action	Stability/harmony
What/content	How/style
Individualism	Belongingness
Independence	Interdependence/dependence
Self-reliance	Reliance upon others

PERCEPTION	
Mind/body dichotomy	Mind and body are one
Monochronic time/action	Polychronic time/action[57]
Linear or segmented time	Nonlinear or comprehensive time
Future orientation	Past or present orientation
Space/objects separated	Continuity of space/objects
Subject-object	Subject-subject
Nonsensual and non-senseful	Sensual and senseful
INTERACTION	
Low-context	High-context[58]
Competition	Cooperation[59]
Verbal emphasis	Nonverbal and verbal
Written or electronic	Face-to-face
Impersonal	Personal
Schizoid/fragmented relationships	Holistic/interdependent relationships
Monological	Dialogical[60]
Practical/aloof	Nonpurposive/involved
Easy to break action chains	Difficult to break action chains[61]
Systematic	Spontaneous

REALISTIC CULTURAL EMPATHY

Intercultural knowledge and intercultural skills overlap and reinforce each other. When we are familiar with another culture our uncertainty is decreased and we believe that we will not make a major cultural *faux pas* upon entering the culture. We also need to develop some applied skills such as the ability to communicate well with people in the culture and to be able to analyze and interpret what might be happening in a cross-cultural conflict situation. Of course, these skills are best learned through experience. This is the reason most intercultural training involves such experiential exercises as simulations, games, role plays, and so on.

The object of good intercultural training is to help participants to develop *realistic cultural empathy*. This is simply the ability to put oneself in another's psychological and cultural shoes—to see the world as that person sees it. If we can understand the beliefs and worldviews of others we can better explain their behavior and, more importantly, we can anticipate how they may respond to what we say or do. This is an essential cross-cultural communication skill.

Realistic cultural empathy is primarily cognitive or intellectual, <u>not</u> affective or emotional.[62] It means understanding how people in a particular culture tend to solve problems and how they view the world. If we want to understand the interests of people in a negotiation, we need to know how they think and perceive reality. People from the same cultural background usually share ways of thinking and perceiving. It does <u>not</u> mean "sympathy" which is indeed emotional and external.

Realistic cultural empathy does not mean "agreement with" people in another culture.[63] There is no need to agree with someone else's political or religious views. But if I want to understand why they said something—and if I want to anticipate how they will react to what I say—I must get inside their heads to understand their political and religious views as well as their values, beliefs, and thought patterns. And realistic cultural empathy does not mean "identification with" or "being like that other person." Nothing is more obnoxious than an Anglo-American who goes to Mexico and tries to act more Mexican than a Mexican. You cannot, and should not, deny your own culture.

Let us turn to an example which involves cultural differences. On November 4, 1979, Iranian students stormed the American Embassy and held 52 employees as hostages for 444 days. Former California governor Ronald Reagan, who was then running for President, told reporters that the way to get the hostages released was to "turn Tehran into a parking lot." In other words, his solution was to bomb Tehran. Would that have gotten the hostages released? Probably not.

In a situation where the hostage takers are motivated to simply take and hold an embassy, the use of force, or even the threat of using force, might very well induce them to give up the hostages. It would be irrational to die holding an embassy. The motives of these hostage takers could only be understood in the context of the situation and the Persian culture.

The worldview of Iranians tends to be more tragic and pessimistic than that of Americans. This may be a result of a history of many wars, invasions, and occupations by other countries, revolution and so on. To be overly idealistic and optimistic when things often indeed "go bad" is to be naïve and even childish. Americans are much more likely to melodramatically believe that good people will usually succeed in their endeavors and everything will end up well in the end. In the old cowboy movies, the good guys all wore white hats and they always won the fights. Only the bad guys with black hats got killed. As the expression goes, Americans "see the glass half full" while Iranians "see the glass half empty."

Added to this tragic perspective was an underlying respect for martyrdom—sacrificing and suffering persecution, even risking death, in the defense of one's religion. Many of the young men who took the American Embassy saw it as a religious act. They believed the United States to be the "Great Satan." If your enemy is the Great Satan, then you must be on the side of God. Your cause must be good and righteous.[64] An expectation of tragedy and the hope for martyrdom may be embedded in the cultural and religious belief systems of those who took the Americans hostage. And if this is true, what is the worst thing then that can happen to a martyr? He lives. Being killed by the Great Satan is not bad news if you really want to be a martyr. Threatening to bomb Tehran would never have gotten the hostages released. It would only have intensified and prolonged the crisis. Realistic cultural empathy is also a matter of knowing what <u>not</u> to do because you can anticipate the possible reactions to your behavior.

DOES CULTURE MATTER?

Some contemporary scholars argue that culture is the key to both economic and democratic development. Lawrence Harrison[65] identifies ten cultural values that he believes are "progress-prone" such as a future time orientation and frugality, a strong work ethic, education especially for women, a sense of community that goes beyond the family, an ethical code, and secularism. Geography and the history of a people can impact development, but cultural values are the most significant variables. Harrison is basically a cultural determinist who believes that a society without these values cannot advance to become a modern democratic nation state with a vibrant and growing economy.

The opposite of progress-prone values are those that are "static"—a past and present time orientation, the desire for immediate gratification, collectivism at the expense of individualism, extreme loyalty to the extended family or tribe, the lack of an ethical code and an all-encompassing emphasis on religion, and with little value placed on education for all. Even if the country has abundant natural resources it will not flourish economically and it is likely to have an undemocratic government.

Cultural determinists clearly emphasize hidden or internal culture at the base of the iceberg model of culture. As mentioned earlier, Marxists would focus on the tip of the iceberg and claim that if we change the means of production and the distribution of wealth, we will change the values culture to produce a more humanistic society. Harrison gives priority to the base of the iceberg. If we change cultural values we change the behavior of citizens in ways that lead to economic growth and democracy.

Harrison's position is an up-to-date version of sociologist Max Weber's *The Protestant Ethic and the Spirit of Capitalism* and social psychologist David McClelland's *The Achieving Society*. Although he provides greater empirical evidence to support his theory and devotes more attention to linking these values to democratic development, he still views "Protestant" values as essential for any growth. In a past-time oriented society there is little planning for the future and change is not welcome. One's loyalty is primarily centered on the extended family or tribe and thus there is less of a chance for a civic culture to develop. People seek to preserve and identify with that which benefits their familial or ethnic group. In turn, this may lead to corruption and practices that benefit one group over another. Outsiders and insiders are clearly delineated.

Static cultures tend to be both traditional and homogeneous which inhibits creativity and innovation that are especially necessary in the modern world. There are few rewards for individual achievement and there is a tendency to maintain the status quo. Countries that are static produce few patents compared with those that are more urban and heterogeneous.

Many critics view these cultural determinist theories as downright ethnocentric. The definition of progress is very Western with an over-emphasis on individualism at the expense of the family or community. Viewed from a collectivist perspective, individualism is simply selfishness. The colonial experience of a country and a lack of abundant natural resources must impact economic growth. It may be no accident that countries with a temperate climate tend to be wealthier and necessarily have a future time orientation. In a temperate climate, crops must be harvested and stored at a particular time or everyone could starve during a severe winter. This requires planning for the future.

Culture certainly *matters* but there are other factors that are perhaps equally important determinants of economic and political development. Exaggerated cultural values may even be harmful to the overall society. While rewarding individual achievement might lead to overall economic growth, a virulent or pathological individualism can weaken the family and the social fabric and collectivist values that hold a community together. Alienation and psychological isolationism in an urban society may be a result of radical individualism.

Conversely, extraordinary loyalty to one's extended family or ethnic group, with an emphasis on traditional and rigid social roles and status, prevents many citizens from achieving their full educational or professional potential. In turn, they do not contribute equally to overall economic growth. A son is obligated to stay in the village to walk in his father's footsteps and never becomes a great political leader or entrepreneur. There may be a clear division and inequality between genders, social roles and status are rigidly ascribed, and there is an enormous distance between subordinates and superiors.

The debate will continue regarding the importance of cultural values and which values are best for a modern society. Perhaps a healthy tension between conflicting values within a society may be good because it leads to synergistic creativity in a rapidly changing world. Traditional values might provide a stability which is necessary to cope with modern technology and increased intercultural interaction. And yet, an acceptance of change and new ways of perceiving reality and solving problems may be necessary to carry a society into an increasingly interdependent world.

SECTION I: Readings

How Cultures Collide

Edward T. Hall and Elizabeth Hall

Elizabeth Hall (for Psychology Today): For years, you've been saying that our ignorance of nonverbal communication threatens international relations, trade, and even world peace. Your new book, *Beyond Culture,* makes your warnings stronger and more specific. Just how, for example, does our ignorance of the silent language of behavior affect our relations with the People's Republic of China?

Edward T. Hall: All human beings are captives of their culture. When dealing with the Chinese, we are apt to try to read their true intentions from what they do rather than what they say. But in so doing, and by assuming that behavior means pretty much the same around the world, we anticipate their actions as if they were Americans—whereas they read our behavior with strong Chinese overtones. That could lead to serious misunderstandings.

One difference between us and the Chinese is in the way action chains are handled. An action chain is a set of events that resembles a dance, except that it is a dance with a goal. If any of the basic steps of the dance are omitted or distorted, the chain is broken and the action must begin all over again. The goal may be sex, marriage, corporate mergers, peace treaties—or something as simple as shaking hands or buying a gallon of paint. I doubt if any

Psychology Today, 10, No. 7, (July 1976): 66, 69, 71–74, 97.

human social action exists that does not involve action chains.

In this culture, chains have clearly defined steps and stages; in China, the steps are not as clear to us. Faced with a troublesome situation, the Chinese will often act as though nothing has happened. They believe that once one acknowledges an event, then one must take action—and action may be very, very serious. This is why the Chinese may seem to ignore our actions in one instance and be hypersensitive in another. We misread their intentions both in Korea and in Vietnam.

pt: And we misread them because we couldn't decipher the steps in their action chains?

Hall: In part, yes. In Vietnam we misread Chinese intentions by thinking they were motivated the way we were and took them too seriously; in Korea we didn't take them seriously enough. They told us where the line was, but we didn't believe them. In the same way, the Chinese may fail to see when we are very serious, and they misread the signs in our action chains. Whenever the members of one culture believe that another possesses no subtlety, as some Chinese apparently believe of us, it is a clear sign that the first culture has grossly misunderstood the second; I know of no culture without subtlety.

pt: We were warned that allowing the North Vietnamese to win would topple the first in a chain of dominoes, that Vietnam would lead to a solidly Communist Asia, just as Munich led toward a Nazi Europe.

Hall: When we went into Asia, we tried to fit events into a pattern that we have seen work in Europe. We confused Vietnam with Munich. The parallels were nonexistent. For we shared a history as well as political and social institutions with the Czechs; we shared none of these with the South Vietnamese. When Hitler marched on Czechoslovakia, it was an authoritarian government opposing a democratic regime; in Vietnam there were two authoritarian regimes.

pt: Do you think that with a better knowledge of the Chinese culture we would have known that some of the actions we took with trepidation would not provoke the Chinese into sending troops?

Hall: Possibly. But with a better knowledge of other peoples, we might not have fallen for our own propaganda. And might have avoided Vietnam in the first place. Clearly we had no idea of what we were getting into.

pt: And if you have a Secretary of State who meets every international situation as if it were an episode in 19th-century European politics . . .

Hall: You have a problem. But it runs deeper than that, for we avoid knowing. Our Department of State rotates its overseas employees every two years. According to one undersecretary in charge of personnel, our policy assumes that when a U.S. citizen knows a country too well, he begins to represent them, not us. This is, of course, a head-in-the-sand attitude.

As far as China goes, we eliminated the old China hands in Joe McCarthy's heyday. When men like John Stewart Service and John Carter Vincent told us what was happening in China, that Mao's Communists were winning, they were drummed out of the State Department as disloyal.

But to return to action chains. Americans, if they are sophisticated, watch other people's behavior to anticipate events. The Chinese do not ignore behavior entirely, but they are apt to pay more attention to where the other person is placed in a social system. They believe that the system will ultimately dictate behavior. This is because China is a high-context culture and we're a low-context culture.

pt: Just what do you mean by high- and low-context cultures?

Hall: Context and communication are intimately interrelated. In some cultures, messages are explicit; the words carry most of the information. In other cultures, such as China or Japan or the Arab cultures, less information is contained in the verbal part of a message, since more is in the context. That's why American businessmen often complain that their Japanese counterparts never get to the point. The Japanese wouldn't dream of spelling the whole thing out. To do so is a put-down; it's like doing your thinking for you.

pt: Like talking down to someone, or explaining something to a child.

Hall: Exactly. This sort of misunderstanding is so common that a few Americans picked up one reliable cue that shows when Japanese diplomats, having tried to get across an important point, realize they've failed. When this happens, they start slugging down Scotch. Remember, however, that in situations such as these, expectations may have significant unconscious overtones. Since much of culture operates outside our awareness, frequently we don't even know that we know. We pick them up in the cradle. We unconsciously learn what to notice and what not to notice, how to divide time and space, how to walk and talk and use our bodies, how to behave as men or women, how to relate to other people, how to handle responsibility, whether experience is seen as whole or fragmented. This applies to all peoples. The Chinese or the Japanese or the Arabs are as unaware of their assumptions as we are of our own. We each assume that they're part of human nature. What we think of as "mind" is really internalized culture.

pt: Let's explore some of the differences between high and low context. How does a high-context culture handle personal responsibility?

Hall: The difference is built in, shared, preprogrammed information as it relates to the transmitted, public part of the message. In general, high-context cultures can get by with less of the legal paperwork that is deemed essential in America. A man's word is his bond and you need not spell out the details to make him behave. One depends more on the power and influence of established networks of friends and relatives. Even in rather mundane matters, the two systems can be seen in contrast. For instance, several years ago I was traveling in Crete and wanted to visit the ruins at Knossos. My traveling companion, who was from low-context, fast-moving New York, took charge of the arrangements. He bargained with a taxi driver, agreed on a price, and a deal was made. We would take his taxi. Without warning, just as we were entering the cab, he stopped, got out and asked another driver if he would take us for less money. Since the second driver was willing, my

friend said, "Let's go." The first taxi driver felt he had been cheated. We had made a verbal agreement and it had been violated. But my friend, coming from a low-context opportunistic culture, felt no moral obligation at all. He had saved the equivalent of 75¢. I can still see the shocked and horrified look on the face of the first taxi driver.

pt: Your friend was accustomed to getting three bids for a job.

Hall: Yes, and insisting on competitive bidding can also cause complications overseas. In a high-context culture, the job is given to the man who will do the best work and whom you can control. In a low-context culture, we try to make the specifications so precise that a builder has trouble doing a bad job. A builder in Japan is likely to say, "What has that piece of paper got to do with the situation? If we can't trust each other enough to go ahead without it, why bother?"

There are further implications of this pattern. A friend of mine in the Middle East was out one evening with a large group of Lebanese men. He happened to mention casually that if he only had some money, he could make a bundle. Much later as the group was breaking up, one of the men whom he didn't know gave him his card and asked him to drop by the next day. When my friend called, the man asked him how much money he needed and for how long, stating that he had some extra money. Upon hearing the amount, he proceeded to write out a check. The Lebanese businessman did not know my friend personally, but knew that he was part of a particular group, and therefore trustworthy.

pt: In other words, he didn't have to run a credit check.

Hall: No. Our low-context approach frequently ties the hands of American bankers in the Middle East. Several years ago, before things deteriorated out there, I interviewed a number of bankers. I was told they just couldn't compete with the local banks. For every loan over a certain amount, the Americans had to send a profit-and-loss statement to New York for an OK. By the time New York passed on the loan, the customer had gone elsewhere.

pt: That would mean that only high-risk loans would be left for American banks. Members of a high-context culture would know by a man's group whether he was a good risk.

Hall: Precisely.

pt: A number of corporations have gotten into hot water by paying bribes to foreign officials.

Hall: Bribery, as far as I know, is not condoned anywhere in the world, even in countries where it is a general practice. For a long time, civil servants in many countries simply did not earn enough to live on. They made a living wage by accepting a little extra to do their official tasks. But it's a long way from tipping an agent for stamping your visa to passing out a million dollars for an aircraft contract.

pt: From what you have been saying, the high-context culture functions on the basis of whom you know, while the American culture functions according to rules of procedure. Maybe American companies who pay off so-called agents are merely trying to buy the friendship network.

Hall: You are so right. However, any American could establish the same network that he tries to buy, but it would take him longer to do it. Most companies are not willing to invest that much time. Instead of building a solid foundation of relationships against the time when we will need them, we take a short cut and use money instead.

pt: How would a high-context culture like Japan have handled Watergate?

Hall: Again there are some interesting differences. In Japan, the man at the top is responsible. Nixon would have committed suicide. In the case of the My Lai massacre, Westmoreland would have taken the rap. In low-context systems, responsibility is kicked as far down the system as possible. In a high-context culture, the top man shoulders the blame.

pt: So the sign on Harry Truman's desk, "The Buck Stops Here," was really a high-context sign. He did take responsibility; he always said that dropping the bomb was purely his own decision.

Hall: Truman had a deep moral sense, a sense of continuity, and was deeply conversant with the presidency as an institution. He came out of a past age. In the days of the Old West, a man's word was his bond in this country, in part because everyone really did know everyone else. Truman belonged to this tradition. Recently our culture has been becoming noticeably more low-context.

pt: I can't disagree. We've had the rise of experts who tell us how to do everything from having sex to rearing children to being assertive—things one would assume people did as a part of being human. And the new marriage contracts specify everything about the bond from who washes dishes to how many nights a week out each partner has.

Hall: One of the complications of a low-context culture is the fragmenting of experience. The plethora of experts testifies that. The marriage contracts may mean that our commitment to each other is diminishing. Commitment is greater in a high-context culture because the mass of the system is so great that you literally cannot escape, and it's almost impossible to change the rules.

pt: Nearly everything we have said shows up the advantages of a high-context culture. What are its disadvantages?

Hall: We've just said that they're very hard to move. Reforms come slowly. They're also likely to have rigid class structures and a family structure that holds people in a vise. You can't escape. The only way for a Japanese woman to get back at her mother-in-law is to wait until her own son marries. There's less mobility. Your occupation may be determined by what your father did. Or you may sign up with an employer for life as they do in Japan. High context cultures are more group-oriented, and they sacrifice individualism. Individuals outside the group are apt to be helpless.

pt: Can you lay out some of the major cultures in terms of their context?

Hall: I would begin with the German-Swiss. They are low-context, falling somewhere near the bottom of the scale. Next the Germans, then the

Scandinavians, as we move up. These cultures are all lower in context than the U.S. Above Americans come the French, the English, the Italians, the Spanish, the Greeks and the Arabs. In other words, as you move from northern to southern Europe, you will find that people move toward more involvement with each other. Look at the difference between a Swedish and an Italian movie.

pt: Sometimes people will discuss a Bergman movie and each will have a completely different motivation for the characters.

Hall: The first thing to remember about a Bergman movie is that no matter what it means to you, it means something else to a Swede. We can't possibly interpret all that's going on there.

pt: You said earlier that each culture also has its own way of dividing up space.

Hall: With space, of course, one has to mentally shift gears. Space is a communication system, and it's one of the reasons that many North Europeans and Americans don't like the Middle East. Arabs tend to get very close and breathe on you. It's part of the high sensory involvement of a high-context culture. If an Arab does not breathe on you, it means that he is consciously withholding his breath and is ashamed.

pt: For the Arabs, then, this part of culture doesn't operate outside awareness.

Hall: For us, much of it does—for the Arabs it's different. They say, "Why are the Americans so ashamed? They withhold their breath." The American on the receiving end can't identify all the sources of his discomfort but feels that the Arab is pushy. The Arab comes close, the American backs up. The Arab follows, because he can only interact at certain distances. Once the American learns that Arabs handle space differently and that breathing on people is a form of communication, the situation can sometimes be redefined so the American relaxes.

pt: In *The Hidden Dimension*, you wrote that each of us carries a little bubble of space around with us and that the space under our feet belongs to us.

Hall: Again, the things we take for granted can trip us up and cause untold discomfort and frequently anger. In the Arab world you do not hold a lien on the ground under foot. When standing on a street corner, an Arab may shove you aside if he wants to be where you are. This puts the average territorial American or German under great stress. Something basic has been violated. Behind this—to us—bizarre or even rude behavior lies an entirely different concept of property. Even the body is not sacred when a person is in public. Years ago, before all the fighting, American women in Beirut had to give up using streetcars. Their bodies were the property of all men within reach. What was happening is even reflected in the language. The Arabs have no word for *trespass,* no word for *rape.* The ego and the id are highly developed and depend on strong controls of the type few Europeans are accustomed to providing.

Space, of course, is one way of communicating; even at home, our language shows it. We say of an intimate friend that he is "close" and that someone who does not get emotionally involved is "standoffish" or "distant." Once I heard a hospital nurse describing doctors. She said there were beside-the-bed doctors, who were interested in the patient, and foot-of-the-bed doctors, who were interested in the patient's condition. They unconsciously expressed their emotional involvement—or lack of it—by where they stood.

pt: We're all becoming aware that the body does communicate. Books on body language have become popular. You can buy books that tell you how to succeed in business, be a smashing success at a cocktail party, or become popular with the opposite sex, all by reading body cues. Are these books generally helpful?

Hall: I think they are dreadful. Unfortunately, a few writers have exploited things that some of us have discovered about human behavior, and have managed to give the field a bad name. When a popularizer writes that sitting with your legs crossed has a certain specific meaning, he's just complicating life for everyone. In the final analysis, human beings have to deal with each other on a real-life basis.

pt: Are you implying that people who read these books will try to change their behavior?

Hall: That's the idea. It's manipulative, and I think it's not good for people to manipulate each other. Women don't like to be regarded as sex objects, because it involves manipulation.

pt: Besides the ethical objections, what about the practicality of such advice?

Hall: It's grotesque, and besides it just doesn't work. People are being taken advantage of, and they should feel quite angry when they find out.

pt: Does the problem lie in the fact that these books take the meaning of body language out of context?

Hall: You've put your finger on the crux of the matter. When body signals are not seen in context, their meaning can only be distorted. The popularizers of body language take a low-context, manipulative, exploitative view of high-context situations. When I speak of silent language, I mean more than body language. I refer to the totality of behavior as well as the products of behavior—time, space, materials, everything.

pt: One of the major differences in behavior you've found comes from a culture's way of handling time. How does time affect the shape of a culture or a person's view of the world?

Hall: Time, like space, communicates. It is not merely a convention, it's an organizing system. Our culture happens to organize most activities on a time base. We talk about time as if it were money; we spend it, save it or waste it. Time patterns are so deeply embedded in our central nervous system that we can't imagine getting along without them. The Western world couldn't function without its linear, one-thing-at-a-time system. Technology requires a monochronic approach. Railroads and airlines couldn't be integrated or run without schedules.

Of course, in the U.S. we don't begin to approach the Swiss in their slavery to time. Wherever a Swiss railroad stops, no matter how far into the mountains, passengers can look out the window at the nearest telegraph pole. On the pole will be a small white sign with a line down the middle and an arrow pointing in each direction, telling how many minutes—not kilometers—it is from the last station and how many it is to the next.

pt: It's apparently no accident that the Swiss are great watchmakers. But what is another way of handling time?

Hall: The Hopi Indians provide us with an excellent contrast because they don't have a single system that integrates everything. They believe that every living thing has its own inherent system and that you must deal with each plant or animal in terms of its own time. Their system is what I call polychronic, which hasn't always worked to their advantage. For example, if the Hopi had a slow-maturing variety of corn that would barely produce edible ears by the end of the growing season, they were apt to accept it. White Americans would be more apt to develop new strains that matured sooner; the old-time Hopi wouldn't think of altering a living time system.

pt: A bit of that polychronic time would help American mothers who become nervous if their children don't walk or talk at a certain age. They've been told each child has its own rate of maturation, but they don't believe it.

Hall: That's because we are wedded to some distant standard against which everything is measured. Even so, housewives have more experience with polychronic time than the rest of us. They must get husbands off to work, children to school, babies bathed and fed, meals ready, and clothes washed and dried. Each of those has its own time system, and it's one reason women have reacted so strongly to their life. A polychronic system tends to minimize individuality at the expense of group needs while a monochronic system can restore feelings of identity sometimes to the extent of narcissism. But if your identity comes from the group, as a Pueblo Indian's does, a monochronic system can be quite destructive because it interferes with group cohesiveness.

pt: Does this difference in time systems contribute to cross-cultural conflicts?

Hall: Of course. It can and has generated all sorts of tension between peoples. For example, 40 years ago when I worked with the Hopi, they were building dams paid for by the taxpayers. The government knew how long it takes to build dams and expected them to be finished in a set period of time. The Hopi felt that a dam had no built-in schedule, and they would not be hurried. Now, if it had been possible to convince the Hopi that inherent in the dam's structure was the fact that it was supposed to be completed in 90 days, for example, the problem would have been solved. But we didn't know enough then.

pt: Do all Western countries run on monochronic time?

Hall: Not entirely. Latin American and Mediterranean countries tend to be polychronic. It goes with high-context cultures. This has caused American businessmen and diplomats some trouble. Both have made appointments with Latin Americans and been kept waiting. Typically the Latin American, left to his own way of doing things, would have an office full of people, each there for a different purpose, showing no favoritism. He fails to devote himself to the North Americans who happen to be there to see him. The North American, running on a monochronic system, almost inevitably believes that the Latin American is telling him that he is not important. The Latin interprets the American's resentment as narcissism.

pt: How does this affect the manufacturing plants that American companies opened in Latin America?

Hall: For years I worked with an American company that tried to run a plant in Mexico. They finally gave up. They had a high-quality product and just couldn't get the Mexicans to produce to their standards. You should understand that the problem was not just time. It was a case of not developing a system that the local people could understand in terms of their own culture.

There's always a solution. Unfortunately Americans frequently fail to find it. Aramco, for example, was losing money on one of their trucking operations in Saudi Arabia. Finally, an Arab was able to buy the franchise and set up his own system. Knowing his own people, he worked out a series of complex reinforcement schedules for each truck and driver. He even penalized them for every valve cap that was missing and rewarded drivers when nothing that was supposed to be there was missing. Oil levels in the crankcase, maintenance schedules, time schedules, everything was examined and recorded.

The cost per ton-mile dropped to a third of what it had been under American management.

pt: Sounds as if he simply imposed a behavior-shaping schedule on the drivers.

Hall: Yes, but he also organized a way of getting quality that the people understood and would accept. You couldn't set up such an arrangement with American drivers. It would be infringing on their territory to tell them how to take care of their trucks. We think of ourselves as successful managers, but the only people we can manage are other Americans, and we frequently don't do too well at that.

pt: How does all this affect our foreign relations in the Middle East?

Hall: Monochronic people tend to get their information from one or two sources, whereas polychronic people gather information from all over. The Arabs read several New York newspapers, *The Washington Post, Foreign Affairs*, everything they can get their hands on, and put the whole thing together. They come up with what they believe is the policy of the U.S. Once when I was in the Middle East during a crisis, I tried to tell Arabs that they had been reading the expression of several special-interest groups, which bore little or no resemblance to the policy of the U.S., but I didn't get very far. Instead of reacting to the policy of the State Department or Kissinger or Ford, they're reacting to some curious amalgam of the views of Kissinger, James

Reston, various U.S. senators, the oil companies, the Anti-Defamation League, and goodness knows what else.

Another difference between Europeans and Arabs concerns disputes and how they are handled. Arabs depend on outsiders to intervene in disputes. In Arab societies, if two people are arguing and one of them gets hurt, the bystander who failed to stop the fight is the guilty party.

pt: Is that why Egypt is open to Kissinger's diplomacy?

Hall: Kissinger has a healthy male ego. Not only is there a meshing of personalities, but Arabs understand personal diplomacy. Remember that the first Arab-Israeli accord came about when Ralph Bunche got both parties isolated on an island and put each on a separate floor of a hotel. He carried messages back and forth between the floors until, finally, things began to work. He was very persuasive. Kissinger has done something similar, but I am under the impression that he didn't design it that way.

pt: Do the different cultural backgrounds of the Arabs and the Israelis complicate the situation?

Hall: Naturally. The Middle East is a village culture, and village land is sacred in a way that is impossible to describe in the U.S. For example, about 25 years ago, a friend of mine conducted a census of a Lebanese village. The villagers claimed several times as many people as actually inhabited the village. People who had emigrated to Mexico and New York and Brazil and who hadn't been back for generations were counted and were still considered members of the village.

Europeans and Americans think in terms of nation states. Israel is a nation state in the midst of a village-culture complex. We're not talking about mere convention. The Palestinian Arabs who were displaced from their land have not forgotten, and they will never forget. They still consider as their sacred home that village their fathers were driven out of 30 years ago.

On top of that, Zionism is a European thing. Israel has some of the same problems with her

Yemenite Jews that she has with the Arabs. Indigenous Jews, as you know, have to be enculturated into a new European tradition.

pt: So before you even begin to talk about religion, you begin with two incompatible traditions.

Hall: It took the Arabs 20 years to discover that. They finally woke up and discovered that they were not fighting Jews, because they had gotten along with Jewish villages for centuries. They were fighting Europeans.

pt: In *The Hidden Dimension*, you have a photograph of a house built by an Arab to punish a neighbor. Do Arab spite patterns affect the conflict between Israel and the Arab States?

Hall: They haven't yet, but they could. That house looks like a big wall, four stories high. The man who built it owned a narrow strip of land along the road, and the man behind him pushed too hard in trying to buy the land, and told the owner his land wasn't worth anything because no one could build a house on it. The owner of the land said, "I'll show you," and he built this house about six-feet thick—and furthermore built it high enough to cut off his neighbor's view of the Mediterranean.

If the Arabs are pushed too far and a Holy War is declared, there will be a disaster. I don't even like to think about it because once an Arab is in the spite response, he's apt to do anything—wreck his life—the lives of his children—he's past caring. No warning is given and, once the spite pattern takes over, nobody can intervene successfully until it runs its course.

pt: Do the cultural differences between blacks and whites in this country cause misunderstandings?

Hall: The data we have show that they do. The black culture is considerably higher in context than the white culture. I'm not talking about middle-class blacks; they're likely to be as low-contexted, compulsive and obsessional as whites.

But take the matter of the way we listen or show that we are paying attention when someone is talking. I once got a young black draftsman a job with an architectural firm, where he almost got fired.

He did his work well but his employer complained about his attitude. This mystified me until once when I was talking to him and noticed I wasn't getting any feedback. He just sat there, quietly drawing. Finally I said, "Are you listening?" He said, "Man, if you're in the room, I'm listening. You listen with your ears." In their own mode, interacting with each other, ethnic blacks who know each other don't feel they have to look at each other while talking. They don't nod their heads or make little noises to show that they're listening the way whites do.

Old-time Pullman porters used to do a lot of head-bobbing and foot-shuffling and yessing, which was a response to their being hassled by whites. In those days, not knowing the nature of the white listening system, they didn't want to take chances and so they produced an exaggerated version of what whites expected, to show their customers that they were paying attention.

pt: What about the feeling many blacks have that they're invisible men?

Hall: That's another cultural difference. Depending upon the part of the country he's from, a white on the street looks at a person until he's about 12 to 16 feet away. Then, unless they know each other, whites automatically look away to avoid eye contact. This automatic avoidance on our part seems to give blacks the feeling of invisibility, because they use their eyes very differently than whites. As high-context people, they're more involved with each other visually and in every other way.

pt: Do blacks and whites handle time differently?

Hall: Their time is apt to be more polychronic than ours, which caused problems in Detroit when they first began to work on assembly lines and wouldn't show up. At times blacks jokingly refer to CPT or colored people's time when dealing with whites. Their system seems to run much closer to the way the body operates as well as being more situational in character.

Blacks also pay more attention than we do to nonverbal behavior. I once ran an experiment in which one black filmed another in a job interview. Each time something significant happened, the watching black started the camera. When I looked at those films, I couldn't believe my eyes. Nothing was happening! Or so I thought. It turned out that my camera-operator was catching—and identifying—body signals as minor as the movement of a thumb, which foreshadowed an intention to speak. Whites aren't so finely tuned.

pt: Since many of our ethnic groups come from high-context cultures, I suppose that our low-context approach has caused problems for them as well.

Hall: There are many such problems, but particularly when urban renewal enters the picture. Planners and politicians are apt to mark ethnic neighborhoods as slums, and classify them for renewal because they do not see the order behind what appears to be disorder. Live, vital, cohesive ethnic communities are destroyed. To make way for a university in Chicago, planners wiped out a Greek and Italian neighborhood, over strong protests. The scars haven't healed yet. It is important to stress that when you scatter such a community, you're doing more than tear down buildings; you're destroying most of what gives life meaning, particularly for people who are deeply involved with each other. The displaced people grieve for their homes as if they had lost children and parents. To low-context whites, one neighborhood is much like the next. To high-context people, it is something else again.

pt: You once said that urban renewal programs were as destructive as enemy bombing.

Hall: That was no mere metaphor. Take a good look at any neighborhood that's been hit by urban renewal. It's like a European city after a bombing raid. Furthermore, wasting communities is the first step in a chain of events that ends in destroying our cities. As a last resort and if absolutely necessary, neighborhoods should be relocated en masse. The whole community should be moved together—local policemen, streetcleaners, shopkeepers, and even postal clerks should be moved as a unit. Of course it will never happen. It would make too much sense.

pt: If I had to sum up our talk, I'd say that your work is a plea for sensing context.

Hall: If I have only one point to make, it is that nothing is independent of anything else. Yet in the U.S. we use a special-interest approach for solving political, economic and environmental problems, which disregards the interconnectedness of events. Unfortunately, our schools are no help because they consistently teach us not to make connections. I feel strongly that there should be a few people at least whose task is synthesis—pulling things together. And that is impossible without a deep sense of context.

The Role of Culture and Perception in Communication

Marshall Singer

Back in the 1960s I argued that every identity group has a culture of its own.[1] I also argued then that every individual is a part of perhaps hundreds of different identity groups simultaneously and that one learns, and becomes a part of, all of the cultures with which one identifies. I will make those same arguments in the pages that follow.

At the time I wrote that article some anthropologists said that I was destroying the concept of culture. If it was to have any meaning it had to be applied only to very large groups like total societies or large language or ethnic groupings. As I saw it, the way the anthropologists viewed the problem forced them to describe the large degree of cultural variation that exists *within* every society as being "subcultural." For me that didn't seem to be a logical or useful way to deal with the problem—particularly when I realized that I was in some ways much closer to some "subcultures" in other societies than I was to many within my own. It seemed to me then—and still does today—much more logical and useful to talk about the culture of each group and then to examine—for each total society—the groups that comprise it. Each society is certainly different from every other society, but that is because no two societies contain all of the same groups and only

those groups. I suppose it's a little like looking at two different kinds of cake. A chocolate cake is certainly quite different from, let's say, a fruitcake, yet they are both still cakes and as such have more in common with each other than either does to, let's say, a chocolate candy bar. But that does not distract from the fact that the chocolate in the cake and the chocolate in the candy bar are much more similar to each other than they are to any of the other ingredients of either the cake or the candy bar.

Culinary analogies notwithstanding, over the course of the decades anthropologists themselves have now independently come to take a position very similar to the position I took then. Certainly they have not done so because of me but rather because of the compelling logic of the argument. In any event, in the pages that follow I hope to show the reader how the individual interacts with the groups of which she or he forms a part and how both the individual and the groups affect each other.

Now with this work, I am about to anger some anthropologists again, because I am pushing the concept still further. I am now going to argue that because no person is a part of all, and only, the same groups as anyone else and because each person

This is a revision of the first chapter of his book *Intercultural Communication: A Perceptual Approach* first published by Prentice-Hall in 1987. It is currently available as *Perception and Identity in Intercultural Communication: An Abridged and Revised Edition*, Boston: Intercultural Press, 1998, ISBN 1-877864-61-7 ranks the attitudes, values, and beliefs of the groups to which he or she belongs differently, *each individual must be considered to be culturally unique.* Notice that I am *not* arguing that every person is a culture unto herself or himself. Culture is, after all, a group-related phenomenon. What I will argue is that each individual in this world is a member of a unique collection of groups. No two humans share only and exactly the same group memberships, or exactly the same ranking of the importance, to themselves, of the group membership they do share. Thus each person must be culturally unique.

If I am correct in this assertion—and I hope to be able to convince the reader in the pages that follow that I am—this means that every interpersonal communication must, to some degree, also be an intercultural communication. The implications of this conclusion, if true, are rather enormous. Some may have difficulty in accepting it. I hope the argument I make is sufficiently convincing that over the course of the next decades most scholars—regardless of discipline—will come to accept this way of viewing interpersonal and intergroup interactions.

There is another important concept I will introduce here. I will argue that every communication relationship has a power component attached to it, and we might as well deal with it openly and consciously. Until now very few communication specialists have been prepared to deal with the power aspect of the communication process. On the other hand, most political scientists until now have failed to recognize the importance of cultural differences in the situations they study. It is one of my most deeply held convictions that the study of intercultural communication informs the study of political behavior. It is also my contention that any study of communication relationships that ignores the power aspect of those relationships is one that misses a very important element of all communications.

One additional point that must be made: I do not believe that "better communication" is a panacea. Conflict at every level of analysis has always persisted and probably always will. I am convinced that to the degree that interpersonal, intergroup,

or international communication can be facilitated (a) there is likely to be less misperception and fear of other actors, and (b) at least the actors can be certain, if they are in conflict, that they both agree on what the conflict actually is about.

In many ways the world is shrinking at an incredible rate. Strange and often frightening groups are coming into contact with each other at ever accelerating rates. Isolation is unthinkable. More people are living and working and studying among people of different cultures today than at any previous time in history. That experience can be made easier, more productive, and more satisfying if we better understand the processes at work. And while intercultural communication may be a difficult task, it is not impossible.

CULTURE: WHAT IS IT?

Of all the animals known to exist, the human animal is perhaps the most social. Particularly in our earliest years, but throughout our entire lives as well, people exist—and must exist—in relationships with other human beings. Each of the humans with whom one comes into contact brings to that relationship his or her own view of the universe. More important, perhaps, each of the groups in which one has been raised or in which one has spent a good deal of time will have conditioned the individual to view the world from its perspective.

As animals, all of us must eat, drink, sleep, find shelter, give and receive affection, and meet all of the other biologic requirements "that flesh is heir to." But what we eat, when we eat, and how we eat are all behaviors we have learned from the groups in which we have grown up. Not only the language I speak and the way I think but even *what* I see, hear, taste, touch, and smell are conditioned by the cultures in which I have been raised.

Benjamin Lee Whorf, the noted linguist, has written: "We are thus introduced to a new principle of relativity, which holds that all observers are not led by the same physical evidence to the same picture of the universe, unless their linguistic backgrounds are similar, or can in some way be calibrated."[2] I would go a step further and substitute the word *cultural* for the word *linguistic*.

Every culture has its own language[3] or code, to be sure, but language is the manifestation—verbal or otherwise—of the perceptions, attitudes, values, beliefs, and disbelief systems that the group holds. Language, once established, further constrains the individual to perceive in certain ways, but I would argue that language is merely one of the ways in which groups maintain and reinforce similarity of perception.

Genetically, we inherit from our parents those physical characteristics that distinguish us as their offspring. Admittedly there is a good deal of individual variation physically and experientially, but there is a good deal of similarity. Given two white parents the overwhelming probability is that the offspring will be white. Given two English-speaking parents the overwhelming probability is that the offspring will speak English. The difference is that physical identity is—within a given range of probability—fixed, while cultural identity is not. The son of two white parents will always remain white no matter what happens to him after birth, but the son of two English-speaking parents may never speak English if immediately after birth he is raised by a totally non-English-speaking group. Thus while physical inheritance is relatively immutable, cultural inheritance is ever changing. The fascinating aspect of cultural conditioning, however, is that while there is theoretically an almost infinite number of possibilities, in fact, the number of group-learned experiences to which most individuals are exposed is amazingly limited. Thus for example, while there may be a whole world to explore, if not an entire universe, the incredibly overwhelming majority of individuals who inhabit this planet never stray more than a few miles from their place of birth. They will, in all probability, speak the language that their parents spoke; practice the religion that their parents practiced; support the political parties that their parents supported; and in broad outline accept most of the cultural perceptions that their parents accepted. In sum, they will perceive the world in a manner strikingly similar to the way their parents perceived the world. That is precisely what makes

them a part of the same broad cultural groups of which their parents formed a part. All will deviate from the perceptions of their parents (some only mildly, others more radically), but that is inevitable because every individual is unique. So too are the experiences that every person has. While most of those experiences will be learned from other groups into which the individual will be socialized in the course of his or her life, some of those experiences will not have been group related.

What is more, cultures themselves are constantly changing (in part because the environments in which people live are constantly changing), and thus people's perceptions of the world around them are also constantly changing. Further, some people—particularly in Western societies—rebel against the attitudes and values of their parents and adopt different group values for themselves. Though most people in the West go through a period of rebellion while in their teens, by the time they are adults the vast majority seem to have returned to the cultures of their parents. Each of us is a member of a finite number of different identity groups, but it is a comparatively small number compared to the incredibly large number that exist in the world. A very large number of the most important groups to which we belong are the same groups to which our parents belonged.

It is a most basic premise of this work that *a pattern of learned, group-related perceptions— including both verbal and nonverbal language, attitudes, values, belief systems, disbelief systems, and behaviors—that is accepted and expected by an identity group is called a culture. Since, by definition, each identity group has its own pattern of perceptions and behavioral norms and its own language or code (understood most clearly by the members of that group), each group may be said to have its own culture.*

Years ago Ruth Benedict said: "The life history of the individual is first and foremost an accommodation to the patterns and standards traditionally handed down in his community. From the moment of his birth the customs into which he is born shape his experience and behavior. By the time he can talk, he is a little creature of his culture, and by the time he is grown and able to take part in its activities, its habits are its habits, its beliefs his beliefs, its impossibilities his impossibilities. Every child that is born into his group will share them with him . . ."[4] And while she was referring there to total societal groups, everything she said then still holds with reference to all identity groups.

The early cultural anthropologists wanted to collect data on how different groups met their biological needs and related to their environments. In order to do that they felt that they had to find remote, isolated, "primitive" groups that had not been "contaminated" by contact with Western societies. Thus they went to the South Pacific, to isolated American Indian reservations, to the Latin American mountains and remote jungles, and to the Asian subcontinent looking for people who were presumed to have been so isolated that they would have been living and doing things the same ways for millennia. In the process they created the impression that it was only those "quaint" and "primitive" peoples who had cultures that were clearly differentiated from one another. Later anthropologists corrected that misconception by rightly demonstrating that all peoples have unique histories, belief systems, attitudes, values, traditions, languages, and accepted and expected patterns of behavior, and that these ensembles constitute culture. But even there the notion persisted that one had to look at a total society in order to understand its culture. Thanks most, perhaps, to the work of Benjamin Lee Whorf and Edward Sapir, the tremendously important role of language in shaping patterns of thinking—and thus the relationship between language and culture—was established. But in so doing they also created the impression that only peoples who spoke distinctly different languages—not dialects—had distinctive cultural patterns. Only in very recent times have scholars come to accept the notion that *every group* that shares a similar pattern of perceptions—with all that implies—constitutes a culture. Since every identity group has somewhat different learned cultural ensembles, in greater or lesser degree, then every identity group may be said to have its own culture.

C.T. Patrick Diamond paraphrases as follows a statement of P. Kay published in *Current Directions in Anthropology:* "The worlds of café society, ethnic and sexual minorities, the social elite, professional or occupational groups and age cohorts each represent a shared but distinct perspective that orders the respective field of experience to provide identification and solidarity for its members. Such groups possess sets of implicit assumptions or bases for discrimination. These conventional understandings provide their culture or their tacit theory of the world."[5] Thus at least some modern anthropologists also share the view that every group has a culture of its own.

Why the importance of making this distinction? Because looking at it this way enables us to apply the tools and techniques of intercultural analysis and communication to all interpersonal, intergroup, and international interactions. Further, it enables us to look at any totality—a small informal group, a large organization, a city, or a tribe or nation—and ask, What are the identity groups present in that unit of analysis? To what degree are there linkages among the groupings? To what degree are the unit identities stronger than the group identities that comprise it? To what degree are the group identities stronger? How can communication between groups be encouraged? These and dozens of similar questions must be answered if the effectiveness of personal, group, or national communication is to be increased. And the effectiveness of those communications will be increased if we constantly keep in mind the cultural differences that must be dealt with.

Henry Hoijer has said: " . . . to the extent that languages differ markedly from each other, so should we expect to find significant and formidable barriers to cross-cultural communication and understanding . . . It is, however, easy to exaggerate . . . the . . . barriers to intercultural understanding. No culture is wholly isolated, self-contained, and unique. There are important resemblances between all known cultures—resemblances that stem in part from diffusion (itself an evidence of successful intercultural communication) and in part from the fact that all cultures are built around biological, psychological, and social characteristics common to all mankind . . . Intercultural communication, however wide the differences between cultures may be, is not impossible. It is simply more or less difficult, depending on the degree of difference between the cultures concerned.[6]

To this Diamond adds the following, this time paraphrasing the psychologist G.A. Kelly:

People belong to the same cultural group not merely because they behave alike nor because they expect the same things of others but especially because they construe their experiences in similar ways. However, people are not helplessly suspended in their culture. The task is to generate the imagination needed to envision the infinity of possibilities still open to people of any group; that is to construe their way out of cultural controls.[7]

PERCEPTIONS AND HUMAN BEHAVIOR

My first conscious awareness of the importance of perceptions to human behavior began with an incident when I was still a graduate student. At that time esoteric foods like chocolate-covered ants, fried grasshoppers, smoked rattlesnake meat, and sweet-and-sour mouse tails, were the culinary fad. Upon moving into a new apartment, I received from a friend (as a housewarming gift) a whole carton of these canned delicacies. Having at that time rather prosaic food habits, I did not proceed to consume the entire carton. Indeed, it sat untouched for the better part of a year while I alternately toyed with the idea of trying one of these less-than-tempting "goodies" myself or throwing the entire carton in the garbage. One evening while putting out a whole array of cheeses and other edibles in preparation for a cocktail party I was about to hold, it occurred to me that my opportunity had arrived. Without saying anything to anyone about what I planned, I opened a can of fried caterpillars into a little white dish and set them out on the table along with the other foods. Then I waited to see what would happen. Halfway through the evening one of the unsuspecting young ladies I had invited to the party came up to me and said, "Marshall, those fried shrimp you put out were delicious." "Fried shrimp?" I asked as innocently as I could. "I didn't serve any fried shrimp." "Yes

you did," she insisted. "They were in a little white plate on the table. In fact, they were so good I ate most of them myself." "Oh," I said, pausing for maximum effect, "those weren't fried shrimp, they were fried caterpillars."

Virtually the moment I said that the smile disappeared from her face, her complexion turned markedly green, and she proceeded to become terribly sick all over my living room floor. I realized immediately—as I was cleaning up the floor—that what I had done was a terrible trick to play on anyone, and I have never done it again. But as I reflected on the incident, it amazed me that a food that could have been thought to be so delicious one moment—when it was *perceived* to be fried shrimp—could be so repugnant the next, when it was *perceived* to be something else. Suppose they really had been fried shrimp, and I had merely been pulling her leg? Would that have changed her physical reaction? I doubt it. In this case, as in most cases involving human behavior, reality was less important than one's perception of reality.

It is not the stimulus itself that produces specific human reactions and/or actions but rather how the stimulus is perceived by the individual that matters most for human behavior. It is perhaps the most basic law of human behavior that people act or react on the basis of the way in which they perceive the external world.

PERCEPTIONS: WHAT ARE THEY?

By *perception,* I mean the process—and it is a process—by which an individual selects, evaluates, and organizes stimuli from the external environment. Perceptions are the ways in which a person experiences the world. They also determine the ways in which we behave toward it. That "world" includes symbols, things, people, groups of people, ideas, events, ideologies, and even faith. In sum, we experience *everything* in the world not "as it is"— because there is no way that we can know the world "as it is"—but only as the world comes to us through our sensory receptors. From there these stimuli go instantly into the "data storage banks" of our brains, where they have to pass through the filters of our censor screens, our decoding mechanisms, and the collectivity of everything we have learned from the day we were born. All of the information stored in the brain—including the "program" we have learned that teaches us how to learn about new data—in turn affects (if not determines) not only what relatively few buts of data we will attend to (from the literally millions available) but also how we will interpret each bit that we do select.

Perceptions, attitudes, values, and belief systems are not all the same thing (although throughout this work I will sometimes refer to *perceptions* as a shorthand way of referring to them all), but they all affect each other and they all constantly interact.

Technically speaking, group-related, learned perceptions (including verbal and nonverbal codes), attitudes, values, and belief and disbelief systems plus accepted and expected codes of behavior, taught by the groups with which we identify, are what constitutes culture. Perceptions that are not group taught (such as individual physical differences in sensory receptors, body chemistry, or individual unique experiences) should not be considered part of cultural perceptions. Neither should physical or environmental factors that affect perceptions. The trouble is that the distinction between these types of perception is extremely blurred.

They are all closely interrelated. G.A. Kelly has argued: "Meaning is not extracted from Nature but projected by people upon it. People's behavior can be understood only in terms of their own constructs; that is, from their own internal frames of reference.... Even people's most familiar constructs are not objective observations of what is really there; they are instead inventions of personal and group culture."[8]

Hence, virtually every message to which we attend will be *at least indirectly* affected by our cultural conditioning. Further, when we have finished discussing all of the factors that affect perceptions the reader will see more clearly, I think, what a profound effect our cultures do have on the way we perceive and what a minor effect (by comparison) other factors have in most cases. Thus if I am somewhat imprecise in the way I sometimes use the terms *culture* and *perceptions* synonymously, I ask the reader to forgive me. It should be understood, however, whenever I do use them synonymously that I am referring to *group-related, learned* perceptions only. I suspect that it will be easier for most readers to forgive some imprecision than it would be for them to forgive having constantly to wade through the phrase "the totality of all of the attitudes, values, beliefs . . ."

Take any stimulus, whatever that stimulus may be—a person, an event, an idea—it doesn't matter. On the basis of all of the previous stimuli that have gone into our data-storage banks and the way we have organized those stimuli, we make judgments about the new stimulus. Those judgments are called attitudes. Something is good or bad, right or wrong, useful or dangerous, beautiful or ugly. Each of the groups into which we have been socialized (and as we shall see shortly, we are socialized into a great many) teaches us *its* attitudes toward those stimuli. Many of the groups with which we identify will teach us conflicting judgments about the same stimuli. In some cases even the same group will, on specific issues, teach conflicting issues. Conflicting or not, what is important to note here is that *every* group teaches its members what *its* preferred attitudes are.

A value on the other hand is a desired event or situation—something we would like to see happen. After twenty-five years of research on human behavior Milton Rokeach says of values: "A *value* is an enduring belief that a specific mode of conduct or end-state of existence is personally or socially preferable to an opposite or converse mode of conduct or end-state of existence. A *value system* is an enduring organization of beliefs concerning preferable modes of conduct or end-states of existence along a continuum of relative importance."[9] He goes on to argue that values can be broken down into two categories: *institutional values,* which concern "desirable modes of conduct," and *terminal values,* which concern "desirable end-states of existence."[10]

Obviously, values are closely intertwined with attitudes. We desire certain events or situations above others because we have learned that they are good, right, and/or useful. Which attitudes and values the individual will adopt as his own will depend in very large part on the ranking he makes of the various group identities he holds at any given time. Yet the complexity of the process is such that those attitudes and values, in turn, will affect our identity, which in turn, will affect how we perceive any new stimulus. *The totality of all of the perceptions, attitudes, values, and identities that we hold—and the way we rank them at any moment in time—is referred to as a belief system.* Holding a particular belief system implies, however, that there are a host of other belief systems that we do not hold. Those are labeled disbelief systems. If, for example, I believe that people are basically hostile and "out to get me," then I do not believe that people are basically friendly and helpful. If I am a Buddhist believer, I am not a Buddhist nonbeliever. Nor will I likely be a Christian, Muslim, Jewish, Hindu, or any other kind of believer.

The totality of all of our group-related, learned perception, attitudes, values, and belief and disbelief systems *plus the ranking we make in any specific context* of all the groups with which we identify (our identities), plus the behaviors we normally exhibit, constitute what I call our personal culture. Some—indeed, even many—of those perceptions, attitudes, values, and identities we hold may be totally (more often partially) contradictory. Despite that, we somehow manage to hold them all and to apply different ones to our behavior in different situations. Further, there are times when our own

behavior can alter those very perceptions, attitudes, values, identities, and beliefs we hold. Thus what I am suggesting is a circle of causality. Each affects the other and is in turn affected by them. (See Figure 1.[11])

Virtually all of these processes, of course, occur completely below our level of consciousness, and they occur continuously from the moment of our birth. We are hardly ever aware on a conscious level that they are occurring at all. They are almost totally involuntary processes despite the fact that they are very largely learned. But learned they are. Particularly in those early, formative years our most basic belief systems and our corresponding disbelief systems are being formed. And once formed, they change only very slowly—or when we are confronted by some event that is so dramatic and/or so discordant with an attitude, value, identity, or belief that we have held dear that we are forced to reevaluate. Most often we are forced to reevaluate when we interact with people who have different attitudes, values, or belief systems. While the ranking of our identities change from context to context, it is probably true that once hardened, attitudes and values change much more slowly than do other perceptions. Our most basic "central beliefs" (almost always held subconsciously) probably never change at all.

Factors That Affect Perception

There are a great variety of factors that affect perception. There is no question that the learned factors are by far the most important. But before we discuss them, there are some other factors that are not unimportant, and we will discuss those first.

Physical Determinants of Perception

The only way we can know about the world outside our own bodies is by the impressions of that outside world picked up by our sensory receptors. While most of us have all of these same sensory receptors, we know that no two individuals are identical physically.

Language: Verbal and Nonverbal

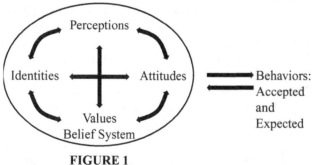

FIGURE 1

For example, empirical evidence has proven that the swirls on the tips of every human's fingers are ever so slightly different from everyone else's. It must then follow that each person's sense of touch must also be ever so slightly different. Yet far more important for the way people view the universe may be the still unanswered questions of physical variations in other sensory receptors. What about the configuration of cones and rods in the retina of the eye, or taste buds on the tongue, or fibers in the ear, or any of the other physical receptors of external stimuli? *If no two individuals have identical physical receptors of stimuli, then it must follow, on the basis of physical evidence alone, that no two individuals can perceive the external world identically.*

Yet physical differences in sensory receptors, while important, may be the least of the factors contributing to differences in perception. Consider for a moment that peculiar combination of physical and psychological factors called personality or temperament that makes each of us unique. Some scholars would argue that temperament is one of the key factors determining how we perceive the external world.[12] While I'm not certain that I would place it in as central a position with regard to perceptions, there is no doubt that it is a contributing factor.

Which of the factors that go into making up temperament are physical, and which are learned— and to what degree they are learned—it is impossible to say at this point in our knowledge. We know that some children are born with incredibly placid personalities, while others are born hyperactive. Certainly that is not learned. What are probably learned, however, are acceptable and unacceptable ways of coping with those physical characteristics. What is learned is that other people react to us in certain ways if we follow one behavior pattern and differently if we follow another.

Before I leave the subject of physical determinants of perception, there are a whole range of other physical differences that make us unique and deserve to be mentioned here because of the ways in which they affect our perceptions. I'm thinking here of the vast array of physical characteristics we inherit at birth. Height, weight, gender, skin color, hair texture, physical handicaps of one sort or another all have an impact on how we will perceive the world. It is not the physical characteristics themselves that necessarily determine our perceptions but rather other people's reactions to these physical characteristics that are so important in shaping our view of ourselves and of the world.

In summary, while I do not believe that physical factors are the most important determinant as to how individuals perceive the world, what I have attempted to show is that physical differences *alone* make it impossible that any two humans could perceive the world identically. That fact by itself would make it impossible for any two humans to communicate with 100 percent accuracy. As we shall see as we proceed, other factors individually and collectively make the probability of accurate communication even more remote and difficult to achieve.

ENVIRONMENTAL DETERMINANTS OF PERCEPTION

No matter how good, bad, or different people's visual sensory receptors are, in the absence of sufficient light no color can be perceived; in the absence of all light no visual images whatever can be received. Similarly if a sound is made above or below the threshold at which the human ear is capable of sensing it, no sound will be heard. (It is important for us to make the distinction, as we will later in greater detail, between stimuli that are received on the conscious level and those that are received below the level of consciousness. What I am discussing here are the factors that affect the perception of the stimuli, whether at the conscious or subconscious level.)

Physical environment also affects the way we perceive things. There is increasing evidence that people who live in tropical areas of the world may see reds and oranges very differently from the way people living in the Arctic see those colors. People living in a desert environment or a rain forest will certainly have very different perceptions of water. It is not an accident that Eskimos have twenty-seven different words for snow. And indeed people who grew up in a big city probably perceive a great many

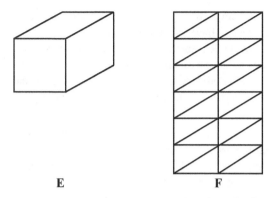

E   F

FIGURE 2 From Willis D. Ellis, *A Source Book of Gestalt Psychology* (New York: Humanities Press, 1967). Reprinted by permission of Humanities Press and Routledge & Kegal Paul Ltd.

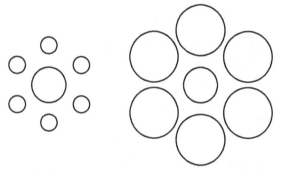

FIGURE 3 From Bernard Berelson and Gary A. Steiner, *Human Behavior: An Inventory of Scientific Findings* (Harcourt Brace Jovanovich, Inc., 1964). Reprinted by permission of the publisher.

things very differently than do people who grew up on a farm in the country.

Relationship of stimulus to surroundings. Bernard Berelson and Gary Steiner say: "Even the simplest experiences are organized by the perceiver; and the perceived characteristics of any part are a function of the whole to which it appears to belong."[13] Observe Figure 2. The figure E is present in F, but it is very difficult to perceive it there consciously because of the surrounding elements in F.

What has been said thus far also applies to size. Look at Figures 3 and 4. Correct! The inner circles in both drawings in Figure 3 are the same size, as are the lines in Figure 4. Once again the surrounding elements (circles in Figure 3, lines in Figure 4) distort and determine what we see. Subconsciously, we may be able to see the similarity in these figures, but on a conscious level we would "swear" that they were different. Everything—including perceptions of reality—is relative and contextual.

All of these figures are presented here merely to demonstrate that we can't always trust our perceptions—even when they are culturally neutral. What we see may very well depend on what surrounds it, or what it is near. But many of the most important of our perceptions—like our attitudes, values, and beliefs—are not culturally neutral. Rather they have been taught by the groups that are most important to us. Further, everything that has been shown here about visual perceptions could

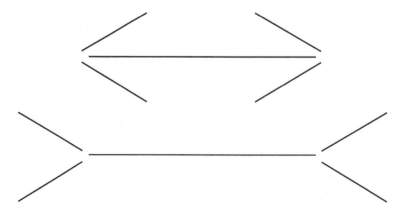

FIGURE 4 The Muller-Lyer illusion. From D. Price Williams, "Cross-Cultural Studies," *New Horizons in Psychology,* ed. Brian M. Foss (Pelican Books, 1966), 398. Copyright © Penguin Books.

be replicated for all of the senses as well. It is just easier to reproduce pictures than it is to reproduce sounds, tastes, or smells.

What is more, different cultures will not even see the same things we do. Go back to Figure 4. Research has indicated that some cultures have no difficulty in seeing that the horizontal lines are of equal length.[14] It is precisely these kinds of differences in perception that are so very difficult to deal with. How do I communicate accurately with someone who perceives differently than I do when it would never occur to me that that person could possibly perceive differently?

LEARNED DETERMINANTS OF PERCEPTION

Far more important than either physical or environmental differences in determining an individual's perceptions of the external world are the *learned* factors involved in the reception, organization, and processing of sensory data.

Even identical twins born into and raised by the same family (and thus presumed to have the same physical and learned inheritance) will not have identical perceptions of the world. If one could accurately measure perceptions, there is no doubt that the degree to which twins share similarity of perceptions would be considerably higher than for most other individuals, but those perceptions would be far from identical. Certainly the younger the identical twins were at the time the test was given the more similar their perceptions would likely be, but even so, anyone who lives with twins knows how different they can be, from the earliest age. Looking in from the outside, someone who is not a part of the family may not notice those differences. Indeed, the outsider is much more likely to be struck by the similarity of the children than by the differences. But a parent or siblings, from the first weeks, have no difficulty telling them apart physically, and by the end of a few months are amazed at the personality differences. Why this is so, is difficult to explain. It's relatively easy to understand that as twins get older their experiences are increasingly dissimilar, but it is startling to see how what appear to be minuscule variations in their exposure to the outside world can produce such profound differences in

even the youngest children. Perhaps one caught a cold and the other did not. Perhaps while the twins were resting outdoors a bird flew close to one and startled it but was unnoticed by the other. Perhaps a dog "nipped" one and not the other. Whatever the specifics there is no question that while their experiences may indeed be far more similar than for most people, they are never identical. And because those experiences are not identical, they simply will not view the world identically.

It would push the concept of "personal culture" beyond credibility to argue that two very young identical twins would have different personal cultures since presumably each would have been exposed to all and only the same group-related perceptions. However, it would not violate the concept to argue that as the twins got older and did things separately their personal cultures would diverge. After all, *all* children are slowly, gradually, but inevitably, socialized into the multitude of cultures of which they ultimately become a part. On the other hand, it would not be incorrect to argue that even at a very early age identical twins do not have identical perceptions.

If for physical and experiential reasons it is not possible for any two individuals to perceive the universe in an identical manner, neither is it possible for them to have absolutely no similarities of perception. In a sense there is a continuum of similarity of perception among individuals. One extreme approaches—but never reaches—zero; the other approaches—but never reaches—100 percent. Actually, degree of similarity of perception can probably best be expressed not as a point on a continuum but as a range of points. For example: A Catholic from a wealthy third-generation Boston family and one from an illiterate and impoverished village in Zaire may share not more than perhaps 10-15 percent similarity of perception, as *Catholics*, but to that degree they are part of a broad identity called Catholics. Teachers, considered as a broad group, may have a 15-20 percent similarity of perception. If we narrow the group to include only college teachers, the range of similarity of perception may increase to 20-25 percent. If we further specify that the group consists only of Irish-Catholic, American, middle-class, urban, white, male, heterosexual, college teachers of quantum physics, with Ph.D.'s from the Massachusetts Institute of Technology, between the ages of 35 and 40, the range of similarity of perception might well increase to 75-80 percent.[15] Notice that while we have decreased the number of people who can be included in our group, we have increased the number of group identities the members share. By so doing, we have greatly increased the likelihood of easy communication among them and thus the likelihood of their sharing still greater similarities of perception in the future. It is no wonder that the smaller the group, the greater its cohesion is likely to be.

In order to illustrate how very different differences in perception of the same stimuli can be, a number of years ago I devised an exercise, which I have since run hundreds of times in many different societies. Allow me to describe it here in some detail to illustrate the enormous differences in perceptions of symbols that actually exist.

In this exercise I put four symbols on the board, one at a time, and ask the seminar or class participants to write on a piece of paper all of the meanings that come to their minds when they see the symbols. When they are done writing, I ask everyone in the

room to tell me the meanings they attributed to the symbols. (See Figure 5.)

The answers I get vary enormously, depending on the participants. There is strong indication that they would vary even more if I could do the exercise in remote villages with unschooled individuals in their own languages. As it is, except on three or four occasions when simultaneous translators were present, I have always done the exercise in English, usually with highly educated participants. This has automatically skewed the sample in the direction of *more* similarity of perception because all of the participants shared a certain similarity of perception as speakers of English and usually as highly educated professionals. (Normally the participants are graduate students in public and international affairs or midcareer civil servants.)

The two most common answers I get for the first symbol are "cross"—in the religious sense—and "plus"—in the mathematical sense. Now, since more than half of the participants I get are educated Christians, that is not really a surprising result. Also, since most come from the more developed parts of developing countries, the third most frequent response—"crossroads"—is not surprising. The surprises, for me at least, usually come because of my own perceptual limitations. I am not really surprised by answers like "the letter T," "quadrants on a map," "the hands of a compass," "check mark" as in *correct*, or "a check mark" as in *incorrect*, the word *yes*, the word *no*, "Red Cross," and "the sign for Switzerland," although they are not answers I would have thought of myself. The first real surprises came for me when I did this exercise at a United Nations school in Costa Rica with a group of senior Central American civil servants from all six Central American Republics and a Spanish interpreter. Virtually every answer I got for that symbol suggested Latin Catholic romantic symbolism: "death and transfiguration," "life after death," "love," "sacrifice," "eternal life," "suffering," "God's son," "redemption," "crucifixion," "resurrection." These were just some of the meanings that were suggested to those people by that symbol. Not having been raised in a Latin Catholic culture, there was no way I could see those meanings in that symbol. From a communication

FIGURE 5

point of view it doesn't matter how *I* was raised. What is important is that *they* were raised in that culture, and those were the meanings that symbol held for *them*.

The second real surprise for me with that symbol came when I did the exercise at the University of Malaya in Kuala Lumpur, Malaysia, with a group of second-year university students. Virtually every Malaysian of Chinese extraction (about half the students were of Chinese extraction) saw the symbol as the Chinese number ten because—as I discovered that day—that indeed is the way the Chinese write the number ten. Not having studied Chinese myself, there simply is no way I could possibly have seen the number ten in that symbol. On the other hand, there is almost no way in which a person born of Chinese parents, who has been taught to read and write Chinese as her first language, could *not* see the number ten in that symbol.[16]

This is just another example of why communication across cultural barriers is so very difficult. If the way in which *you* perceive a stimulus is completely outside *my* perceptual ken, how can I possibly begin to communicate with you?

At the point where all the participants have told me the meanings they saw in the first symbol, I usually ask them which one is correct. Obviously the answer is that all of them are correct—for them. *Symbols have no intrinsic meaning. Meaning resides not in the symbol but in our minds.* If you see this + as the number ten or as a symbol of resurrection or as a red cross, who am I to say that you are wrong? What I can say is that it is not the meaning I had in my mind when I devised the exercise. When I decided to use that symbol I saw it as one horizontal line and one vertical line crossing more or less at the midpoint. But that is only what was in *my* head at the time. It is no more correct or incorrect than any other meaning that people ascribe to it. Yet if two people are to communicate effectively, each has to know with some degree of accuracy what the symbols they use mean to the other. All language, after all, is symbolic. If I attribute different meanings to your words than you do (and most often I probably do), then there is no way we can

communicate accurately. But that is precisely the point being made here. *No two human can communicate 100 percent effectively because no two humans have learned to perceive identically.*

For the second symbol I have gotten responses that in some ways were even more revealing to me. In one group of participants there was a man from Egypt. When I drew this symbol on the board, he violently threw down his pencil on the desk and in an angry voice said, "I will not draw that symbol! I give my life to oppose it! I will not play games with that symbol!"

"But it is only two triangles superimposed upon each other; one pointing down, the other pointing up," I said, surprised not at his perception of the symbol as something representing the State of Israel but by the violence of his reaction.

"No," he said, even more angrily than before, "it stands for everything evil in this world! Death! Destruction! Murder! Torture! Violence! Hate! I will not play games with such a symbol!" Whereupon he rolled back one shirt sleeve and asked, "Do you see that scar?" Pointing to a long, red scar about three inches above his right wrist. "I got that fighting murderous Zionism in Sinai in 1956." Then putting his wrist on his head he said, "I wear it like my halo of thorns! I will not play games with evil."

Now who am I to argue with his perception of that symbol? Obviously for him it really did mean all of those awful things, and nothing that I was going to say could change that perception. I recognized then, for the first time perhaps, at an emotional gut level, why it would be so difficult ever to resolve the Middle East situation.

The more I have thought about that Egyptian's reaction to that symbol, and compared it to other reactions I have gotten from different people with different life experiences, the more amazed I am that any communication at all ever takes place. When I have done this exercise with a group of predominantly Jewish, middle-class, American students from New York City I have gotten answers like "Manischewitz wine," "Mogen David products," "Jewish star," "star of David," "peace," "chicken soup," "high holy days," and many other meanings that only an American Jew could associate with that symbol. Now being a New Yorker myself, none of these meanings really surprised me—not even the chicken soup—though I hadn't thought of them when I designed the exercise. Sharing some degree of similarity of perception with that group, I could certainly understand why they would associate those meanings with that symbol.

The third symbol, I have always drawn carefully the way it appears here. While there is usually some diversity among the answers—depending upon the audience—anywhere from 60 to 100 percent will see it as somehow associated with Hitler, fascism, or Nazi Germany. The fact is that the symbol I put on the board is not a Nazi swastika. Hitler's swastika always points to the right, no matter how it is turned, and it is usually turned like this:

But as the saying goes, "Don't confuse me with facts. My mind is made up." It is stylized enough and reminiscent enough of the German swastika to elicit exactly the same depth of emotion—particularly from older Jews who lost relatives during the Nazi period—that a Nazi swastika would. The fact that it is really an ancient Aryan (Indian) symbol in no way changes the depth of one's perception of it as a Nazi swastika.

The fourth symbol is much more ambiguous than the first three and is open to more interpretation. Still, a great many people see it as a "squiggle" or a "signature" or a "corkscrew." More people from developing countries see it as a "river," a "snake," or a "puff of smoke" then do people from developed countries. I once did this exercise at a graduate school of nursing, and more than 60 percent of the participants in that group saw it specifically as an "interuterine device (IUD)" or simply as a "coil" or a "birth-control device." But if you've never seen an IUD, there is just no way you can know what you don't know.

The last part of that last sentence really is at the heart of this exercise and my lengthy discussion of it here. It is so important and so obvious that it is often overlooked. *We know what we perceive; we don't know what we don't perceive. Since there is no way that we can know what we don't perceive, we assume that we perceive "correctly"—even if we don't.* We tend to assume that almost everyone perceives what we perceive, and that we perceive everything (or almost everything) that everybody else perceives. Thus we engage people in discussion on a very wide range of topics assuming that the people with whom we are attempting to communicate share the same perceptions that we do. The two exceptions to this rule usually are people who look terribly foreign (or don't speak our language) and people who are specialists in fields about which we know nothing.

Beyond those exceptions, however, most of us assume that we know what the other person meant when he said something until we discover, by whatever circumstances or accident, that we do not. I automatically assume that someone else perceives what I perceive until proven otherwise. If I didn't do that even the simplest communication would be exhausting.

The more specific the symbol, the more agreement about its meaning we are likely to find. The more abstract the symbol, the greater the variety of meanings we are likely to find associated with it. A word like *table,* for example, is a symbol. But because it is specific the range of perceptions associated with it are likely to be fairly limited. One may see a wooden table or a Formica table, a round one or a rectangular one. One might see a mathematical table, a statistical table, a water table, or a table of contents. But the range of choices one might—and does—associate with abstract concepts like "God," "justice," or "democracy" are truly mind boggling. There probably are as many different meanings associated with those abstract concepts as there are groups in the world.

ENDNOTES

1 This concept was presented first in an article entitled "Culture: A Perceptual Approach," published originally in *Vidya,* No. 3,

Spring 1969, and more recently reproduced in Larry A. Samovar and Richard E. Porter, eds., *Intercultural Communication: A Reader,* 4th ed. (Belmont, CA: Wadsworth Pub. Co., 1985).

2   From *Collected Papers on Metalinguistics,* quoted by Franklin Fearing in "An Examination of the Conceptions of Benjamin Whorf in the Light of Theories on Perception and Cognition," in Harry Hoijer, ed., *Language in Culture* (Chicago: University of Chicago Press, 1954), 48.

3   Here I am using *language* in the broadest sense. It may include the jargon or symbols used by social scientists or mathematicians, for example, to express the concepts peculiar to their group, or it may include the myriad of nonverbal gestures sometimes referred to as body language.

4   Ruth Benedict, *Patterns of Culture,* 1934; reprint (New York: Mentor Books, 1959), 18.

5   C.T. Patrick Diamond, "Understanding Others: Kellyian Theory, Methodology and Applications," in *International Journal of Intercultural Relations,* 6 (1982), 401.

6   Harry Hoijer, "The Sapir-Whorf Hypotheses," in Harry Hoijer ed., *Language in Culture* (Chicago: University of Chicago Press, 1954), 94.

7   Diamond, "Understanding Others," 403.

8   Paraphrased in *ibid.,* 396, 397.

9   Milton Rokeach, *The Nature of Human Values* (New York: Free Press, 1973), 5.

10   *Ibid.,* 7.

11   Although drawn heavily from anthropological and social-psychological literature, this way of viewing culture is my own and can be used at every level of analysis—personal, group, or national.

12   Richard W. Cottam and Ole R. Holsti are two scholars who come to mind. Cottam in particular, in personal communication to this author, argued the importance of temperament.

13   Cited in D. Price-Williams, "Cross-Cultural Studies," from Brian M. Foss, ed., *New Horizons in Psychology* (New York: Penguin Books, 1966) and reprinted in Larry A. Samovar and Richard E. Porter, eds., *Intercultural Communication: A Reader,* 2nd ed. (Belmont, CA: Wadsworth Publishing Co., 1976), 34.

14   Cited in D. Price-Williams, "Cross-Cultural Studies," from Brian M. Foss, ed., *New Horizons in Psychology* (New York: Penguin Books, 1966) and reprinted in Larry A. Samovar and Richard E. Porter, eds., *Intercultural Communication: A Reader,* 2nd ed. (Belmont, CA: Wadsworth Publishing Co., 1976), 34.

15   All figures used in this example are completely hypothetical and are included merely to illustrate a concept. They are not based on any known research.

16   An interesting variation occurred when I did that exercise in Pittsburgh some time ago. A Japanese student did *not* see the number 10, even though the Japanese write the number 10 the same way the Chinese do. Later when I asked him why, he said that it never occurred to him in the context of a Pittsburgh classroom than an American professor would know Japanese.

On Gemeinschaft *and* Gesellschaft

Ferdinand Tönnies[1]

1. ORDER—LAW—MORES

There is a contrast between a social order which—being based upon consensus of wills—rests on harmony and is developed and ennobled by folkways, mores, and religion, and an order which—being based upon a union of rational wills—rests on convention and agreement, is safeguarded by political legislation, and finds its ideological justification in public opinion.

There is, further, in the first instance a common and binding system of positive law, of enforcible norms regulating the interrelation of wills. It has its roots in family life and is based on land ownership. Its forms are in the main determined by the code of the folkways and mores. Religion consecrates and glorifies these forms of the divine will, i.e., as interpreted by the will of wise and ruling men. This system of norms is in direct contrast to a similar positive law which upholds the separate identity of the individual rational wills in all their interrelations and entanglements. The latter derives from the conventional order of trade and similar relations but attains validity and binding force only through the sovereign will and power of the state. Thus, it becomes one

Reprinted from *Sociology: The Great Statements,* ed. Marcello Truzzi (New York: McGraw Hill, 1971), 145–153.

of the most important instruments of policy; it sustains, impedes, or furthers social trends; it is defended or contested publicly by doctrines and opinions and thus is changed, becoming more strict or more lenient.

There is, further, the dual concept of morality as a purely ideal or mental system of norms for community life. In the first case, it is mainly an expression and organ of religious beliefs and forces, by necessity intertwined with the conditions and realities of family spirit and the folkways and mores. In the second case, it is entirely a product and instrument of public opinion, which encompasses all relations arising out of contractual sociableness, contacts, and political intentions.

Order is natural law, law as such = positive law, mores = ideal law. Law as the meaning of what may or ought to be, of what is ordained or permitted, constitutes an object of social will. Even the natural law, in order to attain validity and reality, has to be recognized as positive and binding. But it is positive in a more general or less definite way. It is general in comparison with special laws. It is simple compared to complex and developed law.

2. DISSOLUTION

The substance of the body social and the social will consists of concord, folkways, mores, and religion, the manifold forms of which develop under favorable conditions during its lifetime. Thus, each individual receives his share from this common center, which is manifest in his own sphere, i.e., in his sentiment, in his mind and heart, and in his conscience as well as in his environment, his possessions, and his activities. This is also true of each group. It is in this center that the individual's strength is rooted, and his rights derive, in the last instance, from the one original law which, in its divine and natural character, encompasses and sustains him, just as it made him and will carry him away. But under certain conditions and in some relationships, man appears as a free agent (person) in his self-determined activities and has to be conceived of as an independent person. The substance of the common spirit has become so weak or the link

connecting him with the others worn so thin that it has to be excluded from consideration. In contrast to the family and co-operative relationship, this is true of all relations among separate individuals where there is no common understanding, and no time-honored custom or belief creates a common bond. This *means* war and the unrestricted freedom of all to destroy and subjugate one another, or, being aware of possible greater advantage, to conclude agreements and foster new ties. To the extent that such a relationship exists between closed groups or communities or between their individuals or between members and nonmembers of a community, it does not come within the scope of this study. In this connection we see a community organization and social conditions in which the individuals remain in isolation and veiled hostility toward each other so that only fear of clever retaliation restrains them from attacking one another, and, therefore, even peaceful and neighborly relations are in reality based upon a warlike situation. This is, according to our concepts, the condition of *Gesellschaft*-like civilization, in which peace and commerce are maintained through conventions and the underlying mutual fear. The state protects this civilization through legislation and politics. To a certain extent science and public opinion, attempting to conceive it as necessary and eternal, glorify it as progress toward perfection.

But it is in the organization and order of the *Gemeinschaft* that folk life and folk culture persist. The state, which represents and embodies *Gesellschaft,* is opposed to these in veiled hatred and contempt, the more so the further the state has moved away from and become estranged from these forms of community life. Thus, also in the social and historical life of mankind there is partly close interrelation, partly juxtaposition and opposition of natural and rational will.

3. THE PEOPLE (*VOLKSTUM*) AND THE STATE (*STAATSTUM*)

In the same way as the individual natural will evolves into pure thinking and rational will, which tends to dissolve and subjugate its predecessors, the original collective forms of *Gemeinschaft* have developed into *Gesellschaft* and the rational will of the *Gesellschaft*. In the course of history, folk culture has given rise to the civilization of the state.

The main features of this process can be described in the following way. The anonymous mass of the people is the original and dominating power which creates the houses, the villages, and the towns of the country. From it, too, spring the powerful and self-determined individuals of many different kinds: princes, feudal lords, knights, as well as priests, artists, scholars. As long as their economic condition is determined by the people as a whole, all their social control is conditioned by the will and power of the people. Their union on a national scale, which alone could make them dominant as a group, is dependent on economic conditions. And their real and essential control is economic control, which before them and with them and partly against them the merchants attain by harnessing the labor force of the nation. Such economic control is achieved in many forms, the highest of which is planned capitalist production or large-scale industry. It is through the merchants that the technical conditions for the national union of independent individuals and for capitalistic production are created. This merchant class is by nature, and mostly also by origin, international as well as national and urban, i.e., it belongs to *Gesellschaft*, not *Gemeinschaft*. Later all social groups and dignitaries and, at least in tendency, the whole people acquire the characteristics of the *Gesellschaft*.

Men change their temperaments with the place and conditions of their daily life, which becomes hasty and changeable through restless striving. Simultaneously, along with this revolution in the social order, there takes place a gradual change of the law, in meaning as well as in form. The contract as such becomes the basis of the entire system, and rational will of the *Gesellschaft*, formed by its interests, combines with authoritative will of the state to create, maintain and change the legal system. According to this conception, the law can and may completely change the *Gesellschaft* in line with its own discrimination and purpose; changes which,

however, will be in the interest of the *Gesellschaft*, making for usefulness and efficiency. The state frees itself more and more from the traditions and customs of the past and the belief in their importance. Thus, the forms of law change from a product of the folkways and mores and the law of custom into a purely legalistic law, a product of policy. The state and its departments and the individuals are the only remaining agents, instead of numerous and manifold fellowships, communities, and commonwealths which have grown up organically. The characters of the people, which were influenced and determined by these previously existing institutions, undergo new changes in adaptation to new and arbitrary legal constructions. These earlier institutions lose the firm hold which folkways, mores, and the conviction of their infallibility gave to them.

Finally, as a consequence of these changes and in turn reacting upon them, a complete reversal of intellectual life takes place. While originally rooted entirely in the imagination, it now becomes dependent upon thinking. Previously, all was centered around the belief in invisible beings, spirits and gods; now it is focalized on the insight into visible nature. Religion, which is rooted in folk life or at least closely related to it, must cede supremacy to science, which derives from and corresponds to consciousness. Such consciousness is a product of learning and culture and, therefore, remote from the people. Religion has an immediate contact and is moral in its nature because it is most deeply related to the physical-spiritual link which connects the generations of men. Science receives its moral meaning only from an observation of the laws of social life, which leads it to derive rules for an arbitrary and reasonable order of social organization. The intellectual attitude of the individual becomes gradually less and less influenced by religion and more and more influenced by science. Utilizing the research findings accumulated by the preceding industrious generation, we shall investigate the tremendous contrasts which the opposite poles of this dichotomy and these fluctuations entail. For this presentation, however, the following few remarks may suffice to outline the underlying principles.

4. TYPES OF REAL COMMUNITY LIFE

The exterior forms of community life as represented by natural will and *Gemeinschaft* were distinguished as house, village, and town. These are the lasting types of real and historical life. In a developed *Gesellschaft,* as in the earlier and middle stages, people live together in these different ways. The town is the highest, viz., the most complex, form of social life. Its local character, in common with that of the village, contrasts with the family character of the house. Both village and town retain many characteristics of the family; the village retains more, the town less. Only when the town develops into the city are these characteristics almost entirely lost. Individuals or families are separate identities, and their common locale is only an accidental or deliberately chosen place in which to live. But as the town lives on within the city, elements of the *Gemeinschaft,* as the only real form of life, persist within the *Gesellschaft,* although lingering and decaying. On the other hand, the more general the condition of *Gesellschaft* becomes in the nation or a group of nations, the more this entire "country" or the entire "world" begins to resemble one large city. However, in the city and therefore where general conditions characteristic of the *Gesellschaft* prevail, only the upper strata, the rich and the cultured, are really active and alive. They set up the standards to which the lower strata have to conform. These lower classes conform partly to supersede the others, partly in imitation of them in order to attain for themselves social power and independence. The city consists, for both groups (just as in the case of the "nation" and the "world"), of free persons who stand in contact with each other, exchange with each other and cooperate without any *Gemeinschaft* or will thereto developing among them except as such might develop sporadically or as a leftover from former conditions. On the contrary, these numerous external contacts, contracts, and contractual relations only cover up as many inner hostilities and antagonistic interests. This is especially true of the antagonism between the rich or the so-called cultured class and the poor or the servant class, which try to obstruct and destroy each other. It is this contrast which, according to

Plato, gives the "city" its dual character and makes it divide in itself. This itself, according to our concept, constitutes the city, but the same contrast is also manifest in every large-scale relationship between capital and labor. The common town life remains within the *Gemeinschaft* of family and rural life; it is devoted to some agricultural pursuits but concerns itself especially with art and handicraft which evolve from these natural needs and habits. City life, however, is sharply distinguished from that; these basic activities are used only as means and tools for the special purposes of the city.

The city is typical of *Gesellschaft* in general. It is essentially a commercial town and, in so far as commerce dominates its productive labor, a factory town. Its wealth is capital wealth which, in the form of trade, usury, or industrial capital, is used and multiplies. Capital is the means for the appropriation of products of labor or for the exploitation of workers. The city is also the center of science and culture, which always go hand in hand with commerce and industry. Here the arts must make a living; they are exploited in a capitalistic way. Thoughts spread and change with astonishing rapidity. Speeches and books through mass distribution become stimuli of far-reaching importance.

The city is to be distinguished from the national capital, which, as residence of the court or center of government, manifests the features of the city in many respects although its population and other conditions have not yet reached that level. In the synthesis of city and capital, the highest form of this kind is achieved: the metropolis. It is the essence not only of a national *Gesellschaft,* but contains representatives from a whole group of nations, i.e., of the world. In the metropolis, money and capital are unlimited and almighty. It is able to produce and supply goods and science for the entire earth as well as laws and public opinion for all nations. It represents the world market and world traffic; in it world industries are concentrated. Its newspapers are world papers, its people come from all corners of the earth, being curious and hungry for money and pleasure.

5. COUNTERPART OF *GEMEINSCHAFT*

Family life is the general basis of life in the *Gemeinschaft*. It subsists in village and town life. The village community and the town themselves can be considered as large families, the various clans and houses representing the elementary organisms of its body: guilds, corporations, and offices, the tissues and organs of the town. Here original kinship and inherited status remain an essential, or at least the most important, condition of participating fully in common property and other rights. Strangers may be accepted and protected as serving members or guests either temporarily or permanently. Thus, they can belong to the *Gemeinschaft* as objects, but not easily as agents and representatives of the *Gemeinschaft*. Children are, during minority, dependent members of the family, but according to Roman custom they are called free because it is anticipated that under possible and normal conditions they will certainly be masters, their own heirs. This is true neither of guests nor of servants, either in the house or in the community. But honored guests can approach the position of children. If they are adopted or civic rights are granted to them, they fully acquire this position with the right to inherit. Servants can be esteemed or treated as guests or even, because of the value of their functions, take part as members in the activities of the group. It also happens sometimes that they become natural or appointed heirs. In reality there are many gradations, lower or higher, which are not exactly met by legal formulas. All these relationships can, under special circumstances, be transformed into merely interested and dissolvable interchange between independent contracting parties. In the city such change, at least with regard to all relations of servitude, is only natural and becomes more and more widespread with its development. The difference between natives and strangers becomes irrelevant. Everyone is what he is, through his personal freedom, through his wealth and his contracts. He is a servant only in so far as he has granted certain services to someone else, master in so far as he receives such services. Wealth is, indeed, the only effective and original differentiating characteristic; whereas in *Gemeinschaft* property it is considered as participation in the common ownership and as a specific legal concept is entirely the consequence and result of freedom or ingenuity, either original or acquired. Therefore, wealth, to the extent that this is possible, corresponds to the degree of freedom possessed.

In the city as well as in the capital, and especially in the metropolis, family life is decaying. The more and the longer their influence prevails, the more the residuals of family life acquire a purely accidental character. For there are only few who will confine their energies within such a narrow circle; all are attracted outside by business, interests, and pleasures, and thus separated from one another. The great and mighty, feeling free and independent, have always felt a strong inclination to break through the barriers of the folkways and mores. They know that they can do as they please. They have the power to bring about changes in their favor, and this is positive proof of individual arbitrary power. The mechanism of money, under usual conditions and if working under high pressure, is means to overcome all resistance, to obtain everything wanted and desired, to eliminate all dangers and to cure all evil. This does not hold always. Even if all controls of the *Gemeinschaft* are eliminated, there are nevertheless controls in the *Gesellschaft* to which the free and independent individuals are subject. For *Gesellschaft* (in the narrower sense), convention takes to a large degree the place of the folkways, mores, and religion. It forbids much as detrimental to the common interest which the folkways, mores, and religion had condemned as evil in and of itself.

The will of the state plays the same role through law courts and police, although within narrower limits. The laws of the state apply equally to everyone: only children and lunatics are not held responsible to them. Convention maintains at least the appearance of morality; it is still related to the folkways, mores, and religious and aesthetic feeling, although this feeling tends to become arbitrary and formal. The state is hardly directly concerned with morality. It has only to suppress and punish hostile actions which are detrimental to the common weal or seemingly dangerous for itself and society. For as the state has to administer the common weal, it must be able to define this as it pleases. In the end it will probably realize that no increase in knowledge and culture alone will make people kinder, less egotistic, and more content and that dead folkways, mores, and religions cannot be revived by coercion and teaching. The state will then arrive at the conclusion that in order to create moral forces and moral beings it must prepare the ground and fulfill the necessary conditions, or at least it must eliminate counteracting forces. The state, as the reason of *Gesellschaft,* should decide to destroy *Gesellschaft* or at least to reform or renew it. The success of such attempts is highly improbable.

6. THE REAL STATE

Public opinion, which brings the morality of *Gesellschaft* into rules and formulas and can rise above the state, has nevertheless decided tendencies to urge the state to use its irresistible power to force everyone to do what is useful and to leave undone what is damaging. Extension of the penal code and the police power seems the right means to curb the evil impulses of the masses. Public opinion passes easily from the demand for freedom (for the upper classes) to that of despotism (against the lower classes). The makeshift, convention, has but little influence over the masses. In their striving for pleasure and entertainment they are limited only by the scarcity of the means which the capitalists furnish them as price for their labor, which condition is as general as it is natural in a world where the interests of the capitalists and merchants anticipated all possible needs and in mutual competition incite to the most varied expenditures of money. Only through fear of discovery and punishment, that is, through fear of the state, is a special and large group, which encompasses far more people than the professional criminals, restrained in its desire to obtain the key to all necessary and unnecessary pleasures. The state is their enemy. The state, to them, is an alien and unfriendly power; although seemingly authorized by them and embodying their own will, it is nevertheless opposed to all their needs and desires, protecting property which they do not possess, forcing them into military service for a country which offers them hearth and altar only in the form of a heated room on the upper floor or gives them, for native soil, city streets where they may stare at the glitter and luxury in lighted windows forever beyond their reach! Their own life is nothing but a constant alternative between work and leisure, which are both distorted into factory routine and the low pleasure of the saloons. City life and *Gesellschaft* doom the common people to decay and death; in vain they struggle to attain power through their own multitude, and it seems to them that they can use their power only for a revolution if they want to free themselves from their fate. The masses become conscious of this social position through the education in schools and through newspapers. They proceed from class consciousness to class struggle. This class struggle may destroy society and the state which is its purpose to reform. The entire culture has been transformed into a civilization of state and *Gesellschaft,* and this transformation means the doom of culture itself if none of its scattered seeds remain alive and again bring forth the essence and idea of *Gemeinschaft,* thus secretly fostering a new culture amidst the decaying one.

ENDNOTE

[1] Tönnies' major work, *Gemeinschaft und Gesellschaft* (first published in 1887), is available in English translation (edited and translated by Charles P. Loomis) as *Community and Society* (1957). It is also available in an earlier edition, which also contained some of Tönnies' later essays, as *Fundamental Concepts of Sociology* (1940). Tönnies' ten other books, of which the major work dealing with sociology is his 1931 *Einführung in die Soziologie (An Introduction to Sociology),* plus most of his essays, still await English translations. A full bibliography of Tönnies' work can be found in: *American Journal of Sociology, 42* (1937): 100–101. He is best remembered for his distinction between two basic types of social groups. Tönnies argued that there are two basic forms of human will: the *essential will,* which is the underlying, organic, or instinctive driving force; and *arbitrary will,* which is deliberative, purposive, and future (goal) oriented. Groups that formed around essential will, in which membership is self-fulfilling, Tönnies called *Gemeinschaft* (often translated as *community*). Groups in which membership was sustained by some instrumental goal or definite end he termed *Gesellschaft* (often translated as *society*). *Gemeinschaft* was exemplified by the family or neighborhood; *Gesellschaft,* by the city or the state.

The Washington Post

Think American, Japanese Are Advised
Government Panel Says Traditional Values Impede Progress

by Doug Struck

Washington Post Foreign Service

TOKYO, Jan. 19—Are the Japanese, too, well . . . Japanese?

For decades, the very traits that have defined Japanese society—conformity, decision-making by consensus, a follow-the-rule orderliness—have been nurtured and praised here as the glue that keeps this nation together.

But now a government-appointed panel has concluded that Japanese society must change. The Japanese should become more independent, the commission said. More tolerant of people who veer from the norm. Less preoccupied with rules, peer pressure and school tests. There should be more immigrants. And more lawyers.

To some, it sounds like Japan should be more like America.

"We shouldn't be afraid of Americanization or globalization," said Makoto Iokibe, a political science professor and member of the commission. When Commodore Matthew Perry and his fleet of American warships forced Japan to open to the world in 1853, Japan thrived, he said. When Gen. Douglas MacArthur and his occupation force forced Japan to embrace American-style democracy. Japan thrived again.

"If we are smart enough, then you will find Japan still very Japanese," he said in an interview today. "On the other hand, if we want to keep our identity, want to 'be Japanese' and refuse American or global impact, we will be miserable Japanese isolated from the world. People will be complaining about how Japan is being bypassed again."

It was just this loss of stature in the world that led to formation of the commission. The prolonged economic doldrums that knocked Japan from its 1980s peak led to what is often called "the lost decade." In March, Prime Minister Keizo Obuchi appointed a panel of the nation's top intellects and leaders—notably excluding the bureaucrats who traditionally guide the government—and charged them with recommending goals for the 21st century.

The headlines in the national press, about the report, released Tuesday, focused initially on its concrete and dramatic proposals: Adopt English as a "second language;" cut the required academic school week to three days so students can take more fun subjects; lower the voting age from 20 to 18; increase the immigrant work force.

But even more dramatic is the underlying theme of the commission's conclusions—a scathing criticism of some of Japan's basic operating tenets. The report laments an "ossified" society in which an allegiance to rules and conformity have "leached Japan's vitality." For Japan to succeed, the group noted; there must be "a spirit of self-reliance and the spirit of tolerance, neither of which has been given sufficient latitude so far."

It recommends a Japan "where people's vitality is not inhibited by precedents, regulations and established interests." In a society where group consensus is preferred over individual initiative, the report recommends "empowerment of the individual" and more support for risk takers.

To Western ears, these sound like routine populist platitudes, served up on any campaign trail. But editorialists here were quick to identify the panel's language as a sweeping indictment. "The report stresses individuality too much," the daily Sankei protested. "We already have a too shallow national unity, and too much respect for personal rights."

Reprinted from *The Washington Post,* January 20, 2000.

There will be opposition, "a contrary wind to reform," warned the newspaper Nikkei. "A lot of people would like to stay where we are and do not want to change."

"We already are being criticized for putting too much emphasis on the individual, for forgetting the critical importance of 'community' and 'Japanese-ness,' acknowledged commission member Yolchi Funabashi, diplomatic columnist for the Asahi Shimbun.

Tadashi Yamamoto, executive director of the commission and president of the nonprofit Japan Center for International Exchange, said the panel made far-reaching recommendations because "our basic premise was that something is basically wrong with society. We needed a sense of urgency."

"We are really advocating a fundamental reorientation of society," he said today. "The system of government that served Japan so well after the defeat in the war doesn't work any more."

Since Japan was forcibly opened to the "modern" world, Yamamoto said, it has made a furious race to "catch up," first to the mechanical weaponry and farm equipment of the West in the 19th century, and then to the democracy and economic power of the West following World War II.

That effort required individual subservience to the common purpose. But that model stifles the kind of creativity that is needed today, Yamamoto said. "The 21st century will be the era of individuals. Individuals have become more important through globalization, the Internet, networking," he said.

During years of poverty following World War II, Japanese looked to the government for all decisions. Now, individuals must take the lead, said Iokibe. "Japanese kids from the very starting point are told about the consensus style and how you should not be different. That kind of education must be changed," he said.

Many of the commission's other recommendations challenge ingrained patterns. The proposal to give all Japanese a "working knowledge of English" is intended to outfit them for the Internet and a global economy, in which English is dominant. But the proposal is being made to a country that ranks near North Korea in its lack of English skills.

The proposal to shorten the compulsory academic school week to three days is intended to make room in the other two days for such pursuits as "personal cultivation and specialized vocational education." But schoolchildren routinely attend classes on Saturday, and from fifth grade on, enroll in night and weekend "cram schools" to pass entrance exams.

The commission noted that Japan's economy will require more immigrant labor in the next two decades to compensate for an aging native population. But its call for policies to "encourage foreigners to want to live and work in this country" comes in a country where some public spas still display "Japanese only" signs.

Even the proposal to train more lawyers sounds strange to Japanese, who tend to avoid the sort of confrontational litigation practiced in the West.

"People ask, 'Do you seriously want to have a bunch of lawyers?'" Yamamoto said. "They see this as Americanization. But we have too many unwritten rules. When we advocate more individualism and individual responsibility, we have to have a much more open system where people can clearly understand the boundaries."

Yamamoto rejects the complaint that these changes reflect "American values."

"I don't think dynamism is an American monopoly," he said. "In a sense, democracy is not necessarily an American thing; it's a universal value."

Culture Matters

by Lawrence E. Harrison

Of the six billion people who inhabit the world today, fewer than one billion are to be found in the advanced democracies. Half or more of the adult population of 23 countries, mostly in Africa, is illiterate. Half or more of the women in 35 countries are illiterate.

Furthermore, the most inequitable income distribution patterns are found in the poorer countries, particularly in Latin America and Africa.

What explains this persistence of poverty and authoritarianism?

The conventional diagnoses offered during the past half century—exploitation, imperialism, lack of opportunity, lack of capital, weak institutions—are inadequate. The crucial element that has been largely ignored is the cultural: that is to say, values and attitudes that stand in the way of progress.

The conclusion that culture matters goes down hard. It clashes with cultural relativism, widely subscribed to in the academic world, which argues that cultures can be assessed only on their own terms and that value judgments by outsiders are taboo.

But a growing number of academics, journalists and politicians are talking about culture as a crucial factor in societal development. Alan Greenspan captured the shift recently when he said, in the context of economic conditions in Russia, that he had theretofore assumed that capitalism was "human nature." But in the wake of the collapse of the Russian economy, he concluded that "it was not human nature at all, but culture."

Over the almost two decades that I have been studying and writing about the relationship between cultural values and human progress, I have identified ten values that distinguish progressive cultures from static cultures:

1. The progressive culture emphasizes the future, the static culture the present or past. Future orientation implies a progressive worldview: influence over one's destiny, rewards in this life for virtue, and positive-sum economics in which wealth expands—in contrast to the zero-sum psychology commonly found in poor countries.

2. Work and achievement are central to the good life in the progressive culture, but are of lesser importance in the static culture. In the former, diligence, creativity and achievement are rewarded not only financially but also with prestige.

3. Frugality is the mother of investment and financial security in progressive cultures.

4. Education is the key to advancement in progressive cultures but is of marginal importance except for the elites in static cultures.

5. Merit is central to advancement in the progressive culture; connections and family are what count in the static culture.

6. Community: The radius of identification and trust extends beyond the family in the progressive culture, whereas the family circumscribes community in the static culture.

7. The societal ethical code tends to be more rigorous in the progressive culture. Every advanced democracy except Belgium, Taiwan, Italy and South Korea appears among the 25 least corrupt countries on Transparency International's "Corruption Perceptions Index."

8. Justice and fair play are universal, impersonal expectations in the progressive

Reprinted with permission © The National Interest, No. 60, Summer 2000, Washington D.C. - Parts excerpted culture. In the static culture, justice is often a function of whom you know or how much you can pay.

9. Authority tends toward dispersion and horizontality in progressive cultures, which encourage dissent; toward concentration and verticality in static cultures, which encourage orthodoxy.

10. Secularism: The influence of religious institutions on civic life is small in the progressive culture; their influence in static cultures is often substantial. Heterodoxy and dissent are encouraged in the former, orthodoxy and conformity are encouraged in the latter.

The ten factors I have suggested are not definitive. But they do at least suggest which elements in the vastness of "culture" may influence the way societies evolve.

CHANGING THE TRADITIONAL CULTURE

Recently, Latin America has taken the lead in contriving initiatives designed to accelerate economic growth, fortify democratic institutions and promote social justice.

Claudio Veliz's 1994 book, *The New World of the Gothic Fox,* contrasts the Anglo-Protestant and Ibero-Catholic legacies in the New World. Veliz defines the cultural current with the words of Peruvian writer Mario Vargas Llosa, "the economic, educational and judicial reforms necessary to Latin America's modernization cannot be effected unless they are preceded or accompanied by a reform of our customs and ideas."

One American of Mexican descent, Texas businessman Lionel Sosa, has also contributed to the new paradigm in his book, *The Americano Dream.* Sosa catalogues a series of Hispanic values and attitudes that present obstacles to achieving the upward mobility of mainstream America:

1. The resignation of the poor—"To be poor is to deserve heaven. To be rich is to deserve hell."

2. The low priority given to education—"The girls don't really need it, they'll get married anyway. And the boys? It's better that they go to work, to help the family."

3. Fatalism—"Individual initiative, achievement, self-reliance, ambition, aggressiveness—all these are useless in the face of an attitude that says, 'We must not challenge the will of God.'"

4. Mistrust of those outside the family, which contributes to the generally small size of Hispanic businesses.

The gender issue has also come to the fore, challenging the traditional machismo culture. Latin American women are increasingly aware of the gender democratization that has occurred, particularly in First World countries, in recent decades, and they are increasingly organizing and taking initiatives to rectify the sexism that has traditionally kept them in second-class status.

To be sure, Latin American values and attitudes are changing, as the transition to democratic politics and market economics of the past fifteen years suggests. Several forces are modifying the region's culture, among them the new intellectual current, the globalization of communications and economics, and the surge in evangelical/Pentecostal Protestantism.

At least one African has come to similar conclusions about progress on his continent. Cameroonian Daniel Etounga-Manguelle's analysis of African culture highlights the highly centralized, vertical traditions of authority; a focus on the past and present, not the future; a distaste for work; the suppression of individual initiative, achievement and saving; and a belief in sorcery that nurtures irrationality and fatalism.

Etounga-Manguelle concludes that Africa must "change or perish." A cultural "adjustment" is not enough. What is needed is a cultural revolution that transforms traditional authoritarian child-rearing practices; transforms education through emphasis on the individual, independent judgment and creativity; produces free individuals working together for the progress of the community; produces an elite concerned with the well-being of the society; and promotes a healthy economy based on the work ethic, the profit motive and individual initiative.

This is not to say that addressing culture will solve all problems. Culture is one of several factors that influence progress. But particularly as we view the longer run, culture's power becomes more apparent.

Nathan Glazer observed that people are made uncomfortable or are offended by cultural explanations of why some countries and some ethnic groups do better than others. But the alternative—to view oneself or one's group as a victim—is worse. Bernard Lewis recently observed in a *Foreign Affairs* article that when people realize that things are going wrong, there are two questions they can ask. One is, 'What did we do wrong?' and the other is 'Who did this to us?' The latter leads to conspiracy theories and paranoia. The first question leads to another line of thinking: 'How do we put it right?'

Yet the role of cultural values and attitudes as obstacles to or facilitators of progress has been largely ignored by governments and aid agencies. Integrating value and attitude change into policies and programs will assure that, in the next fifty years, the world does not relive the poverty and injustice in which most poor countries have been mired during the past half century's "decades of development."

Lawrence E. Harrison is an Associate at Harvard's Academy for International Area Studies.

SECTION II
COMMUNICATING ACROSS CULTURES

COMMUNICATION AND CULTURE

What we communicate and how we communicate are largely determined by our culture. People who come from the same background tend to pay attention to similar media or modes of communication. They also share meanings attributed to those messages they receive. And feedback could be direct and immediate or indirect and delayed depending upon our culture.

There are many types of communication. It can range from a gesture—which has specific meaning only to two people in love—to war between many nations. It involves the sending of messages between members of the same culture (intracultural communication), messages sent between people of different cultures (intercultural communication), to messages sent around the world by nation-states, their institutions, and organizations or representatives (international communication). And it might be face-to-face (interpersonal), via telecommunications such as radio, television, or the internet (mass communication), and texting, sending voicemail messages, or using Facebook and Twitter (social communication).

There are many models of communication but let us begin with a simple cybernetics model to illustrate how the breakdown of communication inevitably takes place as one interacts with people in a new culture. This simple model below may serve as an illustration.

SENDER ▸ ENCODER ▸ MEDIA OR CHANNEL ▸ DECODER ▸ RECEIVER

FEEDBACK ◂

If we communicate with another person, we become both the *sender* and the *encoder*. Thoughts in our head are put into a code or language and molecules of air move between our vocal cords and the other person's ears. The *medium* is sound. The other person is the *decoder* and the *receiver* who speaks our language and the message enters his or her head after which the person reacts with some kind of *feedback*. This is a system and the breakdown of any part of link between parts in the system causes the entire system to break down. It's like some strings of Christmas tree lights: if one bulb breaks, the chain of electricity is interrupted and none of the lights work until the broken bulb is fixed.

This model provides a paradigm for identifying the various components of any cross-cultural interaction and the dynamics of communication. Proponents of this explanation may emphasize any part or link in a communication system as the point of communications breakdown. Some might concentrate on the inefficiencies and misunderstanding brought about by different meanings given to messages. For example, if we consider *the sender and the receiver,* it is clear that we send messages, not meanings. The meanings are in our head. If we come from the same culture or share common experiences, a message will elicit the same or similar meaning. If the sender and the receiver come from different cultures, the same message may elicit completely different meanings in their respective minds.

For example, those who adapt to another culture go through a stressful period of adjustment called culture shock during which they may be disoriented, homesick, sad, or angry. Because of their common experiences they share an intuitive definition of the phrase "culture shock" although they may not know the theoretical explanations for the phenomenon. For those who have never adapted to another culture, the phrase could mean something entirely different or it may have no meaning whatsoever.

In everyday conversation, we use the term "war" very frequently and perhaps too casually with such expressions as "the war on terrorism," "the war on drugs," or "the war on tooth decay." Because of its overuse, the word "war" has lost its meaning. For those who have actually lived through a war on their own soil, the word has very personal and specific meaning which is shared with others who have experienced armed conflict where thousands or even millions of soldiers and innocent people have been killed. They are less likely to use the word so offhandedly.

You can also use this model of communication to focus on the *medium*. When we speak to another person, molecules of air between our vocal cords and the other person's ears are moving and therefore sound becomes the medium. But if the receiver responds with the *feedback*, "I don't understand your point," you could try another medium such as vision and illustrate what you are trying to say with a picture or by writing out the words on a white board.

Not only is the meaning of a message dependent upon the culture of the individual, the medium and type of feedback is equally culturally specific. For example, as we have noted, Americans prefer words and especially written words. They rush to get a negotiation "into writing" as soon as possible. People from more associative, high-context cultures are more likely to prefer face-to-face communications where they might use all of their senses to communicate and build trust—touch, sound, vision, and so on. They would probably only put things "into writing" after they have developed an interpersonal relationship with the other person. To do this too soon might indicate that there is mistrust or the American is too pushy.

Americans often are fairly direct and verbally-oriented. They like unambiguous feedback— "yes" or "no." In cultures where people tend to avoid any kind of offense, negative feedback in particular is indirect and less clear. A subtle gesture could mean "no" or the fact that another person doesn't say "yes," could also mean no. But it is not as abrasive as actually saying "no."

Of course, this is a very simple model and interpersonal communications is much more complex. This model is monological in that messages and feedback flow in one direction. The sender uses the feedback to correct his or her message to be sure that it has the same meaning that he or she intended. If the messages and feedback flowed simultaneously and equally strong in both directions, we would describe the model as dialogue.

In mass communication, the model becomes even more complicated in that the sender and the receiver are usually different people. The media modalities are more limited to perhaps only sound and sight, certainly not smell or touch. And the feedback is often delayed and decayed. A politician might be a sender who wants to persuade the public to support his or her election. He gives a speech at a university that is filmed and recorded by a television network for its national news broadcast in the early evening. The television network is the encoder because it selects out the two minutes of his speech that it wants to broadcast and the anchor person explains the significance of the speech. The politician is anxious to know what the public thought of his ideas and he certainly can't wait until the election to change his message or medium. Thus he hires a pollster to gather feedback from the public.

At the mass communications level, the cultural differences become even more significant because the mass media in one country might be viewed with suspicion because of government control whereas in another country it has enormous credibility. In some countries, newspapers are the primary source of political news and certain papers are viewed as more objective than others whereas in other countries the image of a person on a television screen might be more persuasive and believable because it includes such nonverbal messages as tone of voice, posture, or gestures. The image and nonverbal messages may be much more powerful than words.

And there may be significant generational differences between and within cultures when it comes to the use of digital and social media. Only one in four American adults reads a newspaper every day and even fewer younger people turn to print media for news. The primary source of information for youth today comes from the internet and social media. Social media has great credibility because of its immediacy and apparent lack of filtering by a government or organization. It is imminently democratic. Furthermore, it links generations across national borders as we have seen with the Arab Spring movements in many Middle Eastern countries in 2011 and 2012 and the Occupy Movements (such as Occupy Wall Street, Occupy DC, or even Occupy London and Occupy Moscow).

Verbal and Nonverbal Communication

If we sit with the bottom of our shoe in the face of someone from the Middle East, the message 'sole of shoe toward face' means rudeness and disrespect. In the United States, it is fairly common for people to cross their legs with the bottom of their shoe in the face of a person they are talking with. It is usually quite meaningless and ignored. On the other hand, if someone uses profane language in a business meeting or a university classroom, it quickly gets the attention of every American. What messages we pay attention to and the meanings we give to those messages depend upon our culture.

Language is obviously a key component of communication in any culture. As we noted in the discussion of the Sapir-Whorf hypothesis, it reflects, and perhaps shapes, the values and perceptions of a group of people. As a language becomes more pervasive worldwide, it becomes easier to use and yet also includes a larger vocabulary. It often absorbs words and phrases from other languages. The word "shall" has almost disappeared from everyday American English usage while phases such as *pronto, avant-garde, gung ho,* and *Schadenfreude* are routinely woven into conversations in the U.S. Furthermore, a simplified version of English which locals find easy to use can be found in almost every country. This English *patois* is very useful for commerce with regions such as Asia or Latin America.

Less than 50 years ago, French was considered the language of diplomats and German was the language of chemists and Greek or Latin was used for medical and biological research. Most doctoral students had to master the reading of at least one or two languages other than their native language to conduct their research in diplomatic history, chemistry, or biology. Today, English has become the most common second language in the world. It is used for diplomacy, science, and business and is the common language of the internet. At the same time, there are far fewer verb tenses in English than existed during the time of Shakespeare. When people send messages by text, a word may be represented around the globe by a few simple letters. *LOL* has the same meaning to those who communicate digitally in almost every country.

Language is the principle way in which we describe things and convey information. It is almost impossible to describe a spiral staircase without using words or to explain how to operate a microwave oven without referring to spoken or written instructions. However, if we are communicating feelings, face-to-face communications is the most effective and powerful way of sending messages because we can use *nonverbal communication*—facial expressions, vocal patterns, posture, social distance, and the use of time. A glance or touch can communicate intimate feelings much more clearly than all the poetry or prose that has ever been written.

The study of these ways of communicating includes all of the "ics" in cross-cultural communication—kinesics, proxemics, chronemics, and so forth. Kinesics is the study of human movement or body motions such as facial expressions, gestures, or posture. Proxemics involves how people use space. The distance people maintain between themselves when conversing and even how furniture is arranged are all examples of proxemics. Chronemics is the study of how time is used in different cultures. It ranges from the rhythm or tempo of conversation to the socially acceptable time for arriving late for a party or meeting. But it could also include time-orientation such as focusing on the future and ignoring the past which is typical of the United States. In some other cultures, especially high-context cultures, there is a tendency to focus on the past and the present but to ignore the future.

Nonverbal codes are probably more significant in the breakdown of cross-cultural communication than verbal codes because they are learned implicitly and thus are generally unconscious and the meanings are usually specific to each culture. One can easily identify the breakdown of verbal messages whereas the breakdown of nonverbal messages is less obvious but more significant in that we feel emotionally confused and cut off from others.

Although it is difficult to communicate facts without words, nonverbal messages have greater credibility in all cultures than verbal messages when it comes to social interaction. It is almost as if the body doesn't lie. Regardless of our culture, we may leave a job interview knowing full well that we will not be hired. The interviewer did not formally tell us that we do not have the job, but we read the person's body language and it very clearly communicated, "You don't have the job."

Even if we speak the same language or use interpreters, it is likely there will be a break-down of communication on the nonverbal level if we come from different cultures. In the following chart, which depicts cross-cultural differences in negotiating behavior, we see that the Japanese, Americans, and Brazilians would have difficulty overcoming their different nonverbal ways of negotiating.[1]

The Japanese tend to carefully consider what someone else says whereas Brazilians are much less likely to remain silent. They often will talk over someone else who may be talking. The Japanese also have conversational overlap, but it is usually to affirm what someone else is saying. It is quite common for someone from Japan to continually utter the phrase *hai* which translates as "yes, go on." Both Americans and Brazilians engage in more facial gazing than

CROSS-CULTURAL DIFFERENCES IN NONVERBAL NEGOTIATING BEHAVIOR			
BEHAVIOR (TACTIC)	**JAPANESE**	**AMERICAN**	**BRAZILIAN**
SILENT PERIODS **(Number of silent periods greater than 10 seconds, per 30 minutes)**	5.5	3.5	0
CONVERSATIONAL OVERLAPS **(Number per 10 minutes)**	12.6	10.3	28.6
FACIAL GAZING **(Minutes of gazing per 10 minutes)**	1.3	3.3	5.2
TOUCHING **(Not including handshaking, per 30 minutes)**	0	0	4.7

the Japanese. On the other hand, the Japanese silence and lack of direct eye contact make Americans suspicious and uneasy. Silence often unconsciously communicates rejection to Americans and lack of eye contact indicates a lack of interest in what the other person is saying. They interfere with the intimacy of face-to-face negotiation.

Americans and Japanese would seldom touch in a formal negotiation other than a handshake. Brazilians often touch as a way of communicating friendship and to indicate that they are completely involved in the negotiation. In a negotiation, we can use interpreters and with a back-translation, we can check on the accuracy of the interpretation. However, the meanings we give to these nonverbal messages are usually unconscious and not easy to translate and yet they are vital in the development of our attitudes towards others. Trustworthiness, honesty, sincerity, friendliness, and openness are often determined by these nonverbal messages regardless of what is communicated verbally.[2]

In some cultures people may be more adept in the use of nonverbal communication. For example, both Edward Hall and Albert Mehrabian would agree that people in high-context cultures tend to use more nonverbal messages while low-context people are much more verbally-oriented.[3] In these cultures, there is a greater emphasis on face-to-face communication for information and even entertainment. There is some evidence that women and racial minorities such as African-Americans are much more likely to understand nonverbal messages than mainstream white people. This may be a result of power relationships. This is most probably a result of socialization. These relational skills are highly rewarded among members of these groups. But it may also be in part a result of power differentiation. That is, those who historically have not had power but have been able to "read" the nuances and hidden meanings of nonverbal cues given off by those in power.

Feedback also includes both verbal and nonverbal messages and certainly varies with each culture. In many high-context cultures, feedback is circuitous, subtle, and often nonverbal, whereas Americans prefer direct and unambiguous verbal feedback. Americans want a clear "yes" or "no," not "it is difficult" or simply drawing air through one's teeth when in fact the receiver means "no." Americans do not want to guess at one's response to a question, and indirection, subtlety, or "maybes" are often experienced as inscrutable or deceptive.

In many non-Western, rural cultures, a high premium is placed on social harmony. Thus, if one cannot comply with another's wishes, a flat "no" is discourteous. Such a response is considered abrasive, abrupt, and overly negative. Because everyone wants to say "yes" to maintain good feelings, the absence of an affirmative response is sufficient to communicate "no." In such cultures, people tend to respond negatively with some nonverbal sign or such phrases as "I hope, yes," or "God willing." While perhaps circuitous and ambiguous to an American, such a response is quite clear and polite for many non-Westerners.

We learn the meanings to these nonverbal cues tacitly and often very early in life, simply by participating in social interaction in a given culture. We might not even realize that we attribute meanings to eye contact, touch, or coming late to a meeting because the meanings are almost completely unconscious. We therefore assume that everyone else shares the meanings and yet they are specific to each culture. The internalization of these meanings may be even greater in cultures such as the mainstream American culture where there is such emphasis on written and verbal communication. You can't learn these meanings in most language classes.

American psychologist Paul Ekman found that there are six facial expressions that have universal or common meanings in every culture. All other nonverbal messages elicit meanings that are usually specific to each culture. These facial expressions are happiness, sadness, surprise, fear, disgust, and anger.[4] If we are shown a photo of someone who is sad or happy, we can identify that emotion regardless of the person's culture. However, when it is appropriate to display that emotion may be culture specific. It is possible that a Japanese widow who is receiving visitors who are conveying their condolences might not show the facial expression of sadness because she doesn't want to burden others with her mourning. When everyone leaves, she has the same facial expression of sadness we might observe on the face of anyone who is grieving.

INTERPERSONAL COMMUNICATION AND THOUGHT PATTERNS

Let us now revisit theories we have discussed and bring them together to understand how culture impacts communication, especially at the interpersonal level. Edward Hall's contrast of high- and low-context cultures is a linguistic/communications model. High-context messages are embedded in the culture and their meanings are unconsciously learned by having lived in that culture. There is a greater use of nonverbal communication than in low-context cultures and often numerous sense modalities—such as touch, vision, and sound—are used simultaneously in an interpersonal interaction. High-context people are therefore polychronic and use numerous senses simultaneously and doing many things at the same time.

Low-context people are much more likely to use words that are direct and the connotative and denotative meanings to messages are usually the same. Thus, there is no need to know the culture well to use the language. They tend to dwell on one thing at a time in a linear fashion and they utilize one sense modality at a time to communication. Hall would describe them as monochronic and high-context people as polychronic.

Even low-context people use high-context communication with friends and loved ones with whom they share intense interpersonal experiences. This language implies an intimacy and a strong sense of belonging. When one speaks this code they are "insiders" or "one of us." There is a shared code that ought not to be used by outsiders. A couple might refer to each other as "sweetheart" or "teddy bear" and a simple gesture has great meaning, perhaps even more than hundreds of words.

We also use *situational high-context dialects* with classmates and those who share our occupation or hobby. University students often use acronyms to describe their university, department or major, such as, "I'm an IC major at AU in SIS." Everyone who shares this "culture" knows that this means, "I'm studying International Communication at American University in the School of International Service." Airport controllers use very precise words that pilots understand and yet outsiders may have little understanding of this language. And each sport has its own language and those who are not life-long fans of the sport are often soon found out as newcomers or outsiders because they frequently misuse the terms.

Hall's linguistic model rests on the assumption that we must know internal culture to fully understand communication and especially nonverbal communication because it is high-context and its meanings are usually specific to each culture. There are cognitive psychologists and anthropologists who believe that how we think and solve problems depends upon our internal culture which, in turn, shapes the way in which we communicate. These scholars would argue that our culturally determined systems of logic or thought patterns also tend to fall into two categories along a continuum that roughly parallels Hall's high- and low-context culture model.

Edmund Glenn's associative and abstractive thought patterns, Rosalie Cohen's relational and analytical learning and intelligence, or Ruth Benedict's Dionysian and Apollonian research generally describe the logic of high- and low-context cultures. Bringing together Hall's anthropological/linguistic models with these more anthropological/cognitive models allows us to analyze and interpret interpersonal cross-cultural communication with much greater depth and breadth.

This word game illustrates how a low-context culture still has aspects of high-context communication and the two ways of communicating also are determined by the way in which we think. Here are three phrases in standard American English. Which one does not fit with the other two?

A. Nice weather we're having.

B. Sunny, maximum temperature in the mid-70s.

C. Haven't we met before?

At first glance, many people would say that phrase C does not belong with the other two because phrases A and B deal with the weather and phrase C has nothing to do with the weather. This is especially likely to be the response of those who did not grow up in the U.S. and learn English as their native language.

It is true that phrases A and B relate to the weather. But most Americans would say that phrase B is different than the other two because phrases A and C are informal ways of starting a conversation. When someone says, "nice weather we're having," they don't want a weather report. They are simply saying, "Let's start a conversation." This is also true for the question, "Haven't we met before?" It is an "opening gambit" or way to initiate a relationship. But no one would approach someone in a restaurant and try to engage in informal conversation by saying, "Sunny, maximum temperature in the mid-70s." Phrase B does not have a pronoun or even a verb. It is simply a set of facts.

Although the U.S. is a low-context culture, phrases A and C are actually high-context forms of interpersonal, face-to-face communication. In the context of the American culture, they have almost the same meanings. Of course, this is spoken and informal conversational English that is not taught in language classes and the connotative and denotative meanings are very different. Phrase B is almost entirely low-context. The words mean the same in any language.

Edmund Glenn would describe phrases A and C as *associative* ways of thinking because many things are brought together which can easily change the meanings. He found this thought pattern to be common among people outside of mainstream American and northern European cultures. Rosalie Cohen might identify these phrases as typical of *relational* thinkers because there is an assumption that two people share a relationship and thus common meanings to both verbal and nonverbal messages. In her research on learning styles and gender, she found this to be typical of young girls who are rewarded in American grade schools for their relational skills.

Many things are relevant to the meanings given to the messages. Who says what to whom through what channel is vital to understanding the intended meanings. A young man saying "nice weather we're having" to a young woman he has never met before could mean something very different that the same young man saying "nice weather we're having" to his middle-aged professor. Furthermore, tone of voice or a gesture can easily change the meaning. The phrase must be put in context—gender, age, social class, and accompanying nonverbal messages can alter the meaning of the spoken message.

Phrase B on the other hand is what Glenn would describe as *abstractive* and Rosalie Cohen would identify as *analytic*. The word "abstract" comes from the Latin word *abstractus* and roughly means "to select out" while "analyze" means to divide. Out of a situation where two or more people are communicating is "selected out" that which is relevant to the weather. It makes no difference who is speaking and nonverbal messages have almost no impact. In fact, phrase two might be simply a notice from a weather advisory service that appears as an email or text message. Only the words are relevant—everything else is irrelevant.

Phrases A and C can also be understood as poetic because poetry, by definition, is high-context, associative, and relational which is the reason it is so difficult to translate from one language to another. Poetry is usually shared with others through the spoken word and how the words are said aloud changes their meanings. Phase B is more typical of lawyers or people who write good office memos. It is written, very impersonal, and the words are very precise.

We can contrast these ways of communicating and thinking with the following chart:

A. Nice weather we're having!

C. Haven't we met before?

    High-Context - Relational - Associative

    To Be - Poets

B. Sunny, high in the 70s.

    Low-Context - Analytical - Abstractive

    To Do - Memo Writers/Lawyers

What happens when a poet and a lawyer or memo writer work in the same office? There is often a great deal of misunderstanding simply because they communicate, think, and solve problems very differently. There are some high-context cultures where everyone seems to be a poet. You ask a question and they respond by telling you a story or using many metaphors. They place the answer in context. Metaphors are also images that convey lessons or serve as examples. Words can mean many different things depending upon the situation, nonverbal aspects of the message, and who is communicating to whom.

At most American universities, one is supposed to be very objective, direct, gather quantitative data, and select out those facts that are relevant to your position. This is especially true when writing a paper. Thoughts should be organized according to inductive, linear logic which leads to a rational conclusion. Personal experiences or history might be deemed irrelevant.

In high-context cultures, an answer to a question may require a personal knowledge of those involved and entail delving into the past to understand the present situation. The approach is highly deductive rather than inductive and information is linked together in ways that low-context people might view as irrational.

To illustrate, let us assume that an American is engaged in a joint venture business project in a small village in rural Pakistan. Mr. Jones and his wife arrived yesterday and today he arranged a meeting with Mr. Khan, an elderly man who is the head of a local construction company and also a government official. The purpose of the meeting is to sign an agreement to erect a small building to store supplies for the project. It is important to have the building completed within the next two weeks because the rainy season has nearly begun.

Jones briefly introduces himself and states the reason for his meeting. But before the business discussion gets underway, Khan interrupts and insists that Jones drinks a cup of tea. As the tea is being served, he asks, "How is your family?" Jones is a bit surprised by this personal question and answers, "My family is fine. My wife is at the hotel and in a week or so we should be able to find some permanent housing, but I'm here to discuss the construction of the building." He wants to pull Khan back to what is relevant—the business agreement.

My Khan continues, "I was inquiring about your *real* family." "What do you mean, 'my real family'?" "Your brothers or parents." Mr. Jones is taken aback by this strange question and answers, "Well, my brothers are married and living with their families in the United States, my parents are living on a farm that has been in our family for many years, but I'm here this morning to discuss a construction project."

At this point, a server has poured another cup of tea and Khan asks, "Mr. Jones, is it possible that you are the first-born son in your family—the eldest son?" "Yes, I'm the oldest son." "And your parents are living alone on a farm on which you were raised?" "Yes, they're still on the farm growing crops and raising cows." Mr. Khan looks perplexed and asks, "But why aren't you living on that farm?"

Jones is exasperated with this line of personal and extraneous questioning. He is beginning to reach two conclusions: First, Khan is totally incompetent. What do his parents have to do with this business negotiation? The man does not know how to carry on a business conversation. Second, Jones becomes a bit paranoid and begins to wonder if Khan is trying to avoid discussing business. Is he intentionally sabotaging this negotiation?

"When I was a child, I hated cows. They're dirty, attract flies and I didn't like to get up at 4 in the morning to milk them. When I graduated from high school at the age of 17, my father wanted me to stay on the farm, but I won a scholarship to go to the university. I earned a bachelor's and a master's degree, began working with my company over 25 years ago and I'm now the country manager for this project. And now I'm here this morning to discuss the construction of a building!" He hopes this response will pull the conversation on track.

Khan is shocked by Jones' abruptness, his obvious annoyance with the question, and his attempt to push the conversation into business before they have a chance to get acquainted. Jones has lost confidence that Khan is a competent businessman or knows how to conduct a business negotiation. He is prepared to find another construction company.

Differences in communication style, internal values, and culturally-shaped thought patterns have caused this breakdown of interpersonal communication. Jones is very direct and wants to discuss business as soon as possible. Khan would view this as pushy and rude. Before talking business, one should get to know the other person in terms of character and background. Because Jones is foreign, this means time must be allotted for this personal discussion. If Jones were a local person, chances are that Khan would know a great deal about his family, his trustworthiness, and his record in the local community well before he entered Khan's office.

Jones' way of communicating is direct. He would say that the best way to get from point A to point B in a business meeting is a straight line. Get to the point and stick to that which is relevant to conduct business. If all goes well, he will leave this initial meeting with a signed contract.

A  B

Khan's inquiries are polite ways of saying, "I care about you and what is most important in your life, your family." Every business discussion with a stranger of status would begin with these kinds of questions. They allow him to find out who Mr. Jones *is* as a man, not simply what he *does* as a business person. The conversation also establishes a personal relationship between two men. Because Khan is an associative thinker, he knows that doing business with Jones means that in the eyes of others in the community, they have an affiliation. If Jones is not a good person, this reflects badly on Khan. He is indirectly probing—gathering bits and pieces of information about Jones to answer the questions, "Who are you? What is your character and background?"

Khan is indirect. He goes off on what Jones perceives as irrelevant tangents, but each of these loops or tangents were intended to gather information that Khan deems relevant before they even begin to discuss business.

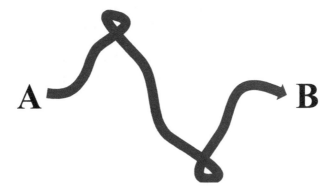

If we bring these two communication styles together, it is clear that Jones is cutting off Khan's loops while Khan appears to be unable to focus his comments on the matter at hand—a business agreement. This is not a good interpersonal conversation.

Jones does not understand why Khan is asking these personal and irrelevant questions which he attributed to incompetence or avoiding conducting business. Khan believes that Jones refuses to engage in this interpersonal repartee because he is rude or perhaps even hiding something.

Jones identifies himself in terms of his individual accomplishments. He earned his scholarships which allowed him to leave the farm, graduate from the university with at least two degrees, and eventually become a successful businessman. Through his own hard work he is now the country manager for this project.

As an older and very traditional rural Pakistani, Khan assumes that every good first-born son would "walk in his father's footsteps" or at least get his father's blessings for whatever he has done during his life. Jones defied his father's wishes for him to stay on the farm and there is no evidence he received his father's blessing for anything he has accomplished. As an associative or relational thinker, Khan views this background information as very useful. If Jones' own father can't trust him, why should Khan trust him? If he would disrespect his own father, he surely would disrespect Khan. It is very unlikely that Khan would sign the agreement.

These cultural differences also impact the pace of a negotiation or a project. Khan would not discuss business specifics until time has been devoted to "getting acquainted" over a few cups of tea. Jones might welcome one cup or even dinner later in the week, but he would like to finish up the business negotiation during this first meeting.

A two-year project for most Americans is often organized according to measureable bench marks. A time line for a two year project might be divided into stages such as this:

Project Timeline

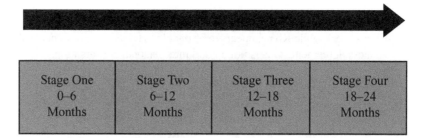

| Stage One 0–6 Months | Stage Two 6–12 Months | Stage Three 12–18 Months | Stage Four 18–24 Months |

In Khan's culture, the first stage would be elongated as they spend time developing a relationship and building interpersonal rapport. Jones might view this as a waste of time and it is quite likely that his company at home would be concerned about his lack of "progress." Many of his days are spent talking with Khan, meeting Khan's associates and family members, and even getting acquainted with aspects of the local culture such as historical sites, food, music, and customs. Much of this first stage requires face-to-face interpersonal interaction. Khan can see him, hear him, and even touch him leading to trust, which is vital for doing business.

Once the trust is established, then communications can move to memos and emails, and business not only can be discussed, the pace actually increases. Let us say that Jones needs to have some work visas processed within the next two weeks or his project will collapse. It is vital to have these visas and yet the office at the Foreign Ministry which normally can process them in a week has slowed down because the supervisor is on leave for his daughter's wedding. Jones is panicked and phones Khan to tell him about the crisis situation.

"Mr. Jones, please calm down. I think I can help you. My cousin works in that office and perhaps can handle the paperwork. Bring the applications to my office and I'll see what I can do." Within two days the visas are available because of the personal relationship between Jones and Khan and the "contacts" Khan has at the Foreign Ministry. The last phase of the project goes much more quickly because time was devoted in the first phase to developing trust. Had trust not been established, it is quite possible the project would be greatly delayed or might fail. Because Jones understood the culture, the project is completed in two years.

Project Timeline

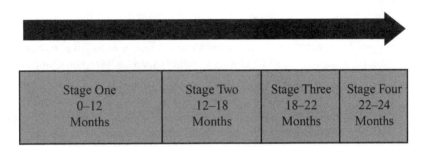

Stage One 0–12 Months	Stage Two 12–18 Months	Stage Three 18–22 Months	Stage Four 22–24 Months

In summary, the way in which we get things done depends upon not only our values and ways of communicating, but also the ways in which we perceive reality and think or solve problems. These are all hidden in internal culture and underpin much of the cross-cultural misunderstanding that occurs during negotiations and meetings.

FRIENDSHIP, DATING, AND ACTION CHAINS

How we develop friendships, date, or conduct ourselves in meetings depend upon our culture. It is not merely a matter of culturally determined differences in ways of communicating, values, beliefs, perceptions, or thought patterns. We carry into these relationships unconscious assumptions regarding the role we play and the steps that are appropriate to accomplish our goal. These assumptions vary with each culture.

In some cultures, an invitation to dinner is comparable to extending the hand of friendship and the beginning step in developing a warm relationship whereas in another culture it is simply a meal shared with others with no other implications. A woman's smile to a male stranger might indicate that she is interested in getting to know the gentleman and thus the beginning of some kind of courting behavior. Yet, in another culture it is just a smile of politeness extended to everyone.

Many animals are biologically programmed to instinctually engage in a series of behaviors that are triggered by a "sign stimulus"—a thing or event—during a particular period of maturation. Often these series of actions allow a species of animals to survive. This process is referred to as "imprinting." For example, a duckling will follow a mother duck shortly after birth during a "sensitive period" that may be only a few hours after birth. The ducklings are biologically programmed to follow the mother duck which provides protection and allows her to keep track of her brood. If the duckling is separated at birth from the mother duck, the instinct to engage in this following behavior still exists and it will follow anything else that moves during that window of time such as a farmer. For the remainder of the duck's life it is likely to continue to follow the farmer around the farmyard.

Very little of human behavior can be explained as a matter of instinct or biology. Humans have the longest maturation period of any animal—the longest amount of time after birth when we need to be cared for by others to survive. Humans have few, if any, instincts and therefore must learn to survive and to accomplish our goals. Being human amounts to being a member of a culture and most of our behavior is socially or culturally, rather than biologically, determined.

There are endless sequences of behavior which we use when interacting with others. Edward Hall refers to them as *action chains*—"a set sequence of events in which usually two or more individuals participate. It is reminiscent of a dance that is used as a means of reaching a common goal that can be reached only after and not before each link in the chain has been forged."[5] A greeting might begin with eye contact, a handshake, mutual questions about the welfare of each other, and a closing comment such as, "See you again soon."

Eye contact means giving our full attention to another, usually accompanied by a smile to nonverbally convey friendliness. We almost instantaneously release our grip after a handshake as we simultaneously utter a greeting such as, "Jim, how are you?" "How is work going?" The encounter is short because we assume the other person is very busy.

In rural Nigeria, a younger person often respects an elder by avoiding direct eye contact and the two hold hands throughout the conversation. Good manners require the use of titles with older people, rather than first names. "Mr. Ukata, how is your family?" To ask about someone's family is perfectly polite and expected whereas an American would find this inappropriate, too personal, and a bit odd, especially if the other person has never met members of his or her family. The greeting ends with a request to take leave of the other person. "I'm sorry, I must catch a bus in a few minutes or I'll be very late for work."

In the United States, people smile while simultaneously making brief eye contact to put each other at ease. It's a friendly nonverbal way for people to exchange salutations without saying anything. This is especially common when encountering strangers in public. Friends are more likely to accompany these gestures with a verbal greeting such as "How are you?" "Fine. How are you?" Not reciprocating a friend's verbal or nonverbal greeting could be rude.

The eye contact and smile between strangers is more typical of rural or southern areas of the United States than in urban areas such as New York City. In other countries, a smile between strangers may be only the first step in developing a friendship and it is not randomly given to strangers because it may set off a friendship action chain.

If an American female student glances at a male student with a friendly smile during the first class of the semester it has little meaning other than a pleasant gesture. Many American men would just return the smile and continue taking lecture notes. There is no implication that a friendship has begun. In some parts of Africa or Latin America, if a young woman smiles at a young man she doesn't know, it might be taken as a nonverbal way of initiating a relationship. He feels obligated to not only return the smile, but to also take the next step in the action chain and begin a conversation. Thus, during the classroom break, he introduces himself, asks her name, and has a casual conversation about each others' backgrounds and why they are enrolled in the course. The relationship has moved beyond a greeting and the young man ends the chat with the question, "Would you like to go to a movie?"

"I appreciate the invitation but I'm not going out this semester with anyone. I want to devote all my attention to my studies." A week later he asks her if she would join him for dinner over the weekend. He assumed that she was just being polite or even coy and her "no thank you" comment really meant, "ask me again." After all, she started the courting action chain when she smiled at him. He had to show his sincerity and persistence by inviting her to go to dinner when it was perhaps more convenient. She is annoyed because she thought she clearly explained that she wasn't going out with anyone and she begins to feel that he is harassing her.

High-context people tend to be more committed to completing an action chain once it has begun. An invitation to someone's home for dinner often is comparable to extending the hand of friendship to another person in Latin America, Africa, Asia, and the Middle East. And this friendship might continue long into the future. You don't invite riff raff into your home to be in the company of family members. In some countries, you wouldn't even extend the invitation unless you were fairly sure that the other person would be free to say "yes" because they would feel very badly if they had to decline it.

In the U.S., an invitation to dinner doesn't necessarily start a friendship action chain. It may simply mean, "I invite you to dinner." And, at the end of the evening, the farewell remark, "Let's get together again soon," means, "Let's get together when it's mutually convenient." In some high-context culture it is confirmation that the friendship action chain has begun and there is a commitment to maintain the relationship. Yet, the American doesn't call for many weeks and they are suspicious that the remark was not only insincere, it was deceptive. Why would a person clearly indicate that he or she is a friend and yet never carry through with further contact?

THE FRUSTRATIONS OF INTERCULTURAL MEETINGS

Intercultural meetings are often painfully frustrating and confusing. Nothing seems to get done and there are endless misunderstandings. It is difficult to pick a leader, set an agenda, and get down to business. While some seem to talk on endlessly about irrelevant matters others are too impatient, pushy, and cold. Gary Althen claims that this is a result of conflicting action chains.[6] Although his observations come from his lifelong experience with university student groups, his findings would apply to any group involving participants from various cultural backgrounds.

Althen theorizes that we carry unspoken assumptions regarding how and when to select a leader, the criteria that ought to be used in selecting a leader, when to stop the chit-chat and "get down to business," how to set an agenda, when to take a vote, and even what kind of vote determines the group's decision—a simple majority or full consensus of the group. These are mostly unconscious action chains which vary with each culture. In an intercultural meeting, they inevitably clash.

Relationships are vital in most high-context cultures and time must be allocated to allow people to get acquainted with each other in any newly formed group. The chit-chat may seem superficial and a waste of time to many low-context people. It is not uncommon for people to go around the room to first identity themselves before they move on to the task at hand. "Tell us who you are," really means, "Tell us what you do," whereas in a high-context culture it could also mean "and tell us about your family background and your experiences." The high-context person is also revealing aspects of his or her personality and skills such as friendliness, charm, articulacy, wit, and so on.

Generally, low-context people are more likely to want to cut off this chit-chat and get down to business more quickly than high-context people. This tendency to quickly move on from the personal to the professional comes across as pushy and uncaring whereas the seemingly endless chatter is sometimes interpreted as incompetence or avoiding the task at hand. These assumptions as to when the chit-chat ends and business begins and the attribution we make of people who do not share our assumptions are mostly culturally determined and unconscious. Low-context people break the "initial get together" action chain of those who are high-context.

Every organization wants competent, skilled, and wise leaders. The process of selecting a leader and the criteria used to determine his or her qualifications depend upon culture. In many low-context cultures what the person has done professionally or academically and what the person will do in the leadership position are the primary factors to be taken into account. This is determined with a written or oral vita which reveals educational background, experience, and skills relevant to the position and the organization. The focus is on accomplishments and potential.

In some high-context cultures, factors such as age, ethnicity, gender, and/or family background are also important when selecting a leader. These criteria might be considered irrelevant in low-context cultures and ought not to be considered because they prevent many qualified people from being selected. It is against the law in the United States to consider these characteristics of a person when it comes to recruitment, hiring, or promotion of employees or when admitting students to universities. In some cases, these personal characteristics can be found on a vita or revealed in an interview.

A task-oriented group within an organization or on a campus will often select a leader more informally. In the United States, a leader is someone that most agree is fair, has good communication skills, and can moderate the group to allow for repartee between members. Almost any member of the group could play this role. In other countries, time must be allowed for casual conversation during which leadership qualities are demonstrated and both professional and personal background is revealed. In traditional cultures in the Middle East, the oldest person who is usually male and has the respect of others would be ranked very high when selecting a leader. In the action chain of picking a leader, more time must be provided for these extensive leadership qualities to become apparent to everyone.

At American University in Washington, students from the same culture were asked what they would do at an initial meeting of a task-oriented multicultural group that would have at least six meetings.[7] Students from the Middle East usually said that they would probably "get acquainted" and allow time for participants to reveal their backgrounds after which they would determine a leader based on experience, age, gender, and so on. The same was true for other high-context students from Africa, Latin America, and Asia. The Americans agreed that very little time is required to get to know each other and anyone could be selected to lead the group. Most students from low-context cultures described the "get acquainted" step in the action chain as mostly an opportunity to greet others and perhaps describe their academic backgrounds or accomplishments.

Most students agreed that a leader could set the agenda for upcoming meetings. However, many low-context students thought that time limits should be placed on the discussion of each agenda item after which a vote could be taken regarding a course of action. Many Asian students were opposed to such time limits and believed that time had to be allocated to each item to allow everyone to speak. The group would make this decision, not the leader. This also would give participants an opportunity to know what the emerging consensus might be before a vote could be taken. Low-context students were much more individualistic. There was no need to have a prolonged discussion. Each person could voice an opinion during the discussion and then vote "yes" or "no." The majority of votes would determine the outcome.

Low-context students valued action as more important than consensus or unity. An individual had the right to disagree before the vote and to be the sole vote in opposition to the majority. Endless discussion was a waste of time and thus a time limit ought to be imposed by the leader or written into the agenda. High-context students tended to view this behavior by low-context students as disrespectful, arrogant, and domineering.

In high-context cultures, there must be sufficient time to allow everyone to voice an opinion. When it is clear that there is agreement, a vote is taken and individuals would vote with the majority to maintain consensus and unity. A good leader would know when this propitious time for a vote would take place. Consequently, it takes much longer to make a decision in high-context cultures. For many low-context students, this elongated step in the decision-making action chain was unnecessary and frustrating.[8]

RACIAL AND GENDER DIFFERENCES IN COMMUNICATION STYLES

Action chains also impact the interaction of different cultural groups within a society. In the 1980s, sociolinguist Thomas Kochman found that his African American and white students had different styles of communication which led to misunderstanding, frustration, and conflict.[9] During a classroom discussion of a controversial issue, black students would often become more "emotional" with raised voices and increased gesturing with hands and arms. White students were often taken aback with the display of emotion and interpreted the gestures as menacing or an indication of being "out-of-control." For black students, their show of emotion was a natural progression in the action chain of a lively discussion and showed their sincerity. The tendency of white students to then become even more controlled in their response was interpreted as withholding true feelings and shutting down the discussion which, in turn, increased the intensity of the emotional responses of black students.

At American University, in the 1970s and 1980s it was not uncommon for black and white students to engage in heated debate in a "teach-in" or open discussion on a current political or social issue. The students were good friends who shared similar goals and yet these meetings often deteriorated into misunderstanding and conflict because of differing communication styles and action chains. Just when black students assumed they were finally freely expressing their deeply held beliefs and feelings some of the white students were panicked by the dramatic display of emotion and wild gestures. These encounters sometimes ended when a white student contacted campus security because they thought there was a "fight" further undermining the trust of black students who believed they were "finally communicating."

It is more than just verbal styles of communication. Kochman found that differences in nonverbal styles also caused misunderstandings. Black males in his classrooms at the University of Illinois tended to break eye contact more frequently than his white students. In the mainstream, white society, the way to nonverbally tell another person "I don't want to listen to you anymore," is to simply break eye contact while the other person is talking. If they still don't get the message, breaking eye contact while glancing at one's watch clearly means, "end of conversation." Many of his black students thought that white people were staring at them all the time which made them uneasy. Many white students thought that black students didn't like them. It might just be a matter of difference in nonverbal communication regarding eye contact.

For many white students, the use of hyperbole, expressive gestures, and loud voices came across as angry and irrational while for many black students it meant sincerity and a willingness to share authentic feelings. On the other hand, many black students interpreted the lack of an emotional response from white students as deceptive. Their linguistic style was not intended to create a confrontation but rather as a way of expressing feelings or "affect."

According to Kochman, among many African Americans, a provocative move or actual physical contact in a hostile situation means things have gotten out of hand and a conflict is taking place. "A 'threat' for Whites then begins when a person says they are going to do something. A 'threat' for Blacks begins when a person actually *makes a move* to do something. Verbal threats, from the Black standpoint, are still 'only talk.'"[10]

According to many linguists the verb "to be" is much more common in Black English than in Standard English which suggests that there are cultural differences between white and black Americans that, in turn, impact the ways in which they communicate. The verb "to do" is one of the most common verbs in standard American English. The associative and even poetic use of spoken words and phrases accompanied with elaborate gestures is very much a part of the traditional African-American culture. Black dance or jazz performances and hip hop music also require the audience to interact with the artist thereby changing each reading or concert. Every performance is unique and there is an intimate oral give-and-take between the artist and the listeners or viewers. This usually does not take place during classical music or ballet concerts with predominantly white audiences.

This interpersonal repartee is demonstrated in a variety of linguistic activities. Black poetry is often read aloud before an audience with hand gestures, variations in tone of voice, and facial expressions that convey intense emotions. Poetic "toasts" or stories such as "Stagger Lee" are handed down from one generation to another with each person adding his or her own distinct variations. Young men often engage in such rhetorical games as "the dozens" or "joning" during which friendly insults are exchanged in front of their friends who give verbal and nonverbal feedback as to whether the response is poetically superior or rather "lame."

Displays of emotion, hyperbole, and the use of metaphors abound in lively discussions and show intense involvement but can also often serve to diffuse interpersonal conflict. Clever use of words and humor might very well prevent a physical conflict. For example, stories such as "Signifying Monkey" are ways of indirectly telling another person that he is arrogant. Biblical references become metaphors which are woven into a debate.

Although these styles of communication are a vital aspect of the traditional Black American culture, they may be dying out with younger generations who have not grown up in predominantly African American social environments. We usually learn our ways of communicating interpersonally from our peers rather than from parents, teachers, or even the mass media. As the overall society becomes more integrated, the use of so-called "black English" and these linguistic styles may gradually diminish among African Americans.

African American political and religious leaders are sometimes deemed "angry" or "manipulative" by white Americans when they use traditional black speaking styles. The hyperbole and emotion is viewed as being out-of-control instead of authentic, honest, and sincere. A black minister might engage in a "call-and-response" oratory style with his or her congregation. "God moved me!" a minister shouts out and the audience responds with a resounding "Amen!" In a black church, this is expected and yet few white ministers would use this audience participation technique.

In the 1980s, Jesse Jackson often used this speaking style when he ran for president.[11] His emotional and often poetic rhetoric rallied black supporters and at the same time scared many white voters. He would often use call-and-response shouting out "I am—" and the audience would enthusiastically finish the phrase with the word "somebody." For the black congregation this was rapport with the congregation and yet for many white people it was demagoguery and manipulation. The more didactic style of many white politicians can communicate control, leadership, and rationality but among black Americans it can also nonverbally communicate lack of authenticity, insincerity, and even dishonesty.

Jackson would often use deductive logic when giving a presentation. He would start with his conclusions and poetically connect anecdotes or personal observations to support his arguments. Many white observers found this to be illogical. They were more likely to inductively frame their positions by gathering as much empirical data as possible and then moving step-by-step through their evidence to finally reach a conclusion in the manner of a lawyer.

In a multicultural society, leaders who can shift their speaking styles to fit the culture of their audiences are usually very successful. Martin Luther King often gave sermons to mostly white audiences using standard American English and delivered roughly the same sermon to a black audience in Black English. Bill Clinton and George W. Bush could also move back and forth using a "folksy" manner with southern audiences or working-class white audiences and formal or "standard" English when on national television. Both were also comfortable using Spanish phrases with Hispanic audiences. Barack Obama is a very skilled style-shifter who can also merge styles thereby winning over both black and white supporters.[12] He can speak as a professor of constitutional law with the intonation of an ordinary person and at a political rally he uses the rhetorical flourishes of black preachers including call-and-response. This fluidity in speaking style is really a form of multilingualism.

There is evidence that American men and women may be socialized to communicate in different ways which lead to misunderstanding and conflict. Sociolinguist Deborah Tannen found in her studies that many female students tend to have a different way of communicating in classrooms than male students.[13] Young girls are socialized to view communication as a way of developing relationships or rapport. They will often say that their best friend is the person with whom they *share* the most secrets. Little boys are often raised to use communication to develop a hierarchy or to compete. Their best friend is often the person with whom they *do* the most.

In the classroom, men enjoy classes during which they can debate others or give reports whereas women are more likely to find that small groups and smaller classes allow them to collaborate with others. The desire for independent success and being at the top is a male characteristic. Cooperation and interdependence are much more feminine traits. Boys are good at analyzing and competing for attention and girls are better when it comes to relational skills.[14]

Going back to our contrast culture continuum, a low-context culture could be described as a masculine culture according to these differences in communication styles. Words become very important and are used to establish control, persuade, and compete with others. A feminine culture is high-context—relationships are valued, nonverbal messages are as important as verbal messages, there is a tendency to avoid interpersonal conflict and maintain harmony.

Hall also describes a low-context culture as "monochronic" and a high-context culture as "polychronic." Men tend to do one thing at a time and use one sense at a time. When they are lost driving, men are perhaps less likely to ask for directions than women because it would clearly indicate that they need help from, or depend upon, others. Women are much more likely to ask for directions. When they are lost, men also tend to turn down the radio to concentrate on finding their way. The radio is a distraction. Women can often multitask and use all of their senses simultaneously—talk on the phone, thumb through a book or magazine, and glance at the television.

Just as the Kochman's observations of African American culture may depend upon region and generation, it is possible that Tannen's findings might not be as true for contemporary female students who grew up in a world with greater equality between men and women. In grade school, boys and girls are equally competitive in classrooms and even in some athletic events. Moreover, women are now the majority in most university classes and therefore are much more confident about being assertive in the classroom, "speaking up," and taking control of discussions.

SECTION II: Readings

Communication without Words

Albert Mehrabian

Suppose you are sitting in my office listening to me describe some research I have done on communication. I tell you that feelings are communicated less by the words a person uses than by certain nonverbal means—that, for example, the verbal part of a spoken message has considerably less effect on whether a listener feels liked or disliked than a speaker's facial expression or tone of voice.

So far so good. But suppose I add, "In fact, we've worked out a formula that shows exactly how much each of these components contributes to the effect of the message as a whole. It goes like this: Total Impact = .07 verbal + .38 vocal + .55 facial."

What would you say to *that?* Perhaps you would smile good-naturedly and say, with some

Psychology Today 2, (Sept. 1968): 145–153.

feeling, "Baloney!" Or perhaps you would frown and remark acidly, "Isn't science grand." My own response to the first answer would probably be to smile back: the facial part of your message, at least, was positive (55 per cent of the total). The second answer might make me uncomfortable: only the verbal part was positive (seven per cent).

The point here is not only that my reactions would lend credence to the formula but that most listeners would have mixed feelings about my statement. People like to see science march on, but they tend to resent its intrusion into an "art" like the communication of feelings, just as they find analytical and quantitative approaches to the study of personality cold, mechanistic and unacceptable.

The psychologist himself is sometimes plagued by the feeling that he is trying to put a rainbow into a bottle. Fascinated by a complicated and emotionally rich human situation, he begins to study it, only to find in the course of his research that he has destroyed part of the mystique that originally intrigued and involved him. But despite a certain nostalgia for earlier, more intuitive approaches, one must acknowledge that concrete experimental data have added a great deal to our understanding of how feelings are communicated. In fact, as I hope to show, analytical and intuitive findings do not so much conflict as complement each other.

It is indeed difficult to know what another person really feels. He says one thing and does another; he seems to mean something but we have an uneasy feeling it isn't true. The early psychoanalysts, facing this problem of inconsistencies and ambiguities in a person's communications, attempted to resolve it through the concepts of the conscious and the unconscious. They assumed that contradictory messages meant a conflict between superficial, deceitful, or erroneous feelings on the one hand and true attitudes and feelings on the other. Their role, then, was to help the client separate the wheat from the chaff.

The question was, how could this be done? Some analysts insisted that inferring the client's unconscious wishes was a completely intuitive

process. Others thought that some nonverbal behavior, such as posture, position and movement, could be used in a more objective way to discover the client's feelings. A favorite technique of Frieda Fromm-Reichmann, for example, was to imitate a client's posture herself in order to obtain some feeling for what he was experiencing.

Thus began the gradual shift away from the idea that communication is primarily verbal, and that the verbal message includes distortions or ambiguities due to unobservable motives that only experts can discover.

Language, though, can be used to communicate almost anything. By comparison, nonverbal behavior is very limited in range. Usually, it is used to communicate feelings, likings and preferences, and it customarily reinforces or contradicts the feelings that are communicated verbally. Less often, it adds a new dimension of sorts to a verbal message, as when a salesman describes his product to a client and simultaneously conveys, nonverbally, the impression that he likes the client.

A great many forms of nonverbal behavior can communicate feelings: touching, facial expression, tone of voice, spatial distance from the addressee, relaxation of posture, rate of speech, number of errors in speech. Some of these are generally recognized as informative. Untrained adults and children easily infer that they are liked or disliked from certain facial expressions, from whether (and how) someone touches them, and from a speaker's tone of voice. Other behavior, such as posture, has a more subtle effect. A listener may sense how someone feels about him from the way the person sits while talking to him, but he may have trouble identifying precisely what his impression comes from.

Correct intuitive judgments of the feelings or attitudes of others are especially difficult when different degrees of feeling, or contradictory kinds of feeling, are expressed simultaneously through different forms of behavior. As I have pointed out, there is a distinction between verbal and vocal information (vocal information being what is lost when speech is written down—intonation, tone, stress, length and frequency of pauses, and so on), and the two kinds of information do not always communicate the same feeling. This distinction, which has been recognized for some time, has shed new light on certain types of communication. Sarcasm, for example, can be defined as a message in which the information transmitted vocally contradicts the information transmitted verbally. Usually the verbal information is positive and the vocal is negative, as in "Isn't science grand."

Through the use of an electronic filter, it is possible to measure the degree of liking communicated vocally. What the filter does is eliminate the higher frequencies of recorded speech, so that words are unintelligible but most vocal qualities remain. (For women's speech, we eliminate frequencies higher than about 200 cycles per second; for men, frequencies over about 100 cycles per second.) When people are asked to judge the degree of liking conveyed by the filtered speech, they perform the task rather easily and with a significant amount of agreement.

This method allows us to find out, in a given message, just how inconsistent the information communicated in words and the information communicated vocally really are. We ask one group to judge the amount of liking conveyed by a transcription of what was said, the verbal part of the message. A second group judges the vocal component, and a third group judges the impact of the complete recorded message. In one study of this sort we found that, when the verbal and vocal components of a message agree (both positive or both negative), the message as a whole is judged a little more positive or a little more negative than either component by itself. But when vocal information contradicts verbal, vocal wins out. If someone calls you "honey" in a nasty tone of voice, you are likely to feel disliked; it is also possible to say "I hate you" in a way that conveys exactly the opposite feeling.

Besides the verbal and vocal characteristics of speech, there are other, more subtle, signals of meaning in a spoken message. For example, everyone makes mistakes when he talks—unnecessary repetitions, stutterings, the omission of parts of words, incomplete sentences, "ums" and "ahs." In a number of studies of speech errors, George Mahl of Yale University has found that errors become more frequent as the speaker's discomfort or anxiety increases. It might be interesting to apply this index in an attempt to detect deceit (though on some occasions it might be risky: confident men are notoriously smooth talkers).

Timing is also highly informative. How long does a speaker allow silent periods to last, and how long does he wait before he answers his partner? How long do his utterances tend to be? How often does he interrupt his partner, or wait an inappropriately long time before speaking? Joseph Matarazzo and his colleagues at the University of Oregon have found that each of these speech habits is stable from person to person, and each tells something about the speaker's personality and about his feelings toward and status in relation to his partner.

Utterance duration, for example, is a very stable quality in a person's speech; about 30 seconds long on the average. But when someone talks to a partner whose status is higher than his own, the more the high-status person nods his head the longer the speaker's utterances become. If the high-status person changes his own customary speech pattern toward longer or shorter utterances, the lower-status person will change his own speech in the same direction. If the high-status person often interrupts the speaker, or creates long silences, the speaker is likely to become quite uncomfortable. These are things that can be observed outside the laboratory as well as under experimental conditions. If you have an employee who makes you uneasy and seems not to respect you, watch him the next time you talk to him—perhaps he is failing to follow the customary low-status pattern.

Immediacy or directness is another good source of information about feelings. We use more distant forms of communication when the act of communicating is undesirable or uncomfortable. For example, some people would rather transmit discontent with an employee's work through a third party than do it themselves, and some find it easier to communicate negative feelings in writing than by telephone or face to face.

Distance can show a negative attitude toward the message itself, as well as toward the act of delivering it. Certain forms of speech are more distant than others, and they show fewer positive feelings for the subject referred to. A speaker might say "Those people need help," which is more distant than "These people need help," which is in turn even more distant than "These people need our help." Or he might say "Sam and I have been having dinner," which has less immediacy than "Sam and I are having dinner."

Facial expression, touching, gestures, self-manipulation (such as scratching), changes in body position, and head movements—all these express a person's positive and negative attitudes, both at the moment and in general, and many reflect status relationships as well. Movements of the limbs and head, for example, not only indicate one's attitude toward a specific set of circumstances but relate to how dominant, and how anxious, one generally tends to be in social situations. Gross changes in body position, such as shifting in the chair, may show negative feelings toward the person one is talking to. They may also be cues: "It's your turn to talk, " or "I'm about to get out of here, so finish what you're saying."

Posture is used to indicate both liking and status. The more a person leans toward his addressee, the more positively he feels about him. Relaxation of posture is a good indicator of both attitude and status, and one that we have been able to measure quite precisely. Three categories have been established for relaxation in a seated position: least relaxation is indicated by muscular tension in the hands and rigidity of posture; moderate relaxation is indicated by a forward lean of about 20 degrees and a sideways lean of less than 10 degrees, a curved back, and, for women, an open arm position; and extreme relaxation is indicated by a reclining angle greater than 20 degrees and a sideways lean greater than 10 degrees.

Our findings suggest that a speaker relaxes either very little or a great deal when he dislikes the person he is talking to, and to a moderate degree when he likes his companion. It seems that extreme tension occurs with threatening addressees, and extreme relaxation with nonthreatening, disliked addressees. In particular, men tend to become tense when talking to other men whom they dislike; on the other hand, women talking to men *or* women and men talking to women show dislike through extreme relaxation. As for status, people relax most with a low-status addressee; second-most with a peer, and least with someone of higher status than their own. Body orientation also shows status: in both sexes, it is least direct toward women with low status and most direct toward disliked men of high status. In part, body orientation seems to be determined by whether one regards one's partner as threatening.

The more you like a person, the more time you are likely to spend looking into his eyes as you talk to him. Standing close to your partner and facing him directly (which makes eye contact easier) also indicate positive feelings. And you are likely to stand or sit closer to your peers than you do to addressees whose status is either lower or higher than yours.

What I have said so far has been based on research studies performed, for the most part, with college students from the middle and upper-middle classes. One interesting question about communication, however, concerns young children from lower socioeconomic levels. Are these children, as some have suggested, more responsive to implicit channels of communication than middle- and upper-class children are?

Morton Wiener and his colleagues at Clark University had a group of middle- and lower-class children play learning games in which the reward for learning was praise. The child's responsiveness to the verbal and vocal parts of the praise-reward was measured by how much he learned. Praise came in two forms: the objective words "right" and "correct," and the more affective or evaluative words, "good" and "fine." All four words were spoken sometimes in a positive tone of voice and sometimes neutrally.

Positive intonation proved to have a dramatic effect on the learning rate of the lower-class group.

They learned much faster when the vocal part of the message was positive than when it was neutral. Positive intonation affected the middle-class group as well, but not nearly as much.

If children of lower socioeconomic groups are more responsive to facial expression, posture and touch as well as to vocal communication, that fact could have interesting applications to elementary education. For example, teachers could be explicitly trained to be aware of, and to use, the forms of praise (nonverbal or verbal) that would be likely to have the greatest effect on their particular students.

Another application of experimental data on communication is to the interpretation and treatment of schizophrenia. The literature on schizophrenia has for some time emphasized that parents of schizophrenic children give off contradictory signals simultaneously. Perhaps the parent tells the child in words that he loves him, but his posture conveys a negative attitude. According to the "double-bind" theory of schizophrenia, the child who perceives simultaneous contradictory feelings in his parent does not know how to react: should he respond to the positive part of the message, or to the negative? If he is frequently placed in this paralyzing situation, he may learn to respond with contradictory communications of his own. The boy who sends a birthday card to his mother and signs it "Napoleon" says that he likes his mother and yet denies that he is the one who likes her.

In an attempt to determine whether parents of disturbed children really do emit more inconsistent messages about their feelings than other parents do, my colleagues and I have compared what these parents communicate verbally and vocally with what they show through posture. We interviewed parents of moderately and quite severely disturbed children, in the presence of the child, about the child's problem. The interview was video-recorded without the parents' knowledge, so that we could analyze their behavior later on. Our measurements supplied both the amount of inconsistency between the parents' verbal-vocal and postural communications,

and the total amount of liking that the parents communicated.

According to the double-bind theory, the parents of the more disturbed children should have behaved more inconsistently than the parents of the less disturbed children. This was not confirmed: there was no significant difference between the two groups. However, the *total amount* of positive feeling communicated by parents of the more disturbed children was less than that communicated by the other group.

This suggests that (1) negative communications toward disturbed children occur because the child is a problem and therefore elicits them, or (2) the negative attitude precedes the child's disturbance. It may also be that both factors operate together, in a vicious circle.

If so, one way to break the cycle is for the therapist to create situations in which the parent can have better feelings toward the child. A more positive attitude from the parent may make the child more responsive to his directives, and the spiral may begin to move up instead of down. In our own work with disturbed children, this kind of procedure has been used to good effect.

If one puts one's mind to it, one can think of a great many other applications for the findings I have described, though not all of them concern serious problems. Politicians, for example, are careful to maintain eye contact with the television camera when they speak, but they are not always careful about how they sit when they debate another candidate of, presumably, equal status.

Public relations men might find a use for some of the subtler signals of feeling. So might Don Juans. And so might ordinary people, who could try watching other people's signals and changing their own, for fun at a party or in a spirit of experimentation at home. I trust that does not strike you as a cold, manipulative suggestion, indicating dislike for the human race. I assure you that, if you had more than a transcription of words to judge from (seven per cent of total message), it would not.

REFERENCES

The Communication of Emotional Meaning.
(Joel Davitz, ed.) McGraw-Hill, 1964.

Expression of the Emotions in Man.
(Peter Knapp, ed.) International University Press, 1963.

Language Within Language: Immediacy, A Channel in Verbal Communication.
M. Wiener, Albert Mehrabian, Appleton-Century-Crofts, 1968.

The Silent Language.
Edward Hall. Doubleday, 1959 (in paperback, Fawcett, 1961).

Cultural Differences in Crisis Communication: One Year After Fukushima

by Motoo Unno

The year 2011 was supposed to be a special one for the Tokyo Electric Power Company (TEPCO). It was the sixtieth anniversary of the company's founding and the fortieth of the construction of its Fukushima Daiichi nuclear power plant by a joint venture with General Electric. Yet on March 11, 2011, triple tragedies struck Northern Japan: a magnitude 9.0 earthquake, a huge tsunami, and a meltdown at the Fukushima plant. This article will analyze how cultural values influence crisis communication by examining U.S. and Japanese officials' communication during and after the accident. It will also assess how cross-cultural elements play a role in crisis leadership. Finally, it will invite discussion on a new issue that has emerged since the accident.

POLITENESS, MODESTY, HARMONIOUSNESS

Japanese schools are highly concerned with their students' morality, stressing the principles of right and wrong behavior. In general, Japanese society tends to evaluate a person based on his or her *politeness, modesty,* and *harmoniousness.* These national values serve as guiding principles in the typical Japanese person's life and are highly appreciated by Japanese society. Following last year's triple crisis, the Japanese people amply demonstrated these core values. For example, people who went to grocery stores after the earthquake picked up goods from the floors, formed a line, and waited politely and patiently to pay for their food.

Later that summer, the Japanese people also showed their modesty. TEPCO and other electric companies asked their customers to conserve electricity as much as possible. Some people, particularly elders who had lived through World War II, were very worried about power shortages; their generation was taught to save everything to win the war. Even though the temperature outside was very high, many felt guilty about using air conditioners and suffered from heatstroke.

The value placed on harmoniousness also influenced the nation's handling of the nuclear crisis. Shortly after it began, a former U.S. task force member in Washington, D.C., who monitored the Fukushima plant for 24 hours, asked an officer at the Japanese Nuclear and Industrial Safety Agency whether or not Japan needed unmanned helicopters. Because of the urgency of the situation, the U.S. official just wanted a "yes or no" answer. Instead, his Japanese counterpart expressed the need to first create a committee to discuss the issue, which would then come to a decision. He pointed out

Dr. Motoo Unno is a professor at Meiji University in Tokyo, Japan, and a visiting professor in the School of International Service at American University in Washington, D.C.

the importance of building consensus to maintain harmony in the Agency. This story suggests that national values became more pronounced in crisis situations.

SHAKY *AMAE*

The Japanese psychiatrist Takeo Doi first published his book, *Amae no Kozo,* "The Structure of *Amae,*" more than 40 years ago. In it, Doi introduced the concept of *amae*—which can be translated roughly as "sweet dependency"—to describe the relationship between parents and their infants. Parents take care of and protect their infants, and infants depend on their parents; trust is at the core of the *amae* relationship. As between parents and their babies, *amae* exists in the relationship between the Japanese people and its government. Traditionally, this means the Japanese people are more likely to depend on and believe a big government than are Americans. It is interesting, for example, to compare Japanese people and Tea Party activists. Unlike the Japanese, Tea Partiers are extremely individualistic, distrust their government, and would prefer a smaller one. Yet after the Fukushima disaster occurred, the *amae* relationship between the Japanese people and their government was severely compromised, and people began to doubt the government's decisions.

First, the Japanese government's official evacuation zone only covered a 12-mile radius around the Fukushima plant. On the other hand, the U.S. government's extended 50 miles. The difference confused people and made many question whether 12 miles was enough.

Second, the Japanese people began to suspect their government's assessment of the accident at the plant. Despite the explosions at reactors 1 and 3 in March, the government's assessment rated the Fukushima disaster a level 5 out of 7 on the International Nuclear and Radiological Event Scale. This placed it at the same level as the incident at the Three Mile Island plant in Pennsylvania in 1979, which did not cause a hydrogen explosion. In April, however, the government raised its assessment from

5 to 7, the worst rating on the scale, putting the disaster on par with the 1986 Chernobyl explosion. Yet the Ministry of Economy, Trade and Industry claimed that releases of radioactive material from the Fukushima plant were only about 10 percent of those at Chernobyl. The Japanese rightly questioned why their government would raise its rating if that were the case.

Third, the government set the allowable radiation exposure level for children in Fukushima prefecture at 20 millisieverts per year. This number is 20 times the standard for the rest of Japan. After the decision, one of then-Prime Minister Naoto Kan's advisors suddenly resigned, explaining in tears that he could not accept the government's decision from a humanistic and moral perspective. Many Japanese watched his press conference in shock, feeling they could no longer rely on their government.

Finally, in May, two months after the disaster, TEPCO admitted to multiple meltdowns at reactors 1, 2 and 3. In June, the Japanese Nuclear and Industrial Safety Agency announced that meltdown occurred only five hours after the accident at the Fukushima plant. Many Japanese people accused both the government and TEPCO of having withheld information about meltdown. In fact, most Japanese people never even saw the actual hydrogen explosions in reactors 1 and 3 on TV, while international channels including CNN, Australia ABC, ZDF and F2 provided continuous coverage of the explosions.

Japanese community members in the Fukushima prefecture were not convinced by their government's decisions and became frustrated at its slow responses. Some even decided to take action themselves, getting rid of radioactive material in schools, parks and roads by monitoring and disposing of soil to protect their children.

GLOBAL LEADERSHIP AND OPENNESS

How should a global leader behave in a crisis? Initially, Prime Minister Kan tried to deal with the disaster by involving only the Japanese. After his resignation, he gave an interview to the newspaper *Mainichi* in which he said he had thought that if Japan did not solve the Fukushima problem by itself, other countries would come to fix it. Kan finally recognized that Japan itself could not find the solution to the disaster and should collaborate with the international community. After all, the nuclear disaster was not only a domestic problem, but also an international one—massive amounts of radioactive material were released into the sea and air. A leader should accept the best people, ideas, technology, wisdom and opinions regardless of race or nationality. That is a global leader. The Fukushima disaster revealed the lack of a global mindset among Japan's political leaders, and showed their weak leadership under crisis.

Furthermore, the Fukushima disaster revealed one Japanese business leader's inability to properly handle a crisis situation. Then-CEO of TEPCO, Masataka Shimizu, was hospitalized because of his frustration after the nuclear accident. Shimizu returned at the beginning of April and repeatedly told the Japanese people that there were no immediate health effects from the radiation leaks. He avoided taking responsibility for the handling of the nuclear disaster, blaming it solely on the tsunami and calling it totally unprecedented. Instead, Shimizu should have been more aggressive in navigating the crisis, and should have shown leadership to the international community.

In addition to a lack of global leadership, a culture of collusion between the bureaucracy and industry in Japan made the government ineffective and dysfunctional. The Ministry of Economy, Trade and Industry, which supports and promotes nuclear plants, has worked closely with both the Nuclear and Industrial Safety Agency and TEPCO for a long time. The Agency should be a watchdog, but its officers usually come from the Ministry. Thus, the Agency is not a truly independent regulator. To make matters worse, TEPCO also hired many ex-officers from the ministry.

This constitutes a Japanese version of the "revolving door." The culture of collusion among these three is tight; an "iron triangle" has resulted, with a high sense of cohesiveness, an "in-group" mentality, closed-mindedness and overconfidence about the safety of Japan's nuclear power plants. They have ignored and excluded scholars who have different viewpoints about nuclear safety. Their organizations lack diverse opinions and ideas and are susceptible to groupthink. This issue must be examined, and cozy ties among the three should be reassessed before another major nuclear disaster hits Japan.

DISCRIMINATION AND STEREOTYPES

The nuclear accident exposed one final issue that must not be overlooked—discrimination. In Iwate Prefecture, a distinct "in-group vs. out-group" mentality, complete with stereotypes and prejudices, has arisen among tsunami victims. Victims who lost their houses take pains to differentiate themselves from those who did not, pointing out that they cannot possibly share the same feelings. They tend to overemphasize their differences, behaving negatively and even displaying open hostility toward those whose houses were saved. A similar mentality has taken hold among the people surrounding Fukushima. Approximately 17,000 children left the prefecture due to a high risk of radioactive contamination; residents of their new home prefectures, who mistakenly believe that radioactive material is transmitted between people, often perceive these children as threats. The children suffer the disrespect that often follows such negative stereotypes.

Additionally, victims of the Fukushima disaster face discrimination in the job market. Some business owners argue that hiring them will raise costs, citing higher insurance fees and fears that money spent on training and education might never be paid back. It is the responsibility of Japanese companies to explicitly discourage discrimination against the victims; Japanese society must also openly discuss the discrimination against these people to reduce stereotypes and prejudices before they get even worse.

CONCLUSION

Crisis communication and cultural values are woven together inextricably. The disaster at the Fukushima Daiichi nuclear plant has opened people's eyes to the dangers of the blind trust inherent in *amae* and cast a new light on the relationship between bureaucracy and industry. It has also laid bare the issue of discrimination in Japan. The country urgently needs strong leadership with a global and open mindset to prepare for future crises.

SECTION III
INTERCULTURAL COMPETENCE:
INTERNATIONAL AND DOMESTIC

LIVING AND WORKING IN A MULTICULTURAL WORLD

The interaction of people from different cultures is greater than at any other time in human history. Modern satellite technology allows us to instantaneously transmit messages and information to all of humankind. We are personally interlinked with cell phones, the Internet, and social media such as Facebook and Twitter. Newer telecommunications technology media will certainly be developed as this book goes to press.

Hundreds of thousands of people move across national borders every day to visit, live, work, or study in a new country. And vast demographic changes are taking place within almost all nations as their inhabitants become increasingly more culturally diverse. European nations that were almost exclusively racially and religiously homogeneous for hundreds of years are now populated with millions of new immigrants from North Africa, the Middle East, and Asia.

There are as many Puerto Ricans living in the mainland of the United States as the entire population of Puerto Rico, and there are more Lebanese in Chicago and Michigan than the city of Beirut. The second largest urban Spanish-speaking population in the world resides in Los Angeles and approximately 500,000 Iranian Americans live in southern California. At least 20% of the residents of Beverly Hills are of Iranian descent. As of 2011, non-Hispanic white people are a minority population in New Mexico, Texas, California, Hawaii, and the District of Columbia. The U.S. Census Bureau predicts that around the year 2050, less than half of all Americans will be non-Hispanic white people.[1]

The ethnic, racial and cultural backgrounds of immigrant groups are constantly changing. In the first decade of the 21st century, the largest group of immigrants coming into the U.S. was from Mexico and yet in 2012, immigrants from Asia outnumbered those coming from Latin America. At American universities, in 2012, the largest group came from China followed by India and South Korea.

Just as the university and workplace are becoming more culturally diverse, the ease of international travel and the proliferation of modern information technology enhance the ability to intermingle and work with others across national boundaries. Multicultural teams—both real and virtual—are now commonplace within national borders and throughout the workforce of international companies. As the society becomes more culturally heterogeneous and companies become more global, businesses and government agencies increasingly try to recruit employees who represent their diverse client base.

The research is abundantly clear that homogeneous organizations are less creative than heterogeneous organizations. In cultures where there is a great power distance between a superior and a subordinate, where there is avoidance of ambiguity, there is also a tendency for everyone to conform to the opinions of those in charge or to maintain consensus. When those sitting around a table represent various perspectives and ways of solving problems, there is greater probability that more innovative solutions to problems will be presented and less likelihood that groupthink will take place. The issue is how to manage the diversity to allow for the greatest creativity and yet maintain enough agreement for everyone to implement a common solution. Because diversity leads to greater creativity, all innovative organizations want a diverse workforce.

INTERCULTURAL COMPETENCE

The probability that a young person today will end up working only with people from his or her own cultural background is very small. We assume that every well-educated person is computer literate and can master the use of the Internet and contemporary electronic communications. In a multicultural world, we also expect all well-educated students and employees to be *interculturally literate*. It is much more than simply knowing about other cultures. In a global economy and with a culturally diverse workforce, supervisors, managers, and leaders are required to be adept at *interacting and working with* people from various backgrounds.

Cultural competence means understanding the behaviors, values, beliefs and worldviews of people from another culture. For some this is primarily a matter of gathering information about the behavior of others—their customs, language, history, religious beliefs, and so on. The focus is on the tip of the cultural iceberg or *external culture*. This knowledge is valuable because it decreases uncertainty when we enter another culture and we have the confidence that we won't make a major cultural *faux pas*. Another broader and more complex level of cultural competence involves understanding what motivates behavior. To understand why people behave as they do, we must focus on hidden culture at the base of the cultural iceberg or at the level of *internal culture*.

To be truly culturally competent, we must have knowledge about the entire vertical iceberg of culture including both external and internal components. This model helps us to better understand the vital importance of hidden or internal culture and the dynamic interrelationship between the various layers of a culture—how values and beliefs shape behavior, how a change in behavior can also change beliefs, how some beliefs are very unconscious while others are conscious, and how people can hold contradictory beliefs. It also allows us to contrast and compare one "iceberg" or culture with another. How do people in Japan greet each other compared to Americans? Why do Japanese bow and Americans shake hands? But cultural competence does not really consider what happens when Americans and Japanese come together.

Cross-cultural communication involves the exploration of how these cultural similarities and differences impact the ways in which people communicate within these various cultures whereas *intercultural communication* focuses on the actual interaction of people from various cultures at the interpersonal, national, and international level. Although these two terms are often used interchangeably, there are subtle and important differences in their meanings.

Intercultural competence requires a combination of cultural competence and cross-cultural communication. It is based upon an understanding of the process of interaction between people from different cultures. While cultural competence focuses on individual cultural icebergs, and cross-cultural communication contrasts and compares these icebergs, intercultural competence involves the use of a horizontal model with which we can predict what will happen when people of different cultures interact—when icebergs collide. Much more is necessary than simply gathering specific information or knowledge about individual cultures or regions of the world. Here the emphasis is also on understanding the process and dynamics of cross-cultural communication, adaptation, and conflict as well as the development of strategies to overcome barriers to effective interaction between people of different backgrounds.

Intercultural competence gives us the expertise to interpret and analyze the interactions of people from different cultures on various levels—the interpersonal, social, political, or economic. We ought to be able to anticipate where conflicts and misunderstandings are likely to occur. In addition, intercultural competence entails an ability to actually interact or communicate effectively with people from various cultural backgrounds. It is more than just knowledge. It is an *applied skill* that cannot be simply acquired didactically by reading books, watching movies, or listening to lectures. The ability to analyze an intercultural encounter and to effectively communicate across cultures also requires experiential or participatory learning with the help of an experienced trainer or coach.

In an effort to more efficiently provide intercultural training to larger numbers of people, hundreds of government and private organizations have developed long-distance learning programs using the Internet, social media, DVDs, and so on. Younger people should be very comfortable using these tools because they use them in their everyday lives. These educational programs are especially helpful for providing area studies or culture-specific cultural competence. However, if they are used without experiential training, they may not be as effective if the intent or purpose is to improve intercultural competency skills.

The acquisition of any applied skill requires hands-on experience. Imagine learning to play soccer by watching a DVD. The narration and images may provide very valuable information and, if well done, could be very engaging and highlight the basics of soccer. It might even provoke us to want to know more about the sport. Nevertheless, if we really want to actually play soccer, we must kick the ball and it is helpful to have a coach who can make real time suggestions as to how we can improve our skills.

It is certainly true that we can appreciate soccer and become great fans without actually handling a ball. We may even understand how to score a goal if we know the speed of the ball, the trajectory, spin, and so on. This theoretical knowledge must be fused together with experiential learning if we want to be effective soccer players.

This is the reason that most intercultural competency training and educational programs include experiential components such as cross-cultural simulations and games. On the other hand, without the didactic knowledge, these exercises can come across as meaningless or even childish. There must be a combination of knowledge and application: real-time learning, modern distance learning and electronic media, and the expertise of an experienced intercultural educator or trainer are necessary to achieve real intercultural competency.

INTERCULTURAL EDUCATION, TRAINING, AND RESEARCH: AN HISTORICAL OVERVIEW

There is a vast body of intercultural research that informs much of the intercultural training provided for diplomats, students, and international business executives working outside their home countries. Experts developed this body of scholarship for very applied and pragmatic purposes: to enhance the effectiveness of sojourners working overseas or with diverse cultural groups within their own societies. It also grew as a result of the changing nature of U.S. foreign policy, the increased involvement of Americans in international negotiation and collaboration, and the demands of a rapidly changing world.

Just as each intercultural relations scholar has his or her own list of seminal thinkers in the field, most can also identify benchmark programs and organizations that contributed to the current study and practice of intercultural communication. Taken together, there are surely hundreds of such programs in many different countries and no one's list could be complete. As a systematic field of study and practice, intercultural relations probably first began in the United States for very practical purposes and the accumulation of research followed the practice of cross-cultural and intercultural training.

International education and the exchange of students and scholars certainly were the earliest concerns of intercultural relations. Most would probably begin their list of benchmark programs with the years 1911 and 1914 when the foreign division of the International Committee of the Young Men's Christian Association (YMCA) and then the National Board of the Young Women's Christian Association (YWCA) organized the Committee on Friendly Relations among Foreign Students to study the problem foreign students face in the U.S.[2]

The American Field Service (AFS) began in 1914 shortly after the outbreak of World War I when young Americans living in Paris volunteered as ambulance drivers at the American Hospital of Paris. AFS participated in every major French battle and carried more than 500,000 wounded during World War I. By the end of the war, 2,500 men had served in the American Field Service with the French Armies. Today AFS has various intercultural programs involved in the exchange of international students and has offices in more than 50 countries.

In 1932 the Experiment in International Living was established in Battleboro, Vermont to foster and support the exchange of high school and college students from around the world. The goal of this program was to bring about better understanding between nations and promote peace. Students lived with host families and attended high schools and universities. Over the years, the program has expanded to include language training and intercultural relations education. It also offers graduate-level degrees and sponsors a wide variety of international visitor, exchange, and development programs. It is now known as World Learning and celebrated its 80th anniversary in 2012. Dozens of other international exchange programs developed since 1932 including Youth for Understanding (YFU) in 1951, which originally was designed to facilitate the exchange of teenagers between the U.S. and Germany but now extends itself around the globe.

At the university level, the exchange of scholars and students across national borders probably goes back to the earliest universities established in Europe during the Holy Roman Empire. These scholars routinely crossed borders and even the academic regalia worn in graduation ceremonies today date back to those years.

In recent history, the Rhodes Scholars program was established in London in 1903 for distinguished scholars from around the world to study at Oxford University. In 1946 the Fulbright Program was created by Congress and grew throughout the 1950s, and in 1947 the Council of Student Travel which is now the Council on International Educational Exchange (CIEE) was founded in New York. Thousands of students and scholars from around the world came to the United States and thousands of Americans traveled around the globe to study, teach, or conduct research. The United States Information Agency (USIA) was established by President Eisenhower in 1953 to provide cultural and educational outreach through American embassies around the world. This was the first organized governmental effort to engage citizens in what today would be termed "public diplomacy."

At the end of World War II, a key component of American foreign policy involved restoring the economic and political stability of countries that were devastated by the war. At the same time, the United States sought to strengthen emerging democracies around the globe as part of the Cold War. The field of international communications grew as it became clear that modern communications technology was a vital aspect of modern international relations.[3]

In the late 1950s, international business began to expand and in 1958, the Business Council for International Understanding (BCIU) institute was established in the School of International Service at American University in Washington to train business executives and their families for relocating overseas.[4] This was also a program supported by President Eisenhower and executives from a consortium of Fortune 500 companies. In 2008, BCIU was renamed the Intercultural Management Institute (IMI) because it expanded its education, training, and research to include diplomatic training for many different countries, multicultural management and diversity training, and various research and training programs around the world. It also began publishing the *Intercultural Management Quarterly* (IMQ).

The Society for International Development was also founded in 1958 to bring together the thousands of civilian and government experts who were involved in political and economic development projects in poor countries. The academic fields of international development and international communications studies were mixed together during the 1950s and 1960s and many of the scholars were experts in both fields. These include Lucian Pye, Wilbur Schramm, Daniel Lerner, and Harold Lasswell.

The 1960s was the "Golden Decade" for the field of intercultural relations. Intercultural training for diplomats, Peace Corps volunteers, soldiers, and business executives and managers became commonplace. Throughout the 1960s, students increasingly traveled across international borders to study and the Peace Corps provided an opportunity for tens of thousands of Americans to assist in development projects around the globe. Training volunteers to serve overseas provided a great deal of research on what techniques were most effective and how people adapt to foreign environments. In 1961 Congress passed the Foreign Assistance Act which led to the creation of the U.S. Agency for International Development (USAID).

The United States was involved in the Vietnam War throughout the 1960s—a war that took place in an area of the world that few Americans understood. The military had to develop new ways of training American soldiers to better work with civilian and military allies in Southeast Asia. At the same time, the U.S. Army was producing detailed cultural, political, economic, diplomatic, and military analysis of most countries with their U.S. *Army Area Handbooks*. These were routinely updated every few years by dozens of scholars.

The Foreign Service Institute (FSI) was established created in 1950 by the U.S. Department of State to provide area studies and language training for American diplomats. During the 1960s, FSI led the way in developing new research on cross-cultural communication and adaptation and more effective ways to train diplomats for working overseas. Many of the seminal scholars in intercultural relations worked at FSI including Edward Hall, Robert Kohls, Edmund S. Glenn, and Glenn Fisher. And many of these scholars and trainers, along with those involved with the Peace Corps, military, international business, and academia, were active in building the field of intercultural relations.

During the 1960s at American University and the University of Pittsburgh courses were first available at the university level in various areas of intercultural relations. These included cross-cultural communication, intercultural communication, and international communication. Throughout the 1970s, intercultural relations scholarship grew and became an academic and professional field of study in universities, various branches of the government, and for-profit and nonprofit organizations involved in overseas work.

In the 1960s, the Peace Corps began to systematically train volunteers for relocating and living overseas. The Center for Research and Education (ERC), one of the major contractors, sponsored a get-together in Estes Park, Colorado for trainers and educators involved in cross-cultural training. Attendees at this 1968 meeting included many of the founders of the field of intercultural relations such as Harry Triandis, Edward Stewart, Stephen Rhinesmith, Albert Wright, and Byant Wedge. This was perhaps the first major conference of intercultural or cross-cultural specialists and led to the formation of a society which they labeled the Society for International Training and Research (SITAR).[5]

In the 1970s this nascent society for intercultural specialists grew to include trainers and scholars such as David Hoopes, Melvin Schnapper, and Michael Tucker. A working conference was held in 1971 during which it was decided that the organization would be completely interdisciplinary and the focus would be more practical than academic.

Many educators were involved in the new organization and there the word "education" was inserted in the emerging organization's name. The newly labeled Society for Intercultural Education, Training and Research (SIETAR) was formerly founded in 1974, a year before the end of the Vietnam War. It is the oldest professional association for interculturalists. The founders of SIETAR were scholars, educators, trainers and practitioners who came from various academic disciplines and professional backgrounds. The organization continues to promote education in the field through the scholarship of its members and the formal acquisition, analysis, and interpretation of intercultural knowledge. This knowledge was completely interdisciplinary and was drawn from the fields of international relations, anthropology, linguistics, psychology, sociology, and so on. The *International Journal for Intercultural Relations* (IJIR), the first professional journal in the field, was founded by SIETAR to bring together this varied scholarship in the field.

SIETAR was also established to promote intercultural *training* which is much more experiential, practical, and applied but also is based upon solid scholarship. It focuses more on skills than abstract knowledge. Many practicing interculturalists would say that intercultural competence is primarily learned through hands-on experience. An example of this kind of training would be a pre-departure workshop which prepares sojourners before they leave overseas by giving them cross-cultural communication, analytic, and interpretive skills through various exercises and simulations.

Although SIETAR is interdisciplinary and includes experts from various professions, at its founding meeting outside Washington, DC, there was tension between so-called scholars and practitioners. Many scholars argued that practitioners often had only anecdotal accounts from which they generalized about all cultures, they did not have enough empirical research or social scientific evidence to support their practices, and they lacked comprehensive theories to explain the behavior of people in different cultures. Many practitioners were returned Peace Corps volunteers or employees of the USAID and the cultural arm of the Department of State, the United States Information Service (USIS). These practitioners, in turn, claimed that scholars did not have field experience and much of their research was abstract and could not be applied.

This conflict between educators and trainers led to the creation of the International Academy for Intercultural Research (IAIR) in 1997, a professional association whose primary purpose is to provide an opportunity for its Fellows, who are published scholars and researchers, to share their findings. At this time, the Academy became the official publisher of the IJIR.

Today, many interculturalists would argue that research and practice go together and complement each other. Much of intercultural knowledge comes from practitioners who have gathered anecdotal and more empirical information from their experiences interacting with people from other cultures. Trainers have also found that qualitative and quantitative scholarship is invaluable for proving or disproving many of their practices. Scholars and trainers must be brought together if the field of intercultural relations is to survive and grow as an applied academic area.[6]

The relationship between interpersonal communication and international communication is almost symbiotic. Anyone involved in international work must have interpersonal intercultural communication skills. This would include international business executives, co-workers in a domestically diverse workplace, diplomats, and soldiers in foreign countries. Moreover, if the field is going to grow, it must continue to be a vital part of international relations and international communications. It cannot simply be limited to the interpersonal.

Cultural differences impact international negotiations, international development projects, and even war. Understanding how culture shapes our image of our own country and images we hold of other countries will allow us to be more effective in our interactions with those of other countries. It may help us better prevent and settle international conflicts. It is vital to understanding the role our country plays in the overall international system of nations.

PUBLIC DIPLOMACY, EXCHANGE OF SCHOLARS, AND STUDY ABROAD

The Cold War began as World War II ended. The United States was concerned with helping countries recover from the devastation of World War II and also to strengthen these countries against what was perceived to be the worldwide threat of expanding Communism. At the same time, there were newly emerging countries which had freed themselves from colonialism and it became vital to American interests to assist those countries in their economic and political development to resist the pull of communism or fascism and at the same time to expand American commercial interests around the globe.

Truman's Marshall Plan (1947) or European Recovery Program to rebuild countries combined with his Point Four Program (1949) which provided technical assistance to "developing countries," was a bold step away from the traditional return to American isolationism after a war. It wasn't just a matter of rebuilding European countries but also Japan and many Asian countries. The Cold War included a protracted military conflict in Korea in the 1950s and the Vietnam War in the 1960s—new cultural areas of the world for Americans.

These programs were based upon the modernity or cultural comparative development theorists such as David McClelland, Wilbur Schramm, Daniel Lerner, and Seymour Martin Lipset. The goal was to help others to adapt American or Western economic and political practice, beliefs, and values during this transitionary period. At the same time there was push back from such cultural relativists as Margaret Mead and Ruth Benedict who took the position that cultures are unique and cannot be understood from outside.

Patterns of development might be found by comparing cultures yet each culture can only be truly understood within its own context. Cultural relativists believed that this required experiential learning through some kind of immersion within a culture by actually going there.[7] This was a logical extension of John Dewey's ideas of pragmatic "hands on" learning through experience and the many participatory training programs that emerged in the late 1940s such as Kurt Lewin's National Training Laboratories T-groups and the Tavistock Institute of Human Relations with its model of learning through intense interpersonal interaction with others in groups.

Most cultural immersion programs involved young people. Exchange programs such as the Experiment in International Living (EIL) founded in 1932, the American Field Service in 1947, and Youth for Understanding in 1951 were all based on the assumption that these immersion experiences led to greater understanding of other cultures. Various universities were offering "study abroad" experiences for their students and faculty, and dozens of student exchange programs such as the British Rhodes Scholars Program and the Fulbright program gave students and faculty the opportunity to not only broaden their studies but also to learn of other cultures.

The Peace Corps, founded by John Kennedy in 1961, was supposed to provide the expertise and assistance of Americans in "community development" projects, although it was mostly an opportunity for young Americans to learn about other cultures. In the beginning, most volunteers were very young generalists who lacked the skills to really provide much help to villages in Africa, Asia, or Latin America. Intercultural scholar Milton Bennett, a Peace Corps volunteer in Micronesia, notes in his own experience, "'community service' was the euphemism for looking around the village where we were living to find some project that might justify the time and effort it took local people to have us around. . . . The local people indulged us in this pretense, even though they were clear in their preference for development workers with big bulldozers and big budgets."[8]

The real reason for embedding young people in villages according to Kennedy's stated goals, was to help "promote a better understanding of Americans on the part of the people served" and to help "promote a better understanding of other peoples on the part of Americans." Although we often think of "public diplomacy" in terms of positive news reports, exposure of scholars and dignitaries on television or radio, or even movies and videos, when it comes to promoting better understanding, face-to-face interaction is required, and the Peace Corps was certainly one of the earliest efforts by the United States in interpersonal public diplomacy.

RACE RELATIONS, IDENTITY MOVEMENTS, AND DIVERSITY TRAINING

Within nations, and especially the United States, there was an explosion of conflict between peoples of different racial and ethnic backgrounds. The two most significant American domestic intercultural issues during the 1950s and 1960s were race relations and counter-cultural identity movements. It was during this period that schools were integrated, the walls of segregation came down, and people of all races increasingly mixed together in neighborhoods and the workplace. This did not happen easily. Civil rights activists demonstrated, picketed, and faced hostile mobs throughout America, especially in the South. Many were harassed, beaten, and arrested. Some were killed.[9]

This was very much a generational conflict. No adult could really tell a young person, "I know what you're going through." Very much like immigrant children, the youth of the 1960s generation grew up in a very different world than their parents. The Cold War brought with it the existential threat of the atomic bomb. Modern communications and travel opened the door to the rest of the world. Young people knew about civil rights marches in the South and an ongoing war in Vietnam. Furthermore, this wasn't just an American generational clash. In 1968, the French government was nearly toppled by student demonstrators and there were violent clashes in other countries such as Germany, Japan, and Canada.

It is true that every generation is different from previous generations. New technology and world events that occur especially during our adolescent years seem to shape the way we view ourselves and the world around us. As adults, the music of our teenage and young adult years becomes the soundtrack of our lives as we recall those events. Although Sigmund Freud and other analytic psychologists would claim that our formative years, before we reach the age of 9 or 10, are the most important in shaping our personality, the adolescent years are perhaps equally important because it is during these years that we struggle with such existential or identity questions as, "Who am I? What's important to me? How am I similar to or different than others? How do I fit into the society without losing my individual identity?" For young people of color, the question became, "How can I keep my black American identity and still be a part of the dominant white, Anglo-Saxon society or dominant culture? Why can't I be black and American?"

While black or African-American youth were challenging the assumption that one had to give up one's differences to fit into the dominant culture, another counter-cultural identity movement was emerging among white youth as they challenged the assumptions of the dominant culture regarding traditional values. It was much more than simply wearing so-called hippie outfits, smoking marijuana, and listening to "acid" music. Although this behavior annoyed many parents, it was really an identity movement that became counter-cultural. They asked such questions as, "Why can't we abolish war? Why can't we eliminate racism? And what price must I pay to gain a piece of the so-called 'American Pie'?"

In the United States, at the same time as the Vietnam War intensified and thousands of young people died or returned home with broken bodies, these counter-cultural identity movements developed among young people. Many college students—both white and those of color—were active in the Civil Rights Movement and rejected not only the war but also what they referred to as "the system" or government. It was truly a counter-cultural phenomenon.

If we were to assess the significant, long-term results of the civil rights and anti-Vietnam War movements of the 1960s, we would probably place at the top of our list the numerous court decisions barring discrimination, the development of massive opposition to the Vietnam War, and the 18-year-old voting age. While all of these developments are indeed important, by far the most significant long-term consequence of both movements was the growth of popular questioning of cultural assumptions held by Americans for generations.[10]

Today a counter-cultural generational conflict may also be taking place around the world. With modern information technology, and especially social media, young people are instantly interconnected within and between nations. In America today, young people have grown up after the Civil Rights Movement and the Vietnam War concluded. They go to fully integrated schools that are both racially and ethnically diverse. Most schools emphasize the values of tolerance and the advantages of cultural diversity. In 2008, these young people overwhelmingly voted for Barack Obama along with both African-American and Latino or Hispanic adult voters. Many who most opposed Obama were older white voters, especially males, from southern states who saw their way of life slipping away.

This was not simply a matter of electing a president named Barack Hussein Obama, whose father was a Kenyan and at one time a Muslim. Of course, this was especially significant because when Obama was born, his interracial parents were legally forbidden to marry in a number of states in the U.S. Both segregation and racism were rampant. Racism in America did not end, but a new era had begun with the election of a black president. It appears that this generation of young people not only believes that a multicultural society free of racism is possible, they supported the election of a man of mixed parentage who identified himself as an African-American with a white mother.

In the Middle East, the so-called Arab Spring Movements at the end of 2010 and into 2011 were led primarily by young people who used social media to instantly mobilize others against what they perceived as outworn and undemocratic regimes in Egypt, Tunisia, Libya and many other countries. They wanted to escape an oppressive past and move into a freer future.

It is perhaps too early to know the full impact of digital or electronic communication on cross-cultural conflicts on the national or international level. Counter cultural movements of youth in the Middle East were abetted by the social media and even the widespread use of Twitter is found in such relatively closed and conservative countries as Saudi Arabia.[11] However, these media also provoke a reaction from those who fear that they threaten traditional values and they nostalgically long for the stability of the past. Islamic political parties gained strength during the Arab Spring just as the identity movements of America in the 1960s and the 1970s led to a return to a very politically and religiously conservative America. Those in the 18–24 age group voted for President Reagan in the 1980 and 1984 elections in a greater percentage than any other age group.

Rapid technological change in communications not only allows for the dissemination of revolutionary and counter cultural ideas and images, it often produces a backlash especially among those who want to restore what they believe was the grandeur and simplicity of the past when social roles and status were clearly defined. During these periods of chaos and uncertainty, ideology provides stability and thus is very appealing. It clarifies an ambiguous and complex reality by often dividing the world into a "*we*-versus-*they*" dichotomy and identifying a distinct enemy intent upon destroying our way of life.

Ironically, the same communications technology can be used to perpetuate a clear enemy-image and mobilize adherents to a reactionary ideology. A video, film, or cartoon that demeans the Prophet Mohammed can be transmitted instantaneously around the globe to incite protests against those who produced such images which they might never have seen without this technology. Furthermore, according to a U.N. report published in the fall of 2012, Facebook, Twitter, and YouTube are increasingly being used by terrorists to recruit sympathizers, spread propaganda, and plan potential attacks.

UNDERSTANDING AMERICAN CULTURE

Studies in cross-cultural communication are mostly a matter of contrasting and comparing both internal and external cultural aspects of different societies, whereas intercultural communication studies focus on the actual interaction of people from different cultures. To explain the behavior of a people and their public policies we need to consider both cross-cultural and intercultural communication.

In cross-cultural communications, we need to begin with some culture that can be used to contrast with others. A culture that most Americans are familiar with is the dominant culture or national culture of the United States. If we take an historical sociological or isomorphic approach, we consider the evolution of this culture with special emphasis on the role of values that date back to the earliest settlers coming to the U.S. shores. In other words, we are viewing the U.S. as a system that develops just as human beings grow from their childhood formative years, through adolescence and young adulthood, until they become mature adults. This is fairly easy when we consider the United States because the nation is so young and we can easily delineate the various stages of growth beginning with childhood. Nations also go through transformative crises just as humans go through the usual trauma and identity crises of adolescence, middle age and the midlife crisis when we become mature adults. Of course, just as we can progress, we can also regress. Some American men who go through a midlife crisis try to recapture the romance, adventure, and freedom of their younger years instead of accepting the responsibility of being mature adults within a family or society.

The primary cultural values and beliefs of individuals develop during childhood and the same may be true for a nation. The formative years are the most important period of human development during which our basic personalities are formed. This is also when we acquire our values. If we compare the evolution of a nation state to that of a human, we could also say that the "formative" or early years in the history of a nation are those during which basic national cultural values emerge to give the citizens a shared national identity.

Since the late 1950s, social scientists have engaged in an ongoing debate regarding the role of cultural values and beliefs as major determinants of national political and economic development. In his book *The Achieving Society* (1961), social psychologist David McClelland provided "empirical evidence" to support the theories of the famous sociologist and political economist Max Weber, author of *The Protestant Ethic and the Spirit of Capitalism* (1904). Weber believed that certain Protestant values and beliefs, such as individualism, delayed gratification and a focus on the future instead of the past, gave people a work ethic which led to rapid national economic growth and a strong democratic civic culture. According to this argument, the underlying basis for capitalism and a liberal and democratic civil society was

Protestantism. This was the major theme in the social philosopher Adam Smith's 1776 capitalist treatise, *The Wealth of Nations*. Smith was a Scottish Calvinist.

According to Weber and McClelland, certain cultural values and beliefs must first exist before economic growth and a strong civic society can emerge. Calvinism, economic capitalism, and political liberalism could be traced back to underlying atypical European values and beliefs such as an optimistic future-time orientation, individualism, and a distrust of an overly powerful central authority. A more contemporary version of this position is advocated by Harvard professor Lawrence Harrison in his book *Culture Matters*.[12] Harrison believes that unless citizens share these progress-prone values there can be no national economic growth or the development of a democratic society. Among the values that distinguish progressive cultures from static cultures are: focus on the future, frugality, education, merit-based advancement, dispersed authority and secularism.[13] In other words, Euro-American or Protestant values lead to economic and democratic growth. This is a very controversial position but one that is widely shared by many in the Euro-American world.

If we refer to our iceberg analogy of culture, those who advocate this cultural explanation for progress would argue that you must change the internal culture if you want to change external culture. If the society is to grow economically and democratically, people must have values and beliefs that encourage and sustain that growth.

On the other hand, sociologist Seymour Martin Lipset[14] claimed that there are certain underlying prerequisites for democracy such as a well-educated populace, a large middle class, and a communications and transportation grid that links citizens within a nation. The economic and education infrastructure or underpinnings that support democratic and economic growth must come first. This fits with Abraham Maslow's famous hierarchy of needs theory.[15] Basic physiological or survival "needs" such as food, water, and security must be first met before a populace can consider such higher order needs as social life, having a democratic society, or reaching one's "full potential" as a human being.

Maslow's hierarchy may apply to Western societies but it is not at all clear that it fits some societies outside the West. For example, in some Middle Eastern cultures, restoring "honor" or avoiding "loss of face" may be much more important than physiological or security needs. People might fight to their deaths to reestablish their family's or even their nation's honor or to regain respect. Maslow would view these as "esteem" needs which are near the top of his rankings of needs.

Lipset's and Maslow's views are almost the inverse of those of Weber, McClelland, and Harrison. They would claim that we can change external culture or the tip of the iceberg and this in turn will change internal culture or the base of the iceberg. In political terms, Lipset is more socialistic, arguing that you must change the means of production and this will change the values of the people.

It is reasonable to conclude that underlying cultural values and various social and physical environmental factors combine in the early years of a nation to produce a national cultural identity. As individuals, when we go through adolescence and enter adulthood, we leave the security of our families and interact with others and this adds another layer to our identities. As a nation interacts with other nations in the international system, it also begins to gain a national image of itself and others. This national identity is also a result of crises such as political upheaval, war, or economic collapse which causes people to come together.

INDIVIDUAL ACHIEVEMENT AND ACTION

The great waves of immigrants coming to America in the 17th and 18th century when the new country was in its formative period were mostly Protestant Christians who were fleeing religious and political persecution in Europe.[16] From the European viewpoint, they were radicals and extremists whose values and beliefs were quite atypical of Europeans at that time. These so-called Protestant or Calvinistic beliefs included an optimism that the future would get better and they would somehow start anew. In addition, everyone would have an equal chance of success in the new land if they worked hard. Originally, this was a religious belief that God would reward the individual who is a good person and works hard with economic success. Today this belief is referred to as "the American Dream." It is the idea that children will have a better way of life than their parents.

These waves of immigrants arrived in a land where there appeared to be unlimited natural resources and vast opportunities to economically excel. At that time in Europe, if you were born poor you died poor. The combination of so-called fundamentalist Protestant beliefs and values that were not typically European, the abundance of resources and opportunities, and the experiences these immigrants had in the so-called New World, created a new set of cultural values that today are viewed as typical of mainstream Americans. They underpin the dominant culture in the United States.

The belief in individual achievement and class mobility was rewarded and reinforced and Americans began to identify themselves in terms of *what they do* rather than their family background or heritage. If you encounter an American at a party, he or she will often greet you with: "Hello, my name is Jim Smith. I'm a lawyer. What do you do?"

People from other cultures might more commonly identify themselves in terms of *who they are*. A Mexican from a village might identify himself to another Mexican by saying, "Hello, I'm Manual Rivera the son of Jose Rivera from Cholula." The primary source of his identity is who he is rather than what he does. He identifies himself in terms of his family or heritage—his father and his birthplace. The past is perhaps as important as the future.

A DISTRUST OF AN OVERLY POWERFUL CENTRAL GOVERNMENT

We can easily see how basic cultural values shape the behavior of people within a society. American individualism and the emphasis on the future explain such expressions as "don't just stand there, do something" and the perception Americans have that they live in a "can do country." The slogan for the Nike shoe company is, "Just Do It!" No politician in the United States would ever say, "Vote for me and I'll keep it the way it is." All politicians claim they will "do something" if elected and the future will get better.

These values also help to explain government and public policies and contemporary political conflict. How much should government help people? If it helps people too much does it take away their individual responsibility to help themselves? But, on the other hand, shouldn't government provide an opportunity for everyone to have adequate health care, to get a proper education and to live in dignity in old age? This is an ongoing political issue in America. What is the role of government in everyday life and especially in determining economic policies?

To understand this continual debate regarding the role of government in the economy and people's lives, we would need to consider such values as individualism, the burden placed upon each citizen to succeed or fail, the belief that hard work will pay off with a better future, and so on. Everyone should also have equal opportunities to succeed and all persons are treated the same in the legal system regardless of family, race, religion, or social and financial status. This explains the tendency to avoid using titles. Even the President is referred to as Mr. or Mrs. President and American ambassadors are not called "Your Excellency." The proper address for an American ambassador is Mr. or Madam Ambassador.

In contrast with the practices in many parts of Europe, the first settlers to come to the shores of America did not want a king, queen, or pope. They were very suspicious and skeptical of an overly powerful central authority. In the words of the great American philosopher Henry David Thoreau (1817–1862), they believed that "less government is better government" and government ought to avoid interfering in the individual citizen's life. Of course, they knew that their "New World" needed a national government to handle foreign affairs and international commerce; matters that impacted everyday life however were deemed largely the responsibility of municipal, county, or state government.

America has never had a national education policy or a national police force. Issues of welfare, law enforcement and adjudication, care for the infirm, and so on, are matters of local or state jurisdiction. And the smallest department of the federal government is the Department of Education because educational policies are determined primarily by the local community or state. Most of the money to pay for public schools comes from local taxes, not federal taxes. America's civil liberties or individual rights such as freedom of speech, freedom of the press, freedom of religion, and so on are found in the Constitution and the Bill of Rights. These documents protect individual freedoms and defend against an overly powerful national government.

Public policies are a balance of authority between the legislative, judicial, and executive branches of the federal government and also a balance of authority between the local and the federal government. Regardless of which branch of government is involved, there is also the balance between the common good and public order and the freedom of the individual. At times this balance is weighted on the side of the common or collective good and there have also been times when it has moved more toward the side of individual rights.

During times of war or economic national crises, the authority of the central government has always increased for the common good and overall national security. After the tragic attacks of 9/11 Americans had to balance their traditional values of individual freedom with the need for national security. Perhaps reluctantly, they gave the federal government more authority to protect the nation. Thus, the federal government became much more powerful with the creation of the third largest department, Homeland Security, and the enactment of laws that gave the federal government more authority to monitor electronic communication.[17] Since 9/11 there has been concern that individual liberties are being sacrificed to provide greater security against terrorism.

Fortunately this debate is ongoing and legal cases are making their way through the judicial system, challenging the authority of the federal government to limit individual civil rights. Gradually there is a restoration of the healthy suspicion that Americans have always had of an overly powerful national government.

In more collectivist countries, one could argue that Americans have "too much" freedom. For Americans, this would seem to be a strange idea. How could someone have too much freedom? It is like suggesting that someone could have too much love. How is this possible? Carried to an extreme, American individualism could be perceived as selfishness in countries where everyone is interconnected by family and community. American freedom of speech and the press allows Americans to publish pornography. But is this good for the overall society? Perhaps citizens ought to sacrifice their individual freedom for the sake of the common good and the community. A young, unmarried individual has enormous freedom to behave in impulsive and self-satisfying ways. However, when one is married, one should give up this freedom for the sake of the family.

In turn, many Americans would claim that if you carry the responsibilities to the community and the family too far, you will sacrifice individual freedom for social stability, and you end up with a caste-like social system where a young man or woman might never achieve his or her full individual potential. How many men must remain in a village to assume family responsibilities and thereby never become great scholars or renowned physicians because they could not leave in order to pursue higher education? How many women living in societies where women's roles are only that of wife or mother, or where women are deemed subordinate to men, will never become great national business or political leaders?

National cultural values can be both positive and negative in any society, especially when carried to their logical extremes. Furthermore, each society decides the proper balance between such values as freedom and order, individualism and collectivism, change and harmony, and so on.

THE MELTING POT MYTH

Until the 1960s, most Americans seemed to believe that all cultures brought to American shores were simply thrown into a gigantic pot.[18] The mixture was stirred and heated until all the cultures melted together. There is some truth to this idea. The United States is certainly a culturally diverse society; however, there is also a dominant culture. Immigrants became a part of this culture by giving up many of their differences so that they could fit into the mainstream of society. In large part, this metaphor of the so-called "melting pot" was a myth. All cultures did not melt proportionately into the "pot." You would need to search carefully to find contributions from Asian, Middle Eastern, Latin American, southern European, or even the American Indian cultures within dominant institutions such as the government, business, media, or universities. The pot actually melted little more than chop suey, shish kebab, tacos, pizza, and corn.

Returning to the analogy of culture to an iceberg, the internal—and largest—part of the American iceberg hidden beneath the water level of awareness was northern European while almost all of the contributions of non-northern European cultures were external and at the tip of our iceberg such as food, music, art and perhaps dress. These overt contributions were easily recognized, and some were very important when it comes to art, music, and literature. Nevertheless, they were fairly insignificant in terms of the totality of American society and its primary institutions during the early days of American history.

A much more accurate metaphor for the early immigrant experience was a cultural "cookie cutter" with a white, male, Protestant, Anglo-Saxon shape or mold. If an immigrant could fit that shape, then he or she easily moved into the dominant culture. But one had to give up those cultural characteristics that would not fit the dominant culture's cookie cutter mold. A Polish Catholic immigrant could become a Protestant, refuse to allow his children to speak Polish outside their home, and change his name from Stripinski to Stevens to fit the mold and thereby become part of the mainstream American society where he could have an equal opportunity to climb the economic ladder. However, Black Americans, most Hispanics, and American Indians couldn't change their skin color or their hair texture. They couldn't fit the cookie cutter mold no matter how hard they tried. Although they may have shared many of the same basic values and beliefs of white immigrants, they were identifiably different and thus were excluded. Racism was also part of American history.

Of course, the United States has changed. Most Americans today would no longer describe the country as a melting pot or a cookie-cutter. In fact, it has become common to describe the United States as a salad bowl with various vegetables. Perhaps a more aesthetic metaphor might be a mosaic or a tapestry which suggests it is acceptable to keep one's differences and still be part of the overall society. What makes a mosaic or a tapestry beautiful are the distinct and contrasting colors and textures. If you remove one piece from the mosaic or one thread from the tapestry, you destroy it.

Differences in gender, race, national origin, ethnicity, religion, and sexual orientation are acceptable and need not be abandoned to have an equal opportunity to achieve your life goals. In fact, these differences contribute to creativity within the society. And when people can bring their full identities into the workplace, they look forward to going to work and they tend to be more productive.

Few Americans would want to eliminate diversity by forcing people to melt into pots or fit into cookie cutters. This is not true pluralism but rather some form of cloning in which we must share the values, beliefs, and behaviors of the dominant culture. Why would any modern manager or teacher want everyone in the room to think like those in the mainstream culture? Most would want diverse views brought into discussions to effectively solve problems. Clones are not creative problem-solvers.

Hyphenated Americans—people with dual or multiple identities—reflect the belief that one can keep one's ethnic, national, religious, or racial identity and still be an American. Mexican-Americans, Irish-Americans, African-Americans or Black Americans, Arab-Americans, Muslim Americans, and American Indians all reflect the practice of being a true American but also maintaining co-identities.

This reflects a multicultural or pluralistic model and the assumption is that not only are differences welcomed, but they are even valued and viewed as strengths. Very few people would want to go back to the past when minorities had to give up their differences to fit into the mainstream culture. Diversity is an opportunity to be embraced, not an obstacle to be overcome. In fact, most Americans believe that diversity enhances creative problem solving and increases productivity.

The issue facing America today is not how to get rid of differences, but rather how to manage a society with so many differences. The United States has always been very diverse, but it is no longer simply a matter of bringing together different European nationalities and ethnic groups. Today, diversity means all races and ethnic groups, various nationalities, men and women, the disabled, employees of all ages, and people of various sexual orientations. Because of the reality of the demographic changes, increasing global interdependence, and the obvious benefits of diversity, Americans will adapt and develop the necessary skills to communicate and work with people of all cultural backgrounds.

About one percent of all Americans are able to say "we were here first." The United States really is a nation of immigrants. Only American Indians can claim they were the original inhabitants of the land. All others came later. In such a diverse society with great importance placed upon the value of individualism, it is surprising that the society can maintain its coherence. Ironically, what ought to destroy the civic culture actually holds it together. The psychological need for a sense of belonging together or collectivism is even greater than in many other countries because of the emphasis on individualism and diversity. This explains the strong civic culture and the urge Americans have to come together during a crisis or a patriotic celebration. The only thing everyone has in common is that they are indeed "Americans." Once the crisis passes or the celebration ends, we get on with our individual lives.

Of course, what also holds the country together is a set of common values and beliefs, the English language and common experiences. Although there are regional and ethnic differences, and most Americans do not fall neatly under one list of values but rather somewhere along a continuum between a so-called "to do" and "to be" culture, most agree that some variation of the "to do" values is basic to the national culture. There is no national or official language in the United States and it is unnecessary because over 98% of Americans speak English.[19] It is the lingua franca of the country and is the language of all public schools. Lastly, the shared immigrant experience and national crises such as wars and natural disasters, give everyone a national image or identity of the United States. The ways in which military, economic, political, and other national crises have been resolved also gives the government both legitimacy and effectiveness in minds of the people.

DIVERSITY IN THE WORKPLACE

There has always been a dominant culture in the United States with a distinct configuration of values, beliefs, behavioral norms, and ways of perceiving and thinking about the world.[20] The workplace has also reflected this mainstream culture. Those who have advanced to management and supervisory positions usually have been white males who could most easily fit into the dominant cultural cookie cutter mold. In fact, there is a "glass ceiling" above which minorities and women could not rise. Well over 95% of all top executives in the private and public sectors are white males. This glass ceiling has hardly cracked in the past twenty years. These managers were highly individualistic, action-oriented competitors who focused on "getting the job done" and planning for the near future. They were "do-ers," not "be-ers."

Successful managers were those who could "get the job done" through aggressive action. These are characteristics attributed to macho American men. In the 1970s and 1980s many companies offered "assertiveness training" courses for women with the assumption that if they could be trained to act like men they could become perfectly competent workers, managers, and supervisors. They might even one day become executives.

Of course, this approach is not pluralism—this is "cookie cutterism." Worse still, it's cloning. In some organizations, Asians comprise a sizable proportion of gifted workers yet few make it to managerial positions. Often the excuse is that "they are too passive." Again, the basic argument is that Asians are unlike white mainstream American males. They aren't assertive enough. But perhaps the more collectivistic ability to develop collaboration and teamwork may be more essential in the contemporary workforce than individual assertiveness. This more "passive" skill and approach may actually increase both productivity and creativity in the multicultural workplace.

Managing diversity means allowing the whole person to come to work each day. With the cookie cutter approach to management, those cultural aspects which do not fit the mold must be left outside the workplace. This diminishes self-esteem for many since only what one *does* is important. A part of their identity must be left at the door. Their gender, race, ethnicity, or sexual orientation is denied, devalued, or marginalized.

When a manager says, "I don't care if my assistant is white, black, Christian, or Muslim, as long as she does the job," the implication is that one's race or religion is irrelevant. Yet, these attributes are essential to one's identity as a whole person. The price you pay to work in the office is to deny your racial or religious identity. Anyone treated in this fragmented, fractionalized, schizoid manner cannot feel like a part of the team, and this sense of alienation will surely impact productivity.

Identity groups based upon gender, race, or ethnicity may help to provide psychological and social support and decrease the sense of alienation non-mainstream employees feel as they transition into the dominant work culture. These groups provide empathetic listeners with whom they may share their experiences. Co-national communities have helped immigrants from Asia or the Middle East to more effectively move into the mainstream American culture. Of course, when these groups become havens where individuals avoid the stress of dealing with the dominant culture they are clearly counterproductive.

Supervisors can encourage employees to bring into discussions ways of viewing problems that may reflect their cultural differences. For example, how might women view a situation in contrast with most men? Would Asian employees prefer to work in teams rather than on individual tasks? And there may be opportunities for employees to bring their ethnicity into the workplace by having a diversity week or special events linked to ethnic heritage.

Management practices might also take into account the needs of different cultural groups, which in turn might increase productivity and decrease turnover. Is flextime preferred by those with small children who may need to drop their children off at school before they come to work? Should Chicano employees be allowed to use their paid leave for their daughter's 15th birthday celebration?[21] Should a location be provided for Muslim employees to pray during working hours?

Almost all American companies, government offices, and universities provide some kind of "diversity training" to help managers, supervisors, and employees to not only understand the benefit of diversity, but also to maximize the productivity and creativity within diverse organizations. As the society becomes more multicultural, the clients these organizations serve require intercultural knowledge and communication skills.

The benefits and problems of diversity depend upon the nature of the group and the nature of the problem the group is facing. If everyone within an organization has the same basic values and beliefs, thinks alike and has a similar way of viewing situations, it is unlikely that the group will be very creative. When faced with a problem, the members may even suffer from groupthink. A group composed of people from various ethnic or cultural backgrounds, different age groups, and with a mixture of males and females, is likely to come up with a longer list of very creative solutions *if they are given enough time and the group is managed to enable them to overcome the difficulties of diversity.*[22] This creativity is especially important when we are brainstorming and trying to come up with new ways of solving problems. The manager must have good intercultural skills and the ability to elicit comments from everyone even when they disagree with the majority of opinion or that of the leadership.

The downside of diversity is that the group may have difficulty coming to any agreements, and there may even be conflict as to how to choose a leader, when to get down to business and stop the chit-chat, or even how to develop an agenda. Each person may have very different assumptions as to the characteristics of a leader, how business ought to be conducted, and the role of team members. These unconscious actions chains are often the source of conflict and confusion when they are brought into the workplace.

When it comes to implementing solutions, the homogeneous group may be more efficient because everyone thinks alike and will move in the same direction. The heterogeneous group might be like a herd of wild horses all going off in different directions. Japan, a very homogeneous society, was able to manufacture transistorized color televisions five years before Americans could get one off the assembly line. The Japanese are very good at implementation. However, Americans actually invented the transistor. Diversity in the United States has contributed to many of its innovative and creative approaches to problem solving.

The word "manage" in the phrase "managing diversity" suggests manipulation or control when in fact the objective is almost the opposite when it comes to multicultural organizations. To ensure both productivity and creativity, a manager must bring about some sort of "cultural synergy"[23] or "diunitality"[24] where the whole is greater than the sum of its parts, and the process of decision-making elicits the widest array of opinions and ideas. We don't want to control or suppress these differences. We want to *facilitate the process* the group takes in making decisions so that we can minimize the inefficiencies and frustrations that diversity causes and in turn enhance or maximize the productivity and creativity of the group.

As has been said, throughout the world in the private and public sectors, the clientele most organizations serve is becoming much more diverse. The ability to relate effectively to people of various backgrounds is necessary for anyone dealing with the public—entrepreneurs, business executives, university professors, and civil servants.[25] Knowledge of intercultural relations and the ability to communicate across cultures will be essential to almost everyone entering the workforce in the next century.

ETHICS AND INTERCULTURAL RELATIONS TRAINING

In any profession one must consider questions of ethics. This is especially true for professionals in the field of intercultural relations. Trainers often engage participants in intense interpersonal interactions and deal with issues that are both highly emotional and controversial. Intercultural training can lead to great interpersonal awareness and growth, deeper understanding of one's own culture and other cultures, and greater intercultural competence. But it can also lead to psychological stress and perpetuate bigotry.

Is the field of intercultural relations harming or helping societies and individuals? Are trainers imparting knowledge or skills in an ethical manner? Does the unethical behavior of an interculturalist damage the profession of intercultural training and education? Who determines what is ethical? These are questions raised by lawyers, doctors, and educators. They also ought to be raised by those engaging in intercultural relations training.

There are overarching ethical issues in any profession. In intercultural relations, these broader questions are usually raised amongst educators and researchers who are concerned with the use of knowledge and the purposes of research. For example, some would argue that the field of intercultural relations provides knowledge that could be used to manipulate others such as powerful Western companies controlling emerging markets. A more recent version of this assertion is that soldiers use this knowledge to advance their military ends. But this could be said of any applied area of study. Chemistry and biology could provide the knowledge and skill for someone to produce a poison or a vaccine. It is true that intercultural relations research could be used unfairly to advance business or to wage war. It could also be used to help nations grow and prosper, to bring about better understanding between people of various backgrounds, and to promote peace and prevent war.[26]

Those who have been struggling with issues of race and discrimination could say that it is unethical to water down these emotional issues by making them simply a matter of cross-cultural differences and misunderstandings. It is true that one of the advantages of dealing with some of these issues in cultural terms is that you may avoid emotionally charged words such as "racist," "sexist," "anti-Semite," "homophobe," or "Islamophobe." A cultural approach is also less judgmental. A culture isn't good or bad; it's just different. On the other hand, this is an ethical problem in that intercultural relations could be twisted into some form of "cultural relativism" where all cultures are "okay." This, in turn, waters down the genuine reality and pain of racism, sexism, anti-Semitism, homophobia, and Islamophobia.

Trying to understand behavior in the context of culture is not the same as finding all behavior relative to the culture and thus acceptable. We are simply saying that all behavior is relative to the culture; not that all behavior is acceptable. For example, there are practices that are becoming universally viewed as unethical regardless of culture because they violate human rights. It would certainly be unethical for scholars and practitioners in the field of intercultural relations to imply that it is acceptable for people in any culture to engage in genocide, the subjugation of women, child abuse, and so on.

In most professions, when it comes to the practice of ethical behavior we are concerned with the behavior of individual practitioners. In intercultural relations, this means trainers. One of the difficulties of ensuring the ethical practice of intercultural trainers is that there is no overall licensing or accrediting body which determines who is qualified to do training or what the ethical standards ought to be for the profession. There are also no formal sanctions that the profession can use to enforce ethical behavior.[27] This is becoming an increasingly more important issue for trainers and the professional.[28]

Over the years, various organizations involved in intercultural relations have developed lists of ethical behavior. A consensus is gradually developing as to what is ethical or unethical practice within the profession. We can easily come up with a few broad ethical guidelines that most professionals would agree ought to be followed to avoid harming clients, organizations, and the profession of intercultural relations.

1. Bad training may be worse than no training. Many organizations require their employees to go through various types of intercultural relations workshops or seminars such as relocation, management, negotiation, race-relations, diversity, or multicultural management training. Cultural and intercultural awareness training and cross-cultural preparation programs for relocating to another culture and returning home are intended to decrease cross-cultural adaptation difficulties and increase effective interaction with those from other cultures. The evidence shows that these training programs usually benefit sojourners and probably save tens of millions of dollars spent on premature returnees, failed business deals or negotiations, and burnt out or browned out employees.

Intercultural management or negotiation training considers how culture might impact a multicultural workplace. In these programs the issue is how a supervisor or manager can increase productivity and creativity by better understanding culture. Negotiation between people of different cultures might eliminate or decrease costly adjudication of disputes and it is clear that mediation requires consideration of cultural differences. Understanding how culture affects crisis negotiation, such as hostage situations, could save lives.

The primary goal of race relations or diversity training is to increase cross-cultural under-standing and to create an environment where differences can be used to increase productivity and creativity; it is also to prevent situations where discrimination might occur. Some of this training is a result of incidents where those who were different were victims of bigotry, intoler-ance, bullying, or hatred, and the assumption is that this training will prevent such incidents.

In all of these training programs, an inexperienced trainer may perpetuate stereotypes instead of useful cultural generalizations. With limited command of relevant data or research to support sweeping generalizations, and without much depth and breadth of theoretical knowl-edge, the trainer used an abundance of personal stories based on his or her limited experience. These anecdotes can be very colorful and entertaining but when taken out of cultural context, they are often caricatures of local people. The examples given may not be relevant to other cultures. Of course all good trainers ought to be engaging and must have good presentation skills but any interculturalist who knowingly perpetuates negative or positive stereotypes simply for entertainment value is engaging in unethical behavior.

Theory and models can be a bit boring, discussing aspects of internal culture such as thought patterns and values can be tedious, and it is easier to just give sojourners a list of dos-and-don'ts. But when the sojourner actually gets into a cross-cultural conflict and assumes everyone fits the stereotypes given by the trainer and then mentally thumbs through the dos-and-don'ts list and discovers the answer to the situation is not there, total panic can set in. The bad training then becomes counterproductive and harmful to everyone.

There are various instruments which are used to assess the flexibility or cultural knowledge of sojourners. These tools are often easy to use and can be "read" by someone certified by the owner of the instrument. They are very useful self-assessment tools which help individuals to consider their knowledge of cultures and characteristics they may have which impede or advance intercultural interaction and adaptation. Many provide a measurement of cultural or intercultural competency.

They may be very useful heuristic devices in pre-departure training programs or even diversity training. Most are very well-researched and have content validity, but they were never intended to be used to select people for overseas study or assignments and they cannot tell an individual if he or she will be effective overseas. Although they may be very reliable they have little or no predictive validity.

The misuse of these instruments could lead to someone failing to get the overseas assignment that might be vital to his or her career. Even worse, individuals may believe they somehow "failed" to prove that they could handle the rigor of living overseas rather than that they simply needed more intercultural knowledge or training to enhance their effectiveness.

2. Don't always give people what they want. It might not be what they need. For those who make a living in cross-cultural training, it is often tempting to create a training design the client wants while knowing full well that it is either ineffective or inappropriate for the needs of the client. Competition in this profession has grown enormously in the past decade and clients can shop around for the training they want.

Some organizations believe they can save money and time if they just cut the training down to a few hours instead of a few days. They want the cultural cookbook without the theory and in-depth understanding. There are trainers who will give them this type of quickie training knowing full well that it is inadequate and participants acquire few, if any, cross-cultural communication, adaptation, or analytical skills. Given the time constraints, the trainer may inadvertently impart misleading, incomplete, and stereotypical information and yet what the trainees really need is intercultural understanding and cross-cultural communication skills.

It is difficult to tell clients that they really are not saving money by providing superficial training especially if the trainer or consultant is offered a good fee and knows the client can find such training elsewhere. Nevertheless we are ethically obligated to inform the client that we believe this type of program is ultimately ineffective and could even be harmful. At the very least, it probably will not increase effectiveness overseas.

Employers are increasingly inclined to send employees on short-term assignments to avoid the costs of relocating. Certainly there is no need to send the entire family overseas for a one- or two-month assignment or to sign a year-long lease for housing. Many universities also offer short term study abroad programs over a summer or winter break instead of an entire semester. The assumption is often made that there needs to be little, if any, pre-departure training for such sojourns.

Exactly the opposite is true. If an employee has only a few months to complete an assignment, the necessity of adjusting quickly is increased. The organization does not have the luxury of allowing the sojourner to have a few weeks to "settle in." Indeed, he or she must "hit the ground running" and move onto the task at hand as quickly as possible. Students may never truly "adjust" to an overseas culture if they realize they are there for only a few weeks. Their cross-cultural preparation is even more vital than those who may have a full semester to get acquainted with local nationals. They do not have a few months to fully understand the internal culture in which they are studying.

Often a client would like to sugarcoat the difficulties of adapting to a new culture or coping with those who are different. This is likely to be the case when it comes to pre-departure workshops. "Everything will be fine. You'll have no difficulties. They're just like us." This feel-good training raises false expectations and perpetuates the assumption of similarities, thereby preventing trainees from anticipating the differences.

The opposite extreme is when a client wants to confront highly sensitive and controversial cross-cultural issues by using a training program that features highly charged emotional confrontations with an intense emotional involvement of trainees. These programs are often some form of diversity training where the goal is to force everyone to "deal with" their real or hidden feelings by bringing them out in the open before others. However, this can sometimes amount to fomenting paranoia and guilt.

This type of cross-cultural training can become so intense that it bears a resemblance to therapeutic encounter groups but in these workshops and seminars people emotionally reveal their intimate or "real" feelings regarding racism, homophobia, anti-Semitism, and/or sexism. However, few trainers are actually certified therapists. One of the problems of many of the race-relations training programs in the 1970s and 1980s in the U.S. was that trainers often forced participants to openly acknowledge their racist perceptions and thoughts. At times, these sessions resembled interrogations where nearly everyone had to emotionally admit that they were racists. And, as in Franz Kafka's *The Trial,* some felt compelled to confess their racism to avoid being accused of not being sincere or withholding information and thereby betraying the group effort.

Cross-cultural training is not therapy and no one should be forced to show emotions or reveal aspects of their personality that are personal and may lead to humiliation and emotional pain. If people want therapy, they should go to a therapist. Nevertheless, it is the responsibility of the professional intercultural trainer to understand the damage that can happen when painful emotions are revealed and the trainer must have the competence to cope with those situations to prevent psychological harm.

Going through severe culture shock changes how we look at ourselves and the world. People claim that they were changed forever because of the intense experience of adapting to another culture. We often produce this kind of transformative growth in an interactive training session. Professional interculturalists must know their audience and realize not only the benefits, but also the hazards they may go through. If it is clear that they are unaware or unprepared for the emotional stress, it would be unethical to put them in this situation.

3. *Primum non nocere.* First, do no harm. Cross-cultural training often includes participatory activities such as games, simulations, or role-plays. Whenever a person engages in these experiential activities, there is always some risk involved that they might embarrass themselves by revealing hidden feelings or attitudes. Although this participatory learning can lead to great personal insight, breakthroughs in self-awareness, a deeper understanding of cultural differences, and the dynamics of cross-cultural interaction and conflict, when carried too far by inexperienced trainers, they can cause psychological harm.

When we move from didactic education to experiential training, participants can certainly learn cross-cultural communication and analytical skills. The hands-on active learning also involves some emotional risk. Some repressed feelings may come to the surface, a participant might feel foolish or childish, and if someone has recently been through some traumatic experience, this activity might be too much to handle. A trainer using participatory exercises needs to protect those who are emotionally fragile from an overly threatening experience and at the same time inform those who are seeking a higher level of cross-cultural and personal awareness that there are personal risks. To put someone in the hands of a trainer who has little experience in handling highly emotionally charged situations is unethical.

Some cross-cultural trainers seek to emphasize the emotional and experiential without due consideration of the ethical responsibility they have to avoid psychological casualties. For example, they may ask a volunteer to engage in a stressful role play simulation that humiliates the trainee. The trainer can then get a few laughs or display his or her superior cross-cultural knowledge and skills. But the trainee feels manipulated and insulted. The chances are that no one else will volunteer to engage in another simulation. Or an inexperienced and unethical trainer may end a simulation before the trainee has psychologically "de-roled." As everyone else goes to lunch, the trainee is still in the role assumed during the game or simulation and is left feeling hurt and disoriented.

Psychologist William Blanchard warned humanistic psychologists who were conducting sensitivity or encounter groups in the late 1960s and the 1970s that any group activity involves risks. In his *Psychology Today* article entitled "Ecstasy without Agony is Baloney,"[29] he pointed out that various human relations trainers were advertising their services to help people to reach their full human potential through expanded awareness. Participants believed that they would experience some kind of "peak experience" or introspective ecstasy by participating in this sensitivity-training, or T-group, which amounted to a form of group psychotherapy. After revealing their souls to others, shedding tears, and revealing intimate details about themselves, many gained enormously heightened self-awareness and freed themselves from their emotional prisons. However, these encounter groups also sometimes resulted in casualties.

Under the guise of "being honest," some participants would sadistically criticize others causing enormous emotional damage. In some cases, those who were psychologically vulnerable and fragile were pushed over the edge and experienced emotional breakdowns. Some participants returned home to their communities and began running similar workshops in community centers, schools, and churches. But they were not trained therapists and had little experience handling the raw and painful emotions that these sessions could arouse.

A T-group is very artificial with its own rules regarding being open and honest. Lessons learned are not always transferable to the workplace. Participants would find great freedom from the fear of being rejected when they found they could tell others how they really felt about them and they were still accepted as members of the group. After an intensive weekend sensitivity workshop, some would return to work on Monday and tell their boss or co-workers what they "really felt" about them. The result was often embarrassment, alienation, and even loss of jobs.

Some "facilitators" believed that the intellect is the enemy of human self-awareness. Participants were seldom asked what they thought but instead were urged to share their feelings with others. Full awareness and enlightenment usually joins together feelings with thoughts, the intellectual with the emotional, and the mind and the body.

This was a part of the counter-cultural movement of the time and was perhaps an over-reaction to the low-context, abstractive society of the U.S. where feelings were often denied or repressed to enhance reason and education was mostly a matter of didactic learning methods. But rather than creating a more holistic person, this created a reverse version of R.D. Laing's "schizoid man." The rational and intellectual were denied to extol the passions and the emotions.[30] At the same time, in the field of cross-cultural training some "facilitators" were so convinced that experiential learning was the only way to develop intercultural awareness and competence that they were also equally anti-intellectual.

4. Professional behavior is ethical behavior. Almost anyone can create a slick webpage claiming to be a great trainer without any hard evidence of education, expertise, or even experience in the field of intercultural relations. Although someone has traveled to Mexico for two weeks, this does not make the person an expert on Mexican culture. And simply attending a workshop does not mean that a person is certified to be a trainer. Clients are increasingly using great due diligence to determine if the trainer or consultant they hire really has the knowledge and experience to provide intercultural services they need. Often they will not only carefully examine the resume or vita of the perspective trainer. They will also consult others who have used the trainer to be sure that the person is not advertising abilities that are unproven.

Unsophisticated trainers sometimes draw from their own narrow experiences overseas and assume they can rely on experiential exercises and anecdotal materials alone. In their briefings, they are able to give some tips on how to deal with people in a specific area of the world. However, as has been mentioned, without an understanding of theoretical approaches to intercultural relations, they end up over-generalizing from their limited experiences and often fail to give trainees a broader understanding of the dynamics of intercultural relations. They often do not have a strong command of relevant scholarship to support their generalizations.

On the other hand, it is difficult to describe the process of adapting to another culture if one has never gone through culture shock. Books may give you a great deal of background on cross-cultural mediation and negotiation, but if you have never actually negotiated or mediated conflicts with those who are culturally different, you would deservedly lack credibility with clients. It is thus tempting to exaggerate your experience.

Ethical trainers do not mislead clients by making false claims of expertise or experience. They do not use the ideas of others and claim them as their own nor do they denigrate the services of others to promote themselves. And they do not foster a dependency relationship, in which people expect specific behavioral advice that they feel they must follow if they are to succeed overseas. Rather, the ultimate goal of training is for each person to assume the responsibility of developing his or her own strategies for effective cross-cultural communication. If you are a good counselor or trainer, the client eventually will no longer need you.

5. Practice what you preach. A good trainer should model the analytical and interpretive skills participants may adopt as they develop their own techniques. The same is true for ethical behavior. If we expect participants to respect different cultures, to treat others with the dignity all humans deserve, and to foster universal human rights, then trainers ought to display this kind of behavior as they conduct training sessions.

If we are conducting diversity training, then our training team ought to be as diverse as possible without compromising competence. If we are dealing with issues of race, gender, or sexual orientation, we should include people of color, both men and women, and gay or lesbian co-workers. Culture specific or area studies training should include presenters from that culture or, at the very least, those who have had culture-specific experience in that region.

If we expect trainees to avoid stereotyping, then the trainer must do the same. Oversimplified categorization of cultures and people may be necessary as we begin to develop theoretical constructs. They allow us to contrast and compare cultures, which is basic to the scholarship of intercultural relations. But we also need to be sure that everyone understands that no human or culture fits neatly into any of these categories. They are simply models that usually represent a continuum along which cultures might fall—between Hall's high- and low-context cultures, Tönnies' *Gemeinschaft* rural communities and *Gesellschaft* urban societies, or Hofstede's individualism and collectivism or high- and low-power distance. Just as we construct models to simplify reality we also must show the complexity of cultures and deconstruct those models.

THE FUTURE OF INTERCULTURAL RELATIONS

The future of intercultural relations as a profession and academic field looks very good indeed. As nations and communities become more culturally diverse and globalization increases, the need for greater competence in intercultural relations will only increase. Although it is possible that eventually this may lead to some kind of "global village," in the next few decades this is more likely to increase awareness of one's own culture and thereby contribute to the fear many have that their traditional way of life will be threatened by the intrusion of people, messages, and materials from other cultures. In the long term, this diversion may eventually lead to greater conversion as people accept the importance of valuing cultural differences and gradually discover the commonalities and similarities between people in the global community of the future.

Interpersonal and international conflict and misunderstanding may decrease with the growth of intercultural relations and competencies. As we learn to more effectively interact with those who are culturally different, we also learn more about them and their cultures. We will discover new ways of perceiving reality and solving problems. Perhaps more importantly, we will also learn more about ourselves and our own culture.

Certainly the areas of cross-cultural negotiation, management, public diplomacy, and conflict will become even more important to lawyers, diplomats, business executives, doctors, and teachers who will work in a much more culturally diverse world. Their professional success will depend upon strong intercultural knowledge and communication skills.

As in any applied field, many scholars and practitioners agree that experience is indeed necessary for all intercultural experts; one cannot simply read books in the field. It is necessary to actually counsel others under the supervision of other more experienced professionals. There are people claiming to be intercultural or diversity experts with very limited depth and breadth of practical, hands-on experience. Eventually, they will be found out. Until then, they discredit the field.

Yet, experience alone is not enough if the field of intercultural relations is to grow both academically and professionally. Practitioners must be able to provide evidence for the efficacy of their work and relate their training to theoretical and conceptual models developed by researchers. A great deal of valuable research has been conducted in the past few decades, and universities are developing rigorous courses in intercultural, cross-cultural, and international communication.

Intercultural relations, as a profession and field of study, will continue to require both practice and research. One is literally contexted within the other. Much of our research comes from formative and summative evaluations of training programs, various case studies, and longitudinal data gathered from sojourners and immigrants.

Research in intercultural relations may be applied to individuals within a particular culture or to nation-states within the international system. The range of application is enormous and growing daily. Educators, counselors, negotiators, managers, and diplomats can freely extrapolate from intercultural research and experience in each other's work.

Intercultural relations will always rely upon interpersonal communication and analytic skills with a focus on face-to-face interactions at the local or domestic level. Diversity training, cross-cultural counseling or ethnopsychiatry, and coaching can only be done by those with good interpersonal intercultural abilities. Even international business and diplomacy requires interpersonal cross-cultural communication skills. However, if the field is to grow as an applied academic field, it must continue to expand its depth and breadth of inquiry even further to consider international issues and applications.

War, mediation, and conflict resolution, international business, public diplomacy, and worldwide health issues are all global concerns that demand much more than interpersonal intercultural competencies. These are big problems that necessitate a global perspective and thinking that is almost Baroque in terms of its interdisciplinary scope.

Intercultural relations must continue to transcend Euro-American experiences and research. Books and journal articles are increasingly more international. Scholarship and practices from around the world can be found in the *Journal of International Communication* and the *International Journal of Intercultural Relations.* Such organizations as SIETAR, AFS, and World Learning now have programs and branches in dozens of countries outside the U.S. and Europe.

The attacks on the United States on 9/11 and the worldwide economic recession in the beginning of the twenty-first century clearly show how interdependent all countries are today. The domestic is now international and the local and global merge when it comes to economics, politics, the environment, and health care. This is especially true for young people who live in a more intercultural world than any other generation. If this field is to grow, it must become more global.

SECTION III: Readings

The Intercultural Meeting

Gary Althen

A common source of frustration for administrators of foreign student programs is the "international student club," or whatever the local organization of foreign (and sometimes U.S.) students is called. "We sent out a notice about an organizational meeting," an FSA might report, "and a reasonable number of students showed up. But the meeting went on and on, and got nowhere." Or, "We have an international

National Association of Foreign Students Affairs Newsletter, (Nov. 1981): 34, 41, 46, 47.

student club, but it doesn't do much. The meetings are exercises in frustration."

From the viewpoint of the adviser who believes it would be salutary to have an active international student club on a campus, it is usually the club's meetings that are the focus of the greatest discontent. The meetings tend to be long, unproductive and often disputational. Why should this be? A look at people's culturally based ideas about meetings might suggest some answers to that question. Before looking at those ideas, though, it is important to mention other possible explanations for the problems advisers face in fostering the development of international student clubs. These have to do with the adviser's and the students' discrepant assumptions concerning such clubs.

An adviser who decides to call an organizational meeting for an international student club is probably making most, if not all, of the following assumptions:

- It would be constructive to have an international student club, to foster interaction between foreign and U.S. students and/or to provide social activities for foreign students.

- It is possible to have an international student club that is divorced from the political interests and viewpoints of the students.

- Students view the staff of the foreign student office as benevolent, apolitical and capable of organizing situations that benefit most foreign students.

- Students from diverse countries see themselves as having important interests in common. They will be able to agree upon objectives for an organization, and will willingly cooperate with each other in seeking those objectives.

All of these assumptions are open to question. But even if they were all accurate, and the international student club idea gets to the point where meetings are held, the problems are only beginning. People with differing cultural backgrounds bring such diverse assumptions and behaviors to

meetings that their gatherings are often rife with misunderstandings.

In *Beyond Culture,* anthropologist Edward Hall offers the notion of "action chains." An action chain is a series of behaviors which people who grow up in a particular culture are taught (usually implicitly) to view as appropriate for a particular situation. People follow their action chains without having to think about what they are doing, or why they are doing it. The situation evokes the behavior.

One situation that evokes certain behaviors is a "meeting." What does the concept of meeting mean to people from different cultures? What behavior is appropriate at a meeting?

To Americans, it seems quite sensible to summon interested people to an organizational meeting for an international student club. It is assumed that interested people will appear at the appointed time and place. There will be a leader, probably elected in some way, or appointed for a temporary period by someone in authority. The leader will moderate the discussion, recognizing people who wish to speak, summarizing people's comments and keeping speakers on the track.

There will be discussion at the meeting. Everyone who wants to talk will have an opportunity to do so. People attending the meeting will seek a common ground (that is, they will compromise), establishing a foundation for subsequent joint action. Agreement will be ratified, probably by means of a vote. If the group is large or the issue complicated, Robert's Rules of Order will be employed to manage the discussion. Otherwise, informality will prevail.

Not everyone has this same action chain concerning meetings. There can be diverse assumptions about several aspects of meetings: why they are held; the means of selecting a leader; the leaders' role; and the role and behavior of those attending the meeting. Some of the various assumptions that people from different cultures make about these topics are discussed here.

Why Meetings Are Held

Americans typically hold meetings in order to share information or to make decisions. More often than Americans, people from elsewhere might hold meetings in order to ratify or formalize decisions that are made elsewhere, or to give people an opportunity to air their views in the absence of an intention to make any decisions. Of course, people who go to a meeting with the assumption that some decisions are to be made will be frustrated if there are others who are at the meeting merely to express their opinions.

Means of Selecting a Leader

Most people make the assumption that a meeting needs a leader, although there are people who do not assume that. Among those who do suppose there should be a leader, there are diverse views about the means by which the leaders should be designated. In some cultures, a person's age and/or social standing would automatically make him or her the leader in the eyes of all those present. In other cultures a formal nomination and election procedure would be employed. Other possibilities for selecting a leader include having someone volunteer to be the leader, waiting for a leader to emerge from the proceedings or having the leader appointed by someone in authority.

At a meeting of students from different countries, especially one held for the purpose of organizing an international student club, these diverse ideas about leadership selection are likely to cause problems. A leader chosen by some people's method may not have legitimacy in the eyes of others. In fact, the others might not even realize that some of the people at the meeting believe a leader has been recognized.

The Leader's Role

Americans typically suppose that a leader who is acting appropriately in the context of a meeting will serve as a moderator—keeping order, calling on speakers, preventing anyone from dominating the proceedings, assuring that everyone who wishes to speak has the opportunity to do so, keeping people's remarks on the subject and helping the group reach decisions. It is often expected that the leader will be neutral with respect to topics of disagreement that arise during the meeting.

In many other societies, the leader is expected to exercise much more authority, and even to make important decisions on behalf of the group. In the eyes of people from such societies, the "democratic" style of group leadership that Americans tend to idealize is likely to seem unsatisfactory. It may give members so much opportunity to present diverse comments that the result seems like chaos. Or the leader's presumably greater wisdom may be seen as getting too little attention.

On the other hand, in societies where it is the norm to reach decisions by consensus, a U.S.-style chairman might seem too obtrusive.

Role and Behavior of Meeting Participants

It is probably the culturally influenced differences in group members' action chains for meetings that account for most of the difficulty at international student club meetings. First, there is the question of the role of people who attend meetings. In general, when a person comes to a meeting, he or she makes some assessment of his or her status in the group, because one's status within the group does much to determine how one is supposed to behave during the meeting. Determining one's status in a meeting of students from diverse countries is essentially impossible because there is no agreed-upon criterion or set of criteria for deciding where group members stand vis-á-vis each other. Possible criteria include age, sex, period of time as a student at the school, previous leadership position within the group, being from a rich or large country, being from the country or region with the largest number of foreign students at the particular school, being an officer in a nationality organization at the school, having a charismatic personality or having some special affiliation with the foreign student office.

With all of these (and no doubt other) criteria being used by different people at the meeting to determine how they fit in, and with these determinations being made in the absence of conscious thought, discrepant conclusions are inevitable. Some people at the meeting will think that others are out of line.

Second, there is not likely to be a shared assumption about the overall function of the meeting. For Americans, as has been said, the unspoken assumption is that people at a meeting will "give and take" to reach compromise agreements that serve as the basis for action. For many others, though, compromise is not seen as natural or desirable. And there is less of an orientation to action. The purpose of the meeting may be to win all arguments, or at least block the progress of those with opposing views or to display one's rhetorical talent. Engaging in what Americans are likely to consider "mere talk" may be, according to some people's assumptions, the basic function of the meeting. People who behave according to these assumptions often seem dogmatic, insensitive and obstructionist in the eyes of those who want to find compromises and make decisions.

A third source of disharmony in meetings of foreign students is differences in what Dean Barnlund calls "communicative style." (See *Public and Private Self in Japan and the United States*.) Only two aspects of communicative style will be discussed here. They are the general manner of interaction in a discussion, and the means by which people reach conclusions in their arguments.

Americans generally prefer a style of interaction that Barnlund labels "repartee." According to that style, no one speaks for very long. A speaker gets to the point quickly, then gives way to another speaker. A person who talks for too long gets a disapproving reaction.

A style prevalent in many other societies encourages much longer presentations from each speaker. Students from those societies are likely to view American-style presentations as superficial, and perhaps lacking in rhetorical skill.

Meetings of foreign students nearly always include some students who, from the viewpoint of others who are present, talk too long. Impatience results.

People from different cultures are likely to manifest different ways of presenting their arguments. In a meeting of foreign students, one student's logic is likely to be another's nonsense. Some speakers will cite what they consider objective evidence to support their views. Others will invoke authorities of some kind. Others will make appeals to sentiment or emotion. Still others will endorse philosophical principles they wish the group to follow.

With two or more different ways of arguing in use at once, failures to understand are inevitable. Impatience and frustration result.

Given all the difficulties confronting an intercultural meeting, it is little wonder that international student clubs are so often dominated by one energetic leader *and* his or her compatriots. They have the same action chain for meetings.

There are things advisers can do to make intercultural meetings more productive. What they can produce at a minimum is learning about cultural differences. If the students attending the meeting can be helped to understand the ideas that appear in this article, they will have learned a good deal about themselves, about other cultures, about the influence of culture on their own and other people's behavior and about the difficulties that beset intercultural encounters. They might be able to work together to surmount those difficulties.

Advisers could use various approaches to helping students learn from the cultural differences that are manifest in intercultural meetings. They could attend the international student club's meetings and offer observations about culturally based behavior they see taking place there. They could have students from a particular country describe to others their action chain for meetings. Better yet, students from particular countries could conduct brief mock meetings that other students could observe, and then there could be discussion of what has been seen.

Such an exercise could sharpen students' ability to observe and analyze manifestations of cultural differences.

Another possibility is to have students from a particular country describe and show how they customarily conduct meetings, and then have all students use that action chain for the meeting. Different groups' action chains could be used at different meetings.

Still another possibility is to have the club's leader explain his or her conception of the leader's role, and his or her expectations of group members. Making these conceptions and expectations explicit can reduce the amount of frustration and anger that result from behavior that others do not understand.

A relatively common approach to the problem of unsatisfactory international student clubs is to try to teach the students the idealized American action chain for meetings. This often takes the name of "leadership training" or "organizational behavior consulting." Such training is best accompanied by explicit acknowledgment of the U.S. cultural assumptions and values on which it is based.

Given all the cultural differences that are manifest in meetings of international student clubs, it is to be expected that such meetings will be unsatisfying for many of the people who attend them. If they are used as occasions for learning about cultural differences, they can be made more productive. If those in attendance are able to find ways to overcome the difficulties that their diverse cultural backgrounds cause them, some very important lessons will have been learned.

The Chinese Practice of Guanxi

M. Cordell Hart

Guanxi is translated into English as "relationship" or "connections" and the Chinese social practice of *guanxi* is similar in some ways to what we of the west have in mind when we say that we "have a friend at city hall." But the Chinese practice is so pervasive, so fundamental to their social ways, that it should be considered a distinguishing feature of the Chinese mindset. Indeed, it is exactly the feature that underlies the primary difference between a western person's sense of self and that of the Chinese.

The Western culture is imbued with the idea of independence and individualism, of the knight errant, of the Lone Ranger, of Polonius's admonition in Shakespeare's "Hamlet:" "This above all: to thine own self be true." In the West, we form associations, to be sure, but we do so for benefits that are specific, definable, not obtainable by the individual self and considered to be of temporary duration—though they may last a lifetime. For

Chinese, constant and close identification with a variety of groups beyond the family is the norm. Conversely, a Chinese person will consider acting independently with about the same frequency and trepidation that a western person will join a fraternal organization or enter into a binding contract.

AN ANCIENT PRACTICE

Guanxi is an ancient consideration among Chinese. The earliest record of the concept comes from the Chou Dynasty, when it was used around 500 B.C. in describing the ethics of certain "natural relationships:" between prince and minister, between father and son, between husband and wife, between brothers, and between friends. However, the *guanxi* addressed in this paper, has rather to do with other, more distant relationships. Even so, note the dates in the several references to *guanxi* (pertinent to this paper) found in just one history text.

a. Commenting on the use of the examination system for the recruitment of officials during the Sui-Tang era (589–907 A.D.): the examination system "did not dominate the process whereby officials were recruited. Recruitment was a social rather than a legal process because in the social scene personal connections ('guanxi') formed the fluid matrix in which candidates for office were advanced and family status was maintained. For example, the Northern Wei established its own list of major clans and made them equivalent to the Chinese list, so that families of nomad background could now move into Chinese life at the top level."[1]

b. Commenting on the great Ming emperor, Hongwu, who reigned 1368–1398: "Finding his prime minister plotting against him in 1380, he had him beheaded, along with everyone in his family or remotely connected, which totaled over the years about 40,000 persons. ('guanxi' networks have their dangers!) Continued beheading of officials and several later purges may have swelled this total to 100,000 victims."[2]

c. Commenting on certain tax surcharges during the reign of Yongzheng, the Manchu emperor who reigned 1722–1736: "Provinces used the proceeds partly to pay higher official salaries to 'nourish honesty.' But the networks of personal connections or 'guanxi' that helped each individual's career were far too deeply inlaid in the structure of government to be eliminated. Today *they* are still a problem."[3]

d. Commenting on the emergence of new leaders of the Chinese Communist Party in the 1950's: "Unlike the democratic egalitarianism and plural opportunities of the American experience, these new power-holders were adept in the creation of 'guanxi' (networks or connections), sycophantic ingratiation with superiors, and authoritarian exploitation of inferiors in the traditional Chinese style."[4]

e. Commenting on production team leaders in modern China: "The team leader was thus the ultimate broker in the grain procurement system, mediating between his team-member inferiors and his brigade-cadre superiors. This function was as old as China's history, a main focus of rural politics and interpersonal village relations. Quite naturally the team leader was involved in patron-client relations with others both above and below his status level. Here was where his connections ('guanxi') came into play. Here was where corruption occurred and often flourished."[5]

It is all too typical, in the western culture, to offer value judgments on the phenomenon of *guanxi* as did the eminent and late sinologist John King Fairbank in paragraphs a.–e. above. And a western generalization regarding organizations holds that inefficiency is present in the degree to which the actual lines of communication and authority do not conform to the prescribed lines, as can be seen in "plumbing" charts. But the Chinese mindset is different, and China's fortunes over the ages seem to have fluctuated for reasons quite apart from the continued practice of *guanxi*. An understanding of *guanxi*, and the other social forms brought to the west by Chinese, may benefit us all.

Surely referring, at least in part, to the criminal manifestations of *guanxi*, one writer notes that "In Chinatown, there is a social order so ruthless that its very existence seems to be against the law. . . but most of the people who live here accept it as normal."[6] But we should recognize, above all, that the purpose of *guanxi* is not friendship, but the exchange of goods and services. Americans, in particular, make this mistake and are shocked to find that their supposed Chinese "friend" has no real affection for them; or the American, because of cultural training not to rely on others, will make few demands of his or her Chinese "friend," thus leading to an impossible situation where the Chinese person is denied an opportunity to fulfill his perceived obligations to the American.

WE AND THEY

Simply put, Asians focus on the group, and Westerners focus on the individual. Asians accept as normal a need to develop and maintain many circles of "useful contacts." They know that each person must deal with a great number of other people in order to make ends meet and get things done. Westerners generally only supplement their more important trust in institutions and law by developing certain personal contacts and favors.

It may not be that Asians cultivate and maintain more relationships with other people than do Westerners, but they surely are more acutely aware of and act on benefits and obligations that attend each relationship. Most importantly, they play personal relationships in a complex and extended way seldom understood, much less practiced, by Westerners. The important usefulness of extension in *guanxi* means that it is possible to receive benefits from other members of a *guanxi* net who may not be immediately known to the person needing the favor, information, etc. A complimentary consideration is that the individual players may not be aware of the total scheme. One authority puts it this way: "Basically, the art of social action in China is a kind of choreography in which 'guanxi' debts are tapped for particular contributions, and the parts woven into an effective whole of which individual contributors may be quite unaware."[7]

Though the Chinese language has all the necessary terms to discuss *guanxi,* and Chinese use them frequently in conversation, many Chinese are oblivious to their own frequent practice of *guanxi*. In some cases, Chinese have simply been unwilling to discuss their social practices with foreigners. According to one ethnic Chinese author, there is something of a collusive mindset among Chinese, at least in their business networks. "The Chinese don't like to talk about networking. It's like they're a sect," he said. "They don't like to be intellectually analyzed. When you describe it, the mystique value

is lost. They think their practices can be learned and used against them."[8] But many Chinese are truly unaware of what they do so naturally. One Chinese police official responded to this writer's request for examples of *guanxi* by stating that he never practices it—but he offered to check the matter out with certain of his colleagues on the force who were of the same ancestral home as he. He could trust them to be candid, he explained.

It is not enough, however, to be merely acquainted with other persons; one must have the mutually-agreed-to privilege of making demands of others. Each party to the *guanxi* bond is convinced that the other(s) has like agreements with still other persons, in sufficient number and of adequate quality, to make this agreement worthwhile. The effectiveness of an individual's "connections" is measured by the amount of his "face" (*mianzi*). Strong *guanxi* gives much *mianzi*. If *A* has *mianzi* with *B,* he can be certain that *B* will render him services on occasion. This bond ensures reciprocity, so that the greater the circle of those with whom "one has *mianzi,*" the better one can counter adversity.[9]

CONTINUING NEEDS

Because the Chinese depend almost exclusively on *guanxi* connections, they must forever seek to maintain and expand their networks of connections. It is most unusual for Chinese people to seek help from an official unknown to them or to expect reliable information from anyone to whom they have not been properly introduced. Since little of consequence is likely to be transacted through anyone outside the network, an individual's *guanxi* relationships will ideally be established in anticipation of foreseeable needs.[10]

One Chinese businessman explained,

An individual wishing to open a Chinese restaurant knows, as a result of existing 'guanxi,' many contractors who are able to do remodeling work, for example. But the restaurant owner must be careful to choose the right contractor. He must choose one who has done remodeling and construction work in the restaurant business. He could choose a contractor who had recently done work for a fruit stand or a butcher shop, and one of the persons he employs only works for him part-time and has a full-time job as a waiter. The waiter, in turn, has a sister-in-law whose father owns an accounting firm [that] has as a client a restaurant supply store. Another contractor that the restaurant owner may know has done work on some restaurants, but concentrates mostly on residential homes. This contractor may have a son who is a doctor, who is married to a computer salesperson. This contractor may also have a good friend in a car dealership. Obviously, the first contractor would be the better choice, because the restaurant owner can then use his 'guanxi' with the contractor to obtain the other services and goods that he will need in the restaurant business. The selection of people with different 'guanxi' for different purposes is key to obtaining goods and services. Also, a fair amount of planning is required to forecast future needs of the project.[11]

Obviously, however, some Chinese will achieve such financial prosperity and wealth of connections that they can afford to relax their efforts to establish new *guanxi*. In those cases, as with the rich and powerful anywhere, they will deign to accept party invitations and other overtures primarily out of a sense of obligation, almost a sense of "noblesse oblige." In the case of a ranking, but not highly paid, Chinese official who needed to guarantee sufficient funds for his son to attend college in the United States, however, the official needed to find a contact who did have the money and who could serve as his son's guarantor. The fact that guarantor actually signed as the father made the transaction fraudulent according to U.S. law and somewhat dangerous to the official for having to rely on someone in a foreign country. The Chinese attitude towards all this could be expressed as "But what are friends for, if not to get things done which cannot be done entirely legally?" Obviously, the guarantor in the

United States acted not out of friendship, but out of his obligation to a *guanxi* partner.

SENIOR-SUBORDINATE RELATIONSHIPS

The main purpose of senior-subordinate relations in *guanxi* is to facilitate the original agreement of terms. Once the senior partner has determined the types of goods and services to be exchanged, the ranking system assumes a passive function. Each partner has equal obligations to honor the agreement. Neither partner may make demands of a type not originally specified. The subordinate partner need not respond to unreasonable requests by the senior.[12]

One investigation of smuggling clearly showed a senior-subordinate relationship: one Mr. Lee "orchestrated an international smuggling ring that included catcher vessels, transport vessels, and holding facilities. Unfortunately, Mr. Lee had no system in place to secretly move large sums of money in foreign commerce. To meet his needs . . . Mr. Lee enlisted the assistance of one Mr. Hsu, a graduate from the same school which Mr. Lee had attended. Mr. Lee was older than Mr. Hsu, and had graduated from the school several years before Mr. Hsu . . . Mr. Hsu was an established businessman, and gave up an honorable life style to accommodate the needs of his higher classmate. It appeared . . . that Mr. Hsu has some sense of 'duty' to help his higher classmate. After Mr. Lee and Mr. Hsu were arrested, 'guanxi' dictated that . . . Mr. Lee confess before the junior member, Mr. Hsu, could talk."[13]

As in *guanxi,* concern for relative rank carries over into other Chinese interpersonal relationships. The Chinese friend of one American sociologist told the American, "I want to be an elder brother to you." The American explained the incident as follows: in order to sustain the role equality that Chinese value in friendship for the emotional involvement it allows, my friend had to apply power differences belonging to the kinship model of voluntary brotherhood in his definition of friendship. He was called upon to enforce predictability in that very relationship he valued for its equities and exchanges of affect. In Chinese friendship, the senior partner is obliged to police the relationship for its social content, making sure that it shall in fact contain role equality. The norm of reciprocity reserved for friendship is ratified by a non-reciprocal obligation on the part of the person in charge of the definition, even though the definition repudiates unequal responsibility.[14]

GUANXI EQUALS FACE

An essential point about *guanxi* is that what we Westerners commonly think of as Chinese concern for "face" is actually Chinese concern for their rank or position in the particular *guanxi*. To lose "face" is to lose position, and this does not mean simply to move down a notch in the hierarchy, it means to lose membership in the group. Whatever a Chinese person may feel about losing "face" does not alter the effect it has on his or her *guanxi* connections. A loss of "face" may be embarrassing, but embarrassment is not loss of "face."

Although *guanxi* is most easily understood as it exists between two persons, it is most often found among several, and each member's position in a *guanxi* is his "face" or *mianzi*. The rules prescribed for "face" behavior differ with each rank, but each has its rules. One rule that all ranks have in common is that each individual must act so as to maintain the structure. Once a *guanxi* arrangement has been established, it is expected to endure a lifetime. No change in positions is envisioned, and no reneging on performance is expected. (One of the easiest ways to lose "face" or position in a network is to go bankrupt. Word of such loss spreads slowly in Mainland China, but quickly elsewhere. It is interesting that word is passed among Chinese subtly, not like the harsh words found in western credit reports. For example, reference to one bankrupt businessman was simply that it "wasn't his own money").

But some people become greedy or selfish or ambitious. If the person who initiates a struggle does not succeed in unseating an adversary, their relationship does not merely return to its previous state. The initiator suffers a loss of "face." If the initiator does succeed, the adversary loses "face." In either case, a loss of "face" means a loss of position, and the loser is ejected from the structure. The outcome of a contest is usually the restructuring of the interrelationships between the remaining members. One possible, though infrequent, outcome is that the entire structure will be dissolved, or transformed drastically.[15] This is utter disaster for all as they can no longer count on the network of social relationships to help them out. That explains many business alliances among Overseas Chinese business people.

One thing is for sure: it is dangerous not to take sides in a "face" fight. If the challenged person succeeds in saving "face," those who should have helped but did not, will probably be cut out of the victor's *guanxi* net. On the grounds that he who is not for me is against me, remaining neutral is equivalent to joining the attack. If the challenger forces the adversary to lose "face," thereby winning the contest, the challenger too will show little enthusiasm towards anyone who stood by quietly on the sidelines. Everyone having a vested interest in the outcome of these attempts at impeachment (except those who may choose to benefit from playing mediator) must choose sides early. As soon as the wall begins to tilt, everyone must start either pushing or pulling.[16]

Note that "face" is situationally defined. It is a semantic construct applicable to a single and specific *guanxi* relationship. What can be created by words can be destroyed by words. For a Chinese, it is not sticks and stones, but words, that break one's bones.[17]

GUANXI IS NEITHER FRIENDSHIP NOR GO-BETWEENS

Americans in particular are prone to confuse *guanxi* with friendship. Chinese use *guanxi* to provide and receive goods and services, while Americans value friendship for its emotional content and, only incidentally, for the practical benefits that may ensue. Although the American's supposed Chinese "friend" in a *guanxi* relationship may be sincere in his relations with the American, it is not affection that he is sincere about.[18] More succinctly, Americans give and take away love; Chinese give and take away face.[19]

The common American explanation for the Chinese use of go-betweens is, understandably, based on American logic. One theory holds that the use of a go-between avoids embarrassment. Another has it that go-betweens present requests in a more persuasive manner than do their sponsors. But go-betweens are employed for rather infrequent matters, such as marriages and, anyway, *guanxi* has neither of the above benefits in mind. A request for services under a *guanxi* arrangement may require the assistance of several people intervening between the requester and the person who has the ability to honor the request, but those intervening are not middlemen or go-betweens, they are members of a *guanxi* network.[20] The compradore system used by European traders until the 1950's was the most successfully institutionalized *guanxi* in business—and reasonably respectable, too.

A Chinese businessman in the United States once solicited investment money from other ethnic Chinese in order to finance a shopping center. One wary potential investor thought to check up on the developer, but he did not contact a credit bureau or a business service such as Dun & Bradstreet. Rather he called an acquaintance in Hong Kong to ask about the developer. The contact in Hong Kong made inquiries of other contacts in other Asian cities and responded to the potential investor that the investor was a bad risk.

American businessmen in China often do hire go-betweens, primarily because they are not sufficiently adept at playing the *guanxi* game. Although American companies operating abroad still have to abide by the strict corruption codes of their country, many apparently hire agents in China who are called upon to do whatever is necessary to make a deal go ahead.[21]

Is *Guanxi* Practiced by Westerners?

By this point, western readers will surely (but mistakenly) be thinking that maybe *guanxi* is not

such a foreign idea. Before considering how the specifics of how Asians practice *guanxi*—and therein lies the real difference between east and west in this matter—let's consider our own ways. Do we of western cultures also have such "bundles" of ties, favors, and obligations as noted above? You bet we do! Beyond blood relations, we have "old Army buddies," classmates, sports teammates, etc., and we participate in unions, fraternities, alumni associations, police fraternal orders, civic associations, political parties, etc.—and we understand what it means to "marry the boss's daughter," to "have a friend at city hall," to "know someone who can get it for you wholesale," and that "a friend in need is a friend indeed." It is not so much that Asians and westerners have any exclusive activities, it is more that the two groups apply varying amounts of resources and degrees of emphasis and skill in doing similar things.

ENDNOTES

[1] John King Fairbank, *China—A New History* (Massachusetts: Belknap Press of Harvard University Press, 1992), 84.

[2] *Ibid.*, 129.

[3] *Ibid.*, 150.

[4] *Ibid.*, 353.

[5] *Ibid.*, 356.

[6] Gwen Kinkead, *Chinatown: A Portrait of a Closed Society,* (New York: Harper Collins Publishers, 1993).

[7] Professor Mark Elvin, Australian National University.

[8] Karl Shoenberger, "Networking Pays Off for Chinese," *Los Angeles Times,* April 6, 1994.

[9] Hu Hsien-chin, "The Chinese Concepts of Face" in Douglas Haring, *Personal Character and Cultural Milieu* (Syracuse University Press, 1956).

[10] Anonymous.

[11] Account of Special Agent Neil Pitagno, U.S. Customs Service.

[12] Anonymous.

[13] Account of Special Agent Richard Severtson, U.S. Department of Commerce.

[14] Leon E. Stover, *The Cultural Ecology of Chinese Civilization* (New York Pica Press, 1974).

[15] Anonymous.

[16] Anonymous.

[17] William K. Carr, "The 'Face' of Mao Tse-tung," *World Affairs,* vol. 131, no. 3 (1968).

[18] Anonymous.

[19] Stover.

[20] Anonymous.

[21] John Kohut, "Going to the War on Graft," Los Angeles *Sunday Morning Post,* April 17, 1994.

Islamophobia and Homophobia

by Robert Wright

As if we needed more evidence of America's political polarization, last week Juan Williams gave the nation a Rorschach test. Williams said he gets scared when people in "Muslim garb" board a plane he's on, and he promptly got (a) fired by NPR and (b) rewarded by Fox News with a big contract.

Suppose Williams had said something hurtful to gay people instead of to Muslims. Suppose he had said gay men give him the creeps because he fears they'll make sexual advances. NPR might well have fired him, but would Fox News have chosen that moment to give him a $2-million pat on the back?

I don't think so. Playing the homophobia card is costlier than playing the Islamophobia card. Or at least, the costs are more evenly spread across the political spectrum. In 2007, when Ann Coulter used a gay slur, she was denounced on the right as well as the left, and her stock dropped. Notably, her current self-promotion campaign stresses her newfound passion for gay rights.

Coulter's comeuppance reflected sustained progress on the gay rights front. Only a few decades ago, you could tell an anti-gay joke on the Johnny Carson show—with Carson's active participation—and no one would complain. (See postscript below for details.) The current "it gets better" campaign, designed to reassure gay teenagers that adulthood will be less oppressive than adolescence, amounts to a kind of double entendre: things get better not just over an individual's life but over the nation's life.

When we move from homophobia to Islamophobia, the trendline seems to be pointing in the opposite direction. This isn't shocking, given 9/11 and the human tendency to magnify certain kinds of risk. (Note to Juan Williams: Over the past nine years about 90 million flights have taken off from American airports, and not one has been brought down by a Muslim terrorist. Even in 2001, no flights were brought down by people in "Muslim garb.")

A few decades ago, people all over America knew and liked gay people—they just didn't realize they were gay.

Still, however "natural" this irrational fear, it's dangerous. As Islamophobia grows, it alienates Muslims, raising the risk of homegrown terrorism—and homegrown terrorism heightens the Islamophobia, which alienates more Muslims, and so on: a vicious circle that could carry America into the abyss. So it's worth taking a look at why homophobia is fading; maybe the underlying dynamic is transplantable to the realm of inter-ethnic prejudice.

Theories differ as to what it takes for people to build bonds across social divides, and some theories offer more hope than others.

One of the less encouraging theories grows out of the fact that both homophobia and Islamophobia draw particular strength from fundamentalist Christians. Maybe, this argument goes, part of the problem is a kind of "scriptural determinism." If religious texts say that homosexuality is bad, or that people of other faiths are bad, then true believers will toe that line.

Reprinted from *New York Times,* October 26, 2010.

If scripture is indeed this powerful, we're in trouble, because scripture is invoked by intolerant people of all Abrahamic faiths—including the Muslim terrorists who plant the seeds of Islamophobia. And, judging by the past millennium or two, God won't be issuing a revised version of the Bible or the Koran anytime soon.

Happily, there's a new book that casts doubt on the power of intolerant scripture: "American Grace," by the social scientists Robert Putnam and David Campbell.

Three decades ago, according to one of the many graphs in this data-rich book, slightly less than half of America's frequent churchgoers were fine with gay people freely expressing their views on gayness. Today that number is over 70 percent—and no biblical verse bearing on homosexuality has magically changed in the meanwhile. And these numbers actually understate the progress; over those three decades, church attendance was dropping for mainline Protestant churches and liberal Catholics, so the "frequent churchgoers" category consisted increasingly of evangelicals and conservative Catholics.

So why have conservative Christians gotten less homophobic? Putnam and Campbell favor the "bridging" model. The idea is that tolerance is largely a question of getting to know people. If, say, your work brings you in touch with gay people or Muslims—and especially if your relationship with them is collaborative—this can brighten your attitude toward the whole tribe they're part of. And if this broader tolerance requires ignoring or reinterpreting certain scriptures, so be it; the meaning of scripture is shaped by social relations.

The bridging model explains how attitudes toward gays could have made such rapid progress. A few decades ago, people all over America knew and liked gay people—they just didn't realize these people were gay. So by the time gays started coming out of the closet, the bridge had already been built.

And once straight Americans followed the bridge's logic—once they, having already accepted people who turned out to be gay, accepted gayness itself—more gay people felt comfortable coming out. And the more openly gay people there were, the more straight people there were who realized they had gay friends, and so on: a virtuous circle.

So could bridging work with Islamophobia? Could getting to know Muslims have the healing effect that knowing gay people has had?

The good news is that bridging does seem to work across religious divides. Putnam and Campbell did surveys with the same pool of people over consecutive years and found, for example, that gaining evangelical friends leads to a warmer assessment of evangelicals (by seven degrees on a "feeling thermometer" per friend gained, if you must know).

And what about Muslims? Did Christians warm to Islam as they got to know Muslims—and did Muslims return the favor?

That's the bad news. The population of Muslims is so small, and so concentrated in distinct regions, that there weren't enough such encounters to yield statistically significant data. And, as Putnam and Campbell note, this is a recipe for prejudice. Being a small and geographically concentrated group makes it hard for many people to know you, so not much bridging naturally happens. That would explain why Buddhists and Mormons, along with Muslims, get low feeling-thermometer ratings in America.

In retrospect, the situation of gays a few decades ago was almost uniquely conducive to rapid progress. The gay population, though not huge, was finely interspersed across the country, with representatives in virtually every high school, college and sizeable workplace. And straights had gotten to know them without even seeing the border they were crossing in the process.

So the engineering challenge in building bridges between Muslims and non-Muslims will be big. Still, at least we grasp the nuts and bolts of the situation. It's a matter of bringing people into contact with the "other" in a benign context. And it's a matter of doing it fast, before the vicious circle takes hold, spawning appreciable homegrown terrorism and making fear of Muslims less irrational.

After 9/11, philanthropic foundations spent a lot of money arranging confabs whose participants spanned the divide between "Islam" and "the West." Meaningful friendships did form across this border, and that's good. It's great that Imam Feisal Abdul Rauf, a cosmopolitan, progressive Muslim, got to know lots of equally cosmopolitan Christians and Jews.

But as we saw when he decided to build an Islamic Community Center near ground zero, this sort of high-level networking—bridging among elites whose attitudes aren't really the problem in the first place—isn't enough. Philanthropists need to figure out how you build lots of little bridges at the grass roots level. And they need to do it fast.

Postscript: *As for the Johnny Carson episode: I don't like to rely on my memory alone for decades-old anecdotes, but in this case I'm 99.8 percent sure that I remember the basics accurately. Carson's guest was the drummer Buddy Rich. In a supposedly spontaneous but obviously pre-arranged exchange, Rich said something like, "People often ask me, What is Johnny Carson really like?" Carson looked at Rich warily and said, "And how do you respond to this query?" But he paused between "this" and "query," theatrically ratcheting up the wariness by an increment or two, and then pronounced the word "query" as "queery." Rich immediately replied, "Like that." Obviously, there are worse anti-gay jokes than this. Still, the premise was that being gay was something to be ashamed of. That Googling doesn't turn up any record of this episode suggests that it didn't enter the national conversation or the national memory. I don't think that would be the case today. And of course, anecdotes aside, there is lots of polling data showing the extraordinary progress made since the Johnny Carson era on such issues as gay marriage and on gay rights in general.*

SECTION IV
CROSS-CULTURAL ADAPTATION

Change, in and of itself, is stressful for all living things—plants, animals, and human beings. Special care must be taken to prepare plants to be relocated to another part of the garden. Each plant must be carefully selected to be sure it can survive the stress of transplantation. Some may be too fragile to cope with the trauma while others might flourish in a new location. As the plants adjust to the unfamiliar soil and light, they may require special attention and care. After an initial transition period, if all goes well, most plants will thrive in the new location.

Animals that are forced to migrate far distances from their homelands usually undergo enormous stress and the weaker often die en route. Even for survivors the move may require yet many more months or years to acclimate to the new physical environment. Adaptation is very daunting for many relocating animals while those who are born in the new location may experience very little stress.

This is also true for human beings. Relocation stress is overwhelming for some and yet for others it is minimal and the relocation may be an exhilarating experience. Furthermore, each member of the family may react differently. Pre-adolescent children are most likely to make friends quickly and learn the local language better than their parents. Some adolescents may find that leaving their friends back home is psychologically very painful and they might find it difficult to develop new friendships. The working spouse may be doing the same work overseas as back home while the nonworking spouse's life may be turned upside down because he or she is totally immersed in the local culture when it comes to shopping, running a household, education of children, and so on. And it is probable that the only pre-departure training and education about cross-cultural adaptation was given to the working spouse.

For those born in the new cultural environment, there may be very little stress except that these children will grow up in a different world than that of their parents and yet they still live with their parents. Parents who move from a small town in America to New York City may find the relocation and adaptation stress to be devastating although their children born in New York adapt very quickly. Somewhat like pioneers in early American history who moved from the East Coast to the western frontier, parents might find it useful to observe how their children adapt. They certainly cannot tell their children, "I know what you're going through," because they will never experience the world in the same way. Each new generation is different and this is especially so today with the impact of rapidly changing technologies. The intergenerational differences are greatly exaggerated when two generations actually grow up in different national cultures.

There are various reasons for leaving one's primary or native culture. Many sojourners relocate voluntarily to find new opportunities for work or study, while others may have no alternative. Today moving to another region of the world would be expected of students and scholars, most executives in multinational organizations, diplomats, or military personnel, although these moves may be only a matter of a few months or years. For those fleeing political violence, economic devastation, or natural disasters such as famine, the relocation may be permanent.

THE DYNAMICS OF CROSS-CULTURAL ADAPTATION

Moving from one culture and entering another, either domestically or internationally, produces the psychological stress known as *culture shock*. We go through this when we leave home to go to college, start a new job in another city, or begin life in the military. Even moving from one organization to another can be traumatic. Of course, the anxiety is magnified many times over when we are relocating to another country. Some of us have great difficulties while others encounter only a brief period of discomfort. Nevertheless, anyone who has adapted to a new social environment went through a stressful period.

Everyone who has adapted to another culture has gone through culture shock. Those who claim that they did not may not have recognized the signs, or perhaps they never really adjusted to another culture. Tourists and those who remain enmeshed within conational groups generally do not experience culture shock. Tourists are short-term sojourners who never actually enter another culture. Many diplomats do not experience culture shock because of their isolation within the diplomatic community and their insulation from the local society. A diplomat who works within the confines of his or her embassy may be doing the same job overseas as back home. The embassy is the sovereign territory of one's home country. The local nationals working for the embassy are usually very bicultural and bilingual. They acculturate to the national culture of the embassy, they know the procedures and practices extremely well, and many have worked at the embassy longer than the diplomats who are only temporarily assigned to the country. On the other hand, the diplomat's family members may go through severe culture shock because they are much more immersed in the context of the local culture.

Once we adjust to a new culture we become somewhat bi-cultural. Of course, to be completely bi-cultural we would have to grow up in two cultures at the same time. When we adapt to a new culture, we don't give up our home culture. In fact, it may become even more important to us when we are overseas. If we remain at home, surrounded by people who share our values and worldviews, we tend to take our home culture for granted. We don't think about it very much. When we leave our home social environment and enter another, we become more consciously aware of our home environment and it may even become more important to us.

Most people eventually adapt to a new culture but some individuals may be predisposed to be unable to tolerate the pressure of culture shock at the time of their relocation. The personality and experience of an individual and the likelihood that they can withstand the stress ought to be considered before sojourners are selected for working in a new culture. They may have gone through recent stressful events and the additional pressure of adapting overseas pushes them over the edge. Selection of personnel for overseas assignments is as important as proper cross-cultural training. Ideally, if we are apprised of the difficulties of cross-cultural adaptation and we realize that the additional stress may be too great, it is best if we could decide not to go overseas. This would also be good for the organization. An analogy might be soldiers who go into battle. Most return home from the stress of warfare fairly unharmed psychologically. However, some are predisposed to be unable to tolerate this kind of pressure and are overwhelmed by the extreme stress of battle. They may go through the psychological breakdown commonly called *shell shock*. It would be better for the soldier and the military if he or she were not put in this situation. But the soldier cannot deselect himself or herself from battle.

Cross-cultural adjustment should be considered a continuum with at least two low periods: entry to another culture and reentry to one's home culture. With awareness of the process of adjustment and recognition of the "symptoms" of stress, individuals can develop their own special coping strategies. Thus, the severity and duration of these stressful periods can be minimized and the entire process can become one of great personal, and even professional, growth.

ENTRY STRESS OR CULTURE SHOCK[1]

The phrase "culture shock," coined by Cora DuBois in 1951, was popularized in the cross-cultural literature by anthropologist Kalervo Oberg to describe problems of acculturation and adjustment among Americans who were working in a health project in Brazil. In his 1960 *Practical Anthropology* article, he described it as "an occupational disease of people who have suddenly been transported abroad [which] is precipitated by the anxiety that results from losing all our familiar signs and symbols of social intercourse."[2]

This illness model is misleading because it assumes that culture shock results from something external such as a "virus" over which we have no control. It implies that it has a distinct set of symptoms, a prognosis, and it lasts a set period of time, and there must be a "cure" of some sort. Worst of all, when we think of a disease our focus is on the pathological aspects rather than on the growth process and positive benefits of having gone through a period of adaptation stress.

Culture shock is not a disease. It is primarily a psychological phenomenon. It is a reaction to the stress of leaving one social environment and entering another. It is not a matter of different food or weather and new social customs but rather how we cope with the new physical and social environment. We all react to stressful events differently and thus the so-called symptoms and prognosis vary with the individual and the nature of the move. Stress produces sleepless nights for some and for others it causes depression or even psychosomatic illnesses. For example, the most common symptom of culture shock for African students studying in the United States seems to be stomach disorders.

Sometimes pre-departure cross-cultural trainers are tempted to list "symptoms" of culture shock that often appear in the research: insomnia, diarrhea, weight loss, and so on. Although this may make the trainer appear very authoritative, it is also very misleading and counterproductive. When experiencing culture shock, some sojourners may find themselves sleeping too much, constipated, and gaining weight. They therefore conclude they are not going through culture shock when in fact there are hundreds of different reactions and no list could include all of them.

Some people can tolerate stress better than others and moving from one house to another in the same neighborhood is much less anxiety-producing than moving from one country to another. Although the critical phases of culture shock may take place for most people during the first month or so overseas, for some they manifest themselves before they walk onto a plane or after they have been in country for a year or more.

Lastly, there is no cure. If there is a disease analogy for culture shock, it might be the common cold. The first time we experience a severe cold, we might panic and assume it is an exotic flu or pneumonia. However, we recover. The next time we have a bad cold, we know that we can minimize the severity and the duration by eating chicken soup, getting plenty of rest, and drinking many liquids. We know that we can prevent colds and definitely have some control over our symptoms. However, we will have many colds during our lifetime.

We experience culture shock whenever we relocate or return home. Experienced sojourners not only recognize the phenomenon as a common occurrence, they anticipate that it will happen and develop ways of minimizing its duration and severity. Former American Secretary of State, Henry Kissinger once remarked that he went through culture shock every time he traveled overseas. And yet, he certainly developed more effective ways of handling it with each venture overseas.

In the past half century, the phrase "culture shock" has become a basic part of the international sojourner's jargon and is now commonly used to describe almost any physical or emotional discomfort experienced by those adjusting to a new environment. "Homesickness," "adjustment difficulties," "uprooting," "culture fatigue," and numerous other terms are often used to describe the same phenomenon as culture shock. While the phrase "culture shock" may be a bit too strong, the other labels fail to focus on cultural factors and are overly euphemistic. Most cross-cultural scholars and trainers use the term culture shock because of historical tradition and the attention-getting value of the words.

The reactions (or symptoms) of culture shock may range from mild emotional disorders and stress-related physiological ailments to psychosis. The types and intensity of reactions to a new cultural environment depend upon the nature and duration of the stressful situation and, more importantly, the psychological makeup of an individual. Some people quickly develop useful coping strategies which allow them to adjust easily while, at the other extreme, some resort to the use of progressively more inappropriate and maladaptive neurotic defense mechanisms which may eventually develop into such severe psychological disorders as psychosis, alcoholism, and even suicide.

Many studies suggest that such severe reactions account for a very small percentage of all sojourners, and it may well be that they were predisposed to an inability to cope with sudden traumatic stress before they traveled overseas. The vast majority of sojourners experience moderate reactions and successfully overcome culture shock. In fact, some may actually come through culture shock more psychologically sound than before they left their own culture.

Over the years severe culture shock has also been measured in terms of so-called "dropout rate" or "premature returns." It has been informally estimated, for example, that the Peace Corps has a dropout rate of between 30 and 40 percent. These are volunteers who return home before completing their terms of service overseas. The implication is that these volunteers terminated their stays because of the stress of cross-cultural adjustment or an inability to adapt overseas. Of course, there may be many other factors to account for such termination including family difficulties, health problems unrelated to stress, or differences with management overseas.

The severity of culture shock is generally much greater when the adjustment involves a completely different culture, because there is a greater loss of Oberg's "familiar signs and symbols of social intercourse" in an entirely new environment. On the other hand, anticipation of a stressful event also affects the severity of the reaction. It seems that if we do not anticipate a stressful event we are much less capable of coping with it. This would explain why we still experience culture shock when entering a slightly different cultural environment or when returning home to our native culture. Most Americans do not anticipate stress when adapting to London and few anticipate the stress of reentering their home culture.

Ultimately the psychological makeup of the individual may be the most important factor. Some people can tolerate a great deal of stress caused by change, ambiguity, and unpredictability while others demand an unchanging, unambiguous, predictable environment to feel psychologically secure. Those who are overly task-oriented and have a high need for individual achievement may be easily frustrated and may have difficulty building trusting relationships with others. And people who are overly closed-minded and inflexible may be unable to develop realistic cultural empathy. These psychological traits, rather than cross-cultural adjustment skills or cultural awareness, may be of primary importance in determining the success with which one adapts to another culture.[3] Again, this is the reason selection is so important.

While Oberg considered culture shock to be an "ailment," some have come to consider it a normal and natural growth or transition process as we adapt to another culture. There is disorientation, ambiguity, and psychological pain but we often come through this state more stable and centered than ever before. The object then is not to eliminate or avoid culture shock but rather to make it a less stressful and more positive experience. Culture shock may be no more harmful than the psychological reactions we experience when adapting to such new environmental situations as entering college or moving to another city in our own culture.

Culture shock is primarily an unconscious phenomenon. Most people have no idea why they are behaving as they are or feeling as they do. By understanding the process of adaptation, one sees that it is a normal reaction to a new cultural environment which everyone goes through to some extent. Furthermore, it can be a very positive experience which allows for great personal insight and growth.

THE U-CURVE OF CROSS-CULTURAL ADAPTATION

For most people, culture shock occurs during the first month or two of a sojourn and may last for five or six months. But for some it will begin before they leave home and others might not experience it until they are in country for a few months. The stress also continues upon return home. If we go overseas again later in life, it will occur once more—again, like the common cold. However, experienced sojourners anticipate that will happen and develop ways of coping with it and they often find that their reactions are very mild.

The graphic below illustrates the usual pattern of adjustment. The perpendicular line represents level of happiness or satisfaction and the horizontal line represents length of time. Upon arrival, most experience that thrill of being overseas. Everything is new and exciting—we meet new friends and are usually welcomed as newcomers to the country. This is the period that Oberg refers to as the "honeymoon" because it is as if we are newlyweds on a honeymoon.[4]

As all married people know, all honeymoons end far too soon. Honeymoons end just as the initial upward trajectory of satisfaction begins to take a downward spiral that we refer to as "culture shock." Disillusionment soon develops as sojourners face the real difficulties of eating the local food, using public transportation, shopping, attending classes, and working with host nationals. Such disillusionment marks the beginning of the U-Curve of culture shock. Of course, those with the greatest disillusionment are those with the greatest illusions. This is the reason it is so important to have realistic expectations. Sugar-coating the experience of cross-cultural adaptation during a pre-departure orientation program is extremely counterproductive because it contributes to this disillusionment.

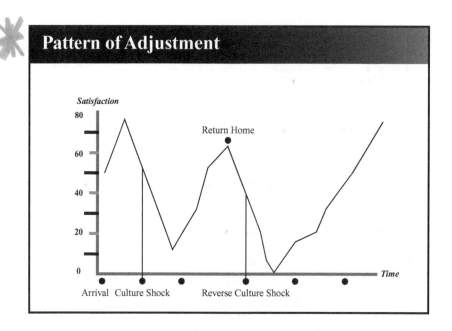

People in the new culture have different beliefs, values, and worldviews. Interpersonal communication is difficult and often breaks down. Cut off from others, sojourners feel disoriented and out of control. They are homesick and long for familiar things from home—friends and family, the weather, food, language. And ways of solving problems that worked so well back home are ineffective in the new culture. They begin to doubt their ability to function in the new culture.

Perhaps 5 or 10 percent of sojourners keep going down in this nosedive and they may have been predisposed to be unable to handle the stress. The overwhelming majority come out of it, which is the reason this is often referred to as the U-Curve of Adaptation. This is when we become accustomed to the food, learn to survive in the new environment, make new friends, and communicate easily with others.[5]

Most sojourners eventually snap out of the downward slide of culture shock as they develop new friendships and begin to feel comfortable with the social and physical environment. They also begin to develop a more adequate, flexible, somewhat bicultural personality. This recovery period completes the U-curve, though sojourners may experience a few other "down" periods before returning home.

CAUSES OF CULTURE SHOCK

What causes culture shock? There are four basic explanations: it is a result of *the collision of internal cultures*, *the loss of familiar cues or reinforcers*, *the breakdown of interpersonal communication*, and *an identity crisis*. All four disorienting states occur in adjustment to any new social environment. However, in a cross-cultural situation, they are greatly exaggerated and exacerbated by cultural differences. While each of these explanations takes a slightly different approach, they are not mutually exclusive nor is any single one adequate to fully understand the phenomenon. Indeed, they overlap and complement each other.

1. Collision of Internal Cultures. The overarching and most comprehensive explanation of why culture shock occurs is the clash of cultures as depicted in the analogy of icebergs colliding in the middle of the ocean. As we have seen, our *external* culture resides at the tip of the iceberg, where we exhibit behaviors. Although the tips of the icebergs may never meet, there is almost certainly a collision taking place well beneath the water level of awareness. Culture shock is a result of the *collision of internal cultures.*

We anticipate the different customs, food, weather, and language especially if the pre-departure training was mostly area studies. We learn the customs and basics of the language and begin to enjoy the food. We even dress like local people. Most people can quickly adjust to these differences and even change their own external cultures, avoiding collision or conflict at the tip of the iceberg.

The real collision occurs at the base of the icebergs, beneath the water level of awareness where we have internal culture—values, thought patterns, worldviews, and higher context language including nonverbal communication. When living in another culture we simply wake up one morning and realize that local people are not playing cards with the same deck that we use back home. They don't share our worldviews, values, and ways of solving problems. We are confused, disoriented, frustrated and even angry. To make matters even worse, this clash was not anticipated unless we somehow replicated this experience with pre-departure experiential exercises. If so, we suddenly have an "ah-ha" reaction—we've been through this before and can realize that the dynamics are very similar. We have been inoculated.

Everyone has experienced this entry stress during the first day of kindergarten, when leaving one's hometown to work or study in another part of the country, or even when entering another organization culture. Although primary culture is always more powerful than secondary cultures, nevertheless each organization has its own shared beliefs or values.[6] These are often found in written documents such as mission statements but most are internal or hidden aspects of the culture which are learned unconsciously as we adjust to the new school or workplace. The collision of organizational cultures can be just as severe as the collision of primary cultures which is the reason many mergers between organizations often fail.[7]

2. Breakdown of Communication. This explanation for culture shock is based upon humanistic psychology with its emphasis on the psychodynamics of human interaction. We are social beings and therefore we must communicate with others. Because most humans communicate quite effectively before the age of three or four, we take the ability to communicate for granted and seldom are consciously aware that the source of much of our pain in human interaction is a result of the breakdown of communication. When we enter a new cultural environment, it is almost inevitable that interpersonal communications will break down and when this happens we feel alienated, isolated and cut off from others. This frustration and distress causes us to react and in a cross-cultural situation, we can describe these reactions as "symptoms" of culture shock.

Going back to our *cybernetics model of communication* in Section I, we can see how cross-cultural communications are bound to break down. The *sender* transmits messages to the *receiver* but not necessarily meanings. *The meanings are in our heads.* If we experienced the world in the same way, then the messages can elicit similar or parallel meaning. But if we come from different cultures, our messages can have very different meanings. As we have already noted, "yes" doesn't always mean "yes" and sometimes "maybe," "it is difficult," or simply looking away from someone when they are talking means "no" or "end of conversation." It all depends on our culture.

Coding is not simply a matter of words. In some high-context languages, words have numerous meanings depending upon the situation whereas in low-context languages the connotative and denotative meanings are usually the same. A person who gets loud and gestures a great deal could simply mean, "I'm very sincere about this." This might be typical of southern Italians or someone from the Middle East. In mainstream America or Sweden this could mean, "He's angry. Call security, he's out of control." This illustration also points out that the greatest part of the message that communicates feelings might not be the words but rather such nonverbal messages as tone of voice, loudness, gestures, posture, facial expression, and so on. And, in a high-context culture, this is even more common. *The meanings we give to nonverbal messages are almost always unconscious and culture-specific.* Thus, the *medium* or *channel* of communication is not simply sound but also sight and, at times, even touch.

Low-context people expect almost immediate and very clear or strong verbal *feedback* while in many high-context cultures where people seek to avoid confrontation—especially with their friends—there is a tendency to give indirect negative feedback in order to maintain the social harmony. Thus, in many high-context cultures people avoid saying "no" and have a tendency to say "it is possible" when they perhaps mean "maybe" or "if I can." Or they may just break eye contact.

Again, there are many parts and links between parts of an interpersonal communication system where a breakdown is likely to occur to produce frustration, misunderstanding, and psychological distress. When we experience pain, as with many animals, we react and these reactions are usually viewed as the so-called "symptoms" of culture shock. Although there are no symptoms that are universal for everyone because we all react to stress differently, there are some basic patterns that we can identify.

3. The loss of cues or reinforcers is the most behavioral explanation in that it primarily focuses on that which is tangible and observable. Everyone is surrounded by thousands of physical and social cues which have been present since childhood and therefore are taken for granted until they are absent. These familiar cues make us feel comfortable and make life predictable. When they are absent we begin to feel like a fish out of water.

Physical cues include objects which we have become accustomed to in our home culture which are changed or missing in a new culture such as food, buildings, pets, and even people. Homesickness is a longing for people back home. We often don't know what we will miss until we get overseas. For example, according to a number of surveys, that which Americans miss the most when overseas is American peanut butter and yet most would never list this as a concern before they leave home.

Social cues, which Oberg refers to as signs and signals, provide order in interpersonal relations. They are signposts which guide us through our daily activities in an acceptable fashion which is consistent with the total social environment. Words, gestures, facial expressions, postures, or customs help us to make sense out of the social world that surrounds us. These cues tell us when and how to give gifts or tips, when to be serious or to be humorous, how to speak to leaders and subordinates, who has status, what to say when we meet people, when and how to shake hands, how to eat, and so on. They make us feel comfortable because they seem so automatic.

They also serve as reinforcers of behavior because they signal if things are being done inappropriately. However, in a new social environment, behavior is no longer clearly right or wrong, but instead becomes very ambiguous. This ambiguity is especially painful for many of those who are accustomed to clear verbal messages and feedback, explicit rules of behavior, and the ability to predict the behavior of others. The directness of some Americans, Dutch, or Germans is often perceived as rude, abrupt, or abrasive in many Asian cultures while the indirect and circuitous response of people in these cultures comes across as ambiguous and sometimes even deceptive.

The low-context, loosely integrated, and heterogeneous nature of Euro-American society is built upon clear, explicit, overt rules of behavior which ensures predictability. In high-context cultures, rules of behavior are often vague, implicit, and buried or embedded deeply within the context of the culture. The society is usually more tightly integrated and homogeneous, and therefore one can infer from his or her own behavior what is appropriate for everyone else.

When familiar cues or reinforcers are no longer elicited by our behavior, we experience pain and frustration. In fact, the loss of a reinforcer or cue is actually a form of punishment in terms of our psychological reactions. Thousands of times Euro-Americans deposit coins into a soft drink machine which results in the drop of a can or cup. If one day no can or cup drops down after depositing their money, they may react to this lack of an expected reinforcer or reward by irrationally kicking the machine. It usually does not cause the can or cup to drop down nor does the machine return the money. But they may feel better because they have vented their anger over the loss of the reinforcer.

4. Identity Crisis.[8] This is by far the most complicated yet the most fascinating explanation of culture shock because it implies that there is genuine and often dramatic psychological or intra-psychic growth that occurs when one successfully overcomes culture shock. Those who have lived overseas often claim that they would not be the kind of person they are today had they not gone through the process of cross-cultural adaptation. Somehow they believe their lives were personally transformed by the experience.

With any transformational experience there is often enormous emotional struggle and the possibility of failure. The so-called existential leap, psychoanalytic catharsis, or the religious experience can be incredibly liberating and exhilarating but there is often great emotional stress. However, no one really grows without some pain. It is also true that some take the existential leap and never make it to the other side of the crevice.

As with the psychoanalytic cathartic event and the existential crisis, there is pain and risk involved in the culture shock experience.[9] A certain percentage of people will be unable to tolerate the stress of giving up an inadequate problem-solving system or an identity which gave them a sense of security and predictability for so long. Very few people who go through culture shock experience such severe reactions as a psychotic breakdown. A great deal depends upon the predisposition of the individual and his or her psychological makeup at the time the stress occurs.

Culture shock tends to bring to conscious awareness the grip that our native culture has had on our behavior and personality. As with psychoanalysis, we can transcend the tyranny of our childhood experiences when we go through some kind of emotional catharsis and become consciously aware of that which has been buried in the unconscious. As adults, we can rationally explore the irrationality of our fears and early experiences that have shaped our personality. We are relatively unaware of the cultural prison we are born into until we leave it and only then can we escape it.

When we enter another culture, the cultural program which has worked so well since childhood is inadequate. The system of selective perception and interpretation no longer wards off the bombardment of millions of new stimuli or cues, and it is no longer clear what the stimuli mean. But this is how we begin to see new relationships and new ways of ordering our perceptual and intellectual world. We are gradually expanding our culturally programmed image system and subjective knowledge structure.

The ways in which we have been programmed by our culture to solve problems or to think no longer work effectively; the environment makes new demands upon us. Finally, we are overwhelmed by the stimuli and demands and must temporarily experience the sense of confusion of not knowing what to pay attention to or how to solve problems. This period may be similar to the transitional stages we experience during other life crises such as adolescence. The ways in which we select out that which is relevant or abstract from our social and physical environment—that which is significant—are obsolete. We are overwhelmed and can no longer cope.

As with any other identity crisis, culture shock allows us to give up an inadequate perceptual and problem-solving system to allow another more expanded and adequate system to be born. It is somewhat of a death-rebirth cycle. This may be similar to an acute schizophrenic episode or crisis—commonly referred to a "nervous breakdown." It is situational and not at all chronic. As with any computer that is overloaded with too much information or with too little programming to sort through that information and solve more complex problems, it crashes. Then we reprogram the computer to handle more information and to cope with more complicated problems.

During severe culture shock, the cognitive devices that allow us to sort out these stimuli and solve problems become dysfunctional. We end up reprogramming ourselves to expand the amount of information we can take in and to solve problems in new ways. In a sense, the identity crisis of culture shock becomes a form of "positive disintegration."[10] It may be as natural and benign as a fever. If allowed to run its course, the normal pattern of adjustment promotes great introspection, self-awareness, and most importantly, a broadened repertoire of problem-solving tools. Those who want to ensure that this is a positive experience can at best psychologically "hold the hand" of the person going through severe culture shock.

In terms of thought patterns and communication, this transitional period is very associative or relational in that everything seems to flow together somewhat chaotically.[11] But this is how we begin to see new relationships and new ways of ordering our perceptual and intellectual world. We are gradually expanding our image system and subjective knowledge structure. We are acquiring a new, expanded and more effective identity.

In her book *Passages*, Gail Sheehy suggests that we human beings are similar to hardy crustaceans. "The lobster grows by developing and shedding a series of protective shells. Each time it expands from within, the confining shell must be sloughed off. It is left exposed and vulnerable until, in time, a new covering grows to replace the old." As with the passages from one stage of human growth to the next, when we go through culture shock, "we must shed a protective structure and are left exposed and vulnerable—but also yeasty and embryonic again; capable of stretching in ways we hadn't known before."[12] The lobster is still fundamentally the same, except more mature. The sojourner who experiences culture shock sees the world in different ways and has a host of new alternatives for solving problems and interacting with others along with enhanced self-awareness.

The overseas experience, like that of an encounter or sensitivity group, offers a new social milieu in which to examine one's behavior, perceptions, values, and thought patterns. An experience close to psychosis may be required to take one outside the collective pressures and assumptions of our culture. We may discover things about ourselves that allow for great personal growth. Yet it may be an ego-shattering experience. Great personal insight can occur for many, while others may find it very destructive. Whether the experience will eventually become positive or negative depends upon one's expectations, adaptability, tolerance for ambiguity and stress, and an understanding that there inevitably will be pain which can be handled and overcome.

The analogy between the overseas experience and the encounter group is even more apropos when we consider that both involve emotional and somewhat irrational situations. Moreover, both demand full participation and emotional involvement. Frustration is only heightened when one attempts to cope with the situation as an aloof, rational, objective observer. It is a total experience of mind and body, the intellect and emotion, and the objective and subjective person.

What are the dynamics of cross-cultural adaptation that explain this phenomenon? The breakdown of communication may be much more profound than simply a matter of disorientation and frustration. It may be more of a breakthrough to new ways of interacting with others and it might give us insight into our own need for human interaction on an authentic level. Ways of accomplishing tasks, solving problems, and thinking which may have worked effectively all our lives may be ineffective in a new culture. When we go through culture shock, we become aware of how our culture has shaped our thinking and perception, and we may become more conscious of our "hidden culture" or internal culture and, in turn, transcend it.

The loss of cues or reinforcers is also disorienting but the uncertainty and confusion frees us from habitual ways of doing and perceiving things and allows us to try new problem-solving methods and to view situations in new ways. Slowly we begin to adopt new cues. Local food and music make us comfortable, new social practices make life predictable and we discover different ways of communicating with our new friends. It is not so much that we are like the proverbial fish out of water as it is that we are thrown into the water and must learn how to swim. We can't simply intellectualize the experience or just watch other swimmers. We must try to swim by moving our limbs in the water—by participating kinesthetically in the aquatic environment. This is much more than a theoretical or intellectual exercise. Eventually we will experience the ecstasy of being able to swim. Some, however, rush to the shore, never to set foot in the water again.

THE REACTIONS OR "SYMPTOMS" OF CULTURE SHOCK AND COPING STRATEGIES

Just as the pattern of adjustment can vary with the individual so do the reactions. For most, the reactions are not severe and yet the quicker we make it through this adjustment period and the less severe the reactions, the more effective we are in a new cultural environment. Although there are an enormous variety of ways in which we respond to stress, we can identify five common stages or phases which are often, but not necessarily, in sequence. Based upon our understanding of these stages and the process of adaptation, we can also identify some coping strategies that might minimize the duration and severity of culture shock.

"Out of Control." People going through culture shock are usually unaware of what is causing them pain or producing their strange behavior. They do not understand that this is a normal result of a communications breakdown. If there is any one reaction that seems to be common for all sojourners, it is a sense of being *out of control*. Rather than behaving rationally, their emotions take over and they become irrational. Sojourners may be frustrated and confused because they cannot engage in simple human interaction. This in turn produces a sense of powerlessness, incompetence, and even childishness. Self-esteem decreases and, if the reaction is extreme, there is sometimes a neurotic feeling of both helplessness and hopelessness. For those who have a strong psychological need to be "in control," this can be quite overwhelming.[13]

This is one of the primary reasons for discussing culture shock in a pre-departure or arrival seminar. Although many may not believe that this would happen to them, discussing the phenomenon during their orientation helps them to anticipate the possibility that it could occur. Understanding that it is normal and simply a result of culture shock actually gives them control when these reactions set in. It allows them to act rather than react and they can develop coping strategies.

Flight. Reactions often overlap and contribute to the sense of being out of control—confusion, frustration, disorientation, anger, and so on. When we experience pain, we tend to avoid or escape from the painful stimulus or engage in *flight behavior*. Nathan Azrin, a behavioral experimental psychologist, conducted a famous experiment to demonstrate this reaction.[14] He placed a rat in a cage with an electric grid on the bottom. When he turned on the electricity, the rat ran out of the cage. Humans react in a similar manner during culture shock. When we experience the pain produced by the breakdown of communication, we avoid those who produce the pain.

This withdrawal from others can be quite unconscious and counterproductive. If one of the primary causes of culture shock is the breakdown of communications, how could cutting off communications with others make it better? On the other hand, temporarily cutting down the bombardment of contradictory messages or stimuli might provide some relief until we can calm down and sort things out. It might be a coping strategy.

Sojourners may begin to believe that going overseas was a big mistake and they find themselves continually thinking about how to go home. They become preoccupied with thoughts about how to "escape" the situation. They may also find themselves to be very sleepy a great deal of the time and yet they get plenty of sleep. This may in part be simply a result of stress but it could also be a kind of unconscious way of dealing with an overload of confusing messages.

For example, when children are overwhelmed by a bombardment of stimuli, they often simply fall asleep and consequently cut down the stimuli. This explains why a four year old child can fall asleep on the sofa in the middle of a raucous party.

Fight. Azrin took his experiment with rats a bit further. He placed two rats in the cage, turned on the electric grid, and then closed the doors of the cage to prevent any escape. The rats tried to get out and then began to attack each other. Interestingly, they would attack anything put in the cage, including a tennis ball. Azrin demonstrated that when the rats were placed in a painful environment from which they could not escape, it produced irrational aggression or *fight behavior*. Of course it was irrational. If the rats were rational they would have tried to attack Azrin.

Many sojourners cannot return home after only a month or two overseas. Some might lose their job, students would need to face friends and family who just recently celebrated their journey overseas, and soldiers cannot simply catch the next flight home. They are trapped in a painful situation as they go through culture shock. Human beings are not rats. We have culture, free will, logic, and so on. Nevertheless, when placed in a painful situation from which we cannot escape, we also engage in neurotic aggression which we often displace onto those who are lower in the social hierarchy. The anger is not directed to supervisors, superiors, or teachers but rather to innocent taxi drivers, waitresses, or clerks. This is somewhat like the child who gets a spanking from a parent and walks out the door of the house and kicks the cat.

This stage of cross-cultural adaptation is especially important because it can become pathological. Individuals who have difficulty expressing or acknowledging their anger can sometimes internalize it thereby leading to psychosomatic stress-related illnesses or even depression. And it may build up to such an extent that it ends in an irrational uncontrolled explosion of rage.[15]

Because of the value placed on rationality in the United States and the overwhelming sense of guilt and loss of control caused by angry reactions, some internalize or deny their anger. This denial actually makes matters worse—depression is often attributed to internalized anger. Adding to the problem, hopelessness and lack of control cause some to feel helpless. They can perceive no way of coping with their feelings and are unaware of what is causing them to behave in such irrational ways. Their sense of hopelessness, helplessness, and lack of control causes them to simply give up trying to control the situation. They learn to be helpless, and learned helplessness is also often considered a major factor in depression.

Filter. This reaction is really a matter of distorting, denying or simplifying the complexity and reality of a painful situation. All of these reactions to culture shock, when carried to extremes, can be highly neurotic and especially this one. *Filter behavior* is similar to a camera lens that you might use when there is a cloudy day. The filter lens distorts the clouds, highlights the darks and the lights, and thereby allows you to have a clearer picture.

Adapting to another culture is initially a complicated dilemma, especially if the cultures are almost opposites in terms of internal values. How can you be a part of a low-context or "to do" culture if you come from a high-context or "to be" culture? Ideally, you would become bicultural and perhaps bilingual. But very few people are completely bicultural or bilingual. You would need to grow up in both cultures at exactly the same time. It is really a matter of degree—some of us are more bicultural and bilingual than others. How could you distort, deny, or simplify this situation to make it more comfortable and decrease the conflict?

There are two basic types of distortions that involve oversimplification and denial. You simply deny that you are in a new culture. Instead of adapting to the new culture you develop a version of your home culture in-country. You speak the local language only when it is an absolute necessity, find restaurants that serve food from home, and hang out in the ex-patriot community with co-nationals. Americans can easily build a "little America" in the middle of Cairo and Egyptians can find a "little Egypt" in the middle of New York City. To justify avoidance of the local culture you may have endless conversations with co-nationals about how terrible it is in the host culture and how wonderful it is at home. This is a distortion because there are wonderful aspects of the host culture and terrible things about back home.

There is an opposite reaction when one denies his or her home culture by over-adapting to the local culture. In a small town in Mexico, an American student from Chicago might grow a moustache within a few weeks after arrival, refuse to speak English with anyone, and avoid interaction with all others from the United States. His Spanish is terrible, he only eats Mexican local food which is so hot that he often finds himself wiping tears from his eyes, and he wears sandals made out of tire treads. Very often he has lively discussions with Mexicans about how wonderful it is in Mexico and how terrible it is in the United States. This is a distortion because there are bad things about Mexico and wonderful things about the United States but these conversations help to justify his denial of his native culture.

This version of filter behavior is often labeled "going native" and is resented by co-nationals and viewed as almost "weird" by local nationals. People from home resent the almost self-righteous assertion that he or she really knows how to adapt when, in fact, they are only denying their home culture and adapting superficial aspects of the local culture—the tip of the iceberg—including language, food, and dress. Locals view this kind of person with amusement because they know the person is from the United States and only people who can't afford real shoes would wear sandals made out of tire treads. These sandals are very uncomfortable.

There is a third kind of filter reaction, which also involves a flight reaction—never really leaving home and letting go of friends and family back home to develop new relationships in a new culture. Modern communications make this form of filter behavior much easier than in the past. With social media and Skype we can communicate instantaneously over thousands of miles. Only a few decades ago, communication back home required expensive phone calls or the delay of letters. It certainly was not a matter of immediate face-to-face communication using a computer.

This lessens the impact of culture shock or homesickness. It also may be a way of escaping the painful reality that you are in another world and thus it can also inhibit adjustment to the new culture. Every student knows of another student who is up all night Skyping with people at home and yet he or she cannot communicate effectively with a roommate. In this situation, modern telecommunications is a way of avoiding the difficulty of interpersonal communication in a new social situation.

FLEX BEHAVIOR—A PROACTIVE RESPONSE TO CULTURE SHOCK

Flight, fight, and filter behaviors are much akin to neurotic defense mechanisms. They are primarily unconscious reactions that allow us to protect ourselves from a painful or ambiguous reality. They control us until we are consciously aware of what is causing our behavior and take steps to control our reactions. *Flex behavior* is mostly a matter of developing conscious ways of minimizing the severity and duration of the stress and developing our own unique ways of overcoming that stress and ultimately adapting to the local culture. These "coping strategies" allow sojourners to do something about culture shock—to face reality and to find various alternative ways of dealing with adjustment difficulties.

It is important to distinguish between *coping strategies* and *defense mechanisms*. Defense mechanisms are unconscious reactions to a stressful or painful reality. The situation controls the individual by causing the reactions.[16] These defenses help us avoid the painful reality through such unconscious neurotic processes as denial, distortion, withdrawal, and repression. They are normal and explicable, but nevertheless ineffective, ways of dealing with the situation and the resultant stress. We can easily recognize such other reactions as displacement of anger, going native, and various psychosomatic illnesses which can be controlled. Simply knowing that these are "symptoms" and not causes eases a great deal of the stress.

There is a thin line between coping strategies and the defensive reactions of fight, flight, or filter. It is often just a matter of time and degree. For example, Skyping or using social media to communicate with family and friends back home may temporarily relieve stress and allow you to catch your breath when overwhelmed with homesickness and a bombardment of new stimuli. In the short term, it is a very reasonable way of coping. If it continues over many months or becomes excessive it might make it too easy to avoid struggling with adapting overseas or communicating with local people. Thus, it becomes flight or filter behavior.

Coping strategies are usually conscious steps that we take to respond effectively to the situation. We begin to take control of our feelings and behavior. We cannot change another culture, and the goal of cross-cultural adaptation is not to avoid the primary source of stress (people in the host culture) but rather to increase our interaction with the local people. Thus, one of the primary ways to minimize defensive reactions, to provide greater self-control, and to maximize effective communication with those in another culture is to develop coping strategies.

A FEW COPING STRATEGIES

While each person must develop his or her own ways of coping, the following brief list of broad strategies may be applied by most sojourners:

1. Understand the dynamics of cross-cultural adaptation. A conscious understanding of the process and pattern of adaptation and the expectation that culture shock will occur eliminates a great deal of the pain caused by ambiguity, uncertainty, disorientation, and lack of predictability. This knowledge allows us to anticipate the stress and allows us to develop conscious positive coping strategies. For some who are overwhelmed by culture shock, it seems as if there is no end. It helps if we know that our reactions are part of the "normal" process of adjustment to another culture and most of us will overcome the stress and may even be better having gone through it.

Feeling "out of control" or helpless is an unconscious reaction. At its extreme, it is often accompanied by the belief that the situation is totally hopeless. The situation controls us unless we understand what is going on. Knowing the process of cross-cultural adjustment or adaptation is probably the best way of overcoming culture shock because we have a sense of control and can act instead of reacting.

The symptoms or reactions cannot be controlled unless there is a clear understanding that culture shock is not some mysterious disease. Moreover, most sojourners will realize that they have gone through this process before, such as their first day of school, summer camp, or boot camp during military training. These parallel experiences were overcome and some of the same coping strategies will work again. We can build upon the reservoir of experiences much as reverse culture shock or reentry/transition stress can be overcome by building upon the experience of culture shock.[17]

Understanding is the beginning step in overcoming a neurosis, but ultimately each individual must develop a sense of control over his or her reactions and must cope with a painful reality which cannot be changed.

2. Control the reactions. If someone is seriously physically injured, the first step is to stop the bleeding or restore breathing. Before you can treat the root causes of culture shock, it is necessary to control the symptoms. If one is paralyzed with frustration and anxiety and feels overwhelmed by stress, it is difficult to perceive alternative ways of behaving or coping. Thus, the first step is to develop first aid techniques which will allow for greater control of the reactions.

Develop your own unique ways of dealing with stress. One American spouse in Venezuela woke up in the middle of the night during her first few weeks in-country and found that she could return to sleep if she scrubbed her kitchen floor. This is a unique kind of flex behavior which is a bit neurotic but harmless and she probably had the cleanest kitchen floor in the community. Gradually, as the stress decreased she could sleep through the night.

If we are overtaken by anxiety, there are positive strategies we can use to cope with it such as getting plenty of rest, eating well, and exercise. There are also negative ways of reducing anxiety that may end up increasing physiological and psychological stress such as eating too much or drinking too much alcohol. People very often gain 10 pounds or more during their first year overseas because they use food as way of decreasing anxiety and occasionally a few alcoholic drinks lead to even more until the individual has a serious alcohol problem.

On the other hand, exercise is a great way to decrease stress. Furthermore, exercise could be combined with increased communication with others through such activities as dance groups or sports teams. As with any stressful situation, relaxing activities and minimizing the number of changes in a short period of time will give the sojourner a sense of control during this adjustment period.

3. Don't just stand there, do something. Communicate. Flex behavior means being more flexible by doing something about culture shock. For example, if the breakdown of communication is one of the primary causes of culture shock, we then realize that by increasing communication with others we are likely to make the situation better. Conversely, if we withdraw even further from others, we are likely to make the situation worse. One cannot change another culture and the goal of cross-cultural adaptation is not to avoid the source of stress (people in the host culture) but to increase interaction with local people which also is a good coping strategy.

When we ask Americans what event seemed to stop the downward spiral of culture shock, one on the most common responses is, "I found a friend." What this really means is,

"I restored interpersonal communication." While under stress we are distracted and therefore cannot be as efficient or effective studying or doing our job as we would be at home. Some then study even harder or work longer hours when perhaps a better coping strategy would be to join a friend for dinner or a cup of coffee, and engage in some conversation with another person. The quicker we can come out of the stress of culture shock, the better we become at accomplishing our tasks.

The lack of human interaction causes us to feel very lonely and long for conversation. This also makes us very vulnerable to attaching ourselves to anyone who communicates with us and yet this person may not be typical of people in the local culture. The need to relate may be so great that we start conversations with anyone who speaks our language. While it may be a good coping strategy to converse more, we also need to be mindful that those with which we can communicate the easiest might not be those with whom we would want to develop a relationship. On many American college campuses, international students are sometimes taken in by hucksters or religious proselytizers.

4. Let go of family and friends back home. Although most coping mechanisms are conscious, some are unconscious. With time, we also give up a temporary coping mechanism when it is no longer necessary. During the first few days or weeks overseas many sojourners write numerous, lengthy emails home or have hours of phone calls or Skype calls with loved ones. Often the conversations are a matter of venting about how difficult it is overseas but unconsciously we are actually compensating for our lack of interpersonal communication. Gradually, as we adjust to the local culture and make friends with local people, the length and frequency of the emails and phone conversations begin to decrease.

Chances are that our friends and family at home don't actually need to know about every activity or adventure we experience overseas, but for the sojourner this is important. It is compensatory behavior—if you can't communicate effectively with people overseas, you over-communicate with people back home. Gradually, as you make friends in the new culture, the emails and calls get shorter and people at home may grow concerned that something is wrong. Indeed, everything is all right because you don't need to communicate so extensively with people at home.

Letting go may take time and should not be a matter of cutting oneself off from loved ones. Abruptly cutting off communication with those at home may be a manifestation of "going native" (filter) and amounts to denying the reality that you are part of two cultures at the same time—your home culture and the overseas culture. You can never really escape your primary culture and you can never be a native in the new culture. There may always be some tension between these two worlds. With time you add a new synergistic cultural layer to your personality where the whole becomes much greater than simply the sum of the parts.

5. Transfer or modify cues. Some sojourners decide to leave behind all reminders of home and start off anew in another culture. However, from our understanding of what happens in the loss of familiar cultural cues, this will actually increase the stress of adjustment. Transferring potent reminders from one's home culture, such as favorite music or photos, may be an effective coping strategy to temporarily ease the pain of loss of cues until new potent ones are adopted.[18] Modifying things in the host environment so that they are somewhat similar to those in the home culture is another coping strategy that might ease the stress. One can make a hamburger of sorts out of almost any meat and with enough spices, American rice somewhat resembles the rice of the Middle East or Asia.

HELPING SOJOURNERS THROUGH THE ADJUSTMENT CYCLE

To help sojourners minimize the duration and intensity of the stress, we ought to begin by providing good pre-departure training that allows those going overseas to understand the process of adaptation and to anticipate the stress. It is tempting for cross-cultural orientation trainers to make suggestions as to what their trainees should do when they get overseas to overcome culture shock. In many cases, these suggestions are very good and there may be others overseas who can serve as mentors. However, if trainers and mentors are successful, trainees no longer need them because well-trained sojourners develop their own coping strategies.

When we are under enormous stress it may seem hopeless. However, if we have been told ahead of time about the U-Curve of adaptation and the dynamics of cross-cultural adaptation, we realize that it won't last forever and there are things we can do to make it better. We are unlikely to panic if we understand that this is a normal part of living overseas and it will end.

When going through culture shock, it helps to have someone to turn to who understands the process of cross-cultural adaptation and can empathize with the experience of the sojourner. Simply maintaining interpersonal communication with those going through culture shock is of enormous help because it allows sojourners to vent their feelings and mentors can assure them that this is a normal process of adjustment. It is a cycle that we all go through as we adapt to a new environment or life-changing situation.

In many respects, the stages in the adjustment cycle are similar to the emotional reactions or steps people go through when they are grieving. The Kübler-Ross model, commonly known as The Five Stages of Grief, was first introduced by Elisabeth Kübler-Ross in her 1969 book, *On Death and Dying*.[19] When someone we care for dies, we often engage in denial (flight), anger (fight), bargaining and depression (filter), and eventually acceptance (flex). These stages do not necessarily come in this order and all stages are not experienced by all those going through culture shock.

Letting go and saying good-bye to family and friends is psychologically beneficial to sojourners and those left at home. We know from studies of death and dying that those who have time to "say goodbye" to a loved one seem to go through the grief cycle much easier than when someone suddenly dies. It allows them to "let go" of the loved one much more easily. Among many American Indian tribes, there are rituals where family members "give away" personal belongings to the friends of someone who has died. These "giving away ceremonies" are psychologically very helpful in dealing with the loss. The same is true when leaving loved ones to go overseas. The going away party is a ritual that makes it easier to let go. And the sojourner might give away house plants, books, and other belongings. This should be incorporated into the pre-departure planning.

SUPPORT FROM HOME AND FROM HOSTS

Cross-cultural training and orientation should be offered to those who remain back home including administrators of programs, co-workers, family members, and even friends. If they understand and empathize with the sojourner's experiences, they can give better support during pre-departure and throughout the stay overseas. Furthermore, in some respects, although they don't leave home, they go through the same cycle of adjustment and grief as the sojourner.

The international human resource specialists of any organization should be well aware of the dynamics of cross-cultural adaptation. Not only are they responsible for preparing the sojourner and his or her family for travel and work overseas, they also provide ongoing support overseas. To do their job effectively requires them to not only understand culture shock and multicultural management, but also to be able to empathize with their overseas employees.

At universities, most staff involved in study abroad programs or managing the exchange of scholars must also be able to empathize with those going through cross-cultural adjustment stress. The study abroad office arranges pre-departure training and often organizes arrival orientation and mentoring for students overseas.

For those who are hosting sojourners it is also vital to provide this training. Host families for international students or *au pairs* and managers or supervisors in offices that hire or manage foreign employees or interns should understand the cycle of adaptation. In the university international student office, for those involved in the management of the exchange of students and scholars, and for teachers and administrators of English as a Second Language programs, this knowledge is crucial for them to do their jobs effectively.

We can best help those going through the trauma of culture shock by maintaining communication with them and showing unconditional positive regard for them—in effect, holding their hand as they learn their own ways of accepting and dealing with the reality of adapting to a new situation. Cutting off communication, except as a temporary escape from an overload of stimuli, is one of the least effective ways of dealing with culture shock and it is usually counterproductive—it makes the situation worse. The sojourner is frustrated, disoriented, and perhaps even angry which causes him or her to say many mean-spirited things about local people. Venting these feelings is not very pleasant for the listener, but with our unconditional, nonjudgmental, positive regard the sojourner feels safe. Of course, gradually the sojourner moves out of this phase and adjusts to the local culture.

The stress of cross-cultural adaptation is not devastating for most people and it may very well lead to enormous personal growth and self-awareness such as enhanced self-esteem and self-confidence. For the most part, the stress is moderate and part of a normal cycle of adaptation. During the downward trajectory of culture shock sojourners may not be as effective as they are at home because they are distracted and under stress, but most come out of it within a month or two and return to their usual emotional state. After they hit the bottom of the U-curve of adaptation, most bounce up again. We can speed up this process and minimize the severity of the reactions by having genuine empathy with the sojourner and with an understanding of the process of cross-cultural adaptation.

Some Danger Signs

There are at least two danger signs that indicate the cycle of adjustment has become pathological and sojourners are perhaps nose-diving rather than pulling out of the downward trajectory. In fact, professional intervention may be necessary. These danger signs are: (1) *extreme withdrawal from others and reality* and (2) *extreme paranoia.* It is really a matter of degree. In their milder forms, these reactions are fairly harmless.

Withdrawing into a co-national community and avoiding local nationals for a few days may be a good way to get your bearings overseas. Even withdrawing from all human interaction for a few days might be a fairly healthy way of dealing with an overload of painful stimuli and calming down in order to more rationally deal with the stress of adaptation. It might be a useful coping strategy of flex behavior. But this is not an unconscious retreat from reality—it is a deliberate strategic withdrawal. There is a clear difference. On the other hand, total self-imposed isolation from all human beings for days on end may be a sign of severe depression.

Sometimes distorting reality or withdrawing from reality to make it a bit more pleasant may be a little neurotic yet relatively harmless. Imagining for a few moments that you are in your home country or with friends and family from home may provide some comfort when you are overwhelmed with loneliness. Creating and living in a fantasy world to avoid an unpleasant reality is a clear sign of possible severe neurosis or even psychosis.

Being fearful of getting lost or becoming the victim of crime when overseas may be a reasonable yet somewhat paranoid way of reacting to a new and unfamiliar environment. When we are miserable and everyone else seems to be oblivious to our suffering, it is easy to imagine that their lack of empathy and care indicates that they like us to be unhappy. But when we believe that local people are intent upon hurting or even killing us, we may indeed be entering the realm of irrational fear or even extreme paranoia.

When these psychological reactions are accompanied by rapid weight loss, an inability to sleep, explosions of rage, or prolonged and deep sadness, it is best to seek out the help of a clinical psychologist or counselor. Many health care workers do not understand the dynamics of cross-cultural adaptation and may not realize that the underlying cause of the behavior is a severe case of culture shock.

The first step is to treat the severe symptoms which may require intensive counseling or even medication. Once the symptoms are controlled, then decisions must be made regarding the probability that adaptation will eventually take place. This may be a very acute but dramatic case of culture shock and intervention actually allows the sojourner to get through the adjustment cycle. Research on shell shock during World War II showed that many soldiers could return to their duties if they had the support and intervention of professional counselors and psychologists who understood the dynamics of battle fatigue.

In some cases, it serves no purpose to keep someone overseas who may be unable to adjust to a new culture. Experienced counselors who know about culture shock are usually able to decide what is best for the sojourner under these circumstances. The premature return home may be a great disappointment to the sojourner but it might also prevent a total psychological crash. Better to have a brown out than a black out.

REVERSE CULTURE SHOCK[20]

Good News—Bad News

Almost all students, business people, development workers, and others who have actually lived in a new culture and intensely interacted with host nationals have experienced some form of culture shock. The good news is that the vast majority handle this stress successfully, with some reliable evidence indicating that they grow from the experience. Most sojourners return home with new cross-cultural communicative and problem-solving skills, greater emotional and intellectually maturity, and a wider global perspective. Other benefits include increased self-confidence, self-awareness, creativity, and flexibility. Many who have lived overseas claim they were "transformed" by the experience and that they would not be who they are today had they not gone through the stress of cross-cultural adaptation. The reactions or "symptoms" of culture shock then were simply the "growing pains" we all go through as we move from one level of intellectual and emotional maturity to another.

It is certainly good news that those who go through culture shock have a profound understanding of the internal aspects of another culture. This could only be acquired experientially through interaction with local people. It would never happen by simply reading books or listening to lectures. The intensity of the personal experience may be more important than the length of time in the culture. There are some who quickly immerse themselves in the new culture and within a short period of time gain this awareness. Others may be in the culture for years but because their experiences are fairly superficial, they never really understand the host culture.

Another piece of good news is that, contrary to popular opinion, long-term sojourners seldom "lose" their native or primary culture while overseas. They instead find their culture by leaving it. The world-renowned Nigerian jazz artist Fela once said that he discovered what it meant to be an African when he left Africa.[21]

In a new culture, sojourners become more aware of what makes them different and consciously examine culturally embedded values, beliefs, and thought patterns. Through the collision of cultural icebergs, they raise to conscious awareness the internal aspects of their home culture including many hidden primary beliefs, values, and ways of thinking. They also return home with a deeper understanding of "self" and what is really important to them as individuals. There is an existential awareness that might not have come about without going through the pain of culture shock.

Now, the bad news. Upon returning home the sojourner passes through another adjustment period often termed "reverse culture shock" or "reentry-transition stress." Most returnees claim that this experience is even more severe and protracted than culture shock and that it sets in much more quickly. Furthermore, those who have adapted best to the life overseas tend to have the most difficulty reentering their home cultures.

A metaphor for this adjustment cycle is provided by the American space shuttle flights. In the early days, the launches were broadcast live around the world because there was great danger during the first few minutes. Extreme stress occurred as the shuttle left earth's atmosphere and *entered* outer space. Once in space, far less stress is exerted on the vehicle and television coverage was cut back. We saw astronauts brushing their teeth and engaging in their tasks. However, live coverage resumed again during *reentry* to earth's atmosphere because this was another very stressful period. In fact, the stress of returning to earth may be even greater than that of leaving it.

THE W-CURVE OF CROSS-CULTURAL ADAPTATION

As we have seen in the graphic of the "Pattern of Adjustment," culture shock can be depicted as a U-curve. But it is not simply a U-curve. When we add the return home, it becomes a less than perfect W-curve with the second half representing reverse culture shock. There are some significant differences in the adjustment patterns and some of the reactions as we readjust to our home culture.

During culture shock, not only do hosts overseas tend to welcome newcomers, they go out of their way to make them feel comfortable as they settle in. Most expect newcomers to make mistakes and be different. They intuitively understand that the sojourner will experience stress adapting to the new physical and social environment and will long for friends and family back home. This honeymoon could last for weeks or even months.

At home, the honeymoon period may last only a few days or a few hours, and often there is no honeymoon. Everyone expects the returnee to fit in quickly. They are much less tolerant of mistakes and have little empathy for the difficulties of reverse culture shock—such problems are not expected or accepted. People at home tend to reject bizarre behavior and have very little understanding of the dynamics of cross-cultural adaptation. They expect the returnee to be fully functional upon return or, as the saying goes, "to hit the ground running."

Again, with the onset of reentry stress, the so-called U-curve thus becomes a W-curve as part of a continuum of adjustment. If one leaves home again and enters another culture, in all likelihood the pattern will continue and culture shock will recur. As with the common cold, recovery does not provide immunity; one can suffer the experience many times. However, with experience, most people find that the severity and duration lessens each time as we develop a repertoire of coping strategies. Many of these same strategies are useful when dealing with reverse culture shock.

WHY IS REVERSE CULTURE SHOCK WORSE THAN CULTURE SHOCK?

Most sojourners who are preparing to return home anticipate little or no difficulty readapting to their native culture. Why should they? They are moving back to family and friends where they will speak their native language and eat food they grew up with. To their surprise, most will actually experience more stress during reentry than during their entry to the overseas culture. Those who adjusted best and were the most successful overseas very often experience the greatest amount of difficulty with reverse culture shock.

A host of factors help explain this phenomenon. The most significant is that few returnees anticipate reverse culture shock. When we expect a stressful event, we can cope with it much better. We rehearse our reactions, think through the course of adjustment, and consider alternative ways to deal with the stressful event. We are emotionally prepared for the worst that could happen. There is evidence that patients who are somewhat anxious about their upcoming surgery recuperate much more quickly and are administered less pain killing medication than those who are assured beforehand that there will be "no problems." Forewarned patients anticipate pain and complications and therefore can even physiologically tolerate the stress much better.

Most returnees are already expecting stress before they leave home. They know they will miss family and friends, and they are anxious about adjusting to new food, a different language, public transportation, and so forth. This is the reason we often try to reassure sojourners during pre-departure training that they can develop coping strategies. On the other hand, few sojourners worry about returning home and repatriation or reentry training often is a matter or encouraging returnees to worry a bit about the stress they may encounter.

Ironically, those who adjust best overseas and are the most successful often have the most severe reverse culture shock. They not only changed the most during their sojourn as they adapted to the overseas culture, they also have more confidence in their abilities to adapt and succeed and thus are the least likely to be anxious about returning home. For example, pre-adolescent children usually adjust very quickly and easily to a new culture, and therefore they tend to experience much greater reentry stress than their parents. A spouse who has learned to run a household overseas may have adapted much more than the employee and therefore could have more difficulties readapting to home.

This may not be true for seasoned sojourners who have gone through numerous bouts of entry and reentry stress. There is evidence that they develop good adaptation skills and coping strategies for dealing with culture shock and also for dealing with reverse culture shock. They learn to adjust well overseas and to re-adjust well upon returning home. They do not necessarily experience the greater difficulty returning home that first-time sojourner often go through.[22]

The Causes of Reverse Culture Shock

The causes of reverse culture shock are quite similar to those of culture shock: the clash of internal cultures including values and thought patterns, the loss of cues or reinforcers, a breakdown of interpersonal communications, and an identity crisis. There is another *collision of internal cultures* in that the values and ways of thinking that worked overseas may no longer be as useful at home and some may even be in conflict with home culture values and thought patterns. We adapted to another culture but it is not a matter of losing our native or primary culture. In fact, we usually return home much more aware of the internal aspects of our primary culture.

The ranking of home culture values may have changed during the sojourn. Some values that were highly rewarded at home might not be rewarded overseas and the reverse is also true. And there may be some kind of overlap of home and overseas values. The point is that although we don't lose our home cultural values, the rankings may change and we return home different inside than when we left.

A survey of over 1500 Nigerian undergraduate students was conducted between 1979 and 1981 as part of a reentry program conducted shortly before they returned home from two or three years of study in small colleges around the United States. They were asked to identify five values they thought were most important to a typical American, five values most important to a typical Nigerian, and their own five most important personal values.

Asking them to make these generalizations was indeed a challenge because these return-ing Nigerians were not "typical" themselves because they had studied in the U.S. They were certainly less than one percent of the population. Nearly one-fifth of all Africans are Nigerian and there are hundreds of different ethnic groups with over 250 different languages spoken within Nigeria's borders. Nigeria is as complex as the U.S., which has over 300 million people and vast regional and ethnic differences.

There was no intent to use this survey to conduct a scientific study of value change. Instead, it was simply a heuristic device to help these returnees consider how they may have changed internally because of their overseas experiences. Many of the so-called values were simply things that "are important" and we forced them to pick only five out of the list of 17 values. Although it was interesting to find out how and why they perceived American, Nigerian, and their personal values the way they did, it was not important if their observations were accurate or supported by any evidence. The underlying purpose of the exercise was to encourage them to anticipate how their personal values might conflict with typical Nigerian values upon their return home.

Most were aware of changes in their overt behaviors because of their stay in the U.S. but they were often quite unaware that they had perhaps changed internally and returned home with a different ranking of values than typical Nigerians. Indeed, there was an "overlap" of values. Of course, they may have arrived in the U.S. with a value structure which was already different than that of the average Nigerian. It was easy to identify such behavioral changes as language, dress, and even such nonverbal cues as social distance, gestures, eye contact, and so on. This exercise was invented to focus on internal cultural changes including values and thought patterns.

A frequent complaint among supervisors of returning Nigerians was that they were "Americanized" and therefore could not fit back into their home culture. For example, they were accused of no longer honoring their elders—a fairly common perception of typical American values and behavior. When asked what behaviors led to this observation, supervisors claimed that returnees would get a cup of coffee when an older person was talking and some smoked cigarettes in front of elders. They were perceived as disrespectful because at times they would publicly disagree with or criticize an older person. These rude behaviors were assumed to be a result of having lived in the U.S.

The findings presented on the next page are based on a sample of 374 respondents but the results are roughly the same as those of over 1500 students.[23] Only one student listed "honor your elders" among the top five values for an average American and yet it was rated by 95.2 percent of respondents as a typical Nigerian value. More significantly, only 42.6 percent listed it among their top five personal values. Religion was picked among the top five values for Americans by only 3.7 percent and yet it was selected among the top five values for Nigerians by 67.6 per cent. As a personal value, only 31.6 percent rated it among their top five[24]. This suggests that there could indeed be a clash of values upon their return home. On the other hand, there were certain values that were viewed as atypical of Nigerians and returnees such as punctuality.

When we concentrate our attention on internal culture, we are also considering ways of thinking and solving problems as well as our worldview, which also impacts such external behavior as rhetorical style. For example, journalists and students who have worked or studied in a high-context culture overseas may have changed their style of writing to be much more associative, relational, or deductive. Their writing might now include more background or context—materials that could be viewed as irrelevant or tangential in a low-context culture. But at home, the sojourner must return to a more direct and inductive way of thinking and communicating. Of course, the reverse may be true of those returning from a low-context culture to a high-context culture—they may need to again organize their thoughts and rhetorical style to be much more indirect and deductive.

It is not as much a matter of giving up values or ways of thinking that were acquired overseas as it is that one must be more flexible and able to easily move from one culture to another or somehow blend the two or more cultures. Just as we return home more bilingual, we also return home more bicultural.

As with culture shock, during reentry there is again a ***breakdown of interpersonal communication*** which causes great frustration and pain. Most returnees do not realize that this

DIRECTIONS: Place an "X" in the boxes indicating the 5 most important values in each column	IN THE UNITED STATES		IN NIGERIA		PERSONAL VALUES	
	Typical American values:		Typical values		For me I value:	
	#	%	#	%	#	%
Honesty	151	40.4	77	20.6	267	71.4
Work hard, be productive	297	79.4	66	17.6	240	64.2
Honor your elders	1	00.3	356	95.2	160	42.6
Patriotism	54	14.4	65	17.4	57	15.2
Freedom	286	76.5	43	11.5	129	34.5
Pursue happiness	59	15.8	70	18.7	66	17.6
Gain goods and wealth	80	21.4	151	40.4	28	7.5
Education	160	42.8	162	43.3	224	59.9
Religion	14	3.7	253	67.6	118	31.6
Know the right people	25	6.7	64	17.1	24	6.4
Help other people	31	8.3	187	50.0	121	32.4
Try new things	132	35.3	12	3.2	59	15.8
Obey the law	120	32.1	88	23.5	87	23.3
Know your heritage	5	1.3	190	50.8	36	9.6
Save time, be punctual	216	57.8	4	1.1	50	13.4
Stand up for what you think is right	142	38.0	27	7.2	125	33.4
Achieve individual success	76	20.3	70	18.7	65	17.4

374 Responses

breakdown is the cause of their distress because much of it has to do with a clash of values, conflicting social cues and especially nonverbal communication. Consequently, they are unaware of what provokes the reactions commonly labeled as "symptoms" of reverse culture shock.

An African sojourner is more conscious of verbal messages in the United States and less aware of nonverbal messages. In the U.S., his verbal abilities are highly rewarded and reinforced while his nonverbal subtlety only leads to confusion. Conversely, an American having spent time in Africa returns home adept at sending and receiving nonverbal messages yet perhaps less conscious of direct verbal messages. Which messages we pay attention to depends upon our culture and the meanings we give to nonverbal messages are almost completely specific to each culture and learned unconsciously.

While in the United States, the African sojourner tacitly learns to maintain an arm's length when talking and to offer a brisk handshake which is almost immediately released. Upon his return home, he is met by family and friends at the airport. His cousin rushes to shake his hand and continues greeting him without releasing his grip. Others crowd around him as they welcome him home. He tries to pull away from his cousin's grip and backs away from those who are talking to him. The returnee suddenly feels as if everyone is very pushy and intruding on his personal space.

His friends and family suddenly realize how he has changed. He no longer takes the time to greet people; he seems cold and standoffish. They consciously notice how he will not hold hands and how he steps back when they try to talk to him. The returnee may be quite oblivious to the nonverbal messages he is sending or why he feels uncomfortable.

Because of the value placed on harmony and politeness, negative feedback in Africa is often indirect and subtle. Briefly avoiding eye contact may be a subtle way of saying "no." And people often say "yes" when they really mean, "I hope I can fulfill your wishes," or "if possible." The returnee is now much more direct and gives unambiguous, verbal negative feedback along with a tendency to avoid saying "yes" unless it is a promise that can be met.

An American returning home from Africa may have picked up these subtleties. Overseas he was highly regarded for his graciousness and efforts to maintain good social relations. To American friends, he seems evasive and indecisive, while to him they appear downright rude.

Friends, food, and music that we enjoyed so much overseas will be missed when we return home and, as with culture shock, there is again a ***loss of cues or reinforcers***. We greeted people in new ways overseas, we gave gifts as locals do, and we learned the way in which people introduce themselves or start conversations. For students or business people who lived in the United States, there may have been a coffee shop that was a great hang-out. Everyone knew your name, the manager greeted you when you came in, and the waiter knew exactly how you wanted your coffee prepared. You could study or review your email there. Although there are wonderful coffee shops in your hometown and some are the same franchise as in the U.S., nevertheless you very much miss the Starbucks in San Francisco or the Cosi in Washington.

In the U.S., greetings are often abrupt. Sojourners from Africa, Latin America, and the Middle East learn that Americans are usually very rushed and thus it is perfectly polite to greet others with a smile and a quick "hi" or a simple, "How are you?" The response is usually to return the greeting with a smile and the word "fine." However, at home, people expect others to engage in more prolonged personal conversation, asking about your well-being and your family. A proper greeting means taking the time to converse including an almost ritualized series of questions about the other person's well-being, family, and health. If this exchange is interrupted, then it may begin all over again until both parties have successfully completed the greeting social action chain.[25]

The returnee may no longer be comfortable engaging in lengthy greetings but these are sincere questions and a polite response would require much more than the word "fine" or others might perceive the returnee as discourteous or even "Americanized." Of course, if the returnee "properly" greeted everyone, he would never get to work on time. On the other hand, perhaps punctuality is not quite as important as in the U.S. and certainly is no excuse for being rude or curt.

During reentry, most sojourners also go through an ***identity crisis***. Their anonymity overseas allowed them to experiment with new behaviors and to accept the practices which were sometimes odd and perhaps unacceptable at home. Because of the enormous intra-psychic growth that occurs overseas, the returnee sees the world differently, develops a repertoire of new problem-solving strategies, and arrives back home with a deeper understanding of his or her values.

As with any identity crisis, culture shock involves a kind of death/rebirth process. The ways of thinking and worldviews that were effective in one's home culture were ineffective overseas. The sojourner gave up some of the old ways to allow new ways to be acquired that were more adequate in the overseas culture. This is somewhat like an adolescent who gives up an immature or more childish way of dealing with the demands of life to grow into more mature behavior with the perceptions and responsibilities appropriate for a young adult. In many cultures, adolescence involves great emotional turmoil and confusion, similar to what takes place during culture shock. There are even puberty rituals that ceremonially celebrate the "death" of the child to allow the adult to be "born." The bar mitzvah for Jews and the confirmation ceremony for Christians are rituals that allow the boy or girl to become a man or woman in the community with a new set of roles and expectations appropriate for an adult.

When sojourners adapt to another culture, they are like the lobster that sheds its skin. Carrying this metaphor a bit further, when we return home we are fundamentally the same lobster we were when we left, but we have grown in ways we never would have had we not gone overseas. We literally are "transformed" intellectually and emotionally. We never really lose our home culture when we adapt to another culture. We just add another cultural layer and return home with a different identity than when we left—one which incorporates the roles and expectations of a person who has lived outside their home culture.

Upon returning home, sojourners must go through another death-rebirth cycle—giving up the identity that worked so well overseas to take on a new one at home. While no one can regress to the pre-departure "self," many will try to deny the impact of their overseas experience. Others may attempt to hang onto their identity acquired while overseas. These two forms of filter reactions won't work at home because they ultimately deny the reality of a changed identity brought about by culture shock. During re-entry, another identity must be developed and new "growing pains" will accompany its birth.

Friends and family members might not have experienced such dramatic growth when the sojourner was overseas. People at home grew older and there were marriages and deaths but the returnee has gone through a very different set of experiences that may be very difficult to share. This is similar to the student who returns from his or her first year away from home to go to college or the returning soldier or Peace Corps volunteer.

The increased global-mindedness of returnees is sometimes accompanied by increased intolerance of parochialism on the part of those at home. While returnees bring with them an enhanced awareness of their home culture, they have also seen it as an outsider while abroad and thus are often more critical of the inconsistencies inherent in any cultural system. In addition, many returnees have highly romanticized their own countries while overseas and are amazed to find that the streets are not as clean as they had imagined, the people are not as warm and friendly, and the efficiency is not as great as seemed the case while out of the country.

Disillusionment sets in quickly for those who glorified their homeland while overseas. This new awareness may come across to others as cynicism. It is probably more a matter of being more consciously and realistically aware of the internal aspects of our primary culture.

The overarching point of Edward Hall's book *Beyond Culture* is that we cannot escape the cultural prison we are born in until we adapt to another culture. Similar to the psychoanalytic experience, through the process of culture shock we raise to conscious awareness that which was unconsciously learned during childhood. We are somewhat intellectually and emotionally "fixated" during our formative years to pay attention to certain messages and ignore others and to give meaning to those messages. We become consciously aware of beliefs, worldviews, values, and ways of thinking that held us captive in our home culture. Consequently we can then go "beyond" them to develop a broader way of thinking and perceiving that may be an overlap of our home and the overseas culture.

Just as adults eventually free themselves from childhood trauma, the sojourner often returns home with a new identity with a clearer awareness of their own values and their home culture. The parochialism of the home society becomes more obvious than ever before to these sojourners, especially in contrast with the more global perspective acquired while away. Although they have discovered many hidden aspects of their own culture by going overseas and have broadened their view of the world, they have also returned more critical of their own society. There are many values, beliefs and behaviors in their home culture that they now realize they do not like but there are also some that they realize are very important to them.

To adapt overseas, sojourners had to be more tolerant of other points of view, change many of their attitudes, and open their minds to new ways of perceiving reality. This tolerance and open-mindedness is not always extended to those back home. While overseas, sojourners were able to accept friends who had religious and political views with which they totally disagreed and yet these same views are intolerable when they are expressed by friends at home.

THE "UNCLE CHARLIE SYNDROME"

The transitional phases of reverse culture shock are remarkably similar to culture shock when we consider causation, reactions, and even coping strategies. There are some differences. For example, the breakdown of communication has little to do with language or even nonverbal communication when we return home. Most returnees quickly adjust to their native language and they gradually re-learn the unwritten meanings of nonverbal messages at home. It is more a matter of what we are trying to communicate. The most significant difference is that most do not anticipate re-entry stress unless they are experienced sojourners who have gone through it before.

Harland Cleveland describes a common experience of returnees. In the words of an American who was interviewed by Cleveland and his colleagues:

> In my hometown, there are probably many people who still don't realize the world is round. I remember when we got home from Moscow people asked me how it was there, but before I could open my mouth; they would begin telling me how Uncle Charlie had broken his arm. They profess interest in things abroad, but they really aren't interested.[26]

Sojourners want to share their overseas experiences, yet trying to do so is a painfully difficult task. After a few days of listening to anecdotes, viewing photos, and receiving gifts, most friends and family members lose interest. Very often the most meaningful experiences really cannot be communicated. These messages have little meaning to those who have never actually lived overseas. It is somewhat like trying to fully share the wonder of a sunset with a blind person.

While Uncle Charlie's broken arm may seem insignificant to the returnee, it was probably a traumatic event for the family. The returnee's lack of interest in Uncle Charlie's broken arm may be very unsettling to those back home.

UNREALISTIC EXPECTATIONS AND NEW ASCRIBED ROLES AND STATUS

A business person or faculty member might become accustomed to the status of "honored guest" overseas. In the afternoon, a server comes around at "tea time" with a cart and asks, "What type of tea or biscuit would you like?" Great care is taken to be sure the type of tea cup is appropriate. When this American returns home, he may find it difficult to even acquire an office or desk. No one brings him tea and, in fact, he gets his own coffee in a Styrofoam cup from the cafeteria.

Many students coming to the United States experience decreased status. Because they are college students, they are viewed as among the elite of their society and yet in the United States their ranking in the society is much lower. They are not special, many professors cannot even pronounce their names, and fellow students have never heard of their home country.

When these students graduate and return home, they may have new roles and even greater status than before they ventured to the United States. Expectations may be quite unrealistic. If they came from poorer countries, they sometimes face envy and resentment from those who did not have the opportunity to travel abroad. Often, the image of America held by those at home is based upon an assumption that everyone there has great wealth, and it may be anticipated that returnees will carry back expensive gifts for all.

These students may have written glowing letters home describing their experiences. Sometimes they failed to describe their financial struggles, thereby reinforcing the perception that they had ample funds. Perceived to be bringing home the "golden fleece," these students may be faced with a host of new obligations—paying school fees for younger siblings, living in a style that becomes a college graduate, providing loans to older family members, and so forth. They cannot hope to fill these new and unexpected roles or to match the new identity ascribed to them by friends and family.

Returnees are often expected to be agents for the so-called "transfer of technology." In many cases, their company or government sent them specifically to gain knowledge and skills that would enhance their organization or national development. Reverse culture shock, however, can interfere with this transfer and sometimes prevent it from occurring. According to Nancy Adler, 20% of business people want to quit their jobs during their first year of returning home.[27] Many Peace Corps volunteers claim that they devoted a great deal of their first year back in the U.S. trying to find another opportunity to go overseas. This is a tremendous potential loss of knowledge and skills acquired overseas.

Long-term sojourners often face a barrier of time separating them from family and friends. To get on with life, some loved ones left at home may go through a cycle of grief for the departed sojourner. This phenomenon is sometimes referred to as "anticipatory grief"—loved ones unconsciously prepare for the possibility that the sojourner may not return or their relationship might end. We see this especially with soldiers whose wives or husbands remain at home and experience the anger and depression that often characterize grief. They psychologically "bury" the sojourner. Upon the sojourner's return, it is as if a ghost has appeared. Intimate relationships cannot simply continue from where they were at departure. They must be evaluated and developed to grow again, taking into account the change that has occurred because of the sojourn.

Reactions or "Symptoms" of Reverse Culture Shock

Most returnees take for granted their ability to effectively communicate with friends and family. The breakdown of communication causes frustration and pain, which, in turn, lead to the physical and psychological reactions associated with stress. Because this stress is not expected, reactions are usually much more severe than those of entry culture shock.

The reactions to reverse culture shock are very similar to those of culture shock. This is the reason for reviewing what people have experienced overseas during any kind of reentry or repatriation training. It not only helps them to realize that they have gone through this stress before and developed coping strategies that may again be useful when they return home, but it also helps them to recognize the "symptoms" as simply a part of the transition to the home culture.

Again, a sense of being *out of control* is very common. Reactions to the situation begin to control returnees and, being unaware of the cause of these reactions, they may not consider alternative ways to cope with the unanticipated breakdown of communication.

Many returnees engage in *flight* behavior. They may withdraw from others, fantasize about returning overseas, or sleep a great deal. Gregarious sojourners may find themselves avoiding others at home. Returnees may suspect that they acquired some illness overseas accounting for excessive sleeping. The returnee is often perplexed by these subconscious reactions to the breakdown of communication.

Returnees to high-context cultures often find this period especially difficult because they cannot flee or avoid others. While there is a great respect for privacy in the United States, this attitude is rare in cultures that emphasize kinship and friendship over the individual. Americans might not find it strange for someone to avoid others for a few days. In many cultures of Africa, Latin America, and Asia, to do so is almost impossible and would be viewed as bizarre behavior.

Flight is usually untenable for returnees. They cannot escape others, sleep away their days, or go back overseas again. They remain trapped in a painful situation that appears hopeless and perhaps endless. At this point, *fight* behavior often develops. While it is perfectly normal to be angry and frustrated under the circumstances, many returnees are confused by their own aggressive feelings which can be very overwhelming. Some even feel guilty, especially returnees to the United States, where anger is often equated with irrationality.

Anger is many times displaced onto those who are lower in the social hierarchy or loved ones who are simply convenient scapegoats. For no apparent reason, a minor disagreement with a taxi driver becomes an emotional blowup or a small marital spat explodes into rage. In extreme cases, this pent up anger can be self-destructive if it is internalized and leads to depression, or destructive to others if it leads to these uncontrollable outbursts of aggression.

Between 2011 and 2013, suicide and spouse abuse rose dramatically among soldiers returning home from Iraq and Afghanistan. The percentage of these kinds of Post-Traumatic Stress Disorder (PTSD) is the highest it has been of any war period. One explanation is that soldiers have experienced a type of war where there are no geographical fronts and it is not clear what "victory" means. Most Americans at home are fairly removed from the reality of the war. Since 9/11, there have been less than 1% of all Americans that have served in the military.

The stress of going through the trauma of battle and returning home to those who have not shared this reality may also be exacerbated by the quick return home. During previous wars such as World War II, the Korean-American War, and the Vietnam War, soldiers often had days or weeks to gradually think through their experiences and anticipate the reactions back home. The return journey often required stops in other countries. Today, soldiers are in a war zone and often return directly to the United States and may be in their home country within 24 or 48 hours. The nature of the warfare and the speedy re-entry may cause them to internalize their frustration and anger until it explodes uncontrollably in self-destructive ways.

Filter reactions to reentry stress manifest themselves in at least three different ways. First, some may simply behave as if they have never been abroad, much like a soldier who refuses to accept the reality of battlefield experience once at home. Such a person denies the impact of the experience and refuses to even try discussing it with others.

The second reaction is the opposite extreme—those who never actually return home, or they deny they are at home. The Nigerian returnee who studied in London wears tweed suits, smokes a pipe, and drinks tea every afternoon and scotch in the evening. He speaks in an affected or exaggerated British accent and drones on constantly about how wonderful everything was in London and how terrible everything is in Lagos. Of course, he forgets the bad times he had while overseas and ignores the many positive aspects of his homeland.

The third reaction is an interesting modification of these distortions and denials and is illustrated by a group of young men in The Gambia who are referred to as the "Been-Tos." They gather nightly in a small bar and unconsciously exclude those who have never sojourned overseas. Conversation is almost entirely about where they have *been to*—some have been to London, others to New York, and so on. They constantly relive their overseas adventures, much like many Peace Corps volunteers who have formed their own "Been-to" cliques in the United States.

A Few Reentry Coping Strategies

During any kind of reentry or repatriation training, time ought to be devoted to reminding returnees that they not only survived culture shock, but returned home with a new set of coping strategies and a greater and more profound awareness of the overseas culture and their home culture. They now know more about themselves, and they have grown in terms of self-esteem, flexibility, problem-solving abilities, and so on.

This debriefing also leads to a clear understanding that cross-cultural adaptation is an ongoing process and reverse culture shock is just the next step. Many of the coping skills or *flex* behaviors that were developed overseas when going through culture shock are equally useful when dealing with reverse culture shock.

1. Anticipate reverse culture shock. Nearly all returnees experience reverse culture shock and report that it was more stressful than culture shock. The most effective way to minimize the severity and duration of reverse culture shock is to anticipate its occurrence. If returnees are aware of the pattern of cross-cultural adjustment, including the reentry phase, they can fairly easily recognize symptoms and develop specific coping strategies.

Re-entry programs are very difficult to organize as a pre-return event or even post-arrival. Most sojourners simply don't see the need for such programs because they are returning to family and friends, food they grew up eating, and using their primary language. At the very least, sojourners can be advised of the stress of re-entry, the process of re-adaptation, and strategies they might use to minimize its duration or severity. This information can be given over the Internet. As with any cross-cultural training, ideally there should be sessions during which they can actually experience what they might encounter at home and these could be offered by the sponsoring institutions and include suggestions and shared experiences of those who have previously returned home.

With pre-departure programs, the goal is to assure everyone that they can cope with culture shock and to allay some of their anxiety. With reentry programs, the goal is to make them more aware of the bumps they are likely to encounter and, in some cases, to increase their anxiety a bit.

You are not the same as when you left home. Your behavior and communication patterns have changed as well as your hierarchy of values and ways of solving problems. Therefore, anticipate where conflict is likely to occur with traditional home behavior, communication, and values.

2. Take time to decompress. When the American Embassy hostages were first released from captivity in Iran in 1981, they were taken to Germany for a few days. The Department of State explained that their brief stay there was not simply for the purposes of debriefing and medical examination, but also for "decompression." This amounted to allowing time for the former hostages to consider how the United States had changed during their captivity. They were encouraged to anticipate re-entry difficulties. In light of the very good adjustment the hostages made after their return to the United States, this stay seems to have served its purpose.

On the other hand, the Department of State chose not to send its employees through a decompression program a decade later when Embassy Kuwait was put under siege during the Gulf War. Eight embassy employees were held hostage for nearly four months in late 1990, and were put on a plane back to the United States as soon as they were out of captivity. Barbara Bodine, one of the captives, wrote that "someone somewhere decided to bring the Embassy Kuwait hostages straight back to the United States. There was . . . no transition out of the world to which we had adapted . . . There was no time or place for a transition from the community that had become our world back to our families, our friend, and our jobs . . . Whatever the reasons, the decision was wrong."[28]

For those who have lived overseas for many years, it is important to realize that your friends and family back home moved on with their lives in your absence. Some are now married and some have grown old or died. Old friends have drifted away and everyone is more concerned with local and personal issues rather than your sojourn. The overall social and physical environment is different than when you left. Buildings have been torn now and new ones put up, the political climate and economy may be quite different than when you left. You may no longer have a job or you now have a new supervisor. Anticipating all of these changes back home is part of decompression.

Re-entry programs are mostly decompression sessions—giving time for people to think through what they have experienced, to consider the strategies they used, and then to anticipate reverse culture shock. Most returnees do not have the opportunity to decompress. They usually must begin functioning in their society immediately upon arrival. Perhaps it would be better if the sojourner could return only via boat or train instead of by airplane, allowing time to think through the process of re-entry. Again, the quick return of American soldiers from Iraq and Afghanistan might not have allowed them the time to go through decompression may have contributed to their relatively high rate of suicide and spousal abuse.

3. Manage stress and control reactions. Use coping strategies you developed overseas. While overseas, most sojourners develop ways of coping with the physical and psychological stress of adaptation through various so-called "stress management" techniques such as exercising, maintaining a healthy diet, and developing daily routines that allow for some escape from the bombardment of stimuli and demands placed on them. These same techniques can be used to cope with the stress of re-entry. Such basic strategies can be especially important because returnees are often quickly immersed in their social and work milieu before they have a chance to "catch their breath."

Culture shock and reverse culture shock are part of a normal adjustment cycle for those who adapt to another culture. Most people return home more self-confident, flexible, creative, and with a widened worldview. For the most part, this adjustment cycle involves reactions that are relatively mild and lead to an expanded sense of identity and self caused by the process of entry and re-entry. We should not try to avoid this stress but rather manage the stress and at the same time minimize its severity and duration.

4. Let go of overseas friendships and rebuild relationships at home.

Take time to say good-bye. Attend all the going-away parties and allow friends to accompany you to the airport. Abruptly ending relationships and leaving a social and physical environment is much more stressful than slowly letting go.

The rituals of "letting go" are important psychologically. The farewell parties are great ways to both reaffirm friendships and at the same time gradually acknowledge that although these relationships will not end, there will be a separation. Those who depart abruptly without taking the time for saying goodbye often find it more difficult to readjust at home. There are accounts of people who were suddenly evacuated for health reasons or perhaps some kind of civil disturbance in the overseas country. In some cases they suffered severe reactions during the re-entry phase such as emotional breakdowns, divorce, and inability to fit back into the community or work and so on.

To cope with the breakdown of communication overseas, sojourners often unconsciously compensate by over-communicating with friends and family back home via letter, phone, email, Skype, social media, and so forth. As overseas friendships developed, the emails and conversations back home grew shorter because the need to communicate intimately was satisfied in the host culture.

Maintaining contact with friends overseas is a very good way to cope with the breakdown of communication during reverse culture shock. Of course, the ultimate goal is to develop good relationships and intimate communication with friends and family rather than to rely on compensatory communication. Gradually, communications overseas will decrease as communication at home increases.

There is no need to totally let go of friends overseas. In fact, many sojourners join clubs or groups of nationals from the overseas culture to build friendships with nationals from the overseas culture, to remind them of the adventures they had, and to continue to improve their language skills. However, if these groups become a way of avoiding reentry and the struggle of communicating with people at home, then they are forms of *filter* reactions rather than *flex* behavior.

Communication with co-nationals who were foreigners in the overseas culture may also be an important way of coping during this phase. Most sojourners discover that other returnees are going through the same process of reentry and can empathize with them. With modern communications and social media, they become a mutual emotional support group. Some of these friendships will last a lifetime.

5. Communicate with others who have gone through reverse culture shock. Find mentors who have successfully readapted. They can suggest ways of overcoming reverse culture shock and they understand how you feel and can empathize with you. While these returnees can be a good support group, be careful that they not become your only friends. Avoid the exclusivity of "Been-to" cliques.

Those who have never been overseas may soon tire of hearing about your adventures. Fellow returnees often want to hear about your overseas exploits and insights, with an interest born from their own multicultural, international experiences. They may also serve as mentors for newly returned sojourners, and can assure these returnees that their reactions are normal and only transitional. Returnees may feel that their adjustment difficulties are the result of personal inadequacies. It is good news indeed to learn that almost all returnees share these difficulties and manage to complete the cycle of adjustment successfully.

6. Transfer cues from overseas and modify cues at home. Bring some of the overseas culture home with you. Many sojourners consciously decide which cues they want to take home—clothing, recipes, a musical instrument. Others transfer cues without knowing it and only realize a cue's real value in easing re-entry transition stress when it is lost. Some returnees would rather have their cell phone or smart phone stolen than the cheap tribal mask they have hanging on their living room wall because the mask is not simply a souvenir. It's a transferred cue—an important reminder of their overseas adventures and friends.

Returnees can't bring people home from overseas, but they can join together in clubs or social events with others who have lived in the overseas culture or with nationals from that culture. The social interactions to which they were accustomed overseas can take place at home. Again, it is important to avoid simply joining these groups to avoid re-entry but they can serve as a modified version of the overseas culture.

Other coping strategies that involve the transfer of cues might include subscribing to publications from the overseas culture, dining at restaurants that feature the host culture food, or reading newspapers or newscasts on the internet from the host country.

Returnees can also modify cues in their home culture, making them similar to overseas cues. With some creativity one can add spices to an American dish to make it similar to traditional Asian food or one could wear a mix of home and host culture clothing.

CROSS-CULTURAL EDUCATION AND TRAINING

Gathering information and knowledge about the culture we are entering reduces our anxiety and gives us confidence that we will not make a major *faux pas* shortly after arrival in a new culture. Some scholars would argue that uncertainty reduction is essential for good adaptation and we can easily measure knowledge acquired in educational programs that provide this kind of culture specific information with a pre- and post-test of information learned. This is what many would call *cultural competence*. This kind of education could be given before departure and it might include face-to-face instruction, modern distance learning, or even various games and simulations that have been developed specially by the U.S. military.

Ideally, we would like sojourners to develop *intercultural competence* which requires both education and training—the acquisition of knowledge of other cultures *and* cross-cultural communicative and analytic *skills*. Preparing sojourners for living overseas is more than just a matter of culture-specific or area studies education to increase cultural awareness, intelligence, or competency. If we want to diminish cross-cultural adjustment stress and increase cross-cultural effectiveness or intercultural competency, it is also necessary to acquire cross-cultural communication, analytic, and interpretative skills. This is often done with well-designed and implemented training programs that include experiential exercises.

Until very recently, cross-cultural preparation was termed *training* because it implied the acquisition of skills and not just knowledge. However, some consider *education* to be more sophisticated and intellectual than training. In their minds education means imparting knowledge whereas skills are abilities—such as repairing an auto or fixing a computer. It would be ideal to have an auto mechanic who is also an engineer. Certainly, when it comes to actual human interaction, we need knowledge and skills. This would be true for a counselor, negotiator, business executive, or someone working in a new culture.

The primary reason for cross-cultural and intercultural education and training is to help sojourners to become more effective overseas and to minimize the severity and duration of cross-cultural adjustment stress. It also reduces failure and the premature return of sojourners.[29] In many international organizations it is now expected by those preparing to go overseas and is routinely offered by the international human resources division of a company or organization, the study abroad office of a university, or as part of military training.

A failed overseas assignment and premature return can be disastrous not only for the employee and his or her organization, but also for the entire family. A vital, highly-skilled and enthusiastic employee who is unsuccessful overseas may return home discouraged and burnt out. The damage to the employee and his or her family might have been prevented with good cross-cultural education and training.

These programs might also minimize critical incidents overseas such as when the sojourner's behavior is so offensive that it jeopardizes negotiations or operations in another country. For example, in the late 1970s two pilots from an American aviation company in Iran were intoxicated and rode their motorcycles through a mosque in Isfahan. This incident impacted the company and all co-nationals. Within a year, the company was asked to leave Iran.[30] One could say that this is simply a matter of common sense but sense is often uncommon when we are outside of our own culture.

The quality of the training is vitally important. Good training increases intercultural competency and may prevent a failed overseas assignment. On the other hand, poor training may be worse than no training at all if it perpetuates stereotypes or gives a false sense of confidence in one's intercultural abilities. The training must include accurate and useful information as well as impart cross-cultural communication skills. Simply knowing the history, economics or politics of a new country is not very useful if one cannot communicate effectively with a local national or lacks the ability to analyze and interpret what is going on in a cross-cultural negotiation or conflict.

TYPES OF PROGRAMS

Cross-cultural education and training should be offered before, during, and after the journey because our informational and skills needs change at different phases of the sojourn. A *pre-departure briefing or orientation program* prepares us and helps us anticipate cross-cultural adjustment difficulties. It may decrease the impact of culture shock. If we know about the country and people we are working with overseas and if we can communicate effectively with local nationals, we have greater confidence in our success.

This type of program is often provided to give sojourners some basic information about the new culture before they leave home. The briefing may reduce uncertainty and give them confidence that they will not make a major mistake, thereby decreasing their anxiety. More importantly, the briefing may paint a realistic picture of people in the new culture, and thus decrease stereotypes and falsely idealistic expectations. By humanizing people in the new culture, there may be less of a tendency to be prejudicial, especially during the stressful period of entry. And the fewer illusions perpetuated by this briefing, the less the disillusionment sojourners may face when they enter the new culture.

Although companies and organizations often provide pre-departure cross-cultural training, few sojourners actually take advantage of the programs. In a nationwide survey conducted by the Employee Relocation Council in 2000, 72 percent of expatriates considered international assignments essential to their careers. Eighty percent of organizations that were surveyed offered at least some type of cross-cultural preparation to employees departing for overseas assignments. According to researcher Tsila Zalcman,

> Even though these cross-cultural programs are pervasive, their utilization by the expatriate population tends to be very low. Managers estimate that, on average, 47 percent of the expatriates take advantage of cross-cultural programs. However, Dynamic Systems Design (DSD) data, based on expatriates' responses, reveal a much lower participation of only 18 percent. When DSD inquired about the low participation in cross-cultural programs, the three most typical reasons given by expatriates were: 1) "I found out about these programs too late" 2) "I had no time to participate before I left for the assignment" and 3) "My manager was not supportive of my participation in the program."[31]

It is tempting to give sojourners a simple list of dos and don'ts and this may be all they really want. Oversimplified descriptions of the destination culture can produce overconfidence and unrealistic expectation. They can end up being stereotypes that are ultimately very harmful.

When faced with a genuine conflict in the new culture, the sojourner might mentally refer to the list. If the answer isn't there, total panic may set in.

Although those going overseas need some culture-specific information, a broader framework that emphasizes internal culture, the process of cross-cultural adaptation and communication, and realistic cultural empathy is probably even more important. To provide a way of contrasting and comparing cultures, it is also essential to help people better understand their home culture and especially basic values, beliefs, thought patterns, and worldviews. Most will forget the destination culture-specific list of behaviors and customs, and they can easily acquire this culture-specific information more accurately after they arrive in country.

If time permits, some basic language training ought to be provided in pre-departure programs—even if it's simply polite greetings and basic questions that are important for public travel, food, security, and so on. Not only will this make everyone a bit more secure, local nationals are likely to welcome the consideration sojourners make to say, "thank you," "good morning," and other such pleasantries.

In-country cross-cultural education and training programs provide ongoing support as we interact with local nationals, improve our language skills and settle into the local environment. Our health, security, and educational needs can be met with good in-country support services and a better understanding of local people. The employee learns how to work with a culturally different workforce and children adjust to new schools and friends. Often some sort of foreign or co-national spouse support group exists to help in the transition.

Re-entry education and training programs may decrease the stress of returning home for both the employee and family. Often reentry/transition stress or reverse culture shock is even greater than culture shock. Many returnees long to return overseas and believe that they are more ineffective at home than they were overseas. Children who grew up overseas during their formative years may not fit back into the culture of their parents. They weren't really totally enculturated to the overseas culture and yet they aren't completely enculturated to their parents' culture. They are third-culture kids (TCKs)—a part of and apart from both cultures.

Parents returning home go through reverse culture shock. For these children raised overseas, the culture of their parents was not the culture in which their personalities were formed. It may not be their primary culture. They are entering their passport culture for the first time and therefore go through entry stress or culture shock. An extreme example of this might be immigrant children who grew up overseas and then return home to the culture of their parents. It is not their home culture.

While most sponsored programs for studying or working abroad include orientation to prepare sojourners for the difficulties of culture shock, few include orientation for reentry. In fact, both sojourners and their sponsors often assume that the journey ends when one arrives home. In truth, the psychological sojourn does not end until one has successfully overcome reverse culture shock. Perhaps greater attention should be given to reentry transition orientation. If not, the stress of this passage may actually defeat the purpose of the sojourn and turn a potentially maturing experience into needlessly prolonged stress and pain.

There are many other types of educational and training programs that could be provided— arrival orientation, process evaluation and briefing during the sojourn, programs for children and spouses, cross-cultural management or negotiation, summative evaluation briefing upon return home, and so on. While these programs may have different purposes that require different approaches and methodologies, they often overlap and include similar training techniques. A briefing may be more didactic and provide cultural information while an orientation may be more interactive and emphasize the development of skills.

The timing of each type of training may be important. As illustrated in the figure below, six months before departure many sojourners are interested in the process of entering and adapting to new cultures and enhancing their communication with local people. They have *interaction and cross-cultural informational needs*. On the other hand, just before they leave or when they first arrive in country, their needs change. They are more concerned with basic *survival informational needs* such as how to use public transportation, the cost of living, visa requirements, adjusting to the food and weather, and security. If we are conducting an entry orientation program when people arrive in country, it is important to realize that their most important informational needs must first be met. More basic survival needs must be addressed before providing for social, cross-cultural, or interactive needs.[32] In fact, although it is important to mention cross-cultural interaction and adjustment in an arrival program, it would probably be even more valuable a month or two after they have arrived. At this time they can share their experiences with others.

In the past decade, many international companies and organizations have increased short-term overseas assignments and decreased the practice of relocating entire families for long terms. Although this cuts relocation costs, ironically it might not actually save money and may diminish the effectiveness of operations overseas. Because there is so little time to adjust to a new culture for employees who are in-country for only a few weeks, they must be fully functional and effective within a matter of days. Pre-departure cross-cultural preparation and training may be even more vital than for those who are moving abroad for more than a year. Furthermore, in some high-context cultures, many deals might

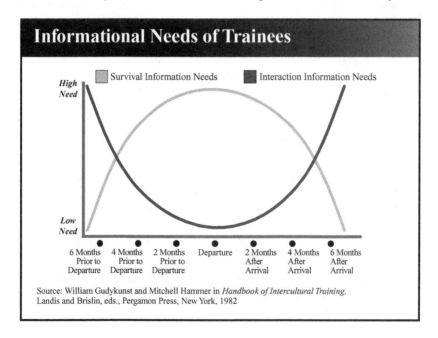

Informational Needs of Trainees

Source: William Gudykunst and Mitchell Hammer in *Handbook of Intercultural Training,* Landis and Brislin, eds., Pergamon Press, New York, 1982

not be settled by short-term sojourners because of the longer time necessary to establish trust and rapport.

A WORD ABOUT SAFETY AND SECURITY OVERSEAS

Relocation orientation programs often include some kind of briefing on safety, health, and security overseas. The ability to communicate across cultures is especially important in a crisis situation or emergency involving safety or health. However, shortly before departure or after arrival, these are basic "survival information needs" that must be discussed before "interaction needs" can be fully addressed.

Most universities, organizations, and companies involved in international work or study abroad provide information on safety and security overseas. During pre-departure programs, sojourners are usually informed of safety, health, and security issues for each country. They are given contact information in case of an emergency, told to update their health insurance policies to be certain they are fully covered for any health problems they might encounter, and alerted to any special safety measures they ought to take while overseas.

For those coming into the U.S. these pre-departure briefings are also increasingly more common and they are a basic part of entry orientation programs. They are often country- or region-specific and geared to the sojourner's particular role as a student, business person, government official, and so on. Study abroad orientation for departing or arriving students is best provided by those professionals who have had years of experience dealing with students whose major concerns may be mostly those regarding health and safety. On the other hand, a business executive might also want to be briefed on security issues and family issues such as providing safe transportation for his or her children to school while overseas, crime, and safety on the street or highway.

Much of the specific information that sojourners need is also available on the internet and most universities and companies have a website for accessing this information. The Department of State routinely posts information on its website regarding safety, health, or security in almost every country and provides workshops on security and safety overseas for those involved in international education and exchange of students and scholars as well as private sector organizations operating overseas. There are also many books and organizations that are devoted to these concerns.[33]

Embassies throughout the world provide support to their nationals who may be dealing with such crises as a serious health problem, safety during a natural disaster, or support if one becomes a victim of crime or violence. Sometimes this means providing emergency financial support or immediate transportation back home. Over 85% of the evacuations back to the U.S. are a result of a medical problem, and the most common injuries are a result of automobile accidents.[34]

SELECTION

Selection of people for overseas assignments is perhaps as important as any kind of training. Care must be taken to carefully select those who are most likely to succeed. Change is stressful for everyone but especially for those who have experienced too many change events in a short period of time. Even when the change events are positive we find that too much within a short window of time can produce a weakened immune system and increased susceptibility to colds or other illnesses.[35] If the changes are mostly negative, people also experience such psychological reactions as depression, insomnia, eating disorders, and so on. Researchers have found that if we can space out change events, we can better cope with them both physiologically and psychologically. It is not a good idea to graduate from college, get married, and move overseas in a two- or three-day period.

Although it is impossible to predict the success of sojourners based upon their personalities there is some evidence that clusters of certain personality traits seem to relate to an inability to adjust well in a new cultural environment.[36] For example, if we consider Geert Hofstede's five dimensions[37] as roughly akin to personality traits, those with a ***high intolerance to ambiguity*** or ***high uncertainty avoidance*** often have difficulty dealing with new or novel experiences such as those we encounter when moving into a new cultural environment. People with a high intolerance for ambiguity tend to be very well organized and they are good at scheduling and planning for the future. Punctuality is important to them and time is viewed as quantitative and linear, allowing them to get things done efficiently. They are highly task-oriented and don't allow themselves to get distracted easily. They clearly have low-context and "to do" characteristics such as being monochronic and having future-time orientation.

In many high-context or "to be" cultures relationships are more important than adhering to rigid schedules. Time is qualitative or nonlinear—it "stretches" depending upon the situation or context. Lunch might take a little longer than usual when an old friend comes to visit and it is certainly qualitatively different than time sitting behind the desk. Re-affirming an old friendship over a leisurely lunch together may be more valuable than returning to the office in a timely manner. What's happening now—present time—or even the past is more important than what might happen in the future. These people are also fairly polychronic and can often do many things at the same time. The old saying, "a bird in the hand is worth two in the bush" would be their slogan.

People with high uncertainty avoidance expect direct responses to their questions, especially those that require only a clear "yes" or "no" answer. In many high-context or "to be" cultures, people try to avoid unpleasant interchanges and are reluctant to say "no," especially to friends. A Mexican friend who cannot come to dinner might respond to an invitation with the phrase *"Ojalá que sí"* which is comparable to the Arabic response, *"insha'Allah."* Both could be translated as "God willing," but they really are indirect ways of saying, "no, I can't come." A Japanese friend might respond by simply saying, "It is difficult" or by sucking air through his or her teeth. These are all polite or nice ways to say, "no." Americans often find these answers to be circuitous or even deceptive. They would simply say "no, I'm sorry I can't come." This may be too direct for some Mexican, Arab, or Japanese friends because it disrupts the social harmony and often comes across as rude and abrasive. To add to the ambiguity, many high-context people often say "yes" when they mean they hope that they will be able to do something, but they're not certain.

People who are *overly task-oriented with a high need for individual achievement*[38] also often have difficulty in adjusting to a new cultural environment. Their primary source of self-esteem comes from being successful in the workplace and they are motivated to be productive because of their individual accomplishments. They might sacrifice friendships and relationships because they are driven to finish their tasks.

In cultures where human relations are vitally important, it would be difficult to build trust. When most of one's time is spent in the workplace, there is little opportunity to develop interpersonal relationships. Local people might unconsciously suspect that this type of person would violate the intimacy and confidence of a friendship just to "get ahead" in the workplace. Until trust is developed, they would keep this person at an "arm's length" providing the minimal amount of support.

These two personality traits might be considered positive and an asset in a culture or organization that is extremely low-context, monochronic, and highly individualistic. In the U.S., employers are often seeking out those who are well-organized, punctual, good at planning and scheduling, punctual, and driven to achieve as individuals. They definitely earn their salary if their productivity is measured in time devoted to getting their job done. On the other hand, in many high-context, polychronic, and collectivistic organizations or cultures these personality traits are often deemed negative. Low-context people who successfully work in a high-context culture ultimately end up being somewhat bicultural. They live in two worlds—the home office and the overseas environment.

Lastly, people who are unsuccessful in cross-cultural adaptation usually are *overly closed-minded and inflexible.* Of course, we all look out at the world through the lenses of our own personal and cultural experiences. People are fairly parochial until they move out of their home culture because they simply don't know that there are other ways of perceiving situations or solving problems. But some are simply closed-minded and cannot accept the possibility that there are values, beliefs, and systems of logic that are neither better nor worse than one's own. They have no capacity for realistic cultural empathy. Some are even downright ethnocentric and consider their way of thinking and their system of values and beliefs as best for the rest of the world. The opposite assumption might be one of "equifinality" where there may be many equivalent ways *(equi)* of working or thinking to reach a goal *(finality)* and the best way might be contingent upon, or relative to, the particular culture or organization.[39]

Surely there are many other personality traits that make it difficult to adjust to another culture or work with those who are culturally different. But chances are that very few people have these traits to such an extent that they would be total failures. With good experiential cross-cultural training exercises and with various cultural awareness surveys or personality inventories, most people can make those adjustments necessary to be effective overseas. These techniques usually lead to greater introspection and self-awareness of one's own personality traits and how they might create difficulties overseas.

A very low-context person who is very punctual and well-organized might find that this trait is counterproductive in a high-context culture where meetings sometimes start 30 minutes late and it is difficult to stick to an agenda. If this is the case, then the sojourner could ease up a bit. Going native and simply accepting the local practices might cause endless frustration. However, what is wrong with allowing meetings to start 10 minutes late and allowing discussions to go a bit off the agreed-upon agenda? With self-awareness, most people can make these accommodations. Of course, there are those who lack introspection or who are so rigid that they will not adapt. They usually fail.

A pre-departure or entry cross-cultural orientation program should give sojourners an understanding of their home culture, their destination cultures, how to effectively communicate and adapt, and a greater awareness of how their personality traits might impact their life overseas. A few who are quite unaware of the difficulties may decide to de-select. Perhaps they are already under stress or they realize that at this time they are not able to make the adjustments that would allow them to be successful. This decision might be best for the sojourner and the sponsoring organization. It serves little purpose to have someone fail overseas. Unfortunately, in some occupations, such as the military, de-selection is not an option for the sojourner.

IMPACT ON THE FAMILY

Cross-cultural orientation programs must include the entire family because each member will go through adjustment difficulties. If members of an employee's family are miserable, the employee not only will be less productive but may decide the overseas assignment is simply not worth it. This is the reason that many organizations today provide cross-cultural training for the entire family, not simply for the employee working abroad. This includes pre-departure, in-country, and re-entry training.

Employees usually go overseas to further their careers. They often do the same type of work overseas that they were trained to perform at home. The rest of the family members are sometimes reluctant sojourners who find that their life has changed dramatically and they must do most things differently overseas. While the employed family member enjoys a daily routine similar to that at home, for spouses and children everything may be different. The children have the continuity and routine of school but they still must develop new friendship at a strange school, sometimes in a different language. Spouses also leave their friends and activities and their lives are disrupted. They may be forced to leave or restructure their jobs or careers to follow their partners overseas.

The most common cause of a premature return home is an unhappy spouse. Two decades ago, most organizations did not provide pre-departure or in-country training for spouses. Today, it is quite common to train the spouse and even children to prevent early returns. If the rest of the family is unhappy, the employee will be impacted. Simply preparing the employee for culture shock or developing cross-cultural skills is not enough.

The social role of a spouse and parent may not be the same as back home. Shopping and arranging social events may be very different than in one's native culture, and managing the household may require intense and prolonged interaction with local nationals. All this leads to greater stress of culture shock for the spouse than the employee. In fact, the most common cause of a premature return of an employee is an unhappy spouse.[40]

In many countries, expatriate groups of spouses would develop their own support network and informal orientation for newcomers. Traditionally, spousal support groups were "wives' programs." Meetings, newsletters, and pamphlets oriented incoming spouses to the local culture and helped spouses to deal with issues such as household management and child-raising in the overseas environment.

Expatriate spouses today are much more than stay-at-home parents. Many are professionals who are concerned about continuing their careers overseas. They often seek jobs overseas or try to further their education. Trailing spouses are not only wives. An increasing number are males and couples are often gay or lesbian. According to data from the Employee Relocation Council (ERC), in 2002 women with trailing spouses were one out of every five relocating professionals.

The wives' groups were not really suited to meet the needs of male spouses. In 1994, a support group run by expatriate trailing males was formed in Belgium and called itself STUDS (Spouses Trailing Under Duress Successfully).[41] Members share their experiences with each other in face-to-face meetings and over the internet. They discuss their new role of managing a household and supervising child care overseas and many suggest ways of continuing their careers.

Not only do husband and wife experience culture shock differently, but each child may experience this stress in ways that vary with age, gender, and personality. Pre-adolescent children may adjust very well overseas because they have not been fully enculturated in their home culture, while adolescent children may have a very difficult time because they must leave their peers to go abroad.

Because members of the family experience culture shock differently when overseas, each goes through reentry stress or reverse culture shock differently upon returning home. The employee who has hardly adjusted to the local culture because his or her work has been similar to that at home may not experience great re-entry stress. Pre-adolescent children often make great adaptations overseas and therefore they may experience greater difficulty returning home.

Many families are afraid that the stress of adapting overseas and returning home will somehow permanently damage the family and yet there is no evidence to support this fear. In fact, the evidence suggests just the opposite—the family becomes closer. If a family is already fragile, such as a couple who are on the verge of a divorce, the additional stress of adapting to a new culture may tip the balance on the relationship and contribute to the divorce. On the other hand, it is probable that some stressful event back home could produce the same result.

The average family will find that the shared journey overseas becomes an adventure which actually draws the family together. Children of sojourners, including third-culture kids, often report that their best friends overseas were their parents.

SECTION IV: Readings

Dimensionalizing Cultures:
The Hofstede Model in Context

Geert Hofstede

INTRODUCTION

Culture has been defined in many ways; this author's shorthand definition is: "*Culture is the collective programming of the mind that distinguishes the members of one group or category of people from others.*" It is always a collective phenomenon, but it can be connected to different collectives. Within each collective there is a variety of individuals. If characteristics of individuals are imagined as varying according to some bell curve; the variation between cultures is the shift of the bell curve when one moves from one society to the other. Most commonly the term culture is used for tribes or ethnic groups (in anthropology), for nations (in political science, sociology and management), and for organizations (in sociology and management). A relatively unexplored field is the culture of occupations (for instance, of engineers versus accountants, or of academics from different disciplines). The term can also be applied to the genders, to generations, or to social classes. However, changing the level of aggregation studied changes the nature of the concept of 'culture.' Societal, national and gender cultures, which children acquire from their earliest youth onwards, are much deeper rooted in the human mind than occupational cultures acquired at university, or than organizational cultures acquired on the job. The latter are exchangeable when people take a new job. Societal cultures reside in (often unconscious) values, in the sense of *broad tendencies to prefer certain states of affairs over others*

(Hofstede, 2001:5). Organizational cultures reside rather in (visible and conscious) practices: the way people perceive what goes on in their organizational environment.

CLASSIFYING CULTURES: CONCEPTUAL DIMENSIONS

In an article first published in 1952, U.S. anthropologist Clyde Kluckhohn argued that there should be universal categories of culture:

> "In principle . . . there is a generalized framework that underlies the more apparent and striking facts of cultural relativity. All cultures constitute so many somewhat distinct answers to essentially the same questions posed by human biology and by the generalities of the human situation. . . . Every society's patterns for living must provide approved and sanctioned ways for dealing with such universal circumstances as the existence of two sexes; the helplessness of infants; the need for satisfaction of the elementary biological requirements such as food, warmth, and sex; the presence of individuals of different ages and of differing physical and other capacities" (Kluckhohn, 1962:317–18).

Many authors in the second half of the twentieth century have speculated about the nature of the basic problems of societies that would present distinct dimensions of culture (for a review see Hofstede, 2001, 29–31). The most common dimension

For: Online Readings in Psychology and Culture January 2006.
Geert Hofstede is Professor Emeritus from the University of Maastricht and Fellow of the CentER for Economic Research at the University of Tilburg, both in the Netherlands.

used for ordering societies is their degree of economic evolution or modernity. A one-dimensional ordering of societies from traditional to modern fitted well with the nineteenth- and twentieth-century belief in progress. Economic evolution is bound to be reflected in people's collective mental programming, but there is no reason why economic and technological evolution should suppress other cultural variety. There must be dimensions of culture unrelated to economic evolution.

U.S. anthropologist Edward T. Hall (1976) divided cultures according to their ways of communicating, into high-context (much of the information is implicit) and low-context (nearly everything is explicit). In practice this distinction overlaps largely with the traditional versus modern distinction.

U.S. sociologists Talcott Parsons and Edward Shils (1951:77) suggested that all human action is determined by five *pattern variables*, choices between pairs of alternatives:

1. *Affectivity* (need gratification) versus *affective neutrality* (restraint of impulses);

2. *Self-orientation* versus *collectivity-orientation*;

3. *Universalism* (applying general standards) versus *particularism* (taking particular relationships into account);

4. *Ascription* (judging others by who they are) versus *achievement* (judging them by what they do);

5. *Specificity* (limiting relations to others to specific spheres) versus *diffuseness* (no prior limitations to nature of relations).

Parsons and Shils claimed that these choices are present at the individual (personality) level, at the social system (group or organization) level, and at the cultural (normative) level. They did not take into account that different variables could operate at different aggregation levels.

U.S. anthropologists Florence Kluckhohn and Fred Strodtbeck (1961:12) ran a field study in five geographically close, small communities in the Southwestern United States: Mormons, Spanish Americans, Texans, Navaho Indians, and Zuni Indians. They distinguished these communities on the following value orientations:

1. An evaluation of human nature (evil—mixed—good);

2. The relationship of man to the surrounding *natural environment* (subjugation—harmony—mastery);

3. The orientation in *time* (toward past—present—future);

4. The orientation toward *activity* (being—being in becoming—doing); and

5. *Relationships among people* (lineality [that is, hierarchically ordered positions]—collaterality [that is, group relationships]—individualism).

Others have extrapolated Kluckhohn and Strodtbeck's classification to all kind of social comparisons, without concern for their geographic limitations without considering the effect of levels of aggregation, and without empirical support.

British anthropologist Mary Douglas (1973) proposed a two-dimensional ordering of ways of looking at the world:

1. '*Group*' or inclusion—the claim of groups over members, and

2. '*Grid*' or classification—the degree to which interaction is subject to rules.

Douglas saw these as relating to a wide variety of beliefs and social actions: Views of nature, traveling, spatial arrangements, gardening, cookery, medicine, the meaning of time, age, history, sickness, and justice. She seemed to imply that these dimensions are applicable to any level of aggregation.

The one- or more-dimensional classifications above represent subjective reflective attempts to order a complex reality. Each of them is strongly colored by the subjective choices of its author(s). They show some overlap, but their lack of clarity about and mixing of levels of analysis (individual-group-culture) are severe methodological weaknesses.

These weaknesses were avoided in an extensive review article by U.S. sociologist Alex Inkeles and psychologist Daniel Levinson (1954). The authors limited themselves to culture at the level of nations, and they summarized all available sociological and anthropological studies dealing with what was then called *national character*, which they interpreted as a kind of modal (most common) personality type in a national society. What I have labeled *dimensions* they called *standard analytic issues*. They proposed:

"To concentrate, for purposes of comparative analysis, on a limited number of psychological issues . . . that meet at least the following criteria. First, they should be found in adults universally, as a function both of maturational potentials common to man and of socio-cultural characteristics common to human societies. Second, the manner in which they are handled should have functional significance for the individual personality as well as for the social system" (1969:44).

From their survey of the literature Inkeles and Levinson distilled three standard analytic issues that met these criteria:

1. Relation to authority;

2. Conception of self, including the individual's concepts of masculinity and femininity; and

3. Primary dilemmas or conflicts, and ways of dealing with them, including the control of aggression and the expression versus inhibition of affect.

As will be shown below, Inkeles and Levinson's standard analytic issues were empirically supported in a study by this author more than 20 years later.

EMPIRICAL APPROACHES AND THE HOFSTEDE DIMENSIONS

In 1949 U.S. psychologist Raymond Cattell published an application of the new statistical technique of factor analysis to the comparison of nations. Cattell had earlier used factor analysis for studying aspects of intelligence from test scores of individual students. This time he took a matrix of nation-level variables for a large number of countries, borrowing from geography, demographics, history, politics, economics, sociology, law, religion and medicine. The resulting factors were difficult to interpret, except for the important role of economic development. Replications of his method by others produced trivial results (for a review see Hofstede, 2001:32–33). More meaningful were applications to restricted facets of societies. U.S. political scientists Phillip Gregg and Arthur Banks (1965) studied aspects of political systems; U.S. economists Irma Adelman and Cynthia Taft Morris (1967) studied factors influencing the development of poor countries, and Irish psychologist Richard Lynn (1971; with S.L. Hampson, 1975) studied aspects of mental health.

In the 1970s this author more or less by accident got access to a large survey database about values and related sentiments of people in over 50 countries around the world (Hofstede, 1980). These people worked in the local subsidiaries of one large multinational corporation: IBM. Most parts of the organization had been surveyed twice over a four-year interval, and the database contained more than 100,000 questionnaires. Initial analyses of the database at the level of individual respondents proved confusing, but a breakthrough occurred when the focus was directed at correlations between mean scores of survey items at the level of countries. Patterns of correlation at the country level could be strikingly different from what was found at the individual level, and needed an entirely different interpretation.

My hunch that the IBM data might have implications beyond this particular corporation was supported when I got the opportunity to administer a number of the same questions to nearly 400 management trainees from some 30 countries in an international program unrelated to IBM. Their mean scores by country correlated significantly with the country scores obtained from the IBM database. So it seemed that employees of this multinational—a very special kind of people—could serve for identifying differences in *national* value systems. The reason is that from one country to another they represented almost perfectly matched samples: they were similar in all respects except nationality, which made the effect of national differences in their answers stand out unusually clearly.

Encouraged by the results of the country-level correlation analysis I then tried country-level factor analysis. The latter was similar to the approach used earlier by Cattell and others, except that now the variables in the matrix were not indices for the country as a whole, but mean scores and sometimes percentages of survey answers collected from individuals in those countries. Analyses of data at higher levels of aggregation are sometimes called *ecological*. Ecological factor analysis differs from the factor analysis of individual scores in that a usual caution no longer applies: the number of cases does not need to be (much) larger than the numbers of variables. The stability of the results of an ecological factor analysis does not depend on the number of cases, but on the number of individuals whose scores were aggregated into these cases. One may even start from a matrix with fewer cases than variables.

Factor analyzing a matrix of 32 values questions for initially 40 countries, I found these values to cluster very differently from what was found at the individual level. The new factors revealed common problems with which IBM employees in all these societies had to cope, but for which their upbringing in their country presented its own profile of solutions. These problems were:

1. Dependence on superiors;

2. Need for rules and predictability, also associated with nervous stress;

3. The balance between individual goals and dependence on the company;

4. The balance between ego values (like the need for money and careers) and social values (like cooperation and a good

living environment). The former were more frequently chosen by men, the latter by women, but there were also country differences.

These empirical results were strikingly similar to the *standard analytical issues* described in Inkeles and Levinson's 1954 article. Dependence on superiors relates to the first, need for predictability to the third, the balance between the individual and the company to the conception of self, and the balance between ego and social values to concepts of masculinity and femininity, which were also classified under the second standard analytic issue.

The four basic problem areas defined by Inkeles and Levinson and empirically supported in the IBM data represent dimensions of national cultures. A dimension is an aspect of a culture that can be measured relative to other cultures. Later, on the basis of research by Canadian psychologist Michael Harris Bond centered in the Far East (Hofstede and Bond, 1988), a fifth dimension was added.

These dimensions were labeled (Hofstede, 1991, 2001):

1. *Power Distance*, related to the different solutions to the basic problem of human inequality;

2. *Uncertainty Avoidance*, related to the level of stress in a society in the face of an unknown future;

3. *Individualism* versus *Collectivism*, related to the integration of individuals into primary groups;

4. *Masculinity* versus *Femininity*, related to the division of emotional roles between women and men;

5. *Long Term* versus *Short Term Orientation*, related to the choice of focus for people's efforts: the future or the present and past.

Each country could be positioned relative to other countries through a score on each dimension. The dimensions were statistically distinct and occurred in all possible combinations, although some combinations were more frequent than others.

After the initial confirmation of the country differences in IBM in data from management trainees elsewhere, the IBM dimensions and country scores were validated through replications by others, using the same or similar questions with other cross-national populations. Between 1990 and 2002 six major replications (14 or more countries) used country elites, employees and managers of other corporations and organizations, airline pilots, consumers and civil servants; see Hofstede and Hofstede, 2005:26.

A breakthrough in the research occurred when country scores on the dimensions turned out to correlate significantly with conceptually related external data. Thus Power Distance scores correlated with a dimension from Gregg and Banks' analysis of political systems and also with a dimension from Adelman and Morris' study of economic development; Uncertainty Avoidance correlated with a dimension from Lynn and Hampson's study of mental health; Individualism correlated strongly with national wealth (Gross National Product per capita) and Femininity with the percentage of national income spent on development aid. These external validations are continued, and the second edition of *Culture's Consequences* (Hofstede, 2001:503–20) lists more than 400 significant correlations between the IBM-based scores and results of other studies. Recent validations show no loss of validity, indicating that the country differences these dimensions describe are, indeed, basic and long-term.

In correlating the dimensions with other data the influence of national wealth (Gross National Product per capita) should always be taken into account. Two of the dimensions, Individualism and small Power Distance, are significantly correlated with wealth. This means that all wealth-related phenomena tend also to correlate with these dimensions. Differences in national wealth can be considered a more parsimonious explanation of these other phenomena than differences in culture. In correlating with the culture dimensions, it is therefore advisable to always include the wealth variable. After

controlling for wealth correlations with culture may disappear. The shared correlation of Individualism and (small) Power Distance with national wealth implies that these dimensions tend to be intercorrelated. However, if national wealth is controlled for, this intercorrelation usually disappears.

Of particular interest is a link that was found between culture according to the Hofstede dimensions and personality dimensions according to the empirically based Big Five personality test (Costa and McCrae, 1992). This test has now been used in over 30 countries, and significant correlations were found between country norms on the personality dimensions (Neuroticism, Extraversion, Openness to experience, Agreeableness and Conscientiousness) and culture dimension scores. For example, 55% of country differences on Neuroticism can be explained by a combination of Uncertainty Avoidance and Masculinity, and 39% of country differences on Extraversion by Individualism alone (Hofstede and McCrae, 2002). So culture and personality are linked but the link is statistical, and should not be used for stereotyping individuals.

Validating the dimensions is of course not only and not even mainly a quantitative issue. Equally important is the qualitative interpretation of what differences on the dimensions mean for each of the societies studied, which calls for an *emic* approach to each society, linking it to the *etic* of the dimensional data.

THE HOFSTEDE DIMENSIONS IN A NUTSHELL

Power Distance has been defined as the extent to which the less powerful members of organizations and institutions (like the family) accept and expect that power is distributed unequally. This represents inequality (more versus less), but defined from below, not from above. It suggests that a society's level of inequality is endorsed by the followers as much as by the leaders. Power and inequality, of course, are extremely fundamental facts of any society. All societies are unequal, but some are more unequal than other. Table 1 lists a

Table 1
Ten differences between small- and large- Power Distance societies

Small Power Distance	Large Power Distance
• Use of power should be legitimate and is subject to criteria of good and evil	• Power is a basic fact of society antedating good or evil: its legitimacy is irrelevant
• Parents treat children as equals	• Parents teach children obedience
• Older people are neither respected nor feared	• Older people are both respected and feared
• Student-centered education	• Teacher-centered education
• Hierarchy means inequality of roles, established for convenience	• Hierarchy means existential inequality
• Subordinates expect to be consulted	• Subordinates expect to be told what to do
• Pluralist governments based on majority vote and changed peacefully	• Autocratic governments based on co-optation and changed by revolution
• Corruption rare; scandals end political careers	• Corruption frequent; scandals are covered up
• Income distribution in society rather even	• Income distribution in society very uneven
• Religions stressing equality of believers	• Religions with a hierarchy of priests

selection of differences between national societies that validation research showed to be associated with the Power Distance dimension. For a more complete review the reader is referred to Hofstede, 2001 and/or Hofstede and Hofstede, 2005. The statements refer to extremes; actual situations may be found anywhere in between the extremes, and the association of a statement with a dimension is always statistical, never absolute.

Power distance index scores were higher for East European, Latin, Asian and African countries and lower for Germanic and English-speaking Western countries.

Uncertainty Avoidance is not the same as risk avoidance; it deals with a society's tolerance for ambiguity. It indicates to what extent a culture programs its members to feel either uncomfortable or comfortable in unstructured situations. Unstructured situations are novel, unknown, surprising, different from usual. Uncertainty avoiding cultures try to minimize the possibility of such situations by strict behavioral codes, laws and rules, disapproval of deviant opinions, and a belief in absolute Truth; 'there can only be one Truth and we have

it.' Research has shown that people in uncertainty avoiding countries are also more emotional, and motivated by inner nervous energy. The opposite type, uncertainty accepting cultures, are more tolerant of opinions different from what they are used to; they try to have fewer rules, and on the philosophical and religious level they are relativist and allow different currents to flow side by side. People within these cultures are more phlegmatic and contemplative, and not expected by their environment to express emotions. Table 2 lists a selection of differences between societies that validation research showed to be associated with the Uncertainty Avoidance dimension.

Uncertainty avoidance scores are higher in East and Central European countries, in Latin countries, in Japan and in German speaking countries, lower in English speaking, Nordic and Chinese culture countries.

Individualism on the one side versus its opposite, *Collectivism*, as a societal, not an individual characteristic, is the degree to which people in a society are integrated into groups. On the individualist side we find cultures in which the ties between

Table 2
Ten differences between weak- and strong- Uncertainty Avoidance societies

Weak Uncertainty Avoidance	Strong Uncertainty Avoidance
• The uncertainty inherent in life is accepted and each day is taken as it comes	• The uncertainty inherent in life is felt as a continuous threat that must be fought
• Ease, lower stress, self-control, low anxiety	• Higher stress, emotionality, anxiety, neuroticism
• Higher scores on subjective health and well-being	• Lower scores on subjective health and well-being
• Tolerance of deviant persons and ideas: what is different is curious	• Intolerance of deviant persons and ideas: what is different is dangerous
• Comfortable with ambiguity and chaos	• Need for clarity and structure
• Teachers may say 'I don't know'	• Teachers supposed to have all the answers
• Changing jobs no problem	• Staying in jobs even if disliked
• Dislike of rules—written or unwritten	• Emotional need for rules—even if not obeyed
• In politics, citizens feel and are seen as competent towards authorities	• In politics, citizens feel and are seen as incompetent towards authorities
• In religion, philosophy and science: relativism and empiricism	• In religion, philosophy and science: belief in ultimate truths and grand theories

individuals are loose: everyone is expected to look after him/herself and his/her immediate family. On the collectivist side we find cultures in which people from birth onwards are integrated into strong, cohesive in-groups, often extended families (with uncles, aunts and grandparents) that continue protecting them in exchange for unquestioning loyalty. Again, the issue addressed by this dimension is an extremely fundamental one, regarding all societies in the world. Table 3 lists a selection of differences between societies that validation research showed to be associated with this dimension.

Individualism prevails in developed and Western countries, while collectivism prevails in less developed and Eastern countries; Japan takes a middle position on this dimension.

Masculinity versus its opposite, *Femininity*, again as a national, not as an individual characteristic, refers to the distribution of values between the genders which is another fundamental issue for any society, to which a range of solutions are found. The IBM studies revealed that (a) women's values differ less among societies than men's values; (b) men's values from one country to another contain a dimension from very assertive and competitive and maximally different from women's values on the one side, to modest and caring and similar to women's values on the other. The assertive pole has been called 'masculine' and the modest, caring pole 'feminine.' The women in feminine countries have the same modest, caring values as the men; in the masculine countries they are somewhat assertive and competitive, but not as much as the men, so that these countries show a gap between men's values and women's values. In masculine cultures there is sometimes a taboo around this dimension (Hofstede *et al,* 1998). Taboos are based on deeply rooted values; this taboo shows that the Mas/Fem dimension in some societies touches

Table 3
Ten differences between collectivist and individualist societies

Collectivism	Individualism
• People are born into extended families or clans which protect them in exchange for loyalty	• Everyone is supposed to take care of him- or herself and his or her immediate family only
• 'We'-consciousness	• 'I'- consciousness
• Stress on belonging	• Right of privacy
• Harmony should always be maintained	• Speaking one's mind is healthy
• Others classified as in-group or out-group	• Others classified as individuals
• Opinions and votes predetermined by in-group	• Personal opinion expected: one person one vote
• Transgression of norms leads to shame feelings	• Transgression of norms leads to guilt feelings
• Languages in which the word 'I' is avoided	• Languages in which the word 'I' is indispensable
• Purpose of education is learning how to do	• Purpose of education is learning how to learn
• Relationship prevails over task	• Task prevails over relationship

basic and often unconscious values, too painful to be explicitly discussed. In fact the taboo validates the importance of the dimension. Table 4 lists a selection of differences between societies that validation research showed to be associated with this dimension.

Masculinity is high in Japan, in German speaking countries, and in some Latin countries like Italy and Mexico; it is moderately high in English speaking Western countries; it is low in Nordic countries and in the Netherlands and moderately low in some Latin and Asian countries like France, Spain, Portugal, Chile, Korea and Thailand.

Long-Term versus *Short-Term Orientation*: this fifth dimension was found in a study among students in 23 countries around the world, using a questionnaire designed by Chinese scholars (Hofstede and Bond, 1988). Values associated with Long Term Orientation are thrift and perseverance; values associated with Short Term Orientation are respect

for tradition, fulfilling social obligations, and protecting one's 'face.' Both the positively and the negatively rated values of this dimension are found in the teachings of Confucius around 500 B.C. So it is not correct to equal Long-Term Orientation with Confucianism; it represents a focus on the future-oriented maxims of Confucianism, at the expense of the past-oriented ones. Also, the dimension applies equally well to countries without a Confucian heritage. Table 5 lists a selection of differences between societies that validation research showed to be associated with this dimension.

Long-term oriented are East Asian countries, in particular in China, Hong Kong, Taiwan, Japan, and South Korea but to a lesser extent also India and Brazil. A medium term orientation is found in most European countries, but the U.S.A. and Britain are more short term oriented. A very short term orientation is found in Africa and in a number of Islamic countries.

186

Table 4
Ten differences between feminine and masculine societies

Femininity	Masculinity
• Minimum emotional and social role differentiation between the genders	• Maximum emotional and social role differentiation between the genders
• Men and women should be modest and caring	• Men should be and women may be assertive and ambitious
• Balance between family and work	• Work prevails over family
• Sympathy for the weak	• Admiration for the strong
• Both fathers and mothers deal with facts and feelings	• Fathers deal with facts, mothers with feelings
• Both boys and girls may cry but neither should fight	• Girls cry, boys don't; boys should fight back, girls shouldn't fight
• Mothers decide on number of children	• Fathers decide on family size
• Many women in elected political positions	• Few women in elected political positions
• Religion focuses on fellow human beings	• Religion focuses on God or gods
• Matter-of-fact attitudes about sexuality; sex is a way of relating	• Moralistic attitudes about sexuality; sex is a way of performing

OTHER APPLICATIONS OF THE DIMENSIONAL PARADIGM

When *Culture's Consequences* appeared in 1980, it represented a new paradigm in social science research: analysing survey-based values data at the national level and quantifying differences between national cultures by positions on these dimensions. Like other new paradigms, it initially met with rejection, criticism and ridicule next to enthusiasm (Kuhn, 1970). By the 1990s the paradigm had been taken over by many others, and discussions shifted to the content and number of dimensions. The paradigm inspired a number of other studies into dimensions of national cultures.

Many studies further explored the dimension of individualism and collectivism (e.g. Kim et al., 1994; Triandis, 1995; Hofstede, 2001: Chapter 5). From all the Hofstede dimensions, this one met with the most positive reactions among psychologists,

especially in the U.S.A. which happened to be the highest scoring country on it. Ind/Col scores were strongly correlated with national wealth which led some people to the conclusion that promoting individualism in other cultures would contribute to their economic development. In fact, data show that the causality is most probably reversed: wealth tends to lead to individualism (Hofstede, 2001: 253). The individualism in U.S. culture also led people to studying it at the *individual* level (comparing one person to another), not at the level of societies. In this case it is no longer a dimension of culture but possibly a dimension of personality. Also there is no more reason why individualism and collectivism need to be opposite; they should rather be considered separate aspects of personality. An extensive review of studies of individualism *at the individual level* was published by Oyserman, Coon and Kemmelmeier (2002). Comparing these studies across societies they found a different ranking of countries from the

Table 5
Ten differences between Short- and Long-Term-Oriented societies

Short-Term Orientation	Long-Term Orientation
• Most important events in life occurred in the past or take place now	• Most important events in life will occur in the future
• Immediate need gratification expected	• Need gratification deferred until later
• There are universal guidelines about what is good and evil	• What is good and evil depends upon the circumstances
• Traditions are sacrosanct	• Traditions are adaptable to changed circumstances
• Family life guided by imperatives	• Family life guided by shared tasks
• What one thinks and says should be true	• What one does should be virtuous
• Children should learn tolerance and respect	• Children should learn to be thrifty
• Social spending and consumption	• Saving, investing
• Unstructured problem solving	• Structured, mathematical problem solving
• In business, stress on short-term profits	• In business, stress on future market position

Hofstede studies; but Schimmack, Oishi and Diener (2005) proved this was due to a methodological error: Oyserman *et al.* forgot to control for acquiescence (response set), and the acquiescence in their data was significantly negatively correlated with the object of their study which made their results random.

The cultural focus on the Individualism versus Collectivism dimension led Triandis (1995) to splitting it into horizontal and vertical individualism. This split overlooks the fact that the Hofstede dimension of large versus small Power Distance already covered the horizontal/vertical aspect quite satisfactorily. From my point of view the horizontal/vertical distinction for Ind/Col as a dimension of culture is redundant. It may be useful at the individual level, but this is for others to decide.

Like individualism and collectivism, the terms masculinity and femininity have also been used for describing values at the individual level. Earlier

studies by U.S. psychologist Sandra Bem (1974) showed already that in this case masculinity and femininity should again rather be treated as separate aspects than as opposite poles.

An important alternative application of the dimensional paradigm was developed by the Israeli psychologist Shalom Schwartz. From a survey of the literature, Schwartz composed a list of 56 values. Through a network of colleagues he collected scores from samples of elementary school teachers and of college students in over 50 countries. (Schwartz, 1994; Schwartz and Bardi, 2001). Respondents scored the importance of each value 'as a guiding principle in my life.' Schwartz at first assumed the same dimensions would apply to individuals and to countries, but his data showed he needed different classifications at different levels. At the country level he distinguished seven dimensions: Conservatism, Hierarchy, Mastery, Affective autonomy, Intellectual autonomy, Egalitarian commitment and Harmony. Country scores for teachers published by Schwartz in 1994 were significantly correlated with the IBM scores for Individualism, Masculinity and Uncertainty Avoidance (Hofstede, 2001, p. 265).

Another large scale application was the GLOBE (Global Leadership and Organizational Behavior Effectiveness) project, conceived by US management scholar Robert J. House in 1991. At first House focused on leadership, but soon the study branched out into other aspects of national and organizational cultures. In the period 1994–1997 some 170 voluntary collaborators collected data from about 17,000 managers in nearly 1,000 local (non-multinational) organizations belonging to one of three industries: food processing, financial services, and telecommunication services, in some 60 societies throughout the world. In the preface to the book describing the project (House *et al.*, 2004), House writes "We have a very adequate dataset to replicate Hofstede's (1980) landmark study and extend that study to test hypotheses relevant to relationships among societal-level variables, organizational practices, and leader attributes and behavior".

For conceptual reasons GLOBE expanded the five Hofstede dimensions to nine. They maintained the labels Power Distance and Uncertainty Avoidance (but not necessarily their meaning). They split Collectivism into Institutional Collectivism and In-Group Collectivism, and Masculinity-Femininity into Assertiveness and Gender Egalitarianism. Long Term Orientation became Future Orientation. They added two more dimensions: Humane Orientation and Performance Orientation. The nine dimensions were covered by 78 survey questions, half of them asking respondents to describe their culture ('as is') and the other half to judge it ('should be'). GLOBE thus produced $9 \times 2 = 18$ culture scores for each country: nine dimensions 'as is' and nine dimensions 'should be'.

In an evaluation of the GLOBE project (Hofstede, forthcoming), I re-factor analyzed the country scores on GLOBE's 18 dimensions. Five meta-factors emerged, of which the strongest, grouping seven of the 18 measures, was highly significantly correlated with GNP per capita and next with the Hofstede Power Distance dimension. Three more meta-factors were significantly correlated with respectively the Hofstede Uncertainty Avoidance, Individualism and Long Term Orientation dimensions. The GLOBE questionnaire contained very few items covering Masculinity in the Hofstede sense, but whatever there was belonged to the fifth meta-factor. The results show that in spite of a very different approach, the massive body of GLOBE data still reflected the structure of the original Hofstede model.

An author sometimes cited as having researched dimensions of national culture is the Dutch management consultant Fons Trompenaars (1993). He distinguished seven conceptual dimensions, the first five borrowed from Parsons and Shils (1951) and the last two from Kluckhohn and Strodtbeck (1961) which he applied to the level of nations (see earlier in this article). Trompenaars collected a database of survey items related to these dimensions, but in the only statistical analysis of his data published so far, applying Multidimensional Scaling to some 9,000 questionnaires, only two interpretable factors emerged, both correlated with Hofstede's Individualism, one of these also with Power Distance (Smith, Trompenaars and Dugan, 1995; Smith, Dugan and Trompenaars, 1996). The only country scores that could be based on Trompenaars' data refer to these two flavors of individualism (Smith, Peterson and Schwartz, 2002). Trompenaars' claim to seven dimensions therefore lacks empirical support.

One large international survey effort that developed independently from the search for cultural dimensions is the World Values Survey led by U.S. political scientist Ronald Inglehart. A study of values via public opinion surveys was started in the early 1980s as the European Values Survey. In 1990 a second round was started, renamed the World Values Survey (WVS). It eventually covered some 60,000 respondents across 43 societies, representing about 70 per cent of the world's population with a questionnaire including more than 360 forced-choice questions. Areas covered were ecology, economy, education, emotions, family, gender and sexuality, government and politics, health, happiness, leisure and friends, morality, religion, society and nation, and work (Inglehart, Basañez and Moreno, 1998; Inglehart *et al.*, 2004). Although the search for dimensions was not a primary purpose of this study, Inglehart in an overall statistical analysis found two key country-level factors which he called: 'Well-being versus survival' and 'Secular-rational versus traditional authority' (Inglehart, 1997, p. 81–98). These were again significantly correlated with the Hofstede dimensions: Well-being versus survival correlated with a combination of Individualism and Masculinity; Secular-rational versus traditional authority negatively with Power Distance. Further analysis of the enormous WVS survey data bank may produce additional dimensions.

DIMENSIONS OF ORGANIZATIONAL CULTURES

The dimensional paradigm has also been applied at the level of organizations. A research project similar to the IBM studies but focusing on organization rather than national cultures was carried out by this author and a team of collaborators in the 1980s (Hofstede *et al.*, 1990). Qualitative and quantitative data were collected in twenty work organizations or parts of organizations in the Netherlands and Denmark. The units studied varied from a toy manufacturing company to two municipal police corps. This study found large differences among units in perceptions of daily practices but only modest differences in values, beyond those due to such basic facts as nationality, education, gender and age group.

Six independent dimensions allowed to describe the larger part of the variety in organization practices. These six dimensions can be used as a framework to describe organization cultures, but their research base in twenty units from two countries is too narrow to consider them as universally valid and sufficient. For describing organization

cultures in other countries and/or in other types of organizations, additional dimensions may be necessary or some of the six may be less useful. The six dimensions were:

1. *Process-oriented versus results-oriented.* Process-oriented cultures are dominated by technical and bureaucratic routines, results-oriented by a common concern for outcomes. This dimension was associated with the culture's degree of homogeneity: in results-oriented units, everybody perceived their practices in about the same way; in process-oriented units, there were vast differences in perception among different levels and parts of the unit. The degree of homogeneity of a culture is a measure of its 'strength:' the study confirmed that strong cultures are more results- oriented than weak ones, and vice versa (Peters & Waterman, 1982).

2. *Job-oriented versus employee-oriented.* The former assume responsibility for the employees' job performance only, and nothing more; employee-oriented cultures assume a broad responsibility for their members' well-being. At the level of individual managers, the distinction between job orientation and employee orientation has been popularized by Blake and Mouton's Managerial Grid (1964). The Hofstede *et al.* study shows that job versus employee orientation is part of a culture and not (only) a choice for an individual manager. A unit's position on this dimension seems to be largely the result of historical factors, like the philosophy of its founder(s) and the presence or absence in its recent history of economic crises with collective layoffs.

3. *Professional versus parochial.* In the former, the (usually highly educated) members identify primarily with their profession; in the latter, the members derive their identity from the organization for which they work. Sociology has long known this dimension as 'local' versus 'cosmopolitan,' the contrast between an internal and an external frame of reference (Merton, 1949).

4. *Open systems versus closed systems.* This dimension refers to the common style of internal and external communication, and to the ease with

which outsiders and newcomers are admitted. This is the only one of the six dimensions for which a systematic difference was found between Danish and Dutch units. It seems that organizational openness is a societal characteristic of Denmark more than of the Netherlands. This shows that organization cultures also contain elements from national culture differences.

5. *Tight versus loose control.* This dimension deals with the degree of formality and punctuality within the organization; it is partly a function of the unit's technology: banks and pharmaceutical companies can be expected to show tight control, research laboratories and advertising agencies loose control; but even with the same technology some units may still be tighter or looser than others.

6. *Pragmatic versus normative.* The last dimension describes the prevailing way (flexible or rigid) of dealing with the environment, in particular with customers. Units selling services are likely to be found towards the pragmatic (flexible) side, units involved in the application of laws and rules towards the normative (rigid) side. This dimension measures the degree of 'customer orientation,' which is a highly popular topic in the management literature.

Dimensionality of Cultures in the Future

The fact that the world around us is changing does not need to affect the usefulness of the dimensional paradigm; on the contrary, the paradigm can help us understand the internal logic and the implications of the changes.

Some critics suggest that the number of dimensions should be extended. Triandis (2004) has defended this position, and the GLOBE project actually tried to extend the five Hofstede dimensions to 18. But additional dimensions are only meaningful if they are both conceptually and statistically independent from those already available, and they should also be validated by significant correlations with conceptually related external measures. There is an epistemological reason why the

number of meaningful dimensions will always be small. Dimensions should not be reified. They do not 'exist' in a tangible sense. They are constructs: if they exist, it is in our minds. They should help us in understanding and handling the complex reality of our social world. But human minds have a limited capacity for processing information, and therefore dimensional models that are too complex will not be experienced as useful. In a famous little article, Miller (1956) argued that useful classifications should not have more than seven categories, plus or minus two. I would go for the minus rather than the plus.

Within the dimensional model cultures can of course change their position on a dimension. Critics argue that Hofstede country scores based on IBM subsidiaries around 1970 are obsolete. But studies correlating the old country scores with related variables available on a year-by-year basis find no weakening of the correlations. A good reason for this is that the country scores on the five dimensions do not provide *absolute* country positions, but only their positions *relative to the other countries* in the set. The relationship of the dimensions to basic problems of societies and the historical evidence of the continuity of national solutions to such problems suggest that even over much longer periods the measures obtained will retain their validity. Influences like those of new technologies tend to affect all countries without necessarily changing their relative position or ranking; if their cultures change, they change in formation. Only if on a dimension one country leapfrogs over others will the validity of the original scores be reduced. This is a relatively rare occurrence.

Some authors predict that new technologies will make societies more and more similar. Technological modernization is an important force toward culture change and it leads to partly similar developments in different societies, but there is not the slightest proof that it wipes out variety on other dimensions. It may even increase differences, as on the basis of pre-existing value systems societies cope with technological modernization in different ways.

Culture change basic enough to invalidate the country dimension index rankings, or even the relevance of the dimensional model, will need either a much longer period—say, 50 to 100 years—or extremely dramatic outside events. Many differences between national cultures at the end of the 20th century were already recognizable in the years 1900, 1800 and 1700 if not earlier. There is no reason why they should not play a role until 2100 or beyond.

REFERENCES

Society, Politics and Economic Development: A Quantitative Approach.
Adelman, I & Morris, C.T. (1967). Baltimore: Johns Hopkins University Press.

Journal of Consulting and Clinical Psychology, 42, 155–62.
Bem, S.L. (1994). The measurement of psychological androgyny.

The Managerial Grid.
Blake, R.R. & Mouton, J.S. (1964). Houston TX: Gulf.

Journal of Abnormal and Social Psychology, 44, 443–69.
Cattell, R.B. (1949). The dimensions of culture patterns by factorization of national characters.

Revised NEO Personality Inventory (NEO-PI-R) and NEO Five-Factor Inventory (NEO-FFI) Professional Manual.
Costa, P.T.,Jr. & McCrae, R.R. (1992). Odessa FL: Psychological Assessment Resources.

Natural Symbols: Explorations in Cosmology.
Douglas, M. (1973). Harmondsworth U.K.: Penguin.

American Political Science Review, 59, 602–14.
Gregg, P.M. & Banks, A.S. (1965). Dimensions of political systems: Factor analysis of a cross-polity survey.

Beyond Culture.
Hall, E.T. (1976). Garden City NY: Anchor.

Culture's Consequences: International Differences in Work-Related Values.
Hofstede, G. (1980). Beverly Hills CA: Sage.

Cultures and Organizations: Software of the Mind.
Hofstede, G. (1991). London: McGraw-Hill U.K.

Culture's Consequences: Comparing Values, Behaviors, Institutions and Organizations across Nations.
Hofstede, G. (2001). Thousand Oaks CA: Sage.

Journal of International Business Studies.
Hofstede, G. (forthcoming). What did GLOBE really measure? Researchers' minds versus respondents' minds.

Organizational Dynamics, 16(4), 4–21.

Hofstede, G. & Bond, M.H. (1988). The Confucius connection: from cultural roots to economic growth.

Cross-cultural Research, 38(1), 52–88.
Hofstede, G. & McCrae, R.R. (2004). Culture and personality revisited: Linking traits and dimensions of culture.

Cultures and Organizations: Software of the Mind, Revised and expanded 2nd edition.
Hofstede, G. & Hofstede, G.J. (2005). New York: McGraw-Hill.

Administrative Science Quarterly, 35, 286–316.
Hofstede, G., Neuijen, B., Ohayv, D.D. & Sanders, G. (1990). Measuring organizational cultures: A qualitative and quantitative study across twenty cases.

Masculinity and Femininity: The taboo dimension of national cultures.
Hofstede, G. with Arrindell, W.A., Best, D.L., de Mooij, M. Hoppe, M.H., van de Vliert, E., van Rossum, J.H.A., Verweij, J., Vunderink, M. & Williams, J.E. (1998). Thousand Oaks CA: Sage.

Culture, Leadership, and Organizations: The GLOBE Study of 62 Societies.
House, R.J., Hanges, P.J., Javidan, M., Dorfman, P.W. & Gupta, V. (Eds., 2004). Thousand Oaks CA: Sage.

Modernization and Postmodernization: Cultural, Economic, and Political Change in 43 societies.
Inglehart, R. (1997). Princeton NJ: Princeton University Press.

Human Values and Beliefs: A Cross-Cultural Sourcebook. Political, religious, sexual, and economic norms in 43 societies. Findings from the 1990–1993 World Values Survey.
Inglehart, R., Basañez, M. & Moreno, A. (1998). Ann Arbor: The University of Michigan Press.

Human Beliefs and Values.
Inglehart, R., Basañez, M., Diez-Medrano J., Halman, L. & Luijkx, R. (2004). Mexico City: Siglo XXI Editores.

The Handbook of Social Psychology IV (pp. 418–506).
Inkeles, A. & Levinson, D. J. (1969[1954]). National character: The study of modal personality and sociocultural systems. In G. Lindzey & E. Aronson (Eds.), New York: McGraw-Hill.

Individualism and Collectivism: Theory, Method and Applications.
Kim, U, Triandis, H.C., Kagitçibasi, C. Choi, S.C. & Yoon, G. (Eds., 1994). Thousand Oaks CA: Sage.

Anthropology Today: Selections (pp. 304–20).
Kluckhohn, C. (1962[1952]). In S. Tax (Ed.), Universal categories of culture. Chicago: University of Chicago Press.

Variations in Value Orientations.
Kluckhohn, F.R. & Strodtbeck, F L. (1961). Westport CT: Greenwood Press.

The Structure of Scientific Revolutions, 2nd edition.
Kuhn, T.S. (1970). Chicago: University of Chicago Press.

Personality and National Character.
Lynn, R. (1971).Oxford: Pergamon Press.

British Journal of Social and Clinical Psychology, 14, 223–40.
Lynn, R. & S.L. Hampson (1975). National differences in extraversion and neuroticism.

Social Theory and Social Structure.
Merton, R.K. (1968[1949]). New York: Free Press.

Psychological Review, 63, 81–97.
Miller, G.A. (1956). The magical number seven, plus or minus two : Some limits on our capacity for processing information.

Psychological Bulletin, 128(1), 3–72.
Oyserman, D., Coon, H.M. & Kemmelmeier, M. (2002). Rethinking Individualism and Collectivism: Evaluation of Theoretical Assumptions and Meta-Analyses.

Toward a General Theory of Action.
Parsons, T. & Shils, E.A. (1951). Cambridge MA: Harvard University Press.

In Search of Excellence: Lessons from America's best-run companies.
Peters, T.J. & Waterman, R.H.,Jr. (1982). New York: Harler & Row.

Personality and Social Psychology Review, 9, 17–31.
Schimmack, U., Oishi, S. & Diener, E. (2005). Individualism: A valid and important dimension of cultural differences between nations.

Individualism and Collectivism: Theory, Method and Applications (pp. 85–119).
Schwartz, S.H. (1994). Beyond individualism/collectivism: New cultural dimensions of values. In U. Kim, H.C. Triandis, C. Kagitçibasi, S.C. Choi & G. Yoon (Eds.). Thousand Oaks CA: Sage.

Journal of Cross-Cultural Psychology, 32, 268–90.
Schwartz, S.H. & Bardi, A. (2001). Value hierarchies across culture: Taking a similarities perspective.

International Journal of Psychology, 30, 377–400.
Smith, P.B., Trompenaars, F. & Dugan, S. (1995). The Rotter locus of control scale in 43 countries: A test of cultural relativity.

Journal of Cross-Cultural Psychology, 27, 231–64.
Smith, P.B., Dugan, S. & Trompenaars, F. (1996). National culture and the values of organizational employees: A dimensional analysis across 43 nations.

Journal of Cross-Cultural Psychology, 33, 188–208.
Smith, P.B., Peterson, M.F. & Schwartz, S.H. (2002) Cultural values, sources of guidance, and their relevance to managerial behavior: a 47-nation study.

Individualism and Collectivism.
Triandis, H.C. (1995). Boulder CO: Westview.

Academy of Management Executive, 18(1), 88–93.
Triandis, H.C. (2004). The many dimensions of culture.

Riding the Waves of Culture: Understanding Cultural Diversity in Business.
Trompenaars, F. (1993). London: Economist Books

Building a "Cultural Index" to World Airline Safety
After Looking at a Dutch Study, Boeing Suggests a Deeper Examination of Regional Issues
by Don Phillips

Do cultural and regional differences play a role in world aviation safety?

The Boeing Commercial Airplane Group, with some trepidation, has raised that question in an update of its authoritative 10-year survey of aviation safety. While offering no final answer, the world's largest airplane manufacturer says initial data suggest the possibility and demand deeper study.

"We're not saying there's anything there, but we think there's something there," said Paul D. Russell, chief engineer for airplane safety engineering. "We ought to study it. We think culture may be a player."

The question is sensitive because it inevitably raises the issue of race and because Boeing runs the risk of inadvertently insulting some of its custom-

---

Don Phillips is a *Washington Post* staff writer. Reprinted from the *Washington Post,* August 21, 1994, A8.

ers. But the initial survey of cultural differences and accident rates offers some surprises.

Boeing relied on a "cultural index" produced by Geert H. Hofstede, an anthropologist at the Institute of International Culture in the Netherlands. Hofstede has rated most countries on four factors: masculinity—the need for "ostentatious manliness;" "uncertainty avoidance"—the extent to which cultures are threatened by the unknown; individualism; and the "power distance"—how much influence a person has over another who is seen as less powerful.

Boeing then compared each factor with each country's accident rate per million departures.

Masculinity and uncertainty avoidance seemed to have almost no relevance to accident rates. But there was a clear correlation between accident rates and the other two factors. Countries with a high rate of individualism had low accident rates, while countries where people in lower positions tend to defer more to superiors had higher accident rates.

Countries with both low individualism and a large "power distance" index appear to have accident rates 2.6 times greater than those at the other end of the scale.

The lowest accident rates were in the United States, Australia, Britain, Canada, New Zealand and most West European countries. In the middle were Japan, India, Argentina, Brazil, Iran, Greece, Turkey and a smattering of other countries. At the top, with the worst rates were most Latin American countries—including Panama, Colombia, and Venezuela—and Asian countries such as Korea, China, Pakistan and Thailand.

"We're not handing this up as the holy grail," said Boeing spokesman Randy Harrison, stressing that the company was relying on someone else's research and that numerous other factors have a bearing on aviation safety.

That was the main theme of Boeing's annual safety survey, entitled "Removing Links in the Accident Chain." Rather than concentrate on the causes of aviation disasters, the company this year asked what would have prevented the accident.

Almost no accidents take place for one reason. Aviation safety professionals often refer to accident causes as a "thin chain"—if any one of the links had been broken, the accident would not have happened. For instance, a captain makes a mistake that the copilot and the air traffic controller do not catch, while on-board warning equipment malfunctions. While "pilot error'" might be the "probable cause," the accident could have been prevented by a change in any of the other factors.

Boeing found a surprise here too. The most serious accidents with the greatest death tolls had the most links in the thin chain, sometimes as many as 20. "The more serious the accident, the more opportunities we had to prevent it," Russell said.

The standard sections of the survey showed that worldwide jet aviation deaths are averaging about 560 a year. Most accidents take place on takeoff or landing, and the greatest type of accident continues to be "controlled flight into terrain"—a crew flying an otherwise airworthy plane into the ground or a mountainside. And, as usual, the primary cause—73.7 percent—has been related to the flight crew.

Other factors rose in importance, however, including the need of Boeing and other manufacturers to better design planes for pilots. Airline procedures, while hardly ever mentioned as a "cause," emerged as an important prevention strategy.

"Don't just point at the flight crews," Russell said. "Everybody's in this game."

There were regional differences. In the United States, Canada and Europe, numerous factors emerged as part of the thin chain, including crew procedure, design, maintenance and inspection. In Latin America and Asia, piloting skills and procedures were the major areas of concern. In Africa, a range of piloting factors emerged, but so did Africa's poor airport infrastructure and weather information availability.

SECTION V
CULTURE AND IDENTITY

The terms culture and identity are almost interchangeable. When we learn a culture through the process of enculturation or acculturation, we also acquire an identity as a member of a group. We take on a social role; there is a sense of belonging to, or identifying with, a group with which we share values and ways of perceiving reality. The relationship between culture and identity is apparent with the comment, "as a young Arab Muslim from Kuwait, I see the situation this way." In an attempt to explain why and how he views the world, he states that his identification with numerous groups (youth, Arabs, Muslims, and Kuwaitis) causes him to see things in a particular way.

Among the numerous definitions of the concept we call "culture" we can add the phrase "shared perceptual group." If we view the world in a similar way as others in a group, we also share an identity. We are one of them. In turn, this mutual perception of reality shapes the way in which we think and solve problems. To return to our computer analogy of culture, what information gets into the computer and how it is programmed to solve problems determines its "output." Marshall Singer claims that people in the same culture share ways of perceiving the world and Geert Hofstede defines culture as the "software of the mind," or the way in which we are programmed by our culture to take in information and organize it to solve problems.[1]

We acquire our primary culture during our youth or formative years through a process of acculturation. During these early years our personality is developing and is shaped by the social environment. Until we go to school, we mostly identify with family members and share their basic values, attitudes, and ways of thinking. In elementary school we interact with peers and teachers who also convey aspects of the dominant culture. In addition, we join numerous other groups or secondary cultures throughout our lives. Our profession, region of the country, or even the university we attend becomes an additional aspect of "who we are."

When we enter a new culture as a mature adult and go through culture shock, we adapt to the new social environment, but this does not necessarily change our identity. Although we might develop realistic cultural empathy with those in the new culture, it does not necessarily mean that we internalize or incorporate aspects of their culture into our personality. However, when we *identify with* a culture there is a sense of belonging or sharing the values, perceptions, and thought patterns of a group. It is much more profound than simply walking in their psychological and cultural shoes. We become a part of that group. We are somehow transformed.

The psychoanalytic catharsis, the existential leap, and even the mystical or religious experience are variations of intense transformative events. There is a sense of rebirth or intensive growth that is not a part of our everyday life. Very often these deeply profound experiences are a result of some kind of journey into the unknown. After a period of being lost and confused, we end up with a new and deeper understanding of who we are and where we are going.

This is much more than the identity crisis phenomenon that many go through with severe culture shock because it is extremely intense and life-altering. It amounts to a death/rebirth cycle where an inadequate problem-solving system is overwhelmed and somehow shuts down to allow a broader and more comprehensive system to emerge. It is synergistic and the new whole person is greater than the sum of the parts of two or more cultures. This is very much like the "positive disintegration" that sometimes takes place when neurotics stop struggling to cope with a painful reality and "give up." Many report that they got worse and then became "weller" than ever before.[2] At that time, they became introspective and developed new coping strategies. Some kind of intrapsychic growth took place.

Overcoming severe culture shock and adapting to a new culture can be transformative, but especially so if we do this during our formative years when our personality and identity are developing. If we live in a new culture during these years the experience actually changes our identity. It is more than a matter of adding another layer to our personality; cultural identification means that we actually change inside and develop a new personality that is a blend of two or more cultures. We are then members of a third-culture or we have a multicultural identity. This cannot necessarily be said of those who adapt to another culture as adults when working overseas, studying abroad, or serving in the Peace Corps. Culture shock and reverse culture shock certainly change people, but it is a matter of degree and timing. Growing up in different cultures has a much greater lifelong impact on our personality. It is an existential phenomenon that shapes the depth of our being.

WHO AM I?

According to Sigmund Freud, during the first 6 or 7 years of life our personality is formed as we reconcile the conflict between our need for gratification or pleasure and the restrictions of the external society. He believed that these are the most important years of life when it comes to identity formation. If we experienced some kind of severe psychological trauma during this period or fail to resolve the emotional conflicts during childhood, they create an *identity crisis* which fixates or freezes us at that stage of emotional growth. The conflict becomes a *leitmotif* for the rest of our lives. For example, if a boy views his father as a threatening rival for the attention of his mother (an Oedipal conflict[3]), he cannot identify with, or become like, his father. This conflict with his father becomes less intense as he grows older and goes to school, but it can last until the age of 10 or 11. If it is not resolved, later in life he might view all men of authority as representational of his father. Male teachers or police officers become threats and rivals. He may also spend a great deal of his adult life trying to develop relationships with women who resemble his mother.

We psychologically repress or "forget" this childhood identity crisis and, unless we can somehow recall it later as an adult through a process Freud called "free association," it is trapped in our unconscious. With psychoanalysis, we can raise to conscious awareness that which has psychologically imprisoned us for so many years and we can finally free ourselves from the grip it has held on our personality for so many years.

This phenomenon is the underlying theme of Edward Hall's book, *Beyond Culture*. His basic premise is that we can never free ourselves from the cultural prison we are born into until we somehow experience being lost in another culture. Because our primary culture is learned so early in life, we are unaware of its existence and yet we remain imprisoned by it until we experience some kind of cathartic event. This often takes place when we leave our culture and discover that the usual ways of looking at the world, interacting with others, and solving problems no longer work. At this time we raise to conscious awareness aspects of our internal culture that were hidden from us. We consciously realize its impact on our perceptions, ways of communicating, and our basic beliefs and values. With this conscious awareness, we can then transcend the control it has had on our lives.

Freud viewed the identity crisis children go through as they try to resolve their ambivalent feelings toward their parents as the most important psychological event that shapes personality. But an identity crisis is not like chicken pox or measles where once you've been infected, it will never happen again. As we go through life, we experience many identity conflicts which change how we view the world and deal with life. These include such events as adolescence when we move from childhood to adulthood, when we get married or have a child, and when we begin to accept the reality that we are growing old and will soon die.[4]

Freud viewed the ages of birth to 6 or 7 as the formative years ending with the beginning of adolescence when boys identify with their fathers and girls identify with their mothers. Developmental psychologist Erik Erikson believed that adolescence is also traumatic and a period of life when our personality goes through enormous change. Both would agree that we learn our primary culture during these early years. Erikson agreed with Freud regarding the importance of early childhood, but he thought Freud put too much emphasis on sexuality and that, although we are continually developing our personality throughout life, our identity is well-formed near the end of adolescence.

Erikson, who is credited with coining the term "identity crisis,"[5] believed that there are eight identity crises and the most important one is that of adolescence when we transition from childhood to adulthood. Between the ages of 13 and 19, we attempt to find out who we are and where we are headed in terms of our roles, responsibilities, profession, and so on. It is also during this phase that we are concerned about how we fit into the society and how others might perceive us. Our peer group becomes especially important in our lives as we develop intense relationships with all the ups and downs of belonging, rejection, loyalty, and betrayed trust. This is the period of life when young people "find themselves."

We go through an emotional or existential crisis when moving from one phase of psycho-social development to another. But there is no fixed age when one ends and the next begins. For example, adolescence could begin at the age of 11 or 12 and end in the mid-twenties. In a homogeneous rural *Gemeinschaft*, where everyone raises their children in the same way and shares the same religion, the end of adolescence is often well-defined with rituals that occur at a fixed age. Almost every religion has some sort of rite of passage when adolescence ends and adulthood begins. Confirmation for Christians or the bar mitzvahs for Jews are two institutionalized ways of moving from one identity to another. The entire community agrees that the initiate has taken on a new identity and status with adult responsibilities. Again, this is a death/rebirth event—the ritualistic and symbolic death of the child to allow for the rebirth of an adult.

In an urban heterogeneous *Gesellschaft* it isn't clear when adolescence ends and adulthood begins. In most cities in the U.S., at the age of 16 you are adult enough to drive a car, but you can't vote or serve in the military until you're 18. Only adults can legally consume alcohol, which usually means that you have reached the age of 21. For those who start a full-time job, leave home, and marry immediately after finishing high school, adulthood begins at 18 or 19. For many Americans, studying at a university may be a way of prolonging adolescence. They do not have the "adult" responsibility of working full time or raising a family. Consequently, graduation becomes their rite of passage with an accompanying identity crisis. In the United States, the definition of an adult is ambiguous and even contradictory. There is no clearly agreed upon end of childhood and beginning of adulthood.

It is increasingly common for many children to grow up in numerous cultures before they reach adulthood. How does this impact the identity of children who are raised overseas outside their parents' culture? Do the children of immigrants develop an identity that is some kind of mix of the new culture and that of their parents? Even adults who leave their home culture to live in another culture often go through the death/rebirth process of cross-cultural adaptation which leads to great personal insight and intrapsychic growth. Their identity is also transformed by the intercultural experience.

With the dramatic increase of international travel and the expanding diversity of today's global workforce, more people than ever before are living and working outside their primary culture and interacting with those who are culturally different. These "global citizens" have unique cultures and identities which allow them to become bridges between different cultures. But they also have some personal psychological and interpersonal difficulties which mono-cultural people do not experience.

THIRD-CULTURE KIDS (TCKS)

Children who are raised overseas during their developmental or formative years, are enculturated to the overseas culture while their parents are enculturated to their passport culture. They become members of both their parents' and their overseas culture and are often described as "Third-Culture Kids" or TCKs.[6] This might also describe characteristics of immigrant children or even children who grew up in an urban area and yet their parents are rural farmers.

To add to their identity confusion and complexity, their parents acculturate to the overseas culture and therefore when they return to their home or passport culture, they go through reverse culture shock. On the other hand, children who are enculturated overseas actually go through culture shock when they travel home with their parents.

There is often great concern that the psychological stress of being a part of two or more cultures simultaneously will cause irreparable damage to the child or the family. The fears are unfounded. Although the child's identity may be very fluid, eventually most end up with some kind of multicultural identity that incorporates aspects of various cultures. When these children are asked, "Who were your best friends when you were overseas?" most answer, "My parents." The family often becomes much closer because of the shared overseas experiences.

Many of these children live outside their passport culture most of their lives. They may move from country to country and consequently have a multicultural identity. When asked, "Who are you?" they might respond with the question, "When? When I was 6 years old, I was Kenyan. When I was 13, I was German. And, after the age of 18, I was an American from New York." Their identity is often in flux and changes depending upon their age. The ranking of these primary culture identities will also often change. These primary cultures are layered onto one another and may blend together. After their personality has developed, if they continue to live in other cultures they will also acculturate to many of these secondary cultures.

The early developmental or formative years of childhood are significant for Freud because it is during this time that we begin to develop a unique personality that is a result of how we resolve the conflict between an infantile desire for immediate gratification and the reality that pleasure is often delayed and limited by others.[7] We resolve this struggle by developing an *ego* or "self" which is a compromise between the urges of the *id* and the restrictions of the dominant society or *superego*. This struggle begins around the age of 5 or 6 but extends through early adolescence—stages of psychosexual development that Freud called Phallic and Latency.

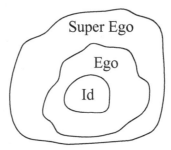

It is also during this period that children acquire their primary culture from their parents, but especially from the father or authority figure who represents the ideal of the society—how we ought to behave. At the same time we develop a conscience and understand what happens when we behave badly. Usually, a son resolves this conflict or crisis by taking on the identity of the father and a daughter takes on the identity of the mother.

Erikson agreed with Freud about the importance of these early stages of development, but thought a greater clash or crisis occurs during adolescence when peers become important to us and we leave the home to interact with others in the overall society. This is when children actually enter the world outside their home and participate in the social life of the local culture.

For children living overseas, the local primary culture is very different than the culture of their parents and siblings. There is often a conflict between these cultures that occurs as the child's personality is still being formed which is very different than when an adult relocates overseas. The adult can adapt to the local culture and leave his or her home culture. It is much more complicated and stressful for the TCK. This collision takes place daily as the child goes to school, develops friendships with others, and then returns home every day to the culture of his or her parents.

TCKs are often caught between cultures that may appear to be in opposition when it comes to basic values, beliefs, worldviews, or practices. They are sometimes living within the classic psychological double-bind where there are conflicting messages.[8] They resolve the conflict or crisis by creating a third culture and their identity then becomes a fusion of the two cultures. For some young people, this is very liberating because they can be part of more than one culture and have a global perspective. For others, it is overwhelming because they never feel they fully belong to a particular culture.

Ruth Useem, an American sociologist and anthropologist, is credited with inventing the term "third culture kids" (TCKs) to describe her three sons who lived with her in India for a year on two separate occasions in the 1950s. She discovered that they incorporated aspects of their birth or passport culture and the overseas or second culture to create a new third culture. As a sociologist she did not devote much attention to Freudian theory of personality formation but instead focused on how children raised outside their passport cultures differed from children who grew up within the culture of their parents. She and her husband John Useem were quantitative researchers who gathered survey data to determine if TCKs were significantly different in their behavior and relationships than non-TCKs.

During her years at Michigan State University between 1952 and 1985, Ruth Useem, along with her husband John and other scholars, conducted extensive research on hundreds of expatriate families overseas in 76 different countries and found that children who spent part of their formative or developmental years overseas had many characteristics that are today recognized as common to TCKs around the globe. Even as adults, TCKs seem to have some common personality traits that are a result of their childhood experiences, and they are referred to as Adult Third Culture Kids (ATCKs).[9]

For research purposes, the definition of a TCK in the early studies was limited to those who lived overseas during their formative years whose parents were sponsored or worked overseas as part of an ongoing program such as serving in the military, the Foreign Service, or as missionaries. They often live in expatriate communities or enclaves. These children are sometimes referred to as "military brats" and "missionary kids." They publicly assume a role as the representative of their parents' sponsor while overseas. This role becomes especially burdensome during adolescence because of the importance of fitting into a local cultural peer group. Dr. Useem would agree with Erikson that these early teenage years are a crucial period when it comes to identity formation. She also believed that these youths should live overseas for at least a year before adulthood begins.

Many scholars are now expanding the definition of TCKs to include children of immigrants or refugees who grow up in a new country or even children whose parents grew up in a rural homogeneous community and yet were raised in a heterogeneous urban society. Certainly many of the identity issues that TCKs confront when they return to their passport countries are faced by these children as they move from one culture to another. But they are not TCKs if we want to keep the purity of Ruth Useem's original definition.

Immigrants, displaced persons, and refugees are not "sponsored" and therefore their children do not necessarily assume the role of representing their parents' passport culture overseas. It is possible that they will never return to their parents' primary culture and they may never really learn the language that their parents grew up speaking. Nevertheless, the identity conflicts they go through during their youth may be similar to those of TCKs.

There are hundreds of articles, books, and even organizations and blogs that describe the experience of those who did not grow up in their parents' culture. Today, the term TCK is often used interchangeably with such phrases as "global nomads" and "hidden immigrants." The image of a "nomad" moving from location to location is a little more romantic than a "kid" and they are "hidden" because they may look like those around them, yet they think differently and have different values, beliefs, and norms.

David Pollock and Ruth E. Van Reken modified the original definition of TCKs to be a bit more comprehensive:

A Third Culture Kid (TCK) is a person who has spent a significant part of his or her developmental years outside the parents' culture. The TCK builds relationships to all of the cultures, while not having full ownership in any. Although elements from each culture are assimilated in the TCK's life experience, the sense of belonging is in relationship to others of similar background.[10]

This broader definition no longer limits these children to parents who have specific jobs and have lived in expatriate communities overseas. It could include children of immigrants or children who grow up in a different region of the country than their parents.

This more comprehensive definition also includes the idea that TCKs have a "sense of belonging in relationships to others of similar background." Central to the concept of culture is the *sense of belonging* that both primary and secondary cultures provide for their members. TCKs are comfortable with other TCKs because of their shared experiences. And if we use Marshall Singer's definition of a culture as a matter of *shared perception,* then TCKs probably view the world in similar ways.[11]

When explaining the TCK phenomenon, we see how psychology, sociology, and anthropology come together like the proverbial elephant and the blind men. Each explores a different aspect and yet, when brought together, we see more clearly the relationship between each of their approaches. Developmental psychologists would tend to concentrate on when and how the personality develops for the TCK in comparison with non-TCKs. Ruth Useem and other sociologists gathered mostly quantitative data to describe the characteristics of the TCK but they were not overly concerned about practical application of their findings or how the findings relate to various theories of personality development.

Cultural anthropologists tend to look for explanations as to how the overseas experience impacts identity and what happens when TCKs move from one culture to another. Interculturalists would draw from the research of all these scholarly fields and take a multidisciplinary approach to better educate and train people for helping TCKs in their adjustment and identity crises. As trainers and counselors, they are the most applied and most likely to use the research for training, counseling, and education.

CHARACTERISTICS OF TCKS

Various scholars have found some unique characteristics amongst TCKs that distinguish them from those who have not grown up outside their parents' culture.[12] Usually these findings come from surveys and interviews of adult TCKs (or ATCKs) who reflect on their lives and the impact the TCK experience has had on their education, careers, attitudes, and relationships.

Although there are commonalities which TCKs share, there are also exceptions. For example, the greatest numbers of subjects in these studies are American and the findings might not be shared by TCKs in all cultures. There are variations among TCKs regarding the amount of time spent in particular cultures, the age during which these experiences took place, and circumstances such as the intensity of interaction with local nationals or whether the TCK attended a local school or an international school. The attitudes of other family members, especially parents, would surely make a difference. Furthermore, each TCK is an individual.

Some find their global identity to be very liberating and they feel special. Others wish they had remained in one culture during their childhood and resent the up-rootedness of being a TCK.

The early research on TCKs focused on American children returning to the U.S. Today, we have a great deal of research from many other countries. For example, in Japan the terms *kagai-shijo* and *kikoku-shijo* means "overseas children" and "returnee children."[13] They are described as the Japanese version of "military brats" or "missionary kids" or simply "TCKs." Professor Momo Kano Podolsky notes that these children were perceived as "deficient Japanese" in the past because they lacked knowledge of Japanese social and cultural norms but in the 1980s and 1990s this view began to change and they were seen as "new elite" in the Japanese media.[14] They were certainly no longer "hidden immigrants." A large network of schools welcomed these children and provided special academic and counseling support.

They were viewed as bridges between cultures with special language and cross-cultural adaptation skills. This was a stereotype. Many did not have outstanding language (mainly English) proficiency and some were embarrassed because they studied in Japanese schools while overseas. Thus, many simply tried to hide their overseas experiences.[15] Today they are no longer viewed as privileged people who need special types of classes and counseling.

Although it is important to dispel stereotypes about Japanese "returnees," nevertheless, most have characteristics that are typical of TCKs in American studies. Regardless of how much exposure they had to a host country's culture or the mastery of the local language, they tend to see themselves as outsiders who were not understood by those who had never lived overseas. They had a global perspective and were more aware of interpersonal relationships than children who had never left their home country.

Japanese TCKs are no longer treated as young people who need special programs in school and yet they are still valued for their apparent cross-cultural communication skills and experiences. However, in 2012, the Japanese government announced that it was creating pre-schools to accommodate the needs of thousands of multicultural families.[16] These are primarily TCKs returning to Japan, many of whom have bi-cultural parents.

We need to avoid stereotypes of all TCKs but nevertheless there are some statistical studies that suggest that these are a few of the characteristics shared by TCKs and ATCKs:[17]

1. Many American TCKs are *lifelong vagabonds*—even academic vagabonds. They often change majors during college and about 45% attend three universities before earning a degree, but they are four times as likely as non-TCKs to earn a bachelor's degree.[18] They usually graduate and marry later than others. They speak at least two different languages and tend to end up in careers that involve international relocation or travel.

    As with any vagabond, there is a sense of *rootlessness*. Although some may long to "settle down" in one place, most are often *restless*. They enjoy new adventures, new friends, and the challenge of a lifelong process of adapting and re-adapting to numerous cultures.

    Their identity is fluid as they move from one culture to another and their sense of self is not grounded in any one culture. With each culture, there is another way of perceiving reality and they have a myriad of worldviews which are often overlapping and in conflict.

If a person remains in one culture until adulthood, the society shapes or defines their identity. If it is a very homogeneous community, chances are parents raise their children in a similar way, everyone has the same religion, and roles are unconsciously, but nevertheless clearly, understood. To begin with, one is the son or daughter of particular parents. There are common rites of passage that determine transitions from childhood to adolescence and adulthood. For the TCK, the burden of defining identity is placed on the shoulders of the child, not the community.

2.   They are *highly adaptable and fit into new social environments easily*. They make friends quickly and yet many view themselves as a bit inauthentic in that they continually adapt and re-adapt to the cultures in which they are living. They never settle down in one place or with one set of friends. They are "becoming" and "unbecoming" or "a part of," and at the same time "apart from," many different cultures. TCKs often describe themselves as feeling as if they are chameleons because they can change easily to fit into the local cultures.

     According to surveys, more than 80 percent said they could relate to anyone, regardless of race or nationality. And they are open to new experiences and tend to adapt very well to various social situations. They often serve as bridges between members of different cultures because of their ability to speak more than one language combined with their global perspective.

     They make friends easily but they are also likely to move on in their relationships because of their continual relocations. The letting-go process of the grief cycle seems to be a part of their personality as they move from community and friends. In fact, some describe themselves as constantly grieving for the relationships that they must give up as they move on to new locations.

3.   They almost always feel *out of sync* with their peers in their passport culture, who seem to be very parochial.[19] On the other hand, many view themselves as rather worldly or cosmopolitan which probably comes across to others as arrogant. Their home country peers are more domestic-minded and are less likely to be interested in hearing about what is going on overseas or to listen to a TCK who continually relives his or her overseas adventures. A local peer might remind the TCK that he is no longer overseas. In an effort to find those who share their worldviews and experiences, they often join groups that include nationals from countries they have lived in or are populated by other TCKs. On many college campuses, these groups are called "Global Nomads."

4.   They are *great observers and listeners*. They are often perceived as somewhat *detached* because they tend to want to hear all sides of an argument from various perspectives before making up their own minds or taking action. Although they are hesitant to make quick decisions, they are likely to be good mediators and negotiators, especially when those involved come from different cultural backgrounds.

     They welcome complexity and nuance and find it difficult to view things in dualistic white-or-black terms. Thus, they appear tentative and overly thoughtful as they weigh different facts and positions presented by others. In this respect, they fit the stereotypes many Americans have of Europeans and Europeans have of Americans. Europeans often perceive Americans as overly impulsive cowboys who act before they think. Americans often perceive Europeans as too thoughtful and indecisive—"They talk, talk, talk and never do anything." TCKs are much more European than American. President Obama, a TCK, is often accused of being overly tentative as he weighs different options before making a decision.

This hesitancy and caution makes it difficult for TCKs to commit to relationships and place until later in life. They find it difficult to settle down in one place. The grass seems to always appear greener somewhere else.

5.   TCKs have a *global perspective*. They enjoy learning new languages and many are multilingual, they pay attention to political situations around the world, and they understand that one can be task-oriented and still take the time to develop relationships.

They are often nonjudgmental and have mastered realistic cultural empathy. Nancy Adler would describe their worldview as one of "equifinality" and "cultural contingency."[20] There are numerous equally valid ways to solve problems and the best way may depend upon the particular culture. This is the opposite of "parochialism"—"our way is the only way." Parochial people are just unaware that there are other ways to solve problems or perceive situations. This is also the opposite of "ethnocentrism"—"our way is the best way." The ethnocentric person might view all other ways as inferior.

MULTICULTURAL PERSONS

People who have fully adapted to numerous cultures, regardless of their parents' jobs or even their ages may increasingly find themselves labeled "multicultural" or "cross-cultural" persons without the designation of "third culture" or "kid." The amount of multiculturalism will depend upon the intensity of the cross-cultural experience and the degree of impact it has had on identity, including perception. Just as one would need to grow up in two cultures at exactly the same time to be fully bicultural, one would need to grow up in numerous cultures at the same time to be fully multicultural. It then becomes a matter of degree. Some are more multicultural than others.

Children of immigrants, refugees, and regional transplants often belong to numerous primary and secondary cultures. As we have noted, they share many of the characteristics that are common to TCKs yet they do not fit the strict definition given by the Useems. They are *multicultural* in that they have lived in various different cultural environments but they may never return to the culture of their parents. By definition, all TCKs are multicultural but a multicultural person is not necessarily a TCK. Some scholars have adopted the term "cross cultural kids" to encompass the wide variety of types of children who grow up outside the culture of their parents.[21]

Immigrant children have many of the characteristics that both the Useems and Peter Adler attribute to TCKs and multicultural persons. For example, Arsalan, a recent graduate of American University, is the son of immigrants. His parents came from Iran to the U.S. in the mid-1970s to study and remained after the Iranian revolution of 1979. He was born in Marin County, California in 1987 and in his pre-school years he socialized primarily with his Iranian relatives and friends. But once he attended school he entered another world inhabited by children and teachers from the overall American culture. He writes of this struggle for identity:

> During elementary school especially, there were times when I hated that my bagged lunch from home was Persian food and not a salami sandwich like all the other kids. I hated that my name was so hard for everyone to pronounce and that we didn't celebrate Christmas. We were different, and I resented it.[22]

Arsalan grew up as a bilingual and bicultural child and he has kept his involvement in both worlds throughout his college years. "Today, I am extremely proud of being an Iranian American and not just an Iranian or an American. I am a multicultural individual, and I would not have it any other way."[23]

A study conducted of Asian gangs in southern California found that many were teenagers or young adults who seemed to be caught between cultures. They often formed gangs in high school when confronted with Mexican and Black gangs as a matter of self-defense. But these gangs also fulfilled an apparent psychological and social need to "belong" to some kind of collective group or surrogate family with which they could identify. An older gang member was treated as a father figure while another member fills the role of older brother. Each person had a role in the gang's "family." Most of these Asian youths did not fit into their parents' culture nor were they fully a part of the American mainstream cultures.[24] Their identities were similar to TCKs but they would probably never return to their parents' homeland and, if they were typical of the children of Asian parents who were born in this country, about a third would marry someone who was not Asian. Most could hardly speak the language of their parents. Even the tattoos of Asian words that some wore were meaningless. Some came from the labels of cans of tuna that came from Asia.

As early as 1974, Peter Adler described a multicultural person as an existentialist whose identity is continually in the process of "becoming" and "unbecoming" and who is a "part of" and "apart from" the many cultures in which he or she lives.[25] In perhaps overstated and optimistic terms, he views this modern cosmopolitan as one whose "identifications and loyalties transcend the boundaries of nationalism and whose commitments are pinned to a vision of the world as a global community."[26] Although multicultural persons adapt well to different cultures, their adjustment is much more than simply mild or even moderate "culture shock" because the overseas experience has a profound impact on their personalities.

The multicultural person's identity is constantly going through a process of dissolution and reformation, or as Kazimierz Dabrowski describes it, "positive disintegration."[27] The person goes through an intense identity crisis as he or she adapts to each culture. And yet, this leads to great intrapsychic growth.

> The seeds of each new identity of the multicultural person lie within the disintegration of previous identities. "When the human being," writes Erikson, "because of accidental or developmental shifts, loses an essential wholeness, he restructures himself and the world by taking recourse to what we may call 'totalism.'" Such totalism, above and beyond being a mechanism of coping and adjustment, is a part of the growth of a new kind of wholeness at a higher level of integration.[28]

Peter Adler was concerned about the role of confusion of true multicultural persons and he believed that they are very vulnerable. To use Erikson's terminology, they could suffer from a "defused or multiphrenic identity" where the configuration of loyalties and identifications is constantly in flux.[29] On the other hand, because they struggle with the question, "Who am I?" so early in life, it is possible they are more "centered" or have a stronger sense of who they are than those who grow up in one culture. In a homogenous community, everyone may raise their children in a similar way with similar values. Movement from one development phase to another is fairly ritualized and regularized. For multicultural people, it all depends upon where they are at a particular time in their life and the burden of self-definitions rests on their shoulders.

Being an outlier or outsider can be extremely stressful and lonely but it also forces a person to become fairly introspective and to define his or her own "self" or identity rather than to rely upon the dominant culture to make this determination.[30] For example, a gay teenager might be forced to answer the "who am I" question well before a straight teenager. He may have the dualistic or existential perspective of an outsider—both a part of and apart from the mainstream culture. To this extent, he may be more mature than other teenagers at an earlier age.

This is true of TCKs and even many ethnic, racial, religious, and other minorities with societies. As we have noted, when we move into another culture, we become more aware of our primary culture—we find it by leaving it. For the TCK it occurs much earlier in life and for a multicultural person this discovery occurs over and over again.

Peter Adler viewed the multicultural man as "a new kind of man," and yet today we can think of numerous people who fit his characterization. Just as TCKs are now quite common in all societies, the same is true of multicultural persons. Moreover, their number is steadily increasing with the vast numbers of people moving their families across cultures both within and between nations. We don't yet know the full impact of the worldwide social media but chances are that they are abetting the multiculturalism especially among younger people.

TCKs AND MULTICULTURAL PEOPLE AS OUTSIDERS

We can think of many multicultural people who became great leaders. Mahatma Gandhi was born in India but went to study in London when he was 19 years old. When he finished his studies at the age of 22, he briefly returned to India and then traveled to South Africa where he practiced law for 21 years. India is extremely multicultural with many different religions even today. Surely Gandhi's experiences living in London and South Africa had a dramatic impact on him.

Although Gandhi was not necessarily a TCK because he left his home culture during his post-adolescent years, he was definitely a multicultural person who was an outsider and not simply a sojourner traveling from one country to another. Civilizations often progress not on the backs of those who behave well and fit in the mainstream culture of a particular society but rather those who challenge the culture in which they live and even cause others to question practices, beliefs, and values that may have been held for many generations.

Gandhi's teachings influenced another multicultural person—Martin Luther King Jr.— who grew up in the segregated deep south of the U.S. He was an outsider in his own society during an era of rampant racism and segregation. Both he and Gandhi were jailed because of their efforts to change their societies. If they had followed the written and unwritten rules of discrimination in their countries, neither would have been jailed. But they challenged the cultural prison into which they were born.

Outsiders are often forced to define their own identities because they are both inside and outside the mainstream culture. They have the double-vision common to those who do not fit into the dominant culture. Modern existentialism arose during World War II when many intellectuals in Europe were jailed or imprisoned in mental hospitals because they opposed fascism, anti-Semitism, and racism.[31] The only real crime they committed was opposing the dominant society at that time. They reasoned that had they simply fit into the dominant culture, they would be considered normal law-abiding and sane citizens. But they would abet the persecution of Jews, gypsies, homosexuals, and other minorities. Simply following the "rules" of the society would give them freedom but it would also be immoral. They concluded that it therefore was up to each individual to define his or her own existence based upon the reactions to their behavior. Often the individual who is deemed deviant or even mad could be moral and sane. It is possible that the dominant culture is immoral and even mad.

The first American existentialist novel, *The Outsider,* was written by the African American author Richard Wright in 1953.[32] It depicted how a black American was almost invisible and yet he had the double-vision of an outsider—he knew the dominant white culture and its duplicitous practices and contradictions, and yet white Americans hardly noticed him.[33] In the land of freedom and equality there was racism and discrimination. Black people did not have an equal opportunity to get a proper education or job. Many other outsiders at that time—women, immigrants of color, homosexuals, and so on—also surely had this existential double vision of outsiders.

Before he died, Wright was self-exiled in Paris and often associated with famous European existentialists such as Jean-Paul Sartre and Albert Camus. He returned to his flat after an evening with his literary friends and wrote in his diary that he didn't quite understand existentialism but he concluded that black Americans were practicing existentialists because they had the outsider vision similar to the European existentialists.

Barack Obama

John Quincy Adams and Benjamin Franklin lived in France and spoke fluent French. Many political leaders in America were multicultural. However, the most famous TCK today is President Barack Obama who describes himself as an African-American with a white mother. As a young man, his father was a goat herder who grew up in Kenya and met his white mother from Kansas during his graduate studies at the University of Hawaii. This university is located in the most ethnically and racially diverse state in the U.S. where Obama was born in 1961 to an 18 year-old Kansan mother. Even during his pre-school years, he certainly had friends whose families came from many ethnic, racial, religious, and national backgrounds.

From the age of six to ten, he lived in Indonesia with his Indonesian step-father and his white, American mother. Although Barack Obama is a Protestant Christian, his father was Muslim. However, he spent very little time with his father who returned to Kenya shortly after he was born. Indonesia, however, is the largest Muslim country and he was exposed to the practices of Islam. He went to local schools, although they were not Muslim. He speaks some Bahasa, a local language of Indonesia.

In his autobiography, *Dreams from My Father,* Obama described his struggle to define his identity as a mixed-race child trying to fit into his black and his white identity. TCKs and multicultural people are often aware that they are "outsiders" and therefore need to define their own unique identity much earlier than others. This process is often described as "centering." Obama describes this in his autobiography:

> I went to the bathroom and stood in front of the mirror with all my senses and limbs seemingly intact, looking the way I had always looked, and wondered if something was wrong with me.[34]

Added to this was the influence of his growing up in a multicultural Hawaii and his years in Indonesia. As President he sought the support and advice of other TCKs such as White House Senior Advisor Valerie Jarrett whose formative years took place in Tehran and London, and Treasury Secretary Tim Geithner who grew up in East Africa, India, Thailand, China, and Japan—and speaks Japanese.[35]

When he was president of the *Harvard Law Review,* Obama seemed to be highly skilled when it came to mediating various viewpoints while remaining removed from the heat of the debate. His aloofness and his skills as an observer[36] are common characteristics of TCKs as well as the perception others have that he is indecisive, detached, and too intellectual. Many of his students at the University of Chicago were unaware of what position he took on an issue until well after he heard the discussion of all points of view coming from students. This eliminates groupthink and the tendency of the students to conform to the views of the professor, but it also can appear to be a sign of uncertainty. One of the criticisms of Obama as President is that he "acts like a professor."

GENERATIONAL CULTURES

The core of one's identity is formed before our teenage years end. Although Freud emphasized the early years, Erikson believed that going through the emotionally tumultuous years of adolescence further shapes our identity as we go through the ups and downs of acceptance and rejection by our peers and discover our "self" outside the security of the home. In his opinion, this was the most important period of identity formation. And it is during this period of life that we identify with, or feel a part of, a particular generation.

Our "generation" usually refers to the period of identity formation between early adolescence and young adulthood. Today this probably means from the age of 12 until perhaps the late twenties. The music we heard during this period becomes the soundtrack for our life. When we hear a song from that period of life, we often recall not only our personal joys and pains when developing friendships, but also significant national and international events. Almost every American who was an adolescent in the early 1960s recalls when President John Kennedy was assassinated. Those in their twenties today remember when the World Trade Center in New York was destroyed by terrorists on September 11th, 2001. Indeed, the events of 9/11 have become a part of the identity of young adults around the world.

COMMUNICATIONS, TECHNOLOGY, AND YOUTH

Freud believed that humans are quite different than other beings because they have the capacity to alter the physical environment. Rather than physically adapting to their environment (autoplastic adaptation) they developed tools with which they could change and even assault that environment (alloplastic adaptation). In cold climates, animals evolved by growing longer coats of fur while human beings made clothing and dwellings to protect themselves from the climate.[37]

The evolution of human civilization is really a matter of developing increasingly more sophisticated technology with which we can alter the environment. Anthropologist Edward Hall labeled these tools "extensions" because they extend human capabilities across time and space. He states, "The study of man is a study of his extensions."[38] They could be used to make the world better or perhaps to destroy others and the physical environment.

Extensions can fragment life and dissociate humans from each other and we can transfer some of our humanness and human responsibilities to these extensions, a process Hall termed "extension transference." Humans transfer a part of their human responsibility to the extension and it takes on a life of its own. When we developed the technology to kill rabbits by pulling a trigger on a gun from a distance of hundreds of feet, it was fun to go hunting. However, if we had to kill rabbits with our bare hands, it is less likely we would enjoy the sport.

Modern military technology provides an example of extension transference. When using drones or missiles, we are removed from the act of violence. We don't hear the screams or see the destruction. Often the bombing is orchestrated from another country or even another continent. This makes it easier to use the technology without pondering the human consequences. It is far different than hand-to-hand combat.

If we consider culture as a system of interrelated parts, then introducing a new technology alters the system. This is true of communications. Before we could read or write, all communications were face-to-face. People perhaps were very adept at nonverbal communication but they could not communicate across distances or time. With writing, they not only could communicate across space but also extend a message into the future without being in the physical presence of another human. But with this new technology, they were removed from the immediate intimate feelings that are sent with our body language and cannot be as easily expressed with words. Thus, the technology takes away some of our humanness.

Introducing new technology to a social system may enhance the quality of life but it can also adversely impact the entire social system. In a remote village, people may find that the primary source of information and entertainment is face-to-face interaction. They join other families in the evening to share tea and stories in the village market. Their interpersonal communication skills are very highly developed. If we introduce computers and television, villagers might remain at home to get their information and entertainment from a screen. They may be better informed but their interpersonal communication skills may diminish. Shops that serve tea in the village market begin to close as the strong communal spirit of the village starts to weaken.

Digital communication is fast and extends humans to almost any place on earth. But it is difficult to communicate feelings and yet it is easy to send messages which perpetuate cruelty, bigotry, and hatred. Even on the interpersonal level, how often has someone sent an angry message via text message or email which they would never send in a face-to-face situation?

Transportation, communication, and information technology have a very dramatic impact on the young. In the U.S., those who grew up in the 1950s and early 1960s are often referred to as the "Baby Boomers." They were born during the dramatic increase in population after

World War II and they were viewed as different from those who grew up during the Great Depression of the 1930s or during World War II. Modern transportation and communications allowed them to move about easily and interact with others in ways that were different from earlier generations. Teenagers had access to telephones, automobiles, and televisions which changed the patterns of social interaction and sources of entertainment and information from all previous generations. And this new technology was spreading across the globe.

We can often distinguish generations based upon technological innovations. Certainly the digital age of modern communications has greatly changed cultures around the world, but especially so for those who were growing up when this technology became popularized. Their parents may never be as proficient in the use of social media and digital communication as their children, who take it for granted. In fact, parents are often "digital immigrants" while their children were born into the digital world. This is very much like the children of pioneers who easily adapted to the frontier because they were born into that environment. Their parents, on the other hand, carried cultural baggage from their earlier experiences which inhibited their adaptation.

When it comes to adopting modern communications technology, this is truly a worldwide youth phenomenon. Consider how social media has brought together young people from around the globe and produced enormous social and political changes within countries such as the 2011 Arab Spring movements in the Middle East and North Africa. Unfortunately, Facebook, Twitter, and YouTube can also be used to spread propaganda, recruit terrorists, and even plan potential attacks.

Communications technology also changes the ways in which people interact. Few teenagers today write letters to friends and family. A new language or dialect has emerged based upon social media, and many get most of their information about the world over the internet rather than through newspapers and magazines. Some may have written their papers in high school and at the university without having ever gone to a library.

As young people around the globe use texting as a primary way of communicating with family and friends, it is possible that their face-to-face interpersonal skills will atrophy. Instead of taking time to exchange pleasantries before getting down to the matter at hand, they become more direct and use codes that are efficient but rather abrupt. These codes are high-context situational dialects that text users around the world might master but they use only written symbols and words and vision. Some human intimacy is lost because they cannot use their other sense modalities. They cannot touch, hear, or even see the person with whom they are communicating.

It is too early to fully assess the impact of digital communications technology on societies although it will surely change social systems. The divide may be primarily generational. Those who have grown up using this technology have discovered ways to retain intimacy just as people raised in New York City use nonverbal practices which allow them to cope with an overcrowded social environment. Some members of the digital generation even speak of their internet "friends" as if they were lifelong intimate relationships although they have never actually met face-to-face with any of them.

CONFLICT BETWEEN GENERATIONS

As we are socialized and enculturated during our preadolescent years, we acquire many of the beliefs, values, and ways of thinking of our parents. During childhood, parents transmit primary cultural values across at least two or three generations. In fact, the greatest predictor of one's political party identification is the political party of parents. The same may be said for religious identity.

During adolescence young people develop their social ties to their peers and struggle intensely with the question, "Who am I?" As adults, we can all look back on the part of our life and recall the difficulties of "fitting in" or being an "outsider," of seeing ourselves as separate from and different than our parents, and of feeling that older people just wouldn't understand us.

Every generation thinks of itself as unique and certainly different from the preceding generation. This is especially true because the generation we identify with is made of those with whom we shared adolescent and early adulthood experiences. During that period of life, young people often wish to conform to the lifestyle of their peers. Even in the late 1960s when "hippies" claimed to be unconventional in their dress, they often carefully selected clothing that identified them as members of the counterculture.

On the other hand, most young people do not want to be the same as their parents when they are adolescents. They know they are in a different generation or time period. When they hear parents talk about, "in our days," they resist the urge to respond by saying, "your days are over with."

> Even very recently, the elders could say: "You know, I have been young and *you* never have been old." But today's young people can reply: "You never have been young in the world I am young in, and you never can be." This is the common experience of pioneers and their children. . . . Today, suddenly, because all peoples of the world are part of one electronically based, interconnecting network, young people everywhere share a kind of experience that none of the elders ever have had or will have.[39]

Anthropologist Margaret Mead wrote these words about the generation of teenagers in the late 1960s. Author Jack Newfield labeled this generation *The Prophetic Minority* [40] because these young people were somehow going to lead the U.S. into a new era of progress and peace. The previous generation was sometimes called the "ungeneration" or "silent generation" because they seemed to only want to fit into the dominant culture.

In the 1960s this was not just an American happening. It was the era of the youth activism around the globe when young people challenged their dominant cultures to eliminate racism, war, poverty, and so on. These movements took place in France, Germany, Japan, and dozens of other countries. They were often referred to as countercultural movements because their behaviors and values appeared to almost the opposite of the dominant cultures in their respective countries.

They were also identity movements.[41] In the U.S., many young Black Americans took pride in their racial and cultural identity. With the Black Identity movement they refused to give up their racial identity simply to have equal opportunities. They couldn't change their skin color or hair texture to fit into the white, male, Anglo-Saxon, Protestant dominant cultural cookie-cutter. But why should they? Young people took the position that one could be both black, Muslim or gay and still be an "American"—a hyphenated American—an African-American, Muslim-American or gay-American. Other identity movements such as the feminist and Chicano movements asserted the right to have multiple identities within the mainstream or dominant culture.

Since the 1960s and 1970s there have been various other generations such as the "me decade" of the 1980s, Generation X and Generation Y, and the new millennials. It is important to realize that a generation doesn't fit neatly into a particular time period—there is overlap between generational cultures. And all young people were not a part of whatever "movement" was taking place within their generation.

In the United States, most young people of high school and college age have grown up in a multicultural society. Many have taken classes where the value of diversity was stressed. They did not attend segregated schools nor did they march in demonstrations demanding equal rights for everyone. Most have never witnessed overt racism or experienced discrimination. Their friends are straight and gay and come from numerous ethnic, racial, religious, and national backgrounds. Through social media, they are connected daily with peers around the globe and they are much more aware of world events than previous generations. They share many of the characteristics of TCKs.

It is perfectly acceptable to have a multicultural or hyphenated identity—African-American, Muslim-American, gay-American, or white-American. On many registration and survey forms, one can check off numerous categories to identify yourself—white, black, Hispanic, Asian, Native American. Increasingly, young people just identify themselves as American without any reference to ethnicity, race, nationality, or religion.

And yet, there is *de facto* segregation in many communities based upon race and social class. Black and Hispanic families are much more likely to be poor and unemployed than white families. It is tempting to simply dismiss race as a factor and view this as only a matter of economic class, but this would not explain why people of color are disproportionally among the poorest—the least educated with the greatest unemployment. It is certainly much more than a matter of economics.

Around the world, the current generation of young people is much more international and multicultural than any previous generation. They are interconnected by social media and they are also crossing borders more frequently. One of the lessons they learned from 9/11 and the decade of economic crisis they have gone through in the late 2000s is that the politics and economics of one country can impact all the others.

Just as the countercultural movements of young people in the late 1960s challenged their dominant culture, young people in 2011 challenged the authorities in their societies in both the Arab Spring and the Occupy Wall Street movements. In many respects, their demonstrations and sit-ins were countercultural in that they wanted the older elite, who held vast economic, political, and even military power, to share their power with the majority of citizens in their respective countries. These movements claimed to reflect the traditional values of their cultures such as fairness, egalitarianism, and democracy.

In the United States, the jeremiad of a new generation somehow leading the country back to its basic values while simultaneously moving into a new and better future is very tradition-ally American. This was the theme of the Massachusetts Bay Colony and the "City on a Hill." The Puritans claimed they would somehow return to the purity of their Protestant Christian roots and at the same time develop a utopian society which would serve as a beacon for the rest of the world.[42]

In the 2008 election there was a clear generational conflict between supporters of President Obama who were overwhelmingly under 40 and the supporters of Senator McCain who were overwhelmingly over 65. The same divisions seem to be true with the 2012 presidential election.

The young tend to be multicultural and multiracial and they have very different views on social issues. Most favor gay marriage, funding education, and immigration. Many very conservative older voters are opposed to same-sex marriages, tend to be more religious, and hold more negative attitudes toward immigrants. To a great extent, they believe their "way of life" is being threatened by the social changes taking place in the society and tend to be more xenophobic. Although young people may have suffered more from the economic downturns of the past five years, they still remain more optimistic than older people.

At the turn of the millennium, very few people would have predicted that the voters of the United States would elect an African-American as their President or that a Puerto Rican female would be approved as a justice on the Supreme Court. These changes are now taken for granted as more interaction between people of different racial and ethnic backgrounds takes place, especially among young people. The same is true for gay Americans. Most Americans have friends or family members who are gay and the majority of young people approve of same-sex marriage. This would have been unthinkable a generation ago.

Homophobia decreases as gay and straight people get to know each other on an interper-sonal basis. It is very difficult to develop an image of someone as a "threat" or an "enemy" once we develop an interpersonal relationship. This may in part explain the current Islamo-phobia.[43] Very few Americans have actually met a Muslim but gradually American Muslims are interacting with non-Muslims around the U.S., especially among young people. As this interaction increases, chances are that the fear of Muslims will be more difficult to perpetuate.

SECTION V: Readings

Third Culture Persons

Kathleen A. Finn Jordan

Ask someone where they are from, and the answer you will expect to receive may be, "Chicago," "New York," "California," or "Kansas." Even when dealing internationally, expected answers can be "Paris," "Milan," or "Tokyo." But increasingly there is another answer being given, "When?" This answer often comes from those who honestly need to know a time frame before they can give you a geographic reference. They might answer something like "Well, I've lived in the Netherlands, France, and Germany, and Mom and Dad are in South Africa right now, but I'm an American." These people are the children of parents who have been assigned to positions overseas, or who have taken jobs overseas. The positions they take can be in any variety of capacities, from government-related postings, military, or international business assignments to missionary work. The positions they hold may be diplomats, teachers, military personnel, artists, oil-riggers, United Nations' staff, bilingual stenographers, reporters, bankers, technical consultants, or multinational corporation executives, but they all have something in common.[1] The children they raise will live in a variety of cultures and places, and none of them will necessarily be the culture or place that the parents call home.

Geoff, a child of missionary parents, lived abroad for fifteen years, moving between Cameroon, England, Zaire, and Taiwan. When he tried to return to the United States after his sojourn, he began to realize just how much his overseas experience set him apart from his peers in the United States.

Academics would have been the easiest transition and social life would have been the most difficult. I had no idea, even after I had come back to the States and left again after the seventh grade, about what Americans in general or American High School students did, how they acted, or what they were instructed in, so it was in essence coming to a new culture because it had been 5 years since I had been in the states, and, even in the seventh grade, I didn't enjoy that year . . . subconsciously I am an American and I readjusted myself to my new home. My home now, always my home on paper.[2]

Geoff and others who have shared his experience of growing up as children of sponsored adults overseas are "third culture kids" (TCKs).[3] These people have had to develop ways of relating the many cultures of which they are a part. In so doing, they create a composite set of values, norms, and social structures for themselves that contains some of all the cultures to which they relate.[4] But, in creating a composite of these cultures, they are actually creating another, distinct "third culture" which is a part of, yet apart from, the other cultures. These third culture persons are not truly members of any of the cultures in which they have lived, but have developed their own separate and distinct culture that exists between those cultures.

There are many things that distinguish the third culture person from those we term monocultural. Monocultural individuals are those who, like the vast majority of the people in the world, were

This article is first published here. Dr. Jordan is a Consulting Educational Counselor in Washington, D.C. and a Research Associate at Michigan State University.

primarily raised in a single culture. They learned the language, norms, behavior patterns and culture that were inherent to the land where they were raised, and this land was most often the land of their ancestors. Throughout their developing years, monocultural people might have changed physical locations within a country or culture, but the culture and country within which they operated remained in large part the same.[5]

A third culture person, specifically a third culture kid (TCK), was raised in more than one country and culture. TCKs were often raised in four, five, or even six or more countries over the course of their development, and rarely were any of these countries or cultures those which their parent's called home. For the TCK, this home identification may be nothing more than a name on his/her parents' passports. A third culture kid may never have seen, or been a part of, this place until they return to the "home" country for a post-secondary education. But growing up and developing in so many environments has, in many cases, led these individuals to develop an understanding not only of those cultures in which they have been raised, but also an understanding and set of skills for dealing with *any* other culture.

CHARACTERISTICS OF THIRD CULTURE PERSONS

Wayne, a TCK of missionary sponsorship, lived abroad for 13 years, and moved through six countries. When he returned to the United States, he noted that for a long time he was an observer.

> By observation it was easier than learning by mistakes 'cause I didn't have to suffer. I began to analyze people. . . . I found that I am adaptable and I can go and live anywhere, but to find out why I live in a certain way takes at least a year. I'm interested in people and because of that I first observe them and try to learn fundamental things about civilization and integrate those things. After that I go into other things.[6]

Wayne knows that he has the skills to live almost anywhere in the world. He can go into a country and adapt to life in that country, but he won't necessarily understand why he does certain things. This is often a problem that TCKs have when entering a new environment, or even returning to a relatively familiar one. They feel both a part of the culture, and apart from it. Their "third cultureness" actually prevents them from being completely a part of any particular culture. They have adapted to moving, to changing relationships and locales, but being adapted to change may preclude any feeling of having roots in a single culture. This is possibly the most common perception among TCKs: that they are part of all of their respective cultures, yet also apart from all of them. Their experiences make them different by changing the way TCKs attribute value and meaning, thus orienting them to a broader, more multicultural context.[7] Their culture is the third culture.

Researchers observing TCKs as they return to the home country for post-secondary education have also been able to identify other common traits in the third culture personality. TCKs seem to develop an identity management that differs from those who grow up in their own countries, including an exceedingly complex sense of identity. This sense of their identity reflects their overseas experience, and affects their social relationships with individuals and groups. When asked about their initial life plans, TCKs almost always include an ambition to return to a mobile, international lifestyle.[8] As a group, they are more comfortable intrapersonally than interpersonally, they function as perceptive observers: slow to jump in, mapping the territory, collecting information and processing it, and, while doing all of that, feeling marginal at the outset of their exposure to any new environment, though constructively so. Their academic skills stand by them as they seek to acquire appropriate social skills. These characteristics are most often seen by researchers when the TCKs return to the home country to attend post-secondary institutions (colleges and universities).

The following is a list of general characteristics and observations pulled from an ongoing study of 696 adult third culture kids (ATCKs) who are between the ages of 24 and 90.[9] All participants have spent at least a year abroad as the minor dependent of an American parent in the Third Culture role, are currently residing in the United States, and were willing to fill in a twenty-four page self-administered questionnaire. It must be noted that third culture kids can come from any country, and their parents from any culture. This study is based on those with United States citizenship solely because of their accessibility to the researchers. Similar results have been noticed among TCKs with other citizenships.

- As children, the TCKs in the study lived in four to six countries by the age of 18–19. They attended private nonprofit or profit-making schools primarily set up for the education of foreigners. Some schools were set up by their parents' sponsor (DoD schools, Joint Embassy Schools, missionary boarding schools) and others by private, not-for-profit or profit-making groups.

- Approximately 82% of this group speaks foreign languages regularly, or occasionally, and these languages often reflect their own personal, mobile history, rather than their own ethnicity.

- On the point of reentry for many, and the coincidence of that point with the commencement of post-secondary school, their academic transitions are more facile than their emotional and affective transitions; TCKs experience prolonged adolescence.

- TCKs' college behavior seems consistent with mobility patterns experienced during their childhood years. Seldom do they graduate in four years from the same college in which they enrolled as freshman, and even more infrequently in the major they first declare. Continuing a pattern of mobility and change, 38% did not graduate from the first college they attended; 45% attended three or more colleges; and 44% of those who earned a bachelor's degree finished after age 22. Over 80% now function

as professionals, semiprofessionals, executives, or managers/officials. TCKs are four times more likely to earn bachelor's degrees than their United States counterparts.

- TCKs, though their behavior is adaptive to the settings they inhabit, never fully adapt to American life; they are somewhat out-of-sync in aspects of their lives outside of education.

- Two-thirds of the sample feel that it is important to have an international dimension in their lives, though they perceive they have more transnational knowledge and skills than they have the opportunity to use; three-fourths of them feel "different" from those who have not had an overseas experience, but they do not feel isolated.

- ATCKs have problems relating to their own ethnic groups. However, they are internationally experienced and continue their international involvement; they are adaptable and relate easily to diversity, they are helpers and problem-solvers.

- Over 40% have completed a graduate degree and some others are close to completion of one. Most report an excellent education in overseas schools; third culture childhood experiences affected 43% greatly (27% somewhat) in their choice of college and experience; 25% chose international majors and many others pursued interests inspired by their overseas posts.

- 25% work in educational settings; 17% in medical or legal fields. An equal number are self-employed—one third are presidents of their own companies. Over 75% participate in volunteer work in their communities, and about half (47%) report those volunteer activities are related to the international area.

DEVELOPMENT OF THE TCK PERSONALITY

The development of the TCK personality is reflective of a series of adjustments and a never quite-completed process of adaptation. These individuals have extraordinary demands placed on them to adapt to new environments, new places, new people, and new cultures. It is the same type of adaptation which is required of those going through culture shock, but without necessarily having the benefit, or baggage, of a culture which they can call home. While this sometimes leads to a very unsettled life, it can also produce an individual who is not easily influenced by the prejudices of others, and who may be extremely open-minded when encountering anything new.

Adaptation involves interaction between an individual's perception of self and perceptions of the environment. TCKs' management of the process of adaptation reflects the complex identities they have developed from their overseas experiences and their patterns of mobility. Their adaptive pattern involves a series of transactions, including: internalizing the fact of change of place, or return to the "home" country; maintaining extensive networks; managing an intense process of grieving; experiencing a purposeful lack of goals and realistic expectations; maintaining the third culture identity; making integrative adjustments; and the experience of culture shock.[10]

In addition to this process of adaptation, some commonalities among TCKs have been observed in both self and perceptions of the environment. They see themselves as:

- unique
- connected with global reality
- enhanced and enriched by their overseas experience
- superior and/or elite
- mobile
- a part of, yet apart from
- open and enjoying diversity
- ambivalent, independent yet dependent, mature in some ways, yet immature in others
- knowledgeable in a world sense, but naive on return to the country of their citizenship.

In the case of the environment, TCKs offered perceptions of both their overseas environments and the U.S. environment. Impressions of their overseas environments were:

- intense appreciation of the third culture
- love of travel
- value of mobility as a lifestyle
- intense interaction in the family
- strong family ties
- enjoyment of a small, enhanced environment with the benefits of a high standard of living
- close personal relationships with teachers and friends
- a deep sense of connectedness with world events
- creativity in the use of leisure time.

Their perceptions of the U.S. environment were a sense of shock at:

- the largeness of scale
- the importance of the media
- the dynamics of the peer social scene
- the materialism and ethnocentrism of most peers they encountered
- the lack of interest in their personal experiences as students who lived abroad, and
- the overall informality and friendliness of the peer environment as they observed it.

For TCKs, the process of adaptation has been facilitated by the role of a sponsoring organization. In many of the studies that have been done on TCKs, their development appears more influenced by the sponsorship role than by the host country or any individual post. The sponsor provides a continuity of structure and roles, and from this structure TCKs develop modes of being and becoming. The importance of parents' roles are communicated as a fixed and significant point in the TCK's life. The loss of meanings and references which are encountered with each new assignment or move may be mediated by this structure. It provides a stability of meaning and value for objects and roles within the sponsoring organization. For the military dependent, this means that the command structure, and his/her place in it, will be the same at any base to which he/she may be transferred. For the Foreign Service dependent, the embassy will always provide a sense of security and continuity with its structure and its support of the family while abroad. This can be very comforting for the TCK, and the whole family, when they are undergoing an instantaneous defamiliarization.[11] During a time when meaning is being stripped from almost all other aspects of their lives, the sponsor remains constant. Life structures, tasks, geographical address and travels all flow from the sponsor. The sponsor ascribes a certain status to both the individual and the family living abroad.

It is the loss of this "ascribed status" of the sponsoring organization that many TCKs lament upon return to the home culture. That status provides a role which is instantly recognized within the sponsorship group, as well as within the greater third culture environment. This status helps to facilitate transition and provide meaning by acting as an anchor point from which to rebuild the lives of the expatriates and their families. It can also contribute to a sense of elitism.

Cheryl, the dependent of a Foreign Service officer, lived abroad in Denmark, Italy, France, and Germany. Because her father was well-respected in the Foreign Service community, and a high ranking Foreign Service Officer, Cheryl grew up accustomed to living in larger homes, meeting important people, and feeling important because of her father's status in the community. Upon return to her "home" in Washington, D.C., Cheryl felt out of place. She spent her 8th grade year in the United States, and couldn't wait to leave. She made no friends at school, was annoyed by how loud Americans appeared to be, and could not understand what seemed to be the more provincial attitudes and prejudices of her classmates. She also missed being special.[12]

Living abroad, she had been special because of both her nationality as an American, and her father's position with the Foreign Service. "It was like being the big fish in a small pond. You feel special." But when she returned to America, she was "just one of many" at her junior high school. She missed living in fine homes, meeting important people, and being connected to the world. She admits now that she was "probably kind of stuck-up," but the sponsorship role that her father's position placed her in gave her an ascribed status that was simply much higher than what was recognized when she was back in the United States. It fostered a sense of elitism. Living in Washington, D.C., particularly, her ascribed status was lost as she became just another child of a Foreign Service Officer.[13]

TCKs and Reentry

Describing reentry with TCKs can be a particularly difficult task. This is mainly due to the fact that reentry is associated with a return to a culture which an individual knew as home prior to a sojourn overseas. The TCK's return to the "home" country may not be a return at all, but just another move to the latest in the series of cultures and countries which comprise their background. A legitimate question can be asked about whether in fact what the TCK experiences on return to the home country is culture shock rather than reentry. For now, however, we will continue to refer to a return to the home country as reentry. It is during the process of reentry that researchers have been able to gain the most information about the ways in which TCKs adapt and react to their new environment.

George, a business dependent, was overseas nine years and reports moves through three countries. He recalls,

> Upon entering college I had trouble getting back into the American style of life. Overseas I played mostly soccer, rugby, and swimming. The first year I just wanted to leave. I had played a lot of soccer in Iran. The whole general malaise I felt bothered me. I just didn't fit in. I had one good friend who lived in my dorm. I had the expectation that it would be great back in the States. I expected some difficulties, but not as many as I had.[14]

George perceives himself as a mobile person, a traveler, and did not identify at all with being in school. He had troubles with the social ambiance, though he notes that his studies were easy for him. Although he enjoyed his time overseas, he feels reentry and entry to college were not experiences he enjoyed or opportunities for growth. He says,

> I experienced a lot of alienation. I was alienated by attitudes people had about things that were different, the group mentality, expressions and ways of doing things. I was only seventeen when I returned and I was just waking up to a lot of things. It was a stage in my life that was passing. Moving all the time you don't have a firm base to set growth in or to look back on. You don't have future goals or an idea for a set job. I did have an interest in the political aspects of things. I just read a lot.[15]

Cheryl, the dependent of a Foreign Service Officer, could not find a place where she felt she belonged in the United States. She started college attending McGill University in Canada, transferred to the University of New Hampshire, back to McGill, and finally ended up at the Catholic University in Washington, D.C. She reports having trouble with finding her place, never feeling like she belonged anywhere. Now at Catholic University, Cheryl still has almost two years left in her studies, at the end of which she knows she will want to leave Washington, because "it'll be time to move on."[16]

Thomas, a business dependent overseas approximately seven years, really enjoyed his overseas experiences. "I liked my experiences," he states. "As a younger adult you do not have as many restrictions and rules as young adults seem to have in the States. I could do pretty much whatever I pleased." Upon entering the college environment, Thomas was first of all impressed with the large size of the place. Secondly, he noted the friendliness of the people. He shared the fact that he had a "wait and see attitude." According to Thomas, "I'm not that open a kind of person. I usually wait for things to happen to me."[17]

Hans, a TCK with a business sponsorship background, lived overseas for approximately five years. Upon his return, he found that his peer group was far more socially outgoing than he, but also very immature. It was his biggest difficulty in returning to the U.S.

> I knew things that people had no idea about. I had seen places that other people had never seen. I thought I had a real good background in terms of what the world was about and how different people view things. I felt I had more culture but I confronted totally different norms and patterns here and I felt unprepared for it.[18]

As with Hans and Cheryl, TCKs often find that on their return they have no ready reference group. Having become accustomed to dealing with adults, they have not developed the appropriate skills to interact socially with their own peer group in the home country. Because of this, many TCKs continue to relate to the past third culture reference group, or imagine a reference group for the future, usually intellectually or career-related. This is just one of the many internal mechanisms which TCKs develop to deal with the difficulties of entering a new culture. These resources serve them well during the reentry process, but as with any other change, it may take them some time to adjust. In many cases, this process may take up to a year, and the TCK will likely never feel fully a part of the home culture.

Another major contributor to the stress felt by TCKs in their initial reentry period is the loss of the ascribed status provided by the sponsoring organization. When the young adult returns to the States at college age, this ascribed status is no longer operative, and the individual must act for him/herself in yet another new world of meanings and roles. But this time they must do it without the benefit of the continuity provided either by the sponsoring organization, or by their family. The time for return for the TCK does not necessarily coincide with the return of the parents, particularly at college age. Thus, the family that has been so close, and the support the family has offered the TCK through their ongoing transitions, may be on the other side of the globe. All of the issues of separation, loss, reentry/culture shock, confrontation with new and novel patterns of behavior in the "home" country combine with ties loss of both ascribed status and the family support in creating a crisis of independent identity in the TCK.

This crisis of identity that occurs during reentry may cause the TCK to have a delayed commitment process. Some have referred to this delayed development of intimacy and commitment as a prolonged adolescence. This delay of commitment is not relegated solely to interpersonal or intimate relationships, but may extend to basic ideology and choice of occupation. The TCK has to play catch up with his/her peer group, never having developed the social skills that are in operation among this group. During the early reentry period, the "observer" role mentioned earlier by several of the TCKs becomes very important as they work to assimilate and apply the skills that have worked for them in the past when entering new environments. They will observe, map out the local environment and its social dynamics, then begin to assimilate that information into their behavior and interactions. Sometimes, unfortunately, even this observer role can have drawbacks as participation, more than observation, is often the valued trait among American youth. Reentry almost always requires a setting aside of the overseas experience in order to assimilate into the home culture, which only increases the intense grieving period which TCKs must manage when they enter a new culture.

A major part of what can be done for returning TCKs, then, is to help them with this intense period of grieving. Many TCKs don't necessarily get the opportunity to grieve, or to acknowledge the fact that they are grieving. There are too many people, family and friends, demanding that the TCK feel happy about returning home, without realizing that "home" for the TCK may have nothing whatsoever to do with the home their parents recognize. One of the ways to help the TCKs with reentry, then, is to give them a time to both recognize the fact that they are grieving, and to grieve for the loss of friends, family, and a familiar environment. They need to go through a period of

accepting the most recent loss, and then they can continue to adapt to the new environment. Many TCKs have developed for themselves a way to manage this grief, but the experience of reentry has also combined the loss of the few stable factors in the TCK's life: the family, the third culture environment, and the sponsorship role and status. Thus, reentry may well be the most intense period of adaptation the TCK experiences.

Elizabeth, a missionary dependent who lived overseas for approximately 10 years, relates, "I've adapted but I still have culture shock when I return to the United States after being out of the country . . . people are very persistent. They have to get things done and tend to rush and push. Overseas, if it doesn't get done, we'll do it tomorrow." Elizabeth feels that people in the United States are insulated from news and events in the rest of the world, and therefore disconnected and uninformed.[19]

Joy Salmons asked early adult TCKs retrospectively to look at their periods of reentry and identify some of the key stresses they encountered during this period. The responses mirrored the results of earlier studies and indicated that the higher the meaningful life, the lower the present stress; the more years since reentry and the higher the intimacy level, the higher the mental health. However, in the area of intimacy, it was found that the level of intimacy was significant in the mental health of men, but did not necessarily contribute to higher mental health in women. Early adult task achievement was affected by the perception of timing, amount of time since reentry, and the degree of intimacy present in their lives.[20]

CONCLUSION

In an ever-shrinking world, the TCK will play an expanding role. As more links are forged, and as communication among members of different cultures becomes more and more common, the skills of adaptation and understanding which are developed by TCKs become invaluable. As the population becomes more mobile, more and more individuals will experience challenges to their self/identity, the need for a concept of home and roots, and the need for strategies for simple adjustment. In order to be able to help these people, we must understand and nurture the TCKs. Having developed between cultures, TCKs are positioned to become the mediators between cultures. Though they may never feel fully a part of a culture, they can be the bridge through which monocultural people learn to appreciate other cultures. These individuals have the resources which are needed to facilitate understanding between cultures with distinct value systems, histories, and norms. With their ability to perceive similarities and differences that might escape the notice of someone not accustomed to looking for cultural cues, TCKs have the potential to bring these groups together to find a common ground. We need the TCKs.

The skills and resources TCKs have developed are not only applicable to the cultures in which they were raised, but can be used across all cultures. As technological society grows, and brings together global society, these skills will be more and more in demand. It will also become increasingly important to understand the TCKs and their needs as their numbers continue to grow.

The greater the interaction among countries and cultures, the greater the instances of families who will live in many other countries and cultures. They could be the facilitators of a global process of "becoming" as global society continues to evolve and needs facilitators who can move through the various cultures. TCKs bring their own unique problems to the international stage, but they also bring skills and an understanding that may be essential for the twenty-first century.

ENDNOTES

1. Ruth Hill Useem and John Useem, "The Job: Stress and Resources of Americans at Work in the Third Culture." Paper presented for the Twenty-Second Annual Meeting of the Society for Applied Anthropology at Albany, New York (1963.)

2. Kathleen A. Finn Jordan, "The Adaptation Process of Third Culture Dependent Youth as They Re-enter the United States and Enter College: An Exploratory Study." (Ph.D. dissertation, Michigan State University, 1981), 95.

3. John Useem and Ruth Hill Useem, and John Donoghue, "Men in the Middle of the Third Culture: The Roles of American and Non-Western Peoples in Cross-Cultural Administration," *Human Organization* 22 (1963): 169–179.

"Third culture" persons, as defined by some researchers, are individuals who find themselves living abroad in certain specific, sponsored roles. These roles include sponsorship by private business, federal agencies, the military, missionary groups, and other categories where the individual assumes a representative, rather than solely individual, role. "Third culture" itself is a generic term used to describe the styles of life created, shared and learned by persons who are in the process of relating their multiple societies. The term "third culture" itself came out of studies done by John Useem in India of Americans participating in various missionary, diplomatic and business programs, and the cross-cultural problems and opportunities that arose from the interaction.

4. John Useem, "The Community of Man: A Study in the Third Culture," *The Centennial Review* 7 (1962):481–498.

5. As we approach the century's end, there are fewer and fewer people in the world uninfluenced in some way by another culture. The use of the term "monocultural" should be understood as merely a matter of the conscious degree of influence other cultures have brought to bear. It is difficult to imagine a completely "monocultural" person and that is not what we wish to convey by use of this term.

6. Kathleen A. Finn Jordan, "The Adaptation Process," 101.

7. Ongoing study of Adult Third Culture Kids undertaken by sociologists/anthropologists Drs. Ann Baker Cottrel of San Diego University; Ruth and John Useem, professors emeritus of Michigan State University, and Counselor/Therapist Kathleen A. Finn Jordan of Washington, D.C.

8. Richard Downie, "Re-entry Experiences and Identity Formation of Third Culture Experienced Dependent American Youth: An Exploratory Study," (Ph.D. dissertation, Michigan State University, 1976).

9. Kathleen A. Finn Jordan, "The Adaptation Process."

10. *Ibid.*

11. I.D. Yalom, *Existential Psychotherapy* (New York: Basic Books, 1980).

12. Cheryl O'Rourke [pseud.], interviewed by Shawn Bates, School of International Service, American University, Washington, D.C., 2 April 1997.

13. *Ibid.*

14. Kathleen A. Finn Jordan, "The Adaptation Process," 115.

15. *Ibid.*

16. Cheryl O'Rourke, interview.

17. Kathleen A. Finn Jordan, "The Adaptation Process," 129.

18. *Ibid.*, 119.

19. *Ibid.*

20. Joy Salmon, "The Relationship of Stress and Mobility to the Psychosocial Development and Well-Being of Third-Culture-Reared Early Adults." (Ph.D. dissertation, The Florida State University, 1987.)

Why Johnny Can't Disobey

Sarah J. McCarthy

Few people are too concerned about whether Johnny can disobey. There is no furor or frantic calls to the PTA, as when it is discovered that he can't read or does poorly on his S.A.T. scores. Even to consider the question is at first laughable. Parents and teachers, after all, are systematically working at developing the virtue of obedience. To my knowledge, no one as yet has opened a remedial disobedience school for overly compliant children, and probably no one ever will. And that in itself is a major problem.

Patricia Hearst recently said that the mindless state of obedience which enveloped her at the hands of the Symbionese Liberation Army could happen to anyone. Jumping to a tentative conclusion from a tip-of-the-iceberg perspective, it looks as though it already has happened to many, and that it has required nothing so dramatic as a kidnapping to bring it about.

Given our experience with various malevolent authority figures such as Adolph Hitler, Charles Manson, Lieutenant Calley, and Jim Jones, it is unfortunately no longer surprising that there are leaders who are capable of wholesale cruelty to the point of directing mass killings. What remains shocking, however, is that they are so often successful in recruiting followers. There seems to be no shortage of individuals who will offer their hearts and minds on a silver platter to feed the egos of the power-hungry. This becomes even more disturbing when one ponders the truism that society's neurotics are often its cultural caricatures, displaying exaggerated manifestations of its collective neuroses. There are enough examples of obedience to horrendous commands for us to ask if and how a particular culture sows the seeds of dangerous conformity.

Political platitudes and lip service to the contrary, obedience is highly encouraged in matters petty as well as profound. Linda Eton, an Iowa firefighter, was suspended from her job and catapulted to national fame for the radical act of breast-feeding at work. A dehumanized, compartmentalized society finds little room for spontaneity, and a blatantly natural act like breast-feeding is viewed as a preposterous interruption of the status quo.

Pettiness abounds in our social relationships, ensuring compliance through peer pressure and disapproval, and enforced by economic sanctions at the workplace. A friend of mine, a construction worker, reported to his job one rainy day carrying an umbrella. The foreman was outraged by his break from the norm, and demanded that the guy never again carry an umbrella to the construction site, even if the umbrella *was* black, since it "caused his whole crew to look like a bunch of faggots."

Another friend, though less scandalizing visibly in his job as a security guard during the wee hours for a multinational corporation, was caught red-handed playing a harmonica. Mercifully, he was given another chance, only to be later fired for not wearing regulation shoes.

Ostensibly, such firings and threats are deemed necessary to prevent inefficiency and rampant chaos at the workplace. But if employers were merely concerned about productivity and efficiency, it certainly is disputable that "yes-people" are more productive and beneficial than "no-people." Harmonicas may even increase efficiency by keeping security guards sane, alert, and awake by staving off sensory deprivation. A dripping-wet construction worker could conceivably be less productive than a dry one. And the Adidas being worn by the errant security guard

Reprinted from *The Humanist* (September/October 1979): 5, by permission of Sarah J. McCarthy.

could certainly have contributed to his fleetness and agility as opposed to the cumbersome regulation shoes. The *real* issues here have nothing to do with productivity. What is really involved is an irrational fear of the mildly unusual, a pervasive attitude held by authorities that their subordinates are about to run amok and need constant control.

These little assaults on our freedom prepare us for the big ones. Having long suspected that a huge iceberg of mindless obedience existed beneath our cultural surface, I was not particularly surprised when I heard that nine hundred people followed their leader to mass suicide. For some time we have lived with the realization that people are capable of killing six million of their fellow citizens on command. Jonestown took us one step further. People will kill themselves on command.

In matters ridiculous and sublime, this culture and the world at large clearly exhibit symptoms of pathological obedience. Each time one of the more sensational incidents occurs—Jonestown, the Mai Lai massacre. Nazi Germany, the Manson murders—we attribute its occurrence to factors unique to it, trying to deny any similarities to anything close to us, tossing it about like a philosophical hot potato. We prefer to view such events as anomalies, isolated in time and space, associated with faraway jungles, exotic cults, drugged hippies, and outside agitators. However, as the frequency of such happenings increases, there is the realization that it is relatively easy to seduce some people into brainwashed states of obedience.

Too much energy and time have been spent on trying to understand the alleged compelling traits and mystical powers of charismatic leaders, and not enough in an attempt to understand their fellow travelers—the obedient ones. We need to look deeper into those who *elected* Hitler, and all those followers of Jim Jones who went to Guyana *voluntarily*. We must ask how many of us are also inclined toward hyperobedience. Are we significantly different, capable of resisting malevolent authority, or have we simply had the good fortune never to have met a Jim Jones of our own?

Social psychologist Stanley Milgram, in his book *Obedience to Authority,* is convinced that:

> In growing up, the normal individual has learned to check the expression of aggressive impulses. But the culture has failed, almost entirely, in inculcating internal controls on actions that have their origin in authority. For this reason, the latter constitutes a far greater danger to human survival.

Vince Bugliosi, prosecutor of Charles Manson and author of *Helter Skelter,* comments on the Jonestown suicides:

> Education of the public is the only answer. If young people could be taught what can happen to them—that they may be zombies a year after talking to that smiling person who stops them on a city street—they may be prepared.

Presumably, most young cult converts have spent most of their days in our educational system, yet are vulnerable to the beguiling smile or evil eye of a Charles Manson. If there is any lesson to be learned from the obedience-related holocausts, it must be that we can never underestimate the power of education and the socialization process.

Contrary to our belief that the survival instinct is predominant over all other drives, the Jonestown suicides offer testimony to the power of cultural indoctrination. Significantly, the greatest life force at the People's Temple came from the children. Acting on their survival instincts, they went kicking and screaming to their deaths in an "immature" display of disobedience. The adults, civilized and educated people that they were, lined up with "stiff upper lips" and took their medicine like the followers they were trained to be—a training that didn't begin at Jonestown.

When something so horrible as Jonestown happens, people draw metaphors about the nearness of the jungle and the beast that lurks within us. It seems that a more appropriate metaphor would be our proximity to an Orwellian civilization with its antiseptic removal of our human rough edges and "animal" instincts. On close scrutiny, the beast within us looks suspiciously like a sheep.

Despite our rich literature of freedom, a pervasive value installed in our society is obedience to authority. Unquestioning obedience is perceived to be in the best interest of the schools, churches, families, and political institutions. Nationalism, patriotism, and religious ardor are its psychological vehicles.

Disobedience is the original sin, as all of the religions have stated in one way or another. Given the obedience training in organized religions that claim to possess mystical powers and extrarational knowledge and extol the glories of self-sacrifice, what is so bizarre about the teachings of Jim Jones? If we arm our children with the rationality and independent thought necessary to resist the cultist, can we be sure that our own creeds and proclamations will meet the criteria of reason? The spotlight of reason which exposes the charlatan may next shine on some glaring inconsistencies in the "legitimate" religions. Religions, which are often nothing more than cults that grew, set the stage for the credulity and gullibility required for membership in cults.

A witch hunt is now brewing to exorcise the exotic cults, but what is the dividing line between a cult and a legitimate religion? Is there a qualitative difference between the actions of some venerated Biblical saints and martyrs and the martyrs of Jonestown? If the Bible contained a Parable of Guyana, the churches would regularly extoll it as a courageous act of self-sacrifice. Evidently saints and martyrs are only palatable when separated by the chasm of a few centuries. To enforce their belief, the major religions use nothing so crass as automatic weapons, of course, but instead fall back on automatic sentences to eternal damnation.

Certainly there must be an optimal level of obedience and cooperation in a reasonable society, but obedience, as any other virtue that is carried to

an extreme, may become a vice. It is obvious that Nazi Germany and Jonestown went too far on the obedience continuum. In more mundane times and places the appropriate level of obedience is more difficult to discover.

We must ask if our society is part of the problem, part of the solution, or wholly irrelevant to the incidents of over-obedience exhibited at Jonestown and Mai Lai. Reviewing social psychologists' attempts to take our psychic temperatures through empirical measurements of our conformity and obedience behavior in experimental situations, our vital signs do not look good.

In 1951 Solomon Asch conducted an experiment on conformity, which is similar to obedience behavior in that it subverts one's will to that of peers or an authority. This study, as reported in the textbook *Social Psychology* by Freedman, Sears, and Carlsmith, involved college students who were asked to estimate lines of equal and different lengths. Some of the lines were obviously equal, but if subjects heard others before them unanimously give the wrong answer, they would also answer incorrectly. Asch had reasoned that people would be rational enough to choose the evidence of their own eyes over the disagreeing "perceptions" of others. He found that he was wrong.

When subjects were asked to estimate the length of a line after confederates of the experimenter had given obviously wrong answers, the subjects gave wrong answers about 35 percent of the time. Authors Freedman, Sears, and Carlsmith stress:

> It is important to keep the unambiguousness of the situations in mind if we are to understand this phenomenon. There is a tendency to think that the conforming subjects are uncertain of the correct choice therefore are swayed by the majority. This is not always the case. In many instances subjects are quite certain of the correct choice and, in the absence of group pressure, would choose correctly 100 percent of the

time. When they conform, they are conforming despite that fact they know the correct answer.

If 35 percent of those students conformed to group opinion in unambiguous matters and in direct contradiction of the evidence of their own eyes, how much more must we fear blind following in *ambiguous* circumstances or in circumstances where there exists a legitimate authority?

In the early sixties, Yale social psychologist Stanley Milgram devised an experiment to put acts of obedience and disobedience under close scrutiny. Milgram attempted to understand why thousands of "civilized" people had engaged in an extreme and immoral act—that of the wholesale extermination of Jews—in the name of obedience. He devised a learning task in which subjects of the experiment were instructed to act as teachers. They were told to "shock" learners for their mistakes. The learners were actually confederates of the experimenter and were feigning their reactions. When a mistake was made, the experimenter would instruct the teacher to administer an ever-increasing voltage from a shock machine which read "Extreme Danger," "Severe Shock," and "XXX." Although the machine was unconnected, the subject-teachers believed that they were actually giving shocks. They were themselves given a real sample shock before the experiment began.

Milgram asked his Yale colleagues to make a guess as to what proportion of subjects would proceed to shock all the way to the presumed lethal end of the shockboard. Their estimates hovered around 1 or 2 percent. No one was prepared for what happened. All were amazed that twenty-six out of forty subjects obeyed the experimenter's instruction to press levers that supposedly administered severely dangerous levels of shock. After this, Milgram regularly obtained results showing that 62 to 65 percent of people would shock to the end of the board. He tried several variations on the experiment, one of which was to set it up outside of Yale University so that the prestige of the University would not be an overriding factor in causing the subjects to obey. He found that people were just as likely to administer severe shock, whether the experiments occurred within the hallowed halls of Yale or in a three-room walk-up storefront in which the experimenters spoke of themselves as "scientific researchers."

In another variation of the experiment, Milgram found that aggression—latent or otherwise—was not a significant factor in causing the teacher-subjects to shock the learners. When the experimenter left the room, thus permitting the subjects to choose the level of shock themselves, almost none administered more than the lowest voltage. Milgram concluded that obedience, not aggression, was the problem. He states:

I must conclude that [Hannah] Arendt's conception of the *banality of evil* comes closer to the truth than one might dare imagine. The ordinary person who shocked the victim did so out of a sense of obligation—a conception of his duties as a subject—and not from any peculiarly aggressive tendencies.

This is, perhaps, the most fundamental lesson of our study: ordinary people, simply doing their jobs, and without any particular hostility on their part, can become agents in a terrible destructive process. Moreover, even when the destructive effects of their work become patently clear, and they are asked to carry out actions incompatible with fundamental standards of morality, relatively few people have the resources needed to resist authority. A variety of inhibitions against disobeying authority come into play and successfully keep the person in his place.

A lack of compassion was not a particularly salient personality factor in the acts of obedience performed by the followers of Hitler, Jim Jones, and the subjects in the Milgram experiments. Nazi soldiers were capable of decent human behavior toward their friends and family. Some, too, see an irony in that Hitler himself was a vegetarian. The People's Temple members seemed more compassionate and humanitarian than many, and yet they forced their own children to partake of a drink laced with cyanide. Those shocking the victims in the Milgram experiments exhibited signs of compassion both toward the experimenter and to the persons that they thought were receiving the shocks. In fact, Milgram finds that:

> It is a curious thing that a measure of compassion on the part of the subject, an unwillingness to "hurt" the experimenter's feelings, are part of those binding forces inhibiting disobedience . . . only obedience can preserve the experimenter's status and dignity.

Milgram's subjects showed signs of severe physiological tension and internal conflict when instructed to shock. Presumably, these signs of psychic pain and tortured indecision were manifestation of an underlying attitude of compassion for the victim, but it was not sufficient to impel them to openly break with, and therefore embarrass, the experimenter, even though this experimenter had no real authority over them. One of Milgram's subjects expressed this dilemma succinctly:

> I'll go through with anything they tell me to do. . . . They know more than I do. . . . I know when I was in the service (if I was told) "You go over the hill and we're going to attack," we attacked. So I think it's all based on the way a man was brought up . . . in his background. Well, I faithfully believed the man [whom he thought he had shocked] was dead until we opened the door. When I saw him, I said: "Great, this is great!" But it didn't bother me even to find that he was dead. I did a job.

The experiments continued with thousands of people—students and non-students, here and abroad—often demonstrating obedience behavior in 60 to 65 percent of the subjects. When the experiments were done in Munich, obedience often reached 85 percent. Incidentally, Milgram found no sex differences in obedience behavior. Though his sample of women shockers was small, their level of obedience was identical to that of the men. But they did exhibit more symptoms of internal

conflict. Milgram concluded that "there is probably nothing the victim can say that will uniformly generate disobedience," since it is not the victim who is controlling the shocker's behavior. Even when one of the experimental variations included a victim who cried out that he had a heart condition, this did not lead to significantly greater disobedience. In such situations, the experimenter-authority figure dominates the subject's social field, while the pleading cries of the victim are for the most part ignored.

Milgram found that the authority's power had to be somehow undermined before there was widespread disobedience, as when the experimenter was not physically present, when his orders came over the telephone, or when his orders were challenged by another authority. Most importantly, subjects became disobedient in large numbers only when others rebelled, dissented, or argued with the experimenter. When a subject witnessed another subject defying or arguing with the experimenter, thirty-six out of forty also rebelled, demonstrating that peer rebellion was the most effective experimental variation in undercutting authority.

This social orientation in which the authority dominates one's psyche is attributed by Milgram to a state of mind which he terms "the agentic state." A person makes a critical shift from a relatively autonomous state into this agentic state when she or he enters a situation in which "he defines himself in a manner that renders him open to regulation by a person of higher status."

An extreme agentic state is a likely explanation for the scenario at Jonestown, where even the cries of their own children were not sufficient to dissuade parents from serving cyanide. Despite some ambiguity as to how many Jonestown residents were murdered and how many committed suicide, there remains the fact that these victims had participated in previous suicide rehearsals. Jim Jones, assured of their loyalty and their critical shift into an agentic state, then had the power to orchestrate the real thing. The supreme irony, the likes of which could only be imagined as appearing in the *Tralfamadore*

Tribune with a byline by Kurt Vonnegut, was the picture of the Guyana death scene. Bodies were strewn about beneath the throne of Jones and a banner which proclaimed that those who failed to learn from the lessons of history were doomed to repeat them.

How many of us have made the critical shift into an agentic state regarding international relations, assuming that our leaders know best, even though they have repeatedly demonstrated that they do not? Stanley Milgram predicts that "for the man who sits in front of the button that will release Armageddon, depressing it will have about the same emotional force as calling for an elevator . . . evolution has not had a chance to build inhibitors against such remote forms of aggression."

We should recognize that our human nature renders us somewhat vulnerable. For one thing, our own mortality and that of our loved ones is an unavoidable fact underlying our lives. In the face of it, we are powerless; and in our insecurity, many reach out for sure answers. Few choose to believe, along with Clarence Darrow, that not only are we not the captains of our fate, but that we are not even "deckhands on a rudderless dinghy." Or, as someone else has stated: "There are no answers. Be brave and face up to it." Most of us won't face up to it. We want our answers, solutions to our plight, and we want them now. Too often truth and rational thought are the first casualties of this desperate reach for security. We embrace answers from charlatans, false prophets, charismatic leaders, and assorted demagogues. Given these realities of our nature, how can we avoid these authority traps to which we are so prone? By what criteria do we teach our children to distinguish between the charlatan and the prophet?

It seems that the best armor is the rational mind. We must insist that all authorities account for themselves, and we need to be as wary of false prophets as we are of false advertising. Leaders, political and spiritual, must be subjected to intense scrutiny, and we must insist that their thought processes and proclamations measure up to reasonable standards of rational thought. Above all, we must become skilled in activating our inner resources toward rebellion and disobedience, when this seems reasonable.

The power of socialization can conceivably be harnessed so as to develop individuals who are rational and skeptical, capable of independent thought, and who can disobey or disagree at the critical moment. Our society, however, continues systematically to instill exactly the opposite. The educational system pays considerable lip service to the development of self-reliance, and places huge emphasis on lofty concepts of individual differences. Little notice is taken of the legions of overly obedient children in the schools; yet, for every overly disobedient child, there are probably twenty who are obeying too much. There is little motivation to encourage the unsqueaky wheels to develop as noisy, creative, independent thinkers who may become bold enough to disagree. Conceivably, we could administer modified Milgram obedience tests in the schools which detect hyper-obedience, just as we test for intelligence, visual function, vocational attributes and tuberculosis. When a child is found to be too obedient, the schools should mobilize against this psychological cripple with the zeal by which they would react to an epidemic of smallpox. In alcoholism and other mental disturbances, the first major step toward a reversal of the pathology is recognition of the severity of the problem. Obedience should be added to the list of emotional disturbances requiring therapy. Disobedience schools should be at least as common as military schools and reform schools.

The chains on us are not legal or political, but the invisible chains of the agentic state. We have all gotten the message that it is dangerous and requires exceptional courage to be different.

If we are to gain control of our lives and minds, we must first acknowledge the degree to which we are not now in control. We must become reasonable and skeptical. Reason is no panacea, but, at the moment, it is all that we have. Yet many in our society seem to have the same attitude about rationality and reason that they do about the poverty program—that is, we've tried it and it doesn't work.

Along with worrying about the S.A.T. scores and whether or not Johnny can read, we must begin to seriously question whether Johnny is capable of disobedience. The churches and cults, while retaining their constitutional right to free expression, must be more regularly criticized. The legitimate religions have been treated as sacred cows. Too often, criticism of them is met with accusations of religious bigotry, or the implication that one is taking candy from a baby or a crutch from a cripple. The concept of religious tolerance has been stretched to its outer limits, implying freedom from criticism and the nonpayment of taxes. Neither patriotism nor religion should be justification for the suspension of reason.

And, on a personal level, we must stop equating sanity with conformity, eccentricity with craziness, and normalcy with numbers. We must get in touch with our own liberating ludicrousness and practice being harmlessly deviant. We must, in fact, cease to use props or other people to affirm our normalcy. With sufficient practice, perhaps, when the need arises, we may have the strength to force a moment to its crisis.

The Obama of "Dreams"

by David Ignatius

The promise of Barack Obama's presidential campaign was that it would transcend the old racial and ideological categories of American politics. Obama was sometimes described as "post-racial" or "the Tiger Woods of politics"—someone who defied the usual dividing lines and, in that sense, could be a healer and a uniter.

The past week has illustrated that race is still a campaign issue. The flap about what the Clintons meant in their comments about *Martin Luther King Jr.* or an *Obama* "fairy tale" on *Iraq* is overdone, but the deeper question of Obama's racial identity is not. He is the first African American with a chance to win the presidency, and many blacks—after initially holding him at a distance—are now treating him as a symbol of racial pride and identity. Amid this heightened sensitivity, the jostling that's normal in a political campaign is taken as a sign of disrespect.

Fortunately, we have Obama to help disentangle the racial threads. I don't mean the candidate we see on the stump—it's too late in the campaign for that—but the one who wrote the book. Obama's first memoir, *Dreams from My Father,* is one of the best political autobiographies I've read, and it deserves to be a modern classic on the subject of the moment—race and identity.

Much of Obama's book is about his own search to understand his life as a mixed-race child of an African father and a white Kansan mother. He describes his early teenage struggles in "trying to raise myself to be a black man in America," shooting pool in the red-light district of Honolulu or learning to trash-talk on the basketball court. "I was living out a caricature of black male adolescence, itself a caricature of swaggering American manhood," he writes.

The book is cited these days because of Obama's frank discussion of his use of drugs in the years when he was dealing with the absence of his father and his uncertain identity: "Junkie. Pothead. That's where I'd been headed: The final, fatal role of the young, would-be black man." He was spared, he writes, in part because of a sense of guilt: "Slipped it into your baby food," his mother told him.

The book is so honest, and so funny and self-aware, that you come away thinking that Obama is that rare politician who genuinely understands who he is. You can't help but worry that once the packagers are done with him, this voice will be blunted.

Certainly, by the time he wrote his second memoir, "The Audacity of Hope," Obama was more into speech-giving mode.

Obama makes clear in *Dreams from My Father* that he brings another valuable gift to politics, in addition to his African American heritage. That's his identity as what sociologists call a "third-culture kid," whose formative years were spent living overseas. Journalist Lee Aitken, who studied the phenomenon when she was editing a special feature for expatriate families called "At Home Abroad" in the *International Herald Tribune*, says that Obama exemplifies many of these third-culture traits.

Third-culture kids learn how to make their way in unfamiliar surroundings. The late Ruth Hill Useem, a former *Michigan State* sociologist who studied them for decades, explained: "They adapt, they find niches, they take risks, they fail and pick themselves up again. . . . Their camouflaged exteriors and understated ways of presenting themselves hide their rich inner lives." In surveys, more than 80 percent said they could relate to anyone, regardless of race or nationality.

It's this voice of a seeker and adapter that you discover in Obama's writings. Describing the years when he was still trying to find himself, "like a salmon swimming blindly upstream toward the site of his own conception," he says he searched for an identity as a civil rights activist and organizer. "Because this community I imagined was still in the making, built on the promise that the larger American community, black, white and brown, could somehow redefine itself—I believed that it might, over time, admit the uniqueness of my own life."

This is the voice I wish I'd heard when the Clinton and Obama camps were trading attack points and "gotcha" lines about race and gender. Clinton has a story to tell about her struggle for identity, just as Obama does. But these candidates are so hunkered down, and their sound bites so pre-chewed, that we begin to lose sight of what makes them trailblazers. What's new gets swallowed up by what's old.

On race, I want to listen to Obama—not his handlers and spin doctors. His journey is inspiring, if he doesn't get lost on the campaign trail.

The writer is co-host of PostGlobal, an online discussion of international issues. His e-mail address is davidignatius@washpost.com.

Foul Shots

Rogelio R. Gomez

Now and then I can still see their faces, snickering and laughing, their eyes mocking me. And it bothers me that I should remember. Time and maturity should have diminished the pain, because the incident happened more than 20 years ago. Occasionally, however, a smug smile triggers the memory, and I think, "I should have done something." Some act of defiance could have killed and buried the memory of the incident. Now it's too late.

In 1969, I was a senior on the Luther Burbank High School basketball team. The school is on the south side of San Antonio, in one of the city's many barrios. After practice one day our coach announced that we were going to spend the following Saturday scrimmaging with the ball club from Winston Churchill High, located in the city's rich, white north side. After the basketball game, we were to select someone from the opposing team and "buddy

Rogelio R. Gomez is a fiction writer living in San Antonio.
Reprinted from *The New York Times* Magazine, 13 October 1991, 24, 69.

up"—talk with him, have lunch with him and generally spend the day attempting friendship. By telling us that this experience would do both teams some good, I suspect our well-intentioned coach was thinking about the possible benefits of integration and of learning to appreciate the differences of other people. By integrating us with this more prosperous group, I think he was also trying to inspire us.

But my teammates and I smiled sardonically at one another, and our sneakers squeaked as we nervously rubbed them against the waxed hardwood floor of our gym. The prospect of a full day of unfavorable comparisons drew us from a collective groan. As "barrio boys," we were already acutely aware of the differences between us and them. Churchill meant "white" to us: It meant shiny new cars, two-story homes with fireplaces, pedigreed dogs and manicured hedges. In other words, everything that we did not have. Worse, traveling north meant putting up a front, to ourselves as well as to the Churchill team. We felt we had to pretend that we were cavalier about it all, tough guys who didn't care about "nothin'."

It's clear now that we entered the contest with negative images of ourselves. From childhood, we must have suspected something was inherently wrong with us. The evidence wrapped itself around our collective psyche like a noose. In elementary school, we were not allowed to speak Spanish. The bladed edge of a wooden ruler once came crashing down on my knuckles for violating this dictum. By high school, however, policies had changed, and we could speak Spanish without fear of physical reprisal. Still, speaking our language before whites brought on spasms of shame—for the supposed inferiority of our language and culture—and guilt at feeling shame. That mixture of emotions fueled our burning sense of inferiority.

After all, our mothers in no way resembled the glamorized models of American TV mothers—Donna Reed baking cookies in high heels. My mother's hands were rough and chafed, her wardrobe drab and worn. And my father was preoccupied with making ends meet. His silence starkly contrasted with the glib counsel Jim Anderson offered in "Father Knows

Best." And where the Beaver worried about trying to understand some difficult homework assignment, for me it was an altogether different horror, when I was told by my elementary school principal that I did not have the ability to learn.

After I failed to pass the first grade, my report card read that I had a "learning disability." What shame and disillusion it brought my parents! To have carried their dream of a better life from Mexico to America, only to have their hopes quashed by having their only son branded inadequate. And so somewhere during my schooling I assumed that saying I had a "learning disability" was just another way of saying that I was "retarded." School administrators didn't care that I could not speak English.

As teen-agers, of course, my Mexican-American friends and I did not consciously understand why we felt inferior. But we might have understood if we had fathomed our desperate need to trounce Churchill. We viewed the prospect of besting a white, north-side squad as a particularly fine coup. The match was clearly racial, our need to succeed born of a defiance against prejudice. I see now that we used the basketball court to prove our "blood." And who better to confirm us, if not those whom we considered better? In retrospect, I realize the only thing confirmed that day was that we saw ourselves as negatively as they did.

After we won the morning scrimmage, both teams were led from the gym into an empty room where everyone sat on a shiny linoleum floor. We were supposed to mingle—rub the colors together. But the teams sat separately, our backs against concrete walls. We faced one another like enemies, the empty floor between us a no man's land. As the coaches walked away, one reminded us to share lunch. God! The mere thought of offering them a taco from our brown bags when they had refrigerated deli lunches horrified us.

Then one of their players tossed a bag of Fritos at us. It slid across the slippery floor and stopped in the center of the room. With hearts beating anxiously, we Chicanos stared at the bag as the boy said with a sneer, "Y'all probably like 'em"—the

"Frito Bandito" commercial being popular then. And we could see them smiling at each other, giggling, jabbing their elbows into one another's ribs at the joke. The bag seemed to grow before our eyes like a monstrous symbol of inferiority.

We won the afternoon basketball game as well. But winning had accomplished nothing. Though we had wanted to, we couldn't change their perception of us. It seems, in fact, that defeating them made them meaner. Looking back, I feel these young men needed to put us "in our place," to reaffirm the power they felt we had threatened. I think, moreover, that they felt justified, not only because of their inherent sense of superiority, but because our failure to respond to their insult underscored our worthlessness in their eyes.

Two decades later, the memory of their gloating lives on in me. When a white person is discourteous, I find myself wondering what I should do, and afterward, if I've done the right thing. Sometimes I argue when a deft comment would suffice. Then I reprimand myself, for I am no longer a boy. But my impulse to argue bears witness to my ghosts. For, invariably, whenever I feel insulted I'm reminded of that day at Churchill High. And whenever the past encroaches upon the present, I see myself rising boldly, stepping proudly across the years and crushing, underfoot, a silly bag of Fritos.

SECTION VI
INTERNATIONAL CONFLICT AND INTERCULTURAL RELATIONS

The field of international relations is usually concerned with peace and conflict between nations. People in every nation want peace, security, and prosperity and seek to maintain their traditional cultural values or way of life. Each nation's foreign policy is based upon its national interests and values but also its perception of the world and the place of the nation in the international system.

Political scientists and international relations scholars often explain the behavior of nations in terms of political, economic, or military power and assume that decisions to be peaceful or to go to war are based upon rational decisions. Leaders decide what action or foreign policy is in the best interests of the nation based upon factual evidence. However, we know that people from different cultures perceive reality differently; they often have conflicting values and ways of thinking. What might be rational in one culture is quite irrational in another.

For example, Maslow's hierarchy of needs theory posits that all human beings must satisfy lower-order needs before they are concerned with higher order needs. Physiological needs—such as food and drink, or security needs such as having a safe place to live—must be met before we are concerned with higher order needs such as having a fulfilling social life, reaching our full potential as human beings, or even living in a country that is democratic. This may be true of many Euro-American cultures. However, there are very clear examples of countries where leaders and their people will fight to the death to restore honor or face, and they may very well sacrifice their physiological and security needs to gain respect from others. Culture is a variable that Maslow did not consider in his theory.

Much of intercultural relations research focuses on the interaction of individuals and how their cultural differences impact negotiation, management, adjustment and conflict. When it comes to international relations, scholars have considered how the personality of individual leaders shapes their foreign policy and the ways in which they negotiate.[1] However, much of this research also ignores culture. Cognitive psychology and psychoanalytic theory are based upon the assumption of similarity between all people. Interculturalists begin with the assumption that there are differences between cultures that must be acknowledged before moving on to the similarities.

Some political psychologists have even gone so far as to explain the invasion of another country based upon the upbringing of a head of state including childhood psychological trauma.[2] This kind of analysis may offer some insight; however, most leaders make decisions regarding foreign policy, and especially military action, based upon rational calculations of costs and benefits and the interests of the state. The personality of a leader certainly influences how that person perceives the world but this is only one of many variables that determine foreign policy. Furthermore, much of this kind of analysis is based upon historical records or information gathered by others rather than the face-to-face interviews that most psychologists would use to determine personality traits.

How do leaders convince their people to support a war? Are people from one culture more likely to be aggressive and warlike than those from another culture? These big questions are important for the field of intercultural relations, but we must be careful when comparing the behavior and motives of individuals with nation states. An individual may be paranoid, but it is uncertain that nations behave in a similar way. On the other hand, if a nation has been invaded by numerous enemies over many decades, it is reasonable to assume that fear of invasion shapes much of its foreign policy. But is this a paranoid or irrational fear, or a realistic one? An individual can die defending some moralistic principle. Perhaps survival of the nation is more important than morality.

FOREIGN POLICY AND CULTURE

Just as an individual's history helps to explain his or her worldview, a country's historical experiences provide an understanding of its foreign policy and how it perceives itself in the international system of nation states. One nation's non-aggressive policy of "containment" could easily be perceived as "encirclement" and a threat by another country that has been invaded numerous times by its neighbors.

If a country believes it is threatened, it might build up its military strength and move troops to the border, which then creates a self-fulfilling prophecy. The increase in military ships, planes and personnel provides *prima facie* evidence that its foreign policy of containment is vital to protect against the impending aggression from surrounding nations. But this policy only increases the sense of threat and hostility in the neighborhood of states.

Foreign policy is very often theory-driven rather than data-driven. If we believe that another country is hostile, our foreign policy toward that country is bound to be defensive and based upon fear. However, there may be very little evidence to support this belief which is often based upon a nation's perception or misperception of reality rather than reality itself. As individuals, if we feel threatened, our heart rate speeds up, we become more anxious, and we prepare to defend ourselves. It makes little difference if this threat is real or imaginary because our reaction will be the same. Our perception of reality may be more important than reality itself.

According to Marshall Singer, those who perceive reality in a similar way also share a culture.[3] Because of their common historical experiences, people in the same nation tend to perceive their country and other countries in similar ways. These shared perceptions, which become their *national image,* are conveyed from one generation to another and become a part of the *national culture* and *national identity.* This national image also shapes foreign policy.

A newly emerging nation often has a self-centered national image. Using an historical sociology or isomorphic approach to explain the evolution of this image and foreign policy, we can draw a parallel with an infant who is unable to have empathy for others and wants immediate gratification of all needs. The child does not yet view himself or herself as part of a social system. As the child matures, there is a greater realization that the child's behavior impacts others and vice versa. At this point, there is an understanding of others and the broader social environment. The child learns to compete or cooperate and can empathize with others.

Economist Kenneth Boulding described the image of a newly emerging nation as an "unsophisticated image."[4] Its foreign policy might not include cooperation with other nations in the international system and there is little empathy for other nations. As the new nation interacts with other nations in the international system, its image becomes more sophisticated. There is an understanding that nations interact with and impact each other—foreign policy can lead to peace or hostility in the region or the entire international system and alter perceptions other nations have of the nation. Leaders especially understand that the nation's behavior affects other nations.

THE IMPACT OF THE MASS MEDIA

The ways in which we are entertained and informed by the mass media both reflect and shape the way we view ourselves, others, and the world at large. For example, surveys consistently show that most Americans believe that the majority of poor people are black, yet most are white.[5] This is because the face of poverty on TV news and in news magazines is overwhelmingly black.

The popular media can dehumanize groups and perpetuate stereotypes. On American TV, people from the rural South in the U.S. are often characterized as hillbillies with funny accents. The men are lanky and unkempt with a taste for moonshine and an aversion for honest work while hillbilly women are either the Granny—a gaunt woman with straight, unkempt hair—or the oversexed and underdressed hillbilly babe.[6] These stereotypes affect not only the way in which others view people from the South, but the way in which people in the South view themselves.

In American movies, blacks are disproportionately cast in roles as criminals, Latin Americans as drug runners, and Arabs as terrorists. Supposedly African-American actor Danny Glover refused to star in the 1989 movie *Lethal Weapon 2* when the "bad guys" were ethnic stereotypes. This was a period of history when the white minority of South Africa, led by the Afrikaners, maintained a segregated society under the policy of Apartheid. Glover did not want to star in a movie that fostered negative stereotypes of African-Americans, Latinos, or Arabs. He understood the power of the entertainment media and therefore insisted that the "bad guys" would be racist Afrikaner diplomats who were involved in drug smuggling and exchanging Krugerands for dollars, which was illegal in the U.S. at that time.

The characters of the "good guys" are usually well developed while stereotypical "bad guys" are portrayed as caricatures, not whole human beings. Thus, when they are eventually killed, no one really cares. The first clear exception was the Oscar winning 1967 movie *Bonnie and Clyde* which was based on two famous bank robbers and their gang. Their characters were very well developed. The audience could easily identify with them as whole human beings who laughed, got angry, made love, frolicked in the field, and yet also killed people. The last scene of this widescreen Cinemascope movie featured a lengthy, bloody gun battle in which they were brutally killed. The police and FBI used Tommy guns filling the widescreen with gore and blood. During this final scene, many Americans stormed out of the theater apparently overwhelmed by the realistic presentation of tragic violence.

The media has a major impact on the way we perceive conflict on the national and international level. Is your image of the world one of conflict between good and evil with good winning out (a melodrama)? Or is it a tragedy where good people sometimes do bad things and bad people sometimes do good things and evil may win out? Are things so black and white that there can be no compromise with your opponent to find a peaceful solution to your differences?

If you see the world as a melodrama and perceive yourself as moral or good and your enemies as less than human and absolutely demonic, it is almost impossible to resolve conflict peacefully. There can be no compromise with evil and during a crisis, such as an international conflict, the pressure on a leader to forcefully take action is greatly increased. The dominant American culture has traditionally valued action, not talk or measured thought. Leaders are expected to decisively act rather than to ponder options, nuances, or subtleties. This dualistic/melodramatic perspective leaves little room for hesitation. In fact, the kiss of death politically for an American leader is to appear to "do nothing."

INTERNATIONAL CONFLICT

International conflict is often caused by a genuine clash of interests between nations which cannot be resolved through peaceful means. For example, a nation may attempt to expand its borders or increase its economic and political power at the expense of another nation. Negotiation, arbitration, and adjudication fail to help it achieve these objectives. After weighing such factors as economic and military capability, the resolve of citizens to support armed aggression, and the strengths and weaknesses of the enemy, a realistic decision is made to engage in war.

However, the primary cause of war may have little to do with such realistic or rational considerations. Perceptions or images of reality may be more important than reality itself when it comes to explaining the dynamics of international conflict. And subjective and irrational drives, such as power, pride, and fear, may be the strongest reasons for conflict. Psychological and cultural factors can also cause, exacerbate, and prolong conflicts between nations.

World War I was largely an accident resulting from irrational fear. When the Archduke Ferdinand was assassinated in Sarajevo in 1914, the balance of power in the international system in Europe collapsed because nations believed that they were going to be invaded by other nations. In fact, the assassination was largely a domestic or regional matter that had nothing to do with the rest of Europe.

As nations built up their military forces along their borders to prevent invasions, this only increased the perception of impending aggression. Rather than deterring war, it may have fueled it. Less than a month after the Archduke was killed, Europe exploded into war. The fear of impending attacks caused nations to engage in pre-emptive strikes against each other until the western world was engulfed in a world war. No nation was motivated by hegemonic aggression. Rather, the underlying motive for using military force was fear. Had nations been able to communicate clearly with each other, or had there been some institution in which they could have debated the "facts," it would have been apparent that there was no real threat from other nations.

Some nations have been genuinely hegemonic. Their aggression was a result of a drive for power over others. War thus became the primary tool for promoting national interests. World War II Germany may be the most outstanding example of such a nation. Hitler was determined to conquer other nations with military force. He was not motivated by fear but rather macho pride and hegemony. He convinced many Germans that Germany was treated unfairly after World War I by France and other countries that demanded reparations. In addition, there were those who were not loyal to Germany.

Hitler really was a genuine "bad guy," or to put it in more biblical terms, he really was evil. He was also a paranoid sociopath with delusions of grandeur and delusions of persecution—a very dangerous combination. He was an anti-Semite and racist who wanted to "purify" the population of Germany. His psychopathology, combined with his rhetorical skills, allowed him to become a charismatic leader who could not have been deterred with talk and reason. Although British Prime Minister Neville Chamberlain believed that Hitler agreed to have "peace for our time" after meeting with Hitler in Munich in September of 1938, this only convinced Hitler that England was weak and ripe for attack. Munich not only didn't deter Hitler, it actually encouraged his aggression.

Knowing the intentions or motives of the adversary is vital to prevent war.[7] If fear of an impending threat is motivating aggression, then communication and negotiation might very well prevent a war. Failure to communicate might actually cause a conflict to spiral out of control as it did during World War I. If hegemonic drive is the cause of the aggression and the intention of a nation or leader is to maximize power over other nations, then communication and negotiation might increase the chance of war. The only deterrence in this case would be the credible threat of countering military action with overwhelming force. Ironically, when an adversary feels threatened, a clear and credible message of being willing to use force only increases the probability of war.

The chart below summarizes much of Robert Jervis' comparison of World War I and World War II.[8] If we consider games or simulations, World War I is analogous to the Prisoner's Dilemma. If states communicate and work together, they could prevent war. If they pursue their own national interests, all states are worse off. Rather than being independent, they are interdependent and ought to develop trust and empathy. Institutions should be created that will minimize misunderstanding and maximize cooperative behavior to the benefit of everyone.

The game of chicken is analogous to World War II—teenagers driving their cars toward each other at a high speed. The driver wins this game by convincing the other that he will kill himself before veering off the highway to avoid a collision. Deterrence amounts to convincing the oncoming driver that he will be killed if he continues speeding ahead.

WORLD WAR I	WORLD WAR II
Used as archetype of idealist worldview	Used as archetype of realist worldview
War was a tragedy	War was a melodrama
Failure to communicate sparked war	Appeasement failed to stop war
Communication may have solved war	Communication may have encouraged war
Driven by pre-emptive strikes/miscommunication	Driven by aggression/hegemonic intentions
Irrational fear spurred on war	Lack of resolve to use force spurred on war
Conflict spiraled out of control	Conflict was not deterred
Game analogy: "Prisoner's Dilemma"	Game analogy: "Chicken"

National leaders portray war as a result of a brazen and unprovoked attack by an enemy and therefore analogous to World War II. In fact, in the past half century, most nations engaged in war for defensive reasons; they were motivated by fear, not aggression. Fear is a psychological phenomenon based upon our perception of reality, not reality itself. How we imagine the world to be motivates our behavior. If we believe that another person intends to do us harm, we defend ourselves even if there is no real threat.

For the sake of illustration, let us consider a very dramatic hypothetical situation. A gunman in a large city begins to shoot people with a high powered rifle from atop a high building. We do not know what is motivating this violence. A clinical psychologist who could interview the man might determine that he is motivated by irrational fear. He is a paranoid psychotic who believes that others will kill him and he is defending himself by engaging in pre-emptive strikes. His intentions are defensive. Of course, he is insane. No one is trying to kill him.

How might we best prevent him from killing more people without killing him? As was mentioned earlier in this book, the only way we can really understand his intentions is to put ourselves in his psychological shoes. Realistic empathy does not mean that we are sympathetic, we agree with him, or that we identify with him. It simply means we understand how he perceives reality. In this case, we would want to decrease his fear. We certainly would not shout up to him with a bullhorn, "Come down from there or we'll shoot you." This would only confirm his worldview that people are trying to kill him. It would make the situation worse.

And we would not walk out in the open with our arms outstretched as we shout up to him, "Look, I'm not armed. Come on down." Chances are that he would think you are trying to trick you or you are a fool. Either way, he might very well shoot you.

The best approach would be to gradually and carefully decrease his sense of fear by reassuring him that you are not a threat. Building trust with him is important and requires empathy, but not sympathy or agreement. And you certainly would not identify with him.

When it comes to the behavior of nations during times of international conflict, empathy is more than just a psychological trait or skill. To be effective in preventing conflict or resolving conflict, we must put ourselves in the cultural shoes of those in another nation. *Realistic cultural empathy* means understanding their national image, traditional values and ways of thinking.

Both American involvement in Vietnam in the 1960s and Soviet involvement in Afghanistan in the 1970s were motivated more by fear than by any hegemonic, aggressive drive. Both countries asserted that their aggression was defensive. The U.S. claimed it was protecting South Vietnam from North Vietnamese aggression and the Soviet Union claimed it was supporting the government of Afghanistan from a CIA-led takeover. Whether these threats were real or imagined is largely irrelevant. The consequence was the same—war.

NATIONAL IMAGES

A national identity or image is a result of how a people overcame national crises across many generations. The history of a nation is a vital part of this image because it is based upon events which are selected, highlighted and organized in a way that makes the country special when compared with others. Going through wars, natural disasters, and economic depressions gives people a sense of shared experiences and shapes the way they view their nation. These experiences are also positive. Having national leaders such as Mahatma Gandhi, Martin Luther King, Jr., or Nelson Mandela, who are renowned around the globe, becomes a source of great national pride.

When the people within a nation come together to overthrow a colonial power or a ruthless dictator, the shared struggle creates nationalism and a national culture with a system of internal values that become a part of the national identity. To understand and predict the behavior of an individual, we must consider that person's history. While we must be cautious in drawing parallels between individual and national behavior, it seems reasonable that if we are to understand and predict national behavior, we must also consider the history that people share in a nation.

Someone who experienced a traumatic childhood with an authoritarian father who exercised strict discipline based upon severe punishment or the threat of punishment may be exceedingly fearful as an adult. He or she might even be somewhat paranoid. In the paranoid's worldview, everyone else is seen as a threat. Paranoids may engage in irrational *possibilistic* thought rather than realistic or *probabilistic* thought.[9] While it is possible that the world is intent on doing harm to a person, it is not very probable.

The Soviet Union was invaded numerous times by other countries including Germany during World War II, leading to the deaths of millions of civilians. The leaders of the USSR during the Cold War went through the purges of Stalin and the deaths of millions more innocent people. Given this history, it is understandable that the leaders of the USSR during the Cold War believed it was entirely *possible* that the U.S. was intent upon destroying their country and the American policy of containing communism under the German Marshall Plan was perceived as encirclement. The deployment of nuclear missiles in Germany increased this sense of fear. Most Americans would argue that this was paranoia because they would never support an invasion of the USSR.

On the other hand, when nuclear missiles were installed in Cuba, many Americans believed that this was an act of aggression and part of the Cold War. When the USSR reminded American leaders that there were American nuclear missiles in Turkey, the U.S. claimed that their missiles were defensive and the Soviet missiles in Cuba were hostile and offensive. However, given the national image of the USSR, its fear was understandable.

In a nation where most share the same child raising practices, if the role of the typical father is authoritarian, we might speak of an "authoritarian society." In this type of society the divisions between superiors and subordinates are clearly drawn and there are fairly rigid social hierarchies. A son is expected to obey his father and when he becomes an adult his children will obey him. Or, to put it in the framework of Geert Hofstede's dimensions, there is a great power distance between subordinates and superiors.

People with an authoritarian personality[10] are usually fairly close-minded and they tend to make clear distinctions between insiders and outsiders. They are intolerant to ambiguity and they tend to believe that those who do not share their way of life are a threat. This national paranoid image may be reinforced by actual threats from other nations. This is perhaps the national image of North Korea in today's world.

Sometimes paranoids engage in preemptive attacks and strike out at others before they are assaulted. They do not see this as offensive behavior. Instead, it is consistent with their image of the world as hostile; they are simply defending themselves from the potential aggression of others. To understand and predict the behavior of paranoids we must get inside their heads to know how they perceive reality. This does not mean we agree with their motives, accept their behavior, or share their reality world.

MELODRAMA AND TRAGEDY

Our national image and national identity becomes more important during a war because our in-group membership gives us a sense of ego support. The in-group/out-group distinction between "us" and "them" becomes clearer as we try to eliminate the ambiguities. We become good and peaceful as they become increasingly more evil and aggressive. We perceive our aggression as defensive, while their aggression is offensive. This dualistic oversimplification is found in most major international conflicts.

An *enemy image* develops to give a sense of belonging and to clarify a complex reality. This melodramatic perspective is somewhat like the old American cowboy movies, where the "good guys" are clearly identifiable because they wear white hats and are absolutely angelic, while the "bad guys" wear black hats and are completely demonic. Of course, the good guys always win.

The American people may be more susceptible to melodramatic imagery than Europeans or others because it is a young country that did not go through a feudal period or fight numerous lengthy wars on its own soil. The dualistic thinking of fundamentalist Protestantism (good and evil, heaven and hell, angels and devils, etc.) and the impact of melodramatic themes and images in the mass media both reflect and reinforce the traditional tendency to perceive the world as a melodrama.

A classic example of this melodramatic/dualistic and even escapist national image is the science fiction movie *Independence Day* which is often shown on television late at night even today. It was the number one move in theaters during the summer of 1996 and the storyline was very simple: aliens from outer space were trying to conquer Earth. The President of the United States, who just happened to be an ace jet fighter pilot, flew the plane that led the attack against them. Thousands of other pilots from around the earth joined in this attack.

When the alien space ships were being destroyed and crashed down to earth, audiences around the United States broke out in spontaneous cheers as if they had just won World War III. This is American. An individual leader takes decisive action and rids the world of an evil threat. It wasn't just a science fiction movie—this was cowboy melodrama! Many Europeans thought it was a satire and ironically it was directed by a German.

In that same year, Americans were glued to their television sets watching the O.J. Simpson murder trial on CNN—"the news channel." In spite of this label, most Americans do not watch CNN for their national or international news. They tend to watch network newscasts in the afternoon on ABC, NBC, CBS, and FOX. If you remove the advertisements, it amounts to about 20 minutes every day.

The American mass media, including the news media, is a commercial media. What appears on television and in newspapers often depends upon what sells products. Events that are dramatic and sensational are usually featured because they attract viewers and readers. People who take clear positions who are entertaining are often interviewed and, because of time and space limitations, most are not in-depth.

CNN made a brilliant business decision when it carried the O.J. Simpson trial live. Their viewership increased over 800 percent.[11] In part this was because most Americans knew Simpson as an athlete and movie actor, but the primary reason was the way in which the trial was presented. It was never simply news or information. It was melodramatic entertainment.

Most of the lawyers, and even the judge, became instant celebrities and many later became famous authors, television personalities, and popular "experts" featured on news shows that cover major crimes.

To make the trial even more melodramatic, at the end of each day, colorful and very articulate legal experts were featured in news shows to give their opinions as to who lost and who won—the prosecutor or the defense—somewhat like a football game. But this was not a melodrama, it was a tragedy. Innocent people had been murdered.

Americans have always enjoyed trials because they are melodramatic—someone wins and someone loses.[12] There is no compromise or mediated settlement. Americans often remember an historical event because of a famous trial such as the "Scopes Monkey Trial" in 1925 which raised the question of whether evolution could be taught in grade schools or the 1935 Lindbergh Baby Kidnapping trial which made kidnapping a federal crime.

Violent conflict, especially when it is international, is much more of a complex tragedy than a simple dualistic melodrama. It is usually quite rare for one party to be completely bad and the other good. We often assume that aggression is a matter of malevolent intent or the hostility of our enemy, and yet fear may be a much more powerful cause for the attack. The tragic reality is that in war all combatants lose.

Aspects of an individual's, or a nation's, image include experience or history, the influence of the mass media and traditional cultural values, ways of perceiving reality, and thought patterns. A nation with a history of actual continued aggression from others, or the perception of ongoing external threat, is predisposed to view the world as hostile. Because the nation has survived in this hostile and threatening world, the national self-image may be one of noble endurance. Delusions of persecution and grandeur may coexist.

The educational system may very well stress past wars and the heroism of one's own people, while the mass media often reinforce this melodramatic enemy image. Children grow up hearing folk tales of the inhuman aggression of invaders and the stoic and morally superior resistance to such hostile acts. When the nation was made to use force, it was always defensive. It was not simply to promote one's own national interests but ultimately or for the sake of others and humankind—"A war to end all wars" or "A war to make the world safe for democracy."

This sometimes is much more than the bravado of nationalistic narratives that enhance pride in one's nation. It can easily become Orwellian indoctrination and doublethink. Those who question the heroic tales become traitors and contrary information that might challenge the patriotic stories is forbidden in the educational system and the mass media. An extreme example could be North Korea.

Enemy soldiers are often dehumanized and portrayed as ignoble animals, which makes them easier to kill.[13] And their violent deaths are sometimes abstract or removed from reality. We talk of tonnage dropped, sorties, or tanks destroyed without considering bodies torn apart and grieving families. The 1991 Persian Gulf War was viewed somewhat like a video game for some Americans, who saw few dead bodies or Iraqi soldiers or civilians on television, yet were entranced by the high-tech precision of American missiles. The current use of drones to kill enemies involves weapons that few have ever seen. We imagine harmless toys, remote guided airplanes that we knew as children, but now they have missiles. There is an assurance that they only kill "targeted" enemies and very seldom harm innocent civilians.

These "smart" weapons do kill innocent people, they are terrifying because they can't be seen or heard from the ground, and it is just a matter of time before many nations begin to use them. The British invented the first battleship with huge guns and it was only a few years later that the navies of many nations had such ships. The U.S. and Soviet Union developed atomic bombs and now many nations have atomic weapons. It is unlikely that only America will have drones.

Historic enemies often have a mirror image of each other.[14] This was certainly true throughout the Cold War and it is true of most international conflicts today. We often see in others the very things we deny in ourselves. Through projection and other defense mechanisms we view our enemy as aggressive, a nation led by evil leaders intent on destroying us. In turn, we are good. Our enemy often views us in the same way.

Underlying these enemy image perceptions is the fundamental attribution error where we have situational explanations for our aggressive behavior and trait explanations for our enemy's aggression. When we engage in military action, it is always defensive and when our enemy engages in military action it is always offensive and based upon hegemonic drive. When we seek to negotiate instead of fight it is because we are a peaceful people. When they agree to negotiate it is because of our vast military might—they had no choice. We twist our perception and explanation of reality to fit our enemy image.

Once fighting has begun, it is very difficult to turn to peaceful ways of resolving a conflict. If we wish to avert a war, the appeal to negotiation or mediation is best made before any blood has been shed. This goes back to Festinger's theory of cognitive dissonance.[15] If our behavior or action contradicts our beliefs, we feel dissonance. We cannot deny or take back the action. The only way to create consonance is to change our beliefs. Once the fighting begins, we change our beliefs to fit our actions. "We are using military power against them because they deserve to be attacked. The enemy must be responsible for the war because we are peaceful."

INTERCULTURAL ASPECTS OF CONFLICT

The psychological approach to understanding conflict tends to emphasize *similarities* among people. For example, the dynamics of perception and cognition found in image theory apply to everyone. All humans respond to inescapable pain by engaging in aggression. Political scientists and international relations experts often assume that there are also common factors and causes for international conflict. Political, economic, and military power and its distribution and security are the primary concerns of states. War is simply a way of asserting power or preserving security when peaceful means no longer work.

A cultural approach assumes *differences*; each culture is unique and human behavior cannot be explained without understanding the impact of culture. While many psychologists and political scientists believe that the commonly held principles of conflict and negotiation are universal and applicable to all societies, culturalists believe that these principles are often specific to particular cultures. They must always be considered in the context of each culture and the dynamics of intercultural communication and interaction.

There are intercultural aspects to all human conflicts on the interpersonal, community, national, or international level. It is increasingly difficult to separate these levels of conflict because the world is shrinking and the interpersonal and local issues are interrelated with both national and global issues. And there are more ethnic cultures within countries. Today many of the civil wars within nations involve ethnic and cultural differences. They tend to spill over into other regions of the world and involve other countries.

Wars between countries are no longer simply regional but instead involve combatants from very different cultures or civilizations. Religion and basic cultural values may be replacing traditional issues of political power and economics as causes of international conflict. However, it is important to realize that today there are more conflicts within civilizations than between civilizations. Harvard professor Samuel Huntington claimed that after the Cold War the world would devolve into a "conflict of civilizations," with each civilization identified with a particular religion such as Christianity, Islam, Confucianism, and so on.[16] He took us from the Cold War back to the Holy Crusades. The new enemy becomes the non-West in terms of religion and civilization.

Huntington's theory of oncoming violent conflict between civilizations has not been proven true. In fact, there is evidence that we are becoming more peaceful in spite of conflicts taking place around the globe. Armed conflict worldwide is actually decreasing in scale.[17]

Huntington believed that Islam was a threat to American civilization. (Of course, America does not have a civilization. It has a national culture which is part of Western Civilization.) There is no evidence to support his assertion. The largest Muslim country in the world is Indonesia and yet it is a very moderate country that is a friend of the United States.

During the Cold War, extremists such as Senator Joseph McCarthy claimed that Communism was like cancer, you need to cut the pink out with the red because there were many "pinkos" in the American film industry, academia, and even at the Department of State. On the other hand, in 1963, President John F. Kennedy gave a commencement address at American University when he announced the first above ground atomic test ban treaty between the Soviet Union and the United States and used the phrase, "making the world safe for diversity." Kennedy did not see the Cold War in dualistic terms and believed that there were different gradations of communism. Yugoslavia was different than the USSR and Cuba was different than China. Communism was not a monolith.

Although Huntington certainly viewed the world in terms of the dualistic "free world" and the "communist world," he was not an extremist. He believed it was in the interests of the U.S. to be engaged with the USSR and to understand the national culture of the Soviet Union. When the Cold War ended, Huntington was concerned that American national identity would be weakened because it had no clear enemy. This need for an enemy is reminiscent of Osama bin Laden who thought that the Western world was a threat to the purity of Islam and all Muslims in the world would unite to fight this common enemy. Both Huntington and bin Laden were wrong.

INTERCULTURAL ASPECTS OF NEGOTIATION

Whether it is a low-keyed business meeting or a life-and-death crisis scenario such as a hostage negotiation, interactions between people of different cultures are frustrating because of differences in communicative styles, conflicting values, and interests, and even such simple assumptions as to how and when to elect leaders, set agendas, or get down to business. The way in which we regard interpersonal conflict and negotiation also varies with culture, yet most people believe everyone deals with conflict in the same way.

Rural Southerners in the United States are much more likely to want to develop rapport during the first few minutes of an initial group meeting. They value harmonious group relations, are often indirect and circuitous in their conversation, and they seem to be rather relaxed or "laid back." Time devoted to maintaining and cultivating good relations with others is perhaps more important than simply doing a job and, in fact, it allows business to progress more smoothly when it is time to get down to business. This would be true of a business meeting in many parts of the non-Euro-American world such as countries in Africa or Latin America. It is part of their negotiation action chain.

A good conversation is like a dance where there is a specific tempo or pace. When people of different cultures come together, they are often out-of-sync in conversational style. How people communicate, not simply what they communicate, is determined by their culture. And conversational style may be even more important than the content of conversation in cross-cultural communication. During discussions, people from New York City not only cut off conversational loops, they often interrupt sentences of others or even complete them. A sign of rapport among New Yorkers is when someone cuts into your conversation. To a rural Southerner this is aggressive, abrasive, abrupt, and disrespectful.

The tendency of the Southerner to speak slowly and drag out the pronunciation of words may strike New Yorkers as childish or unsophisticated. The rapid, staccato speech pattern of New Yorkers may sound like machine gun fire to the rural Southerner. Differences in rhythm or synchrony of conversation, in and of themselves, create misunderstanding and discomfort.

High-context, associative thinkers or *Be-ers* tend to be much more adept at using and translating nonverbal messages. Mainstream American, low-context, abstractive thinkers or *Do-ers* concentrate on words and even more on written words. *Be-ers* prefer the physical presence of another person so that they can relate nonverbal messages to verbal messages and use all their senses to know if the other person is honest, sincere, committed, and so on. They feel very uncomfortable with telephone conversations or memos unless they are supplemented with face-to-face encounters.

When should a group get down to business? In "to be" cultures, where group harmony is highly regarded, there is often a premium placed upon developing rapport before discussing business. To begin doing business before getting to know all members would be very rude. It would imply that no one cares who you are and you don't care who they are.

During this get-acquainted phase, it would be impolite to engage in a formal question and answer format. This would resemble an interrogation. Time ought to be allowed for all to reveal aspects of their character and status in a rather natural, almost poetic fashion. As in any polite conversation, room must be allowed for the very articulate to go off on tangents that may reveal subtle aspects of their character and abilities.

Indeed the style with which a person presents him or herself and interacts with others provides a very good hint as to leadership capabilities, maturity, intelligence, sophistication, and insightfulness. Almost everything that is spoken and how it is presented is relevant to leadership skills. All of this information is somewhat intuitively tied together to create a picture of the whole person, not simply what he or she does in a meeting.

How do we know if there is a full-blown conflict or just a disagreement? How do we know if the conflict is escalating or deescalating? When is it time to resolve the conflict? How do we resolve it? And when is it beyond resolution?[18] Most of the answers to these questions we tacitly learn simply by growing up in a particular culture. They are unconsciously acquired so early in life that they are taken for granted and held to be universal or true of everyone. In fact, they are only true for those within our own specific culture. We usually first become aware that others may not share our assumptions regarding conflict and negotiation when we encounter those who are culturally different.

What could be perceived as a genuine conflict in one culture may be just a lively disagreement in another. For example, mainstream white Americans usually state arguments in a *factual-inductive* manner.[19] Relevant facts are sequentially presented in a fairly unemotional way leading to a conclusion. The greater the number of facts at the onset, the more persuasive the argument. Black Americans tend to be more *affective-intuitive* or deductive. They begin with an emotional position followed by a variety of facts somewhat poetically or metaphorically connected to support their conclusions.

These differences in rhetorical style result in whites being viewed as insincere, impersonal, and deceptive by black Americans while blacks are perceived as irrational, too personal, and abrasive by white Americans. Arguments develop, and many times are lost, because of these differences in style, not substance or content.

When Rev. Jesse Jackson was running for president in 1984, he was often perceived by white Americans as angry, too emotional, and manipulative whereas amongst African-Americans he was seen as sincere and capable of developing good rapport with his audiences.[20] He would often start his speeches at rallies with his conclusions, which was "irrational" in the eyes of many white people. His affective-intuitive arguments were always emotional and quite often members of his black audience would spontaneously join in with comments of encouragement, agreement, and support. This call-and-response pattern between speaker and audience is often a part of the traditional Black Church and truth and sincerity are communicated with emotional intensity. To whites, black Americans probably appeared to be on the verge of a confrontation and united in a clique or even an unruly mob.

This is primarily a result of cultural differences. For example, at a jazz club, the audience and artists become one with constant verbal interaction between them. As the musicians excite the audience, they shout out encouragement—"Right on!" "Go for it!" and so on. This, in turn, changes the way in which the music is performed. In a classical music concert, the audience remains quiet throughout the performance.

In a negotiation with an African-American, when the discussion becomes emotional or heated, white Americans sometimes reactively withdraw into a super factual-inductive mode in an effort to settle things down before they get out-of-hand. "Now let's just calm down and consider the relevant facts in this matter." This is said rather matter-of-factly, without much emotion, to encourage calm and rationality. The white emphasis on facts, logical presentation, and lack of emotion comes off as cold, condescending, patronizing, and further evidence that whites do not really want to hear the views of blacks.

White Americans often assume that there is a short distance between an emotional, verbal expression of disagreement, and a physical conflict, whereas for black Americans there is a much greater distance.[21] Stating a position with feelings is a sign of sincerity for most black Americans and truth is much more important than being polite. However, it might be interpreted as an indication of uncontrollable anger or instability for white Americans and, even worse, an impending confrontation.

Threatening words usually indicate *intent* for white Americans, while they may be used as *affect* among black Americans. For mainstream white Americans, this is true in interpersonal or international conflict. To show feelings and to get another person's full attention, black Americans may overstate the situation and use hyperbole. There really is no "fight" unless someone makes a menacing move. Words are simply used for affect.

White Americans treat words very seriously. They are low-context communicators who depend upon verbal interaction. Nevertheless, there are times when white Americans speak a situational high-context dialect and use words for affect. Perhaps when a child did some mischief, his mother threatened him with mild bodily harm. "If you do that again, you're going to get a real spanking!" In the context of your relationship, the child knew her words were designed to show her feelings, sincerity, and genuine displeasure. It got the undivided attention of the child, who did not call 911.

In some "to be" or high-context cultures, people try to "keep a lid on" disagreement to maintain harmony within the community or group. This is often true for Latin Americans or Arabs. This internalization of negative feelings means that when they erupt, their expression will be very emotional. And because everyone knows everyone else, any conflict affects the entire group.

If a Mexican offends a friend, nothing may be said. Because they know each other so well, there is an unspoken and perhaps unconscious assumption that the offender will intuitively sense the other person's hurt or anger from subtle, nonverbal cues. If the offended person must explicitly verbalize feelings, the offender was obviously too insensitive to "read" the other's feelings. Furthermore, the commitment to a personal relationship is so strong that the Mexican would rather lose an argument than lose a friend.[22] The whole person is unconditionally accepted as a friend—good and bad, rational and irrational. An argument is no grounds for terminating a friendship.

When there is an explosion of emotions, it does not mean that everything is breaking down or that the person has reached the proverbial "end of the rope." Instead, it means "I tried to keep a lid on this. I thought you'd know how I felt and I would never have to directly put my feelings into words. Now I've exposed my feelings. I'm hurt. And everyone else knows how I feel. Let's begin negotiation." But for many white Americans there is a belief that the offended party should have said something much earlier before it became so emotional. The display of emotion means that negotiations have broken down and the friendship is seriously damaged.

Among Mexicans, until there is an exchange of sincere emotional words, no negotiations are taking place. They might assume they are beginning the process of negotiation with their emotional outburst while Anglos believe that the situation is beyond resolution or it is indeed at "the end of the rope."[23]

Most Anglos' friendships are conditional on the rule that friends remain rational or "civil." An emotional expression of anger is equated with irrationality and consequently the termination of a relationship. Of course, when Anglos abruptly withdraw from a relationship after an outburst of genuine anger, many Mexicans begin to doubt the sincerity of the friendship in the first place.

CULTURE AND CONFLICT RESOLUTION

In close-knit communities, if harm should come to another, and you could prevent it but do not, then you are held indirectly responsible for the harm. This assumption of *indirect responsibility* demands that a third-party intermediary must step in to resolve disputes. Furthermore, an intermediary must be associated with the disputants, trusted and esteemed by all, and strive to bring about compromise so that everyone wins. After all, they must continue to live and work together after everything is settled. There is a natural inclination to search for win-win solutions. This is very different than within the American legal system where people go to court to "win" a case and the judge must be totally neutral. The jury can have no relationship with any parties involved in the court case.

In traditional American Indian courts, the object of adjudication is to mediate a case to satisfaction of all involved, not to establish fault or guilt and then to punish.[24] The court ensures restitution and compensation to the victim and his or her family so that harmony is restored within the community. The court plays the role of third-party intermediary.

Intermediaries might be elders or others who are highly regarded and are personally known to everyone involved in the conflict. If the disputants must handle the conflict themselves, there is no way that they can resolve their disagreements without losing face. However, when others assume the role of intermediary it allows everyone to maintain his or her honor. Consequently, when others fail to intervene, they are sometimes held accountable. The assumption is, "you should have stopped me before this got out of hand. Because you didn't step in, you are responsible for this fight."

In Western, urban societies there is no assumption of indirect responsibility and disputes are usually resolved by the parties directly involved. If a matter must be resolved by intervention, the judge or jury must appear neutral or uninvolved. Resolution is often determined by a decision of right or wrong based upon the facts or merit of the case. Compromise is seldom a desired goal. It is a win-lose proposition.

The 1978 Camp David Accords were negotiated in ways that were exceedingly culturally adept. Prime Minister Menachem Begin of Israel and President Anwar Sadat of Egypt met with President Jimmy Carter, a trusted third-party, long before they came to the U.S. Perhaps because Carter is from rural Georgia—a high-context culture—he intuitively understood the cultural dynamics of negotiation in the Middle East. In addition, he was perceived as a sincere, moral, and religious man by almost everyone. These are qualities that are highly regarded in the Middle East.

Both Begin and Sadat were warriors and heroes in their own country and Egypt and Israel fought numerous wars with great loss of life. They certainly did not like each other and there was absolutely no chance that they would simply sit down and begin negotiations. An intermediary who was known and trusted by both of them was essential if anything was to become of a meeting.

Carter spent time developing interpersonal rapport with both heads of state before they left their countries. Sadat journeyed to Jerusalem and met with former Israeli Prime Minister Golda Meir. They discussed their grandchildren and other personal matters. While this may not appear to be essential to negotiation of the end of a conflict between states, it was the first step in the conflict resolution action chain. Sitting down, "drinking tea together," and developing personal rapport was the vital step to the eventual successful negotiation. And what could be more personal than talking about grandchildren?

At Camp David, Carter not only used his good offices to resolve this conflict, but he also played the traditional Middle Eastern role of *waseet* or *wasta*—a third-party intermediary who helps to get things done and also to resolve conflicts. This allowed both heads of state to avoid any loss of face or unpleasantness in direct face-to-face negotiation and yet provided for peaceful and serious resolution.

INTERCULTURAL RELATIONS AND GLOBALIZATION

As people from different cultures increasingly come together within and between countries there is great likelihood that conflict and misunderstanding will also increase. Some will fear that their way of life will be permanently altered or destroyed. This fear, in turn, can lead to defensive aggression and even international conflict.

With time, younger generations will be born into a world of diversity. They will casually interact with people from very different backgrounds in face-to-face encounters and over the internet. Contemporary social media certainly bring people together and this may lead to greater understanding and acceptance of different values and ways of life. But it can also be used to perpetuate enemy images and incite hatred. The naïve idea of a "global village" that would necessarily result from worldwide use of the new media has not yet happened.

In the long run, chances are that young people who use this media for interpersonal interaction with others around the globe will end up overcoming the fearful stereotypes and prejudice. Just as most viewers of television recognize the distortions of advertisements intended to sell products. As we become more accustomed to communicating interpersonally across national borders in real time we begin to trust our own experiences with others rather than the propaganda of enemy imagery.

One of the best ways to change the enemy image we hold of others is to get to know them as human beings rather than dehumanized, demonic caricatures. When we can look another person in the face and we see our mother, father, sister, or brother, we view them as real human beings with whom we can empathize. Electronic media allows us to have these kinds of interactions. But they still cannot have the impact of exchange programs where we are physically present with others and can engage in intensive face-to-face intercultural communication.

Study abroad, exchange of scholars, and international visitors programs are relatively inexpensive ways of bringing about better understanding between people while at the same time decreasing the appeal of simplistic stereotypes that perpetuate international conflict. Public diplomacy through these international interpersonal encounters not only directly benefits the individuals involved, it also changes national images.

We know how to better prepare people for these encounters in order to increase the ease with which they adjust to new cultures and their effectiveness in intercultural communication. More importantly, these sojourns are no longer simply a matter of traveling overseas to work or learn a new language. They can become opportunities to learn more about our own cultures and other cultures. We realize the cultural differences and we may even value them more with these encounters. But we also discover the similarities between people around the globe.

The research is abundantly clear that people who go through an in-depth intercultural experience claim they end up being more flexible with greater self-reliance and self-esteem. They also discover aspects of their own personality that would never be apparent had they remained in their home cultures. The intercultural communication skills they acquire stay with them for the rest of their lives and they are likely to become the informal diplomats who will prevent international conflict in the future.

SECTION VI: Readings

The Face of the Enemy
Jerome D. Frank

An ingenious experiment by J. W. Bagby of New York's Roosevelt Hospital illustrates the phenomenon of perceptual filtering. This psychologist asked American and Mexican school teachers to look into a device that showed simultaneously a different picture to each eye. One eye saw a picture of a baseball player and the other saw a bullfighter.

An overwhelming proportion of the Americans "saw" the baseball player; the overwhelming proportion of Mexicans "saw" the bullfighter. What these teachers saw, of course, was mostly determined by their cultural filter.

No psychiatrist or psychologist would be so rash as to claim that one can make solid inferences about the behavior of nations from that of individuals, but it is startling how often similarities between the man and his country emerge when one starts looking carefully.

One psychological principle certainly is highly relevant to international affairs: a person's beliefs and his expectations largely determine how he thinks and how he behaves. Since citizens of a nation tend to share the same beliefs and expectations, this principle is important if we are to understand how nations see each other and behave toward one another.

Characteristic of each nation's self-image is the belief in national sovereignty, territorial rights and national strength. Each nation believes in its right to pursue vital interests regardless of the effects on other nations.

Reprinted from *Psychology Today,* November 1968. Copyright © 1968, Sussex Publishers, Inc.

The degree of fear in which one nation holds another nation depends upon perception of adversary ability and intent to harm. Whether the people of one nation perceive those of another as enemies depends primarily upon the nature of relations between the two countries. Thus it is when national interests clash and nations are in conflict that the enemy image begins to take its menacing shape. Because of the universal and innate distrust of strangers, a foreign power easily can arouse a sense of threat. Once the opinion-makers have singled out the threatening nation, this innate distrust is focused.

The Russian invasion of Czechoslovakia was portrayed by the American mass media as an unprovoked rape of a country struggling toward freedom; the Russians justified it as necessary to forestall a takeover by anticommunist forces imperiling the security of the Warsaw Pact nations. With the U.S. invasion of the Dominican Republic, the shoe was on the other foot. To us, the action was necessary to remove a Communist threat to our security. To Russia, it was an unprovoked assault on the freedom of that little country.

Enemies create anxiety leading to a progressive simplification of their image in our eyes, and this results in formation of what has been called the mirror image of the enemy. These reciprocal images differ, of course, in the relative prominence of particular features. But to a surprising degree, enemies attribute the same virtues to themselves and the same vices to their opponents.

One excellent study of Russian and American self-images—as expressed in a selection of articles in both mass and elite publications of each nation—shows that virtually 100 percent of the articles described the adversary's goal as international domination or expansion.

Each nation's press portrayed the other nation as aggressive and treacherous, and neither Americans nor Russians accepted the idea that the other was motivated by self-preservation.

Americans tended to be more realistic about their own motives for offering foreign aid, with 42 percent of the articles in American periodicals indicating that the purpose of foreign aid was to strengthen their own side. But in Soviet Union publications, 95 percent of the articles claimed that their own foreign-aid programs were just to be helpful, or else to make it possible for the countries to maintain neutrality. The press on both sides was virtually unanimous in claiming that the *other* side offered foreign aid not to help, but to strengthen a power position and to weaken that of their opponent.

The reciprocal images differed sharply in one respect—foreign policy. Some 69 percent of the Russian items regarded international events as predictable, while only seven percent of the American items took this view. Strangely, this general view was contradicted by the way each side saw the other's specific behavior. The Russians described American foreign policy as a wild and unpredictable response to events, and the Americans tended to see Russian foreign policy as a masterful part of a deep-laid plot. Practically no articles in either American or Russian publications stated that national military measures would bring about the other's downfall, and so there was reinforcement for the peaceful self-image of each nation.

In addition, the press of both nations indicated belief that internal weaknesses and contradictions in the other's system would lead to its eventual downfall. This finding is supported by Urie Bronfenbrenner of Cornell, a Russian-speaking psychologist, who did some informal but careful interviewing of people from different walks of life during a visit to the Soviet Union.

The Russians he interviewed believed that the people of the United States were being deluded and exploited, that they did not fully support the U.S. Government, that American leaders could not be trusted, and that U.S. foreign policy bordered on madness. (Many Americans reflect the flip side of the coin in their view of the Russians.)

Bronfenbrenner also found that nearly all of the Russians who came up to him and began a conversation expressed considerable discontent with life in the Soviet Union. On the other hand, more than

75 percent of the Russians who did not speak until he had initiated the conversation identified fully with the Soviet way of life and the U.S.S.R. worldview.

Another American scientist, Konrad Krauskopf of Stanford University, who visited the Soviet Union about the same time as Bronfenbrenner, had an opportunity for long, informal conversations with his Russian counterparts. He reported: "The Westerner regards the Russians as controlled for the most part without their knowledge, by an oligarchy of rapacious and malevolent men who seek constantly to foment world revolution. The Russian is equally convinced that the West (in Russian eyes, the West is the United States, and all other Western countries are American satellites) is victimized by a small group of profit-mad monopolists who pull the strings that control the government and the communications media, and who try to instigate wars in order to sell munitions . . . it was impossible to resolve this difference in viewpoint. Each of us was repeating what he had read in his own newspapers, and each was suspicious of the other's sources."

A striking feature of the enemy mirror which Americans and Russians hold is the perception that it is *leaders* who are the real villains, and that the general population of the other country is either well disposed to one's own nation—or if they are not, it is because their leaders have misled them. Concomitant with this view is the belief that the masses in the other nation are discontented and would overthrow their leaders if only they could.

This combination is wonderfully consoling for citizens of both countries. It creates a positive image of one's own nation as a savior, and it simultaneously provides convenient, visualizable devils—the leaders—on whom to focus hostility and hate. This is illustrated by the Communists' monomania with "capitalists and monopolists" and with their intellectual concern for the "oppressed masses." And it is shown in the American tendency to focus on enemy leaders as targets—the Kaiser in World War I, Hitler in World War II, Stalin in the Cold War and more recently Castro, Mao, and Ho Chi Minh.

Contributing to the formation of the mirror image of the enemy is the need men have to reduce cognitive dissonance. When our perceptions of the enemy do not fit our preconceived image, anxiety is created and builds up. The effort to reduce this anxiety accounts for many phenomena in human thinking and behavior, and as there is continual effort to make our worldview emotionally consistent, even if it is not logically consistent.

In order to survive, every person must organize the flood of experiences pouring in on him so that he can predict the effects of his behavior both upon people and upon other things. This organizing process starts as soon as he is born, and it is guided by his experiences with his family and with other people in his society.

In general, we filter and interpret incoming information to fit our preconceptions. Value systems are usually abstract enough so we can interpret events to fit beliefs, and also reinterpret our own behavior to make sure that it is consistent with those beliefs. The strain toward consistency tends, of course, to *reinforce* the enemy image.

But the same process also can help destroy the enemy image when a former enemy becomes a needed ally. This is illustrated by a *long* series of public opinion polls on how Americans characterize people in other countries. In polls, respondents often are asked to choose from a list of adjectives the ones which best describe the people of another nation. In 1942, the first three adjectives chosen to characterize the Germans and the Japanese were: warlike, treacherous and cruel. Not one of these adjectives was among the top three describing the Russians, but by 1966, all three adjectives had disappeared from American descriptions of the Germans and Japanese, and the Russians were seen as warlike and treacherous. Predictably, the Communist Chinese by 1966 had become "warlike" and "treacherous" and "cruel." (Interestingly, the characterization "hardworking" rates high among descriptions of all these countries, whether friends or foes. A hardworking enemy is more to be feared, and a hardworking ally is a greater source of strength.)

A change in the American view of the Germans and Japanese followed their *total* defeat. The enemy ceased to be dangerous, and our demand for consistency required that the enemy image be altered. A factor supporting the change was the American belief that these former enemy nations were needed to help combat the spread of Communism.

Thus, in the eyes of many Americans the "warlike, treacherous, cruel, slant-eyed, bucktoothed little Japs" of World War II have become a highly cultivated, industrious, charming, and thoroughly attractive people.

The American image of the German people is even more remarkable—it has flipped four times in less than half a century. Americans admired the Germans before World War I for their industry, their culture and their scientific know-how. Then during the war, Germans became the hated "Huns." Next, the Germans of the Weimar Republic, a democracy, were regarded favorably. The Nazis changed that. Today the Germans once more are staunch allies, even though many of the government officials are former Nazis.

By and large, the Germans today are the same people the Americans hated yesterday. Our change from hostility to friendliness has been made easier by the Germans' formal renunciation of Nazism. But, in retrospect, it may be observed that if these individuals were true Nazis, their change is suspect; and if most were not true Nazis, then they did not warrant our earlier hatred.

The strain to develop a consistent worldview may lead nations with contrasting ideologies to exaggerate the differences in their behavior, and this raises the hopeful possibility that national value systems need not actually change much in order to permit acceptance of coexistence.

A study of American and Russian value systems by R. K. White of George Washington University shows that the American capitalist system which Soviet citizens have been taught to fear is not actually so very different from the "Good Society" that the Russians themselves would like to see

develop in the U.S.S.R. Both systems are relatively modest variations on themes that seem to be among the common great aspirations of the human race.

In stressing how the group to which a person belongs determines his worldview, I do not mean to imply that his view cannot be transcended by reflection and self-awareness. Today, human survival may depend on those individuals who can surmount a tribal outlook and appreciate the worldviews of people of other cultures.

A psychologically crucial part of the worldview of any group is its ideology, and ideological differences contribute to the dehumanization of the enemy. Humans differ from other creatures primarily in the power to symbolize, so that we respond not only to physical violence but to psychological threats to our ideology or self-esteem.

Since nations cannot exist without ideologies, periodic "holy wars" may seem to be inevitable. But two factors mitigate this gloomy prospect. It is more satisfying psychologically to convert members of a rival belief system than to kill them. Conversion confirms superiority.

In addition, ideologies do not have to proclaim that they have exclusive possession of the truth. Some religions, such as Hinduism, declare that all religions have tapped some aspect of the Truth, and some secular ideologies, such as the American one, value diversity of viewpoints in many areas. Adherents of worldviews like these can coexist with others indefinitely without resorting to armed conflict to protect their beliefs.

In the Vietnam War, ideological issues have become crucial. The North Vietnamese and the Viet Cong see themselves as fighting neocolonialism, as well as furthering the Communist ideology.

From a strictly materialistic viewpoint, Vietnam is of minor strategic importance to the United States.

The United States Government sees its action in Vietnam as part of a worldwide commitment to prevent the spread of Communism. And the U.S. also is motivated by a determination to show the world that we are steadfast, that we stand by our commitments.

The Vietnam War has assumed the ideological characteristics of a holy war. Throughout history, such holy wars usually end in mutual exhaustion after tremendous carnage, and with the survivors on both sides still clinging to their beliefs. Psychologically speaking, the notion that making people suffer causes them to abandon their beliefs is a hangover from the days of the Crusades.

Nations at war could be said to resemble children for whom punishment brings contrition only under certain conditions. As every parent knows, one can control behavior by punishment, but whether the punishment alters a basic attitude depends mainly on the child's belief that it was deserved.

There are studies that have attempted to relate personality attributes of individuals to their international attitudes, and most of these studies have dealt with an authoritarian character pattern whose dynamic core is the result of repressing strong hostility to parents and to other authority figures. The person with such character pattern exaggerates the importance of power, of force, and of domination and submission in human affairs. He displaces his hostility to safer targets than the authority figures at home. He projects his internal psychological conflicts onto external enemies, and he expresses his bottled-up aggressive and sexual feelings indirectly by over concern with the "immoral" behavior of foreigners and of the "out" groups in his own society.

People with authoritarian personalities score high on the "F-Scale," which consists of a series of statements like: "What youth needs most is strict discipline, rugged determination and the will to work and fight for family and country;" "Most of our social problems would be solved if we could somehow get rid of the immoral, crooked and feeble-minded people;" "People can be divided into two classes, the weak and the strong." The greater the number of such statements a person agrees with, the higher his score, and a high F-score correlates positively with extreme nationalism.

Within each country, individuals differ in the degrees that they see foreigners as enemies. At one extreme are those we might call xenophobic, those who hold a morbid dislike of foreigners and the other extreme are the xenophiles, who display an excessive acceptance of protestation of peaceful intent on the part of a foreign power, as well as holding hostility toward the leaders of their own country. Both extremists are likely to be hostile toward authority figures, but the xenophobe displaces his aggression to a foreign group and the xenophile focuses on his own leaders.

Since an enemy is seen as a threat to the survival of one's own nation, to change the enemy's image implies dropping one's guard. And the enemy's image has certain dynamic properties that make it resistant to change. First, an enemy mobilizes a nation's sense of solidarity and strength. He becomes a convenient scapegoat for internal problems. Second, the image that a nation holds of its enemy eventually will bring about behavior from the enemy that makes the image a reality.

The view that the actions of the other nation always are based on hostile motives may create a self-fulfilling prophecy. This term refers to the fact that a person's expectations come true. . . . A classic example of this is the international arms race. Each side anticipates that the other will add to its armament. In response to this expectation each increases its own arms, thereby fulfilling the expectations and convincing the other side that its fears are justified—which leads naturally to another round of arms increases.

Leaders on each side fear that their own people are so naive that they easily can be misled by enemy propaganda. The temptation to break off entirely or to restrict communication with the enemy is a strong one. Since the enemy is untrustworthy, if we communicate with him, he may trick us or learn something about us that we do not want him to know.

Another source of distortion of the enemy's characteristics is what G. Icheiser called the "mote-beam phenomenon." People who harbor unacceptable feelings may try to relieve their anxiety by projecting these traits to others, and then attacking them for possessing those traits. A person who tries to hide his own aggressiveness from himself is usually quick to spot aggression in others. In the same way, some Americans who turn a blind eye to the inequities in civil rights for Blacks are very concerned about the restrictions of freedom in the Soviet Union.

Bronfenbrenner showed some American fifth and sixth graders photographs of Russian roads lined with young trees. When he asked why the Russians had planted trees along the road, two of the answers were: "So that people won't be able to see what is going on beyond the road" and "It's to make work for the prisoners." When he asked why American roads have trees planted along the side, the children said "for shade" and "to keep the dust down."

The distorted image of the enemy acts, finally, to block acceptance of his genuine conciliatory moves. An apparently friendly gesture tends to be seen as either evidence of the enemy's weakening, or an effort to create dissension within one's own ranks. These responses are apparent in the Vietnam War. The Viet Cong interpret American gestures of peace as evidence of a weakening will to fight, while the American government sees the enemy's proposals as propaganda aimed at creating dissension in the United States.

An experiment done in a boy's camp by Muzafer Sherif of Pennsylvania State College some years ago suggests that activities requiring cooperation have a powerful effect in reducing antagonism between two hostile groups. When the boys arrived at camp, they were divided into two groups. Then the groups were made enemies through athletic competitions. In time, they became like two hostile nations. Members in each group chose friends only from among themselves, looked down on boys in the other group, and the two groups fought at every opportunity.

Once when a member of one group tried to act as a peacemaker, he was promptly ostracized by his fellows.

Then the camp director surreptitiously arranged events to force cooperation between the two groups. For example, he secretly arranged to have the camp water supply interrupted, and the whole camp had to work together to make necessary "repairs." A truck carrying food for an overnight hike "unaccountably" ran into a ditch. It took all the boys to pull it out with a tow-rope. A series of such events finally broke down hostility between the two groups, and friendly relations eventually were restored.

I would hesitate to generalize from boys in conflict to nations in conflict were it not for certain obvious parallels. In a sense, the nations of the world are in the same predicament today as the boys in that camp. Nations have to cooperate in order to survive, and the international scene contains many opportunities for cooperative activities, like those in the boys' camp, in yielding mutual benefits which one nation alone cannot attain. The International Geophysical Year is a good example.

The first step in contacting the enemy is psychologically the most difficult, and it takes considerable courage to make contact with a distrusted adversary, because this means exposure to dangers not only from the enemy but from one's own side. Here perhaps we can take advantage of what psychiatrists have learned about establishing communication with a frightened, angry and suspicious person. The first step, we have found, is simply to show persistent willingness to listen and to refuse to be discouraged by rebuffs. While you firmly defend yourself against physical attack, you ignore mere verbal abuse. It does not pay to be too friendly. The hostile person is convinced that you mean him no good, and so he is prone to interpret an overly friendly manner as an effort to deceive him. A firm and reserved, but not unfriendly manner, gets farther in reaching out to him.

Communication is only the first step. From a psychological standpoint, a central long-term task is learning how to foster cooperative projects among nations.

The chief danger of the distorted enemy image is that it makes false perceptions as hard to change as if they were true. Only by becoming highly aware of the psychological process that forms images can we hope to dispel the false aspects of an image. Otherwise, the difficulties in communicating with the enemy progressively harden our image of him. Fantasy fills the gaps left by insufficient information, and the face of the enemy reflects our own fears.

Faces of the Enemy
Sam Keen

The world, as always, is debating the issues of war *and* peace. Conservatives believe safety lies in more arms and increased firepower. Liberals place their trust in disarmament and nuclear freeze. I suggest we will be saved by neither fire nor ice, that the solutions being offered by the political right and left miss the mark. Our problem lies not in our technology, but in our minds, in our ancient tendency to create our enemies in our own imagination.

Our best hope for avoiding war is to understand the psychology of this enmity, the ways in which our mind works to produce our habits of paranoia, projection, and the making of propaganda. How do we create our enemies and turn the world into a killing ground?

We first need to answer some inevitable objections, raised by the advocates of power politics, who say: "You can't psychologize political conflict. You can't solve the problem of war by studying perception. We don't *create* enemies. There are real aggressors—Hitler, Stalin, Qaddafi."

True: There are always political, economic, and territorial causes of war. Wars come and go; the images we use to dehumanize our enemies remain strangely the same. The unchanging projection of the hostile imagination is continually imposed onto changing historical circumstances. Not that the enemy is innocent of these projections—as popular wisdom has it, paranoids sometimes have *real* enemies.

Nevertheless, to understand the hostile imagination we need to temporarily ignore the question of guilt and innocence. Our quest is for an understanding of the unchanging images we place on the enemy.

THE ENEMY AS CREATED BY PARANOIA

Paranoia is not an occasional individual pathology, but rather it is the human condition. History shows us that, with few exceptions, social cohesion within tribes is maintained by paranoia: when we do not have enemies, we invent them. The group identity of a people depends on division between insiders and outsiders, us and them, the tribe and the enemy.

The first meaning of *the enemy* is simply the stranger, the alien. The bond of tribal membership is maintained by projecting hostile and divisive emotions upon the outsider. Paranoia forms the mold from which we create enemies.

In the paranoid imagination, *alien* means the same as *evil,* while the tribe itself is defined as good: a single network of malevolent intent stretches over the rest of the world. "They" are out to get "us." All occurrences prove the basic assumption that an outside power is conspiring against the community.

Reprinted from *Esquire,* vol. 101, February 1984, 67–72. Copyright © 1984 by The Hearst Corporation.

THE ENEMY AS ENEMY OF GOD

In the language of rhetoric, every war is a crusade, a "just" war, a battle between good and evil. Warfare is a ritual in which the sacred blood of our heroes is sacrificed to destroy the enemies of God.

We like to think that theocracies and holy wars ended with the coming of the Industrial Revolution and the emergence of secular cultures in the West. Yet in World War I the Kaiser was pictured as the devil; in World War II both Germany and the U.S. proclaimed Gulf mit uns, "In God We Trust"; each accused the other of being Christ-killers. Sophisticated politicians may insist that the conflict between the U.S. and the U.S.S.R. is a matter of pragmatic power politics, but theological dimensions have not disappeared. President Reagan warns us against "the aggressive impulses of an evil empire" and asks us to "pray for the salvation of all those who live in totalitarian darkness, pray they will discover the joy of knowing God."

By picturing the enemy as the enemy of God we convert the guilt associated with murder into pride. A warrior who kills such an enemy strikes a blow for truth and goodness. Remorse isn't necessary. The warrior engaged in righteous battle against the enemies of God may even see himself as a priest, saving his enemy from the grip of evil by killing him.

THE ENEMY AS BARBARIAN

The enemy not only is a demon but is also a destroyer of culture. If he is human at all, he is brutish, dumb, and cruel, lower on the scale of evolution than The People. To the Greeks he was a barbarian. To the Americans he was, most recently, a "gook" or "slant." To the South African he is a black or "colored."

The barbarian theme was used widely in World War ll propaganda by all participants. Nazi anti-Semitic tracts contrasted the sunny, healthy Aryan with the inferior, dark, and contaminated races—Jews, Gypsies, Eastern Europeans. American soldiers were pictured as Chicago-style gangsters.

Blacks were portrayed as quasi-gorillas despoiling the artistic achievements of European civilization. One poster used in Holland warned the Dutch that their supposed "liberators" were a mélange of KKK, jazz-crazed blacks, convicts, hangmen, and mad bombers. In turn, the U.S. frequently pictured the Germans as a Nazi horde of dark monsters on a mindless rampage.

The image of the barbarian represents a force to be feared: power without intelligence, matter without mind, an enemy who must be conquered by culture. The warrior who defeats the barbarian is a culture hero, keeping the dark powers in abeyance.

THE ENEMY AS RAPIST

Associated with the enemy as barbarian is the image of the enemy as rapist, the destroyer of motherhood.

As rapist, the enemy is lust defiling innocence. He is according to Nazi propaganda the Jew who lurks in the shadows waiting to seduce Aryan girls. Or in the propaganda of the Ku Klux Klan he is the black man with an insatiable lust for white women. In American war posters he is the Jap carrying away the naked Occidental woman.

The portrait of the enemy as rapist, destroyer of the Madonna, warns us of danger and awakens our pornographic imagination by reminding us of the enticement of rape. The appeal to sexual adventure is a *sine qua non* in motivating men to go to war: To the warrior belong the spoils, and chief among the spoils are the enemy's women.

THE ENEMY AS BEAST, INSECT, REPTILE

The power of bestial images to degrade is rooted in the neurotic structure of the hostile imagination. Karen Horney has shown that neurosis always involves a movement between glorified and degraded images of the self. In warfare we act out a mass neurosis whereby we glorify ourselves as agents of God and project our feelings of degradation and impotence upon the enemy. We are superhuman; therefore they must be subhuman. By destroying the bestial and contaminated enemy we can gain immortality, escape evil, transcend decay and death.

THE ENEMY AS DEATH

In the iconography of propaganda, the enemy is the bringer of death. He is Death riding on a bomb, the Grim Reaper cutting down youth in its prime. His face is stripped of flesh, his body a dangling skeleton.

War is an irrational ritual. Generation after generation we sacrifice our substance in a vain effort to kill some essential enemy. Now he wears an American or Soviet face. A moment ago he was a Nazi, a Jew, a Moslem, a Christian, a pagan. But the true face of the enemy, as Saint Paul said, is Death itself. The unconscious power that motivates us to fight for peace, kill for Life, is the magical assumption that if we can destroy this particular enemy we can defeat Death.

Lying within each of us is the desire for immortality. And because this near-instinctive desire for immortality is balanced by the precariously repressed fear that death might really eradicate all traces of our existence, we will go to any extreme to reassure ourselves. By submitting to the divine ordeal of war, in which we are willing to die or kill the enemy who *is* Death, we affirm our own deathlessness.

THE RELUCTANT KILLERS

It is easy to despair when we look at the human genius for creating enemies in the image of our own disowned vices. When we add our mass paranoia and projection to our constantly progressing weapons technology, it seems we are doomed to destroy ourselves.

But the persistent archetypal images of the enemy may point in a more hopeful direction. We demean our enemies not because we are instinctively sadistic, but because it is difficult for us to kill others whom we fully recognize as human beings. Our natural empathy, our instinct for compassion, is strong: society does what it must to attempt to overcome the moral imperative that forbids us from killing.

Even so, the effort is successful only for a minority. In spite of our best propaganda, few men and women will actually try to kill an enemy. In his book *Men Against Fire,* Brigadier General S.L.A. Marshall presents the results of his study of American soldiers under fire during World War ll. He discovered that *in combat* the percentage of men who would fire their rifle at the enemy *even once* did not rise above 25 percent, and the more usual figure was 15 percent. He further discovered that the fear of killing was every bit as strong as the fear of dying.

If it is difficult to mold men into killers, we may still hope to transform our efforts from fighting an outward enemy to doing battle with our own paranoia. Our true war is our struggle against the antagonistic mind. Our true enemy is our propensity to make enemies. The highest form of moral courage requires us to look at ourselves from another perspective, to repent, and to reown our own shadows. True self-knowledge introduces self-doubt into our minds. And self-doubt is a healthy counterbalance to the dogmatic, self-righteous certainty that governs political rhetoric and behavior; it is, therefore, the beginning of compassion.

Cognitive Dissonance and International Relations

Robert Jervis

The theory of cognitive dissonance can explain a number of puzzling misperceptions. The basic outlines of the theory are not startling, but some of its implications are contrary to common sense and other theories of cognitive consistency. The definition of dissonance is relatively straightforward: "two elements are in a dissonant relation if, considering these two alone, the obverse of one element would follow from the other." For example, the information that a Ford is a better car than a Chevrolet is dissonant with the knowledge that I have bought a Chevy.

The basic hypotheses are: "1. The existence of dissonance, being psychologically uncomfortable, will motivate the person to try to reduce dissonance and achieve consonance. 2. When dissonance is present, in addition to trying to reduce it, the person will actively avoid situations and information which would likely increase the dissonance."[1]

The basis of dissonance theory lies in the postulate that people seek strong justification for their behavior. They are not content to believe merely that they behaved well and chose wisely—if this were the case they would only have to maintain the beliefs that produced their decisions. Instead, people want to minimize their internal conflict. This leads them to seek to believe that the reasons for acting or deciding as they did were overwhelming. The person will then rearrange his beliefs so that they provide increased support for his actions.

Knowledge of the advantages of rejected courses of action and costs of the chosen one will be a source of uncomfortable dissonance that he will try to reduce. To do this he will alter his earlier opinions, seeing more drawbacks and fewer advantages in the policies he rejected and more good points and fewer bad ones in the policy he adopted. He

may, for example, come to believe that the rejected policy would not satisfy certain criteria that he originally thought it would, or that those criteria are less important than he originally believed, or that the chosen policy will not cost as much as he first thought. The person may also search out additional information supporting his decision and find new reasons for acting as he did and will avoid, distort, or derogate new dissonant information.

If doubts nevertheless creep in, he will redouble his efforts to justify his decision. As a result, "Following a decision there is an increase in the confidence in the decision or an increase in the discrepancy in attractiveness between the alternatives involved in the choice, or both."[2] This is known as the "spreading apart of the alternatives" because of the perceived increase in the gap between the net advantages of the chosen policy and those of the rejected ones.

As the last quote implies, the theory has been developed only for post-decision situations. Two further conditions are necessary. First, there must be a "definite commitment resulting from the decision. . . . It seems that a decision carries commitment with it if the decision unequivocally affects subsequent behavior."[3] Second, the person must feel that his decision was a free one, i.e. that he could have chosen otherwise. If he had no real choice, then the disadvantages of the policy will not create dissonance because his lack of freedom provides sufficient justification for his action.

Making such a decision will, according to dissonance theory, greatly alter the way a person thinks. Before reaching his decision the individual will seek conflicting information and make "some compromise judgment between the information and his existing cognitions or between bits of

Excerpted from Robert Jervis, *Perception and Misperception in International Politics* (Princeton: Princeton University Press, 1976), Chapter 11, 382–406.

information inconsistent with each other and with his existing cognitions." But once the person has reached a decision, he is committed and "cannot process information and make some compromise judgment."[4] Quite the contrary, the person must minimize the extent to which the evidence pointed in the opposite directions.

An ingenious demonstration, an anecdote, and an international example illustrate the meaning of this phenomenon and show that it occurs outside the laboratory. Immediately after they place their bets, race track bettors become more confident that their horse will win. A few hours after deciding to accept a job offer that he had agonizingly considered for several months, a professor said, "I don't understand how I could have seriously thought about not taking the job." And the doubts of British Liberals about whether to go to war in 1914 were almost totally dissolved after the decision was reached.[5]

Many decision-makers speak of their doubts vanishing after they embarked on a course of action, or they say that a situation seemed much clearer after they reached a decision. Evidence that would have been carefully examined before the decision is rejected at later stages.

The American decision not to intervene in Vietnam in 1954 was followed by a spreading apart of the alternatives. When they were considering the use of force to prevent a communist victory, Dulles and, to a lesser extent, Eisenhower believed that a failure to act would expose the neighboring countries to grave peril. When the lack of Allied and domestic support made intervention prohibitively expensive, American decision-makers altered their perceptions of the consequences of not intervening.

Although they still thought that the immediate result would be the fall of some of Indochina, they came to believe that the further spread of communism—fear of which motivated them to consider entering the war—would not necessarily follow.

They altered their views to reject the domino theory, at least in its most deterministic formulation, and held that alternative means could save the rest of Southeast Asia. It was argued—and apparently believed—that collective action, which had initially been sought in order to hold Vietnam, could stabilize the region even though part of Vietnam was lost.[6] By judging that military victory was not necessary, the decision-makers could see the chosen policy of not intervening as greatly preferable to the rejected alternative of unilateral action, thereby reducing the dissonance aroused by the choice of a policy previously believed to entail extremely high costs.

ENDNOTES

[1] Leon Festinger, *A Theory of Cognitive Dissonance* (Stanford: Stanford University Press, 1957): 13, 31; *also see* Jack Brehm and Arthur Cohen, *Explorations in Cognitive Dissonance* (New York: John Wiley & Sons, 1962): 16.

[2] Morton Deutsch, Robert Krauss, and Norah Rosenau, "Dissonance or Defensiveness?" *Journal of Personality,* 30 (1962): 27.

[3] *Ibid.,* 83.

[4] Brehm and Cohen, *Explorations in Cognitive Dissonance,* 106.

[5] Robert Knox and James Inkster, "Postdecision Dissonance at Post Time," *Journal of Personality and Social Psychology,* 8 (1968): 319–323; Cameron Hazlehurst, *Politicians at War,* London: Jonathan Cape (1971): 46–48, 92–117.

[6] Melvin Gurtov, *The First Vietnam Crisis* (New York: Columbia University Press, 1967): 119–122.

International Negotiation: Cross-Cultural Perception

Glen Fisher

The process of negotiating internationally is assuming ever greater importance for all of us, whether treating large or small matters. As our real world becomes a more and more interdependent one, a larger range of problems that heretofore might have been resolved domestically now have to be negotiated internationally. Therefore, the questions for the concerned citizen include: what difference does it make when negotiators and their general publics reflect contrasting national experiences, cultures, and patterns of thinking, and how well are we addressing this special dimension in conducting world affairs?

Too often, if we follow the international negotiation process at all, we focus primarily on substance, tactics, strategy, the obvious interests to be served. But after all, negotiation is a study in social psychology—but in the international case, a study that must also include the psychology of cross-cultural communication. As people turn to dealing across national boundaries, it becomes less likely that even the most cosmopolitan negotiators will reason from the same starting assumptions, the same images of the world, or even the same patterns of logic. Ultimately, in understanding any negotiation process, one needs to anticipate how the issue will in fact be perceived. The new challenge is to enter the cross-cultural factor into the equation.

One might recall certain essentials of perceiving and responding. We know that people do not react to events and issues on the basis of some empirical reality but on the basis of their *images* of it—which almost always will be something a bit different. We like to think in our scientific age that our enlightened images of what is going on will coincide with reality. But psychologists insist that

our perceptual habits are locked in much more than we usually realize and that, as our mental computers are programmed to add context and meaning to that which our senses receive, we tend to perceive the world and its events as we expect it to appear.

A brief classroom-type example of physical perception illustrates the points. A group is asked to describe the shape of a table top located in the corner of the room. All agree that it is rectangular. Yet there would be no rectangle on the retina of any eye in the room—no one would be so positioned to actually see a rectangle. But everyone there has had a lot of experience with table tops and with right angles. So the mind of each supplies what the retina cannot, and the table top is perceived as a rectangle. In fact, this perceptual habit is so locked in that it becomes almost impossible to perceive anything else if in fact the top were not rectangular. This, of course, is the basis for the fun and games that psychologists pursue in optical illusions.

This ability to add to the picture is handy; it would be awkward to have to position oneself so that a full rectangle could be perceived each time the object came to one's attention. When events and issues are more abstract, when they include ideas, beliefs, plans, and institutions, the need to add meaning from the data and experience banks of the mind is all the greater. And effective meaning is all the more subject to experiential differences such as those that are supplied by being socialized in varying cultures and circumstances. Because it is normal to take much of this programming for granted when it is learned largely out of awareness, it is also normal to project this same "common sense" onto others with whom one is interacting. When the interaction is cross-national, the chances

Reprinted from *The Humanist* 43 (November/December 1983): 14–18. Reprinted by permission of Glen Fisher, Monterey Institute of International Studies.

for error, for misperceptions, or for misattributing motives increase enormously. All this strikes at the very heart of international negotiation. Yet it is the subject of relatively little studied analysis.

CULTURAL PREDISPOSITION

Do cultural predispositions really count? Actually, it is difference in cultural traditions or belief systems such as religion that often is the issue, as in the Middle East. But the international observer who is tuned to look for it can often find enough havoc played by less obvious cultural conflict to cause concern for our competence in bridging it. For example, cultural conditioning enters into American-Japanese business negotiation. Americans feel comfortable with lawyers, precise contractual arrangements, and legal remedies; Japanese consider the need for lawyers an unfortunate fallback solution when trust and sincerity fail to sustain a business relationship. Thus, even when a contract is signed, the subjective meaning and the assumptions regarding performance can be at least a few degrees out of synchronization.

I recall the prolonged debate that took place regarding the fall session agenda as the United Nations General Assembly organized one September when I was a junior member of the U.S. delegation. The General Assembly had to decide what issues to include, what they would be titled, and to what committee they would be assigned. The American delegation had a hard time getting very interested in prolonged detailed negotiation on all these matters after the basic decision was reached to include a given item at all. Once that was decided, they did not care very much what the issue was called; they were pragmatic on assignment to committees. Not so the Latin Americans, the French, the Russians, or the Indians. They would argue endlessly, to the great frustration of the Americans, as to precisely how an issue would be labeled and by what principle it would be assigned to committee. To them, it made a real difference; for by stating the principle and by defending the issue at the start, the logic by which the matter would substantially be treated would have been set—the deductive approach. The Americans were more inclined to see this as a waste of time, preferring the inductive approach: what difference does it make what you call it? We will look at the facts and details when the time comes.

Thoughtful translators and interpreters find that culturally based inclinations toward the deductive pattern on the one hand or the inductive on the other will affect their efforts to transmit equivalent meaning and nuance. Does the statement "The subject of the meeting is aggression" mean the same as "Aggression is the subject of the meeting"? In one, the immediate, less abstract item is placed first— the meeting—while in the other the principle to be decided gets first place. Perhaps this is too fine a distinction to count, but such style preferences have been studied, and specialists find that, when you put a full range of all such differences in patterns of thinking together, negotiators may be talking past each other to a serious degree. I have talked with colleagues who have participated in disarmament talks with the Soviets. They report that months have been wasted in a standoff between the Soviets' insistence on debating general principles first, only then letting the facts fall into place as convenient to the agreed principles, while the Americans start with emphasis on details and numbers and a need to agree on the facts that in final agreement will lead up to the guiding principles.

CULTURE AND LANGUAGE

We could gain much appreciation of the cultural gaps which have to be closed by paying closer attention to the relationship between culture and language, including the varicolored meanings that words and expressions take on in translation. In negotiation practice, the degree to which languages are taken to be equitable is alarming. The naïve negotiator uses interpreters like mechanical devices. You put an idea in here and it comes out there. They may even report that the interpretation process provides an advantage—it gives them more time to think. Better yet, if the counterpart speaks English, however imperfectly, communication is assumed to be assured! Such an approach represents a disgracefully superficial understanding of language and culture in an age when so much depends on it and when English itself is used extensively as a second language in so many differing cultural settings.

I recall the reflections of one of our outstanding official interpreters who had been the other person in the room with three different American presidents as they conferred privately with heads of other states. The languages involved were English, French, Polish, and Russian. He felt, as he reflected on the linguistic and cultural factors, that, while he was self-assured in knowing that he was one of the most competent interpreters in the business, frequently the principals for whom he was trying to bridge the language gap were not even talking about the same issues and that there was nothing that he could do about it short of taking over with extended explanatory lectures to each party and, even then, leaving much to fall between the cracks. "It loses something in translation" can be equivalent to international misunderstanding.

Examples come quickly to mind. Consider the subjective feeling that goes with the word *compromise* as translated into the cultural contexts of differing countries. To Americans, it is a positive matter; an agreement gains moral sanction by having resulted from compromising. To Spanish speakers, it is more probable that by compromising something is lost, honor is not upheld, principle is diluted. Or consider the idea patterns which go with the English "fair play"—try translating that into any other language. If it can be done at all, what happens to the idea patterns that go with it? Do they survive intact? I understand that the French get along on *le fer plé*. Latin Americans play soccer in possibly more decorous fashion with *juego limpio*. But one is forced to the conclusion that "fair play" cannot translate in full depth of meaning when there is no equivalence in the thoughts and assumptions that go with the expression. At least, this makes it a bit difficult to assume "fair play" in a negotiation process!

Language, culture, and communication style mix together to complicate understanding. It is difficult to politely say "no" in Japanese, and in practice a direct "no" is avoided in a number of languages. Even what the outsider would assume to be "yes" in Japanese is better taken as "I hear you—go on. I am listening." Such differences in style can inject serious confusion in anticipating intentions or judging agreement in a negotiation process or even in conducting routine business. In fact, when Masaki Imai, a Japanese Internationalist from the corporate world, wrote a book for the benefit of English-speaking managers to help them in their dealings with the Japanese, the title of his book was *Never Take "Yes" for an Answer.*

All this forces us to consider how profound the consequences of national character can be when it comes to conducting all the international dialogue by which our ever increasing elbow-bumping is managed. We can only be suggestive here. However, a sampling of contrasting value orientations that might significantly affect the way that issues are confronted is well worth pursuing.

Long Term, Short Term

When Americans are involved, consider the value placed on time. Some observers think that in international negotiations Americans tend especially to look toward quick answers and short-range solutions. Americans want to get on with the matter at hand directly, put a solution in place, and proceed to the next matter of business. In policy decisions, they pay less real attention to consequences that are five years down the line and much less to those that are several generations away. Even the French, who in world perspective are in many ways culturally very close to Americans, tend to think in longer range, to attack problems for the enduring future, to seek solutions that will evolve over a more extended period. Consequently, in debate the two nations may well have conceptualized negotiating problems in differing ways—including how to deal with the communists or the volatilities of the Third World.

It may be recalled that in the Vietnam conflict the time element was taken into account in totally different ways. Americans wanted to do their thing quickly, resolve in short order the issue of who would govern and by what principles, and get out. The Viet Cong saw the conflict in much longer range. They talked of outlasting the Americans, of seeing their objectives enduring over generations. After the Americans departed, the thought, even expressed explicitly by President Ford, was to "get Vietnam behind us," to go on forthrightly to new problems without brooding over that which had passed behind.

So much for learning from history. This kind of thinking is a world apart from Argentine conceptions of the past as reality, by which they were so highly motivated as to try to regain the Malvinas Islands despite the decades over which the British had seen them established in all practicality as the Falklands. The Soviets also base strategy on a special time perspective that goes with their ideology—their analysis of the course of history makes ultimate change in their favor "inevitable."

In world affairs, it is not surprising that Americans are the activists; an optimistic, activist outlook is central to our achievement-motivated culture. We once joked around the State Department that there is one option in international relations that Americans simply never have: that is, to do nothing. This is not a possible choice in our strategy, despite the probability that in many cases doing nothing, or waiting for someone else to address a problem, would be the best solution. Such is not the American way. Foreign Service officers routinely suffer in the estimation of activistically oriented presidents when they want diplomacy to take a longer course or urge that other than quick direct action be taken to address an international crisis of the moment.

Americans like to be problem solvers, to slay problems as knights slay dragons. This outlook contrasts with that of many other national characters. Americans see world events as arenas in which one should intervene and in which actions have results, in which they are the cause of effects,

where fatalism has little place, where "God helps those who help themselves." This worldview makes failure exceptionally painful. American "credibility" is seen to be established in success and achievement, in steadfastness in achieving the objective. If, in fact, all the effort turns out not to be successful, it seems more natural to look for the person who "goofed" than to think that the task could not have been done or that some combination of larger forces prevailed over the direct action assumptions by which Americans made their plans and conducted their operations. Obviously, this worldview has many advantages and will serve the interests of a world in which problem-addressing leadership is a crucial asset. The post-World War II Marshal Plan was so achieved, as was the very creation of the United Nations. The U.S. AID program rests on this pattern of thinking. Yet some would argue that this outlook can be counterproductive. It lends itself to the short-range strategy noted above or to a tendency to try to resolve problems too superficially by seeking technological fixes or by throwing money at international matters that need repair on the assumption that, if enough resources are expended, a favorable solution is assured.

THE VALUE OF LIFE

Examples of fundamental differences in values and in ways of thinking extend to the most basic assumptions about life and death. In World War II, the Japanese pursued a policy of suicide bombing that would not have been thinkable in American strategy. In effect, in this most dramatic of cross-culture encounters, it confirmed American readiness to perceive the Japanese as subhuman. Yet Japanese culture and expectations did supply a value and attitude pattern to support the kind of sacrifices involved, and this had to be understood to make sense out of Japanese behavior.

After the 1973 Israeli-Egyptian war, something of the same kind of contrast was suggested by a group of American psychiatrists of both Israeli and Arabic ethnic background, who had been in the area at the time. They were brought together to compare notes by the Institute of Psychiatry and Foreign Affairs—a small organization dedicated to exploring the psychological dimension of international interaction, which then sponsored their informal reporting to the State Department. One factor that seemed to stand out was the differing ways in which the fact or prospect of battlefield casualties were taken into account in military strategy and in reaction by the two publics. The Israelis reflected far more emphasis on strategy that avoided loss of life: they were more shaken by battlefield death, more ready to calculate strategy to minimize the death tally. The Egyptians, on the other hand, while clearly feeling a sense of human loss, nevertheless were more stoic and fatalistic in the event. Martyrdom in the cause was more religiously sanctioned; strategy calculation proceeded with a readiness to accept substantial casualties.

In hindsight, it is apparent that American strategists made errors in Vietnam war calculations in assuming that the North Vietnamese would hold similar views of casualties as American tacticians would. At one stage, Secretary Rusk pointed out that the North Vietnamese loss of seven hundred thousand would be the equivalent to an American loss of ten million. It was judged that the enemy simply could not go on much longer. This reasoning went astray, as we know. Americans projected their "common sense" in these matters onto their counterparts; their expectations were not borne out.

Another subtle but highly important difference in assumptions is that regarding the worth and importance of the individual. Contrasts here lead to substantial variance in reasoning about human rights and even the objectives of government itself. In the Anglo-American tradition, fundamental value is placed on the individual, on the individual's "pursuit of happiness," on self-reliance and achievement, personal political independence, and right to private ownership. From a differing perspective, the value might be placed first on the group and on its well-being—from which the individual's well-being and identity will be enhanced. This is more congenial to the thinking of traditional societies. In that view, an individual cannot be given too much

license to do his or her own thing; the group comes first. It becomes more comfortable in such societies to think in terms of socialistic solutions to national problems: government is implicitly charged with protecting the collective interests of the larger group and with keeping individual excesses from prejudicing the collectivity. In that case, single-minded protection of individual freedom and a set of laws to ensure the maximum of individual maneuverability tend to defy conventional wisdom. This makes a considerable difference in reasoning about human rights.

It might be recalled that when the Declaration of Universal Human Rights was debated in the early days of the United Nations, a standoff took place between Eleanor Roosevelt, the American negotiator, and her Russian counterpart. To the Americans, human rights were few, essentially political, and person-oriented. To the Soviets, they were many, more economic, directed toward the integrity and prosperity of the group. The Soviets were outvoted, if unconverted.

Assumptions and values are part of the social milieu into which people are socialized. Thus they define what is sanctioned and what is not, what "ought" to be, what feels right and wrong. All this becomes sustained by emotional charge, which adds even more rigidity to thinking as international dialogue is conducted. Take, for instance, the American value on contracts in business affairs noted previously. Honoring the letter of a contract can become a moral matter sustained by American ideas of what defines good people and bad people. The legal system sustains it; religion adds its support. These feelings make the system work, for by far the largest part of commercial transactions and related conduct of business rests on a pattern of normal expectations rather than enforcement by the threat of formal legal reprisal. As previously noted, this traditionally has not been the basic Japanese feeling about contracts—more dependence typically was placed on feelings of trust and cooperation between the parties, which would endure as changes needed to be made in arrangements toward obtaining their mutual objectives. In this perspective, a contract would be a counterproductive straight-jacket, even immoral. Hence, when Americans and Japanese differ on the desirability of complying with exact contractual wording, it is easy to see that their respective sense of righteous indignation will soon come into play, and emotions will soon further estrange the relationship. The Japanese then are seen as devious in the first place; the Americans, as insincere and overbearing.

Meaning of the Message

This calls attention to a final point I wish to offer. It is normal, as established in communication psychology, for motives to be attributed, consciously or not, in understanding the meaning of a message. This is especially true in negotiation. It is recalled, probably apocryphally, that, during an international negotiation many years ago, the head of one national negotiation team died. Immediately, the other delegation assembled to try to calculate darkly what strategic motive was behind that! In any case, perhaps nothing so complicates effective international negotiation as inaccurate attribution of motive. The complication is the greater as it becomes unlikely that the full degree of misattribution will ever be fully realized.

It can be argued that completely accurate perception of the other side's intention might not bring a peaceful and happy solution. It might make the situation worse as a real conflict is made starker and the impossibility of accommodation made clearer. Still, the prospects for problem solving are clearly enhanced when the counterproductive effects of misperception and misattribution of motive are held to a minimum.

Thus we all have a vested interest in international negotiators achieving the ability to understand other cultures and their accompanying inner logic. We also have an interest in their cultivating that capacity to recognize that much of what they and their own group take as common sense and "normal" human logic constitutes, in fact, a special cultural lens, and that understanding the uniqueness of one's own basis for perception, however valid, is an essential part of managing negotiation communication. It is not an easy task to know one's self in a cross-cultural sense, as so much of one's conventional wisdom is learned out of awareness and reinforced through a lifetime of sharing the conventionalities of one's own society. Perhaps one of the greatest rewards of international exposure is that, by seeking to understand other cultures in depth, a cultural mirror is provided by which one can come to recognize more clearly the values and inner assumptions by which one's own system works.

Endnotes

SECTION I: WHAT IS CULTURE?

[1] Samuel Huntington confuses these terms in almost all of his publications when he claims that many Mexican immigrants refuse to *assimilate*. He believes they refuse to learn English or accept mainstream American values and beliefs. Learning another language is a process of *acculturation,* not assimilation. A white American might not accept the Mexican as an equal, even when he or she has acculturated. Less than half of the children of Mexican immigrants who are born in this country can speak Spanish and there is no evidence that either documented or undocumented Mexican immigrants do not share the values of average Americans. See Samuel P. Huntington, *Who Are We?* (New York: Simon & Schuster, 2004).

[2] This is true of many post-colonial racist, white societies. Those who advanced the easiest were those who most clearly resembled the colonizers. This was true of the United States, Algeria, and even Mexico. See Andrea L. Rich and Dennis M. Ogawa, "Intercultural and Interracial Communication: An Analytic Approach," in *Intercultural Communication: A Reader, 3rd ed.* Eds. L.A. Samovar and R.E. Porter, (Los Angeles County Museum of Art, 1982): 43–49. Also in Gary R. Weaver, *Culture, Communication and Conflict: Readings in Intercultural Relations, revised 2nd ed.* Gary R. Weaver, (Boston: Pearson, 2000), Pp. 54–59.

[3] One of the earliest studies of this phenomenon is by Ithiel de Sola Pool, Suzanne Keller, and Raymond A. Bauer, "The Influence of Foreign Travel on Political Attitudes of American Businessmen," *The Public Opinion Quarterly* 20 (Spring 1956): 147–161. The dynamics and psychological stress of "culture shock" are comparable to the psychoanalytic catharsis that occurs during therapy. Both often lead to greater personal growth, self-awareness and transformation. Some would even describe them as akin to an identity crisis or, for the more philosophical, an existential leap.

[4] Although we may not watch the snow come down, when we awake in the morning and find snow on the ground we *infer* that it must have snowed. This deductive logic is found in many of the social sciences and is the basis for many social constructs such as gender or race. What is considered a feminine or masculine characteristic depends upon one's culture. Although race is often determined by skin color, perhaps 99 percent of all humans share the same genes, and less than 1 percent of those genes determine skin color. Indeed we are all part of the same human "race" almost 100 percent of the time. Race is defined differently in each culture but seldom in terms of biology. Skin color is mostly determined by melanin in one's skin and a "white" person with only a very tiny fraction of so-called "black" blood could have very dark skin. And yet those with darker skin could be discriminated against because of their "race."

[5] The earliest scholar of kinesics is Ray L. Birdwhistle, *Introduction to Kinesics* (Louisville, KY: University of Louisville Press, 1952).

[6] See Edward Hall, *The Dance of Life: The Other Dimension of Time* (Garden City, NY: Anchor Press/ Doubleday, 1983). Some scholars have even referred to culture as almost a form of human DNA because it is acquired so early in life and determines so much of our human behavior. For example, see Dorothy Guy Bonvillain and Gary McGuire, "American Cultural DNA," *Intercultural Management Quarterly,* Spring, 2010, Vol. 11, No. 2, 16–18.

[7] There are other explanations of his behavior such as the possibility he was autistic or schizophrenic. Many books and articles, both fiction and nonfiction, describe Victor or other similar feral children. The original account of Victor was first written by Jean Itard in 1801 in his article "Rapport premier developpements du jeune Sauvage de l'Aveyron." In D.M. Bourneville, ed., *Rapports et Memoires sur le Sauvage de l'Aveyron.* (Paris: Alcan, 1884).

[8] In this section Marshall Singer's chapter ("The Role of Culture and Perception in Communication") gives us another way of looking at culture. When we share a way of perceiving reality with others, we are a member of a "culture." As we go through life, we belong to numerous groups with which we share a way of looking at the world. To this extent we are all "culturally unique."

[9] Margaret Mead was a systems theorist in cultural anthropology who was greatly influenced by Norbert Wiener, as was Gregory Bateson. Margaret Mead, ed. *Cultural Patterns and Technical Change,* (New York: UNESCO, reprinted as a Mentor Book, The New American Library, 1955).

[10] David McClelland, *The Achieving Society* (New York: Free Press, 1961).

[11] T.W. Adorno, et al., *The Authoritarian Personality: Part I & Part II* (New York: John Wiley & Sons, Inc., Science Editions, 1964.) Copyright by The American Jewish Committee, 1950. Also see, Erich Fromm, *Escape from Freedom* (New York: Holt, Rinehart and Winston, 1941).

[12] This is the approach in Gary R. Weaver and Adam Mendelson, *America's Midlife Crisis: The Future of a Troubled Superpower* (Boston/London: Intercultural Press/A Nicholas Brealey Publishing Company, 2008). It is also an approach in the writings of such international relations theorists as Raymond Aron and Stanley Hoffmann.

[13] Reinhold Niebuhr, *Moral Man and Immoral Society: A study of Ethics and Politics* (New York: Charles Scribner's Sons, 1932).

[14] Ralph Linton, *The Cultural Background of Personality* (New York: Appleton-Century-Crofts, 1945), Clyde Kluckhohn, *Mirror for Man* (New York: McGraw-Hill, 1949) or Edward T. Hall, *Beyond Culture* (Garden City, NY: Anchor Press/Doubleday, 1977). It is not clear that Hall actually uses the analogy of an iceberg to depict culture but his thinking regarding internal or hidden culture and external culture was surely influenced by his experiences as a staff member at the National Institutes for Mental Health which was when he first wrote and developed this idea in his classic book *The Silent Language* (Greenwich, CN: Fawcett Publications, Inc., 1959) on pages 64–66. Hall describes how the theories of Sigmund Freud and Harry Stack Sullivan are presented using the "analogy of an iceberg" to explain the relationship between conscious and unconscious mind. Ironically, both psychoanalytic theorists were very much influenced by anthropological theory. In turn, the anthropologist Hall uses psychoanalytic theory to explain his concept of internal or hidden culture. However, Hall and Kluckhohn realized that the iceberg was an oversimplification because it did not allow for consideration of all the nuances of culture. Both referred to explicit and implicit culture.

I further developed the iceberg "analogy" by considering where beliefs, values, or thought patterns might appear on the model and how they interrelate to better explain culture. In addition, I also considered what happens when cultures come together and where the "collision" actually takes place—at the internal level or the part of the iceberg below the water level.

[15] This graphic with the interrelated "layers" was first introduced in the paper and presentation, "The Nigerian Experience: Overseas Living and Value Change," Gary R. Weaver and Phil Uncapher, SIETAR

(Society for International Education, Training and Research) Conference, Vancouver, BC, Canada, March 11, 1981. It is also found in Gary Weaver, "Understanding and Coping with Cross-Cultural Adjustment Stress" in *Cross-Cultural Orientation: New Conceptualizations and Applications* edited by R. Michael Paige, (Lanham, MD: University Press of American, 1986), 135.

[16] A cybernetics system is a group of elements interconnected by communication links and the whole operating as one to reach a goal. This definition is often credited to Norbert Wiener (1894–1964), a mathematician who developed a communications model for understanding the automatic aiming and firing of anti-aircraft guns during World War II. Weiner formalized the idea that feedback is essential for correcting the message in every type of system in biology, physics, the organization of society, computer science, and even philosophy. Norbert Weiner, *The Human Use of Human Beings* (New York: The Riverside Press, Houghton Mifflin Co., 1950).

[17] David McClelland, *The Achieving Society* (New York: Free Press, 1961). Lawrence Harrison and Samuel Huntington, eds. *Culture Matters: How Values Shape Human Progress* (New York: Basic Books, 2000). Lawrence E. Harrison, *The Central Liberal Truth: How Politics Can Change a Culture and Save It From Itself* (Oxford: Oxford University Press, 2006).

[18] Leon Festinger, *A Theory of Cognitive Dissonance* (Stanford, CA: Stanford University Press, 1957).

[19] Ibn Khaldun, *The Muqaddimah: An Introduction to History,* 3 vols (tr. Franz Rosenthal), Bellingen Series XLIII, (Princeton: Princeton University Press, 1967).

[20] Ferdinand Tönnies, "On Gemeinschaft and Gesellschaft," in *Culture, Communication and Conflict: Readings in Intercultural Relations, 2nd ed.,* rev., ed. Gary R. Weaver (Boston, MA: Pearson Publishing, 2000), 66–71.

[21] The terms "developing" or "emerging" has replaced the more offensive phrase "underdeveloped" which was commonly used by modernists in the 1950s and 1960s. This paradigm of culture carried to its extreme amounted to a form of social Darwinism.

[22] In the U.S., this idea is sometimes implied in the phrase the "city on a hill." John Winthrop, the founder of the Massachusetts Bay Colony meant this to suggest that his colony would "purify" Protestantism by returning to basic values which were corrupted in Europe. In turn, the New World would become a beacon or *example* for the rest of the world. But some followers were much more fanatic and sought to *impose* these beliefs on other countries. Today this missionary zeal is often perceived by other countries as a bit ethnocentric and arrogant.

[23] More contemporary versions can be found in the theories of development and modernity in the writings of David McClelland and Lawrence Harrison. However, they date back to social philosopher and political economist Adam Smith's (*The Wealth of Nations*) ideas of the link between Calvinist values and capitalism and sociologist Max Weber's (*The Protestant Ethic and "The Spirit of Capitalism"*) writings on Protestant values and economic and democratic growth development.

[24] Franz Boas, often referred to as the "father of American Anthropology," took the position that the comparative approach was Western-centered, hierarchical, racist, and ethnocentric. He is described as a "cultural relativist" or, in modern academic jargon, an advocate of post-modern relativity and "contextualism." This is also often accompanied by the idea of *historical particularism* which argues that there are no universal principles of development and each society is unique. See Milton J. Bennett,

"A short conceptual History of Intercultural Learning in Study Abroad" in W. Hoffa and S. Depaul (Eds.), *A History of U.S. Study Abroad: 1965–Present.* Special publication of *Frontiers: The Interdisciplinary Journal of Study Abroad,* (2012), 419–449.

[25] Clifford Geertz, *The Interpretation of Cultures,* (New York: Basic Books, 1973). "The concept of culture I espouse . . . is essentially a semiotic one. Believing, with Max Weber, that man is an animal suspended in webs of significance he himself has spun, I take culture to be those webs, and the analysis of it to be therefore not an experimental science in search of law but an interpretative one in search of meaning." 4–5.

[26] See David G. Mandelbaum. ed. *Selected Writings of Edward Sapir in Language, Culture, and Personality.* (University of California Press, 1983).

[27] Geert Hofstede refers to culture as the "software of the mind." Geert Hofstede and Gert-Jan Hofstede, *Cultures and Organizations: Software of the Mind.* New York: McGraw-Hill U.S.A., 2004. Edward Hall also describes culture as "mind" in his book. Edward Hall, *Beyond Culture.* Garden City, (NY: Anchor Press/Doubleday, 1977), 166.

[28] Friedrich Nietzsche, *The Birth of Tragedy* (1872).

[29] Ruth Benedict, *Patterns of Culture* (New York: Houghton Mifflin, 1934). Benedict (1887–1948) was categorized as a member of the "culture and personality" school of anthropology which included Margaret Mean (1901–1978), Clara DuBois (1903–1991), Clyde Kluckhohn (1905–1960) and others.

[30] For a continuum model, see Gary Weaver, "Contrasting and Comparing Cultures," in *Culture, Communication and Conflict: Readings in Intercultural Relations, revised 2nd edition,* (Boston, Pearson Publishing, 2000), 72–77.

[31] Linguist Deborah Tannen describes how young American academics often assume that critical thinking means attacking someone else's ideas, even if they are ideas that the person doesn't hold. Some of these young critics end up on television talk shows where ratings seem to depend upon a good fight rather than an intellectually useful and honest discussion of various points of view. Deborah Tannen, *The Argument Culture: Stopping America's War of Words,* (New York: Random House/Ballantine, 1998).

[32] Daniel Lerner, *The Passing of Traditional Society: Modernizing the Middle East* (Glencoe, IL: The Free Press, 1958), Wilbur Schramm, *Mass Media and National Development: The Role of Information in Developing Countries* (Stanford: Stanford University Press, 1964) and Lucian Pye, *Politics, Personality, and National Building* (New Haven: Yale University Press, 1962).

[33] Some people seem to believe that the intercultural approach which acknowledges differences is somehow responsible for conflict in the world. In the United States, this accusation was sometimes followed with the admonishment that, "You people are going to Balkanize America!" I often discovered that many people who made this charge had very little understanding of the conflict in the Balkans and often had no idea which countries are considered part of the Balkans. The conflict certainly was not a matter of some interculturalists claiming that there are cultural differences within the Balkan region.

[34] Crosby Burns, Kimberly Barton, and Sophia Kerby, "The State of Diversity in Today's Workforce," *Center for American Progress,* July 12, 2012, http://www.americanprogress.org/issues/labor/report/2012/07/12/11938/the-state-of-diversity-in-todays-workforce. Women represent 47 percent of the current labor force in the United States, however in 1950 the number was at 29.6 percent.

[35] Irving Janis, *Groupthink, 2d. ed.* (Boston: Houghton Mifflin, 1982).

[36] Edmund Glenn, *Man and Mankind: Conflict and Communication Between Cultures,* (Norwood, NJ: Ablex Publishing Corporation, 1981). Some anthropologists would use the Greek terms Apollonian and Dionysian to describe Western and non-Western thought and research respectively. This distinction is also found in the philosophy of Friedrich Nietzsche and his discussion of tragedy.

[37] Edward T. Hall, *Beyond Culture.* Garden City, (NY: Anchor/Doubleday, 1977).

[38] Edmund Glenn, *Man and Mankind* (Norwood, NJ: Ablex, 1981).

[39] Ferdinand Tönnies, *Gemeinschaft and Gesellschaft* (Tubingen: Mohr, 1937).

[40] Friedrich Nietzsche, *The Birth of Tragedy,* trans. by William A. Haussmann, from *The Complete Works of Friedrich Nietzsche,* Oscar Levy, ed. (New York: Russell and Russell, Inc., 1964).

[41] Geert Hofstede, *Culture's Consequences: International Differences in Work-Related Values,* Abridged Edition (Beverly Hills, CA: Sage Publications, 1984). His framework is a multipolar rather than bipolar model and includes such continua as individualism/collectivism, masculine/feminine, high-/low-power distance and weak/strong uncertainty avoidance.

[42] Everett Hagen, *On the Theory of Social Change* (Homewood, IL: Dorsey Press/Massachusetts Institute of Technology, 1962).

[43] Hofstede, *Culture's Consequences.*

[44] Florence Kluckhohn and Fred Strodtbeck, *Variation in Value Orientations* (Evanston, IL: Row, Peterson, 1961).

[45] S.I. Hayakawa, *The Use and Misuse of Language* (Greenwich, CT: Fawcett, 1962).

[46] Robert Lindner, *Must You Conform?* (New York: Grove Press, 1956).

[47] Edward C. Stewart and Milton J. Bennett, *American Cultural Patterns: A Cross-Cultural Perspective* Revised Edition (Yarmouth, ME: Intercultural Press, 1991).

[48] R.D. Laing, *The Divided Self* (London: Tavistock Publications; New York: Pantheon, 1960).

[49] McClelland, *The Achieving Society.*

[50] Jean Piaget, *Success and Understanding* (Cambridge, MA: Harvard University Press, 1978).

[51] Hofstede, *op. cit.*

[52] Hall, *Beyond Culture.*

[53] Philip Slater, *Earthwalk* (New York: Doubleday, 1974).

[54] Hofstede, *op. cit.*

[55] Rosalie Cohen, "Conceptual Styles, Culture, Conflict and Nonverbal Tests of Intelligence," *American Anthropologist* 71, (1969): 828–856.

[56] Kluckhohn and Strodtbeck, *Variations in Value Orientations.*

[57] Hall, *op. cit.*

[58] *Ibid.*

[59] Theodore Isaac Rubin, *Reconciliations: Inner Peace in an Age of Anxiety* (New York: The Viking Press, 1980).

[60] Floyd W. Matson and Ashley Montagu, eds., *The Human Dialogue: Perspectives on Communication* (New York: The Free Press, 1967).

[61] Hall, *op. cit.*

[62] I use the phrase "realistic *cultural* empathy" to include both a cognitive psychological and cultural perspective. Ralph White, a cognitive psychologist, views realistic empathy as an intellectual phenomenon and a matter of social learning. He ignores culture in his definition of what he termed "realistic empathy." Ralph White, *Psychology and the Prevention of Nuclear War.* (New York: New York University Press, 1986). 550–553. Cross-cultural communications expert Milton J. Bennett has a more humanistic or existential psychological view. He believes that it means the ability to enter someone else's head *and* heart. Effective cross-cultural communication is a matter of thinking and feeling as others do. Milton J. Bennett, "Overcoming the Golden Rule: Sympathy and Empathy" in *Basic Concepts of Intercultural Communication: Selected Readings,* Milton J. Bennett, editor, Yarmouth, Maine: Intercultural Press, 1998. 191–214. White might consider realistic empathy as a way to understand an adversary's viewpoints and ways of thinking to more effectively anticipate how he or she would react to you, while Bennett seeks to foster dialogical communication.

[63] This is "cultural relativism" where we assume that the only way we can explain the behavior of people in another culture is to accept the reality that it is "relative" or "contingent upon" their culture. Many people seem to define cultural relativism as "accepting" the behavior of people in all cultures. This is a straw man position that may be a result of confusing ethical relativism with cultural relativism.

[64] In Iran the majority of Muslims are Shiites. About 85% of all Muslims around the world are Sunnis. One of the significant differences between a Shiite and a Sunni Muslim is the issue of who is the proper spiritual descendent of the Prophet Muhammad. Shiites would say that Ali, the son-in-law and cousin of the Prophet Muhammad, was assassinated before he could rightly assume his position as the descendent of the Prophet. From the Shiite viewpoint, he was a martyr. Ali's eldest son Hassan, and his other son, Hussein, were also later assassinated. Had they not been killed the line of descendents of the Prophet Muhammad would have gone in a completely different direction. Shi'a Muslims seem to incorporate the idea of sacrifice, or martyrdom, into their religious beliefs.

[65] See Lawrence E. Harrison and Samuel P. Huntington, eds., *Culture Matters: How Values Shape Human Progress* (New York: Basic Books, 2000). This is a fairly controversial collection of essays debating the impact of cultural values on economic and political development. Other books by Harrison include *The Central Liberal Truth: How Politics Can Change a Culture and Save It From Itself.* (Oxford: Oxford University Press, 2006) and *The Pan-American Dream: Do Latin America's Cultural Values Discourage True Partnership with the United States and Canada?* (New York: Basic Books, 1997).

SECTION II: COMMUNICATING ACROSS CULTURES

[1] Based on John L. Graham, "The Influence of Culture on the Process of Business Negotiations: An Exploratory Study," *Journal of International Business Studies,* Vol 16, Issue 1, (March 1985), 81–96.

Chart in Nancy J. Adler, *International Dimensions of Organizational Behavior, 3rd edn.* (Cincinnati: South-Western College Publishing, 1997), 218.

2 This is a very strong reason for using simultaneous instead of consecutive interpretation. As we await a consecutive interpretation, we may appear to be unengaged or disinterested in the negotiation. Also it is important to maintain eye contact with the person who is speaking rather than with the interpreter.

3 See Edward Hall, *The Silent Language,* (Garden City, NY: Doubleday, 1959) and Albert Mehrabian, "Communication Without Words," in *Psychology Today 2,* (September 1968), 145–153.

4 Although his findings are accepted by most psychologists, there are psychologists who are not convinced of their universality. Paul Ekman, ed., *Darwin and facial expression: A century of research in review.* (New York: Academic Press, 1973).

5 Edward T. Hall, *Beyond Culture* (Garden City, NY: Anchor Press/Doubleday, 1977), 141.

6 Gary Althen, "The Intercultural Meeting," *National Association of Foreign Students Affairs Newsletter,* (November, 1981), 34, 41, 46 and 47. In Gary Weaver, *Culture, Communication and Conflict: Readings in Intercultural Relations, revised 2nd edition* (Boston: Pearson, 2000), 158–161. Also see Gary R. Weaver, "The Multicultural Child Care Staff: Meeting the Needs of a Diverse Client Population," *CYLC* (Fall, 1988), 49–55.

7 Dr. Gary Wright was the Principal Investigator for this project entitled "Experiment in Multi-Cultural Small Group Communications" which was funded by a NAFSA CO-OP grant in 1982–83. The goal was to determine if group members carried unconscious action chains into their intercultural meetings which caused much of the frustration in communication. Videotaped interviews supported Althen's theory. Wright was the Foreign Student Advisor at American University and Althen served in the same position at the University of Iowa.

8 This was one of the reasons for government of Japan's slow in reaction after a tsunami destroyed nuclear reactors in 2011. See Motoo Unno, "Cultural Differences in Crisis Communication: On Year After Fukushima," *Intercultural Management Quarterly,* Vol. 13, No. 1, Spring 2012, 3–6.

9 Thomas Kochman, "Black and White Styles in Pluralistic Perspective," *Test Policy and Performance: Education, Language, and Culture,* (Boston: Kluwer Academic Publishers, 1989), 259–296. Also in Weaver, *Culture, Communication and Conflict, revised 2nd edition,* 283–298.

10 *Ibid.,* in Weaver, 297.

11 Jesse Jackson was often perceived as angry and demagogic when he ran for president in the 1980s. See Juan Williams, "Missing the Message," *The Washington Post,* 9 February 1986, 1, 8 (B).

12 "'Obama can turn on that black dialect when he wants to and turn it off,' Rush Limbaugh once fumed" according to H. Samy Alim and Geneva Smitherman, "Obama's English," *The New York Times,* 9 September 2012, Sunday Review Section, 5. These linguistic scholars also note that President Obama can bring together "white syntax" with "black style."

13 Deborah Tannen, "Teachers' Classroom Strategies Should Recognize that Men and Women Use Language Differently," *The Chronicle of Higher Education,* 37, no. 40 (10 June 1991), B1, B3. Also in Weaver, *Culture Communication and Conflict, revised 2nd edition,* 279–282.

[14] Rosalie Cohen found in the late 1960s that girls are socialized to develop "relational skills" and boys "analytic skills." This explains how boys are often better at mathematics and sciences while girls were better at group activities and the social or behavioral sciences. "Conceptual Styles, Culture, Conflict and Nonverbal Tests of Intelligence," *American Anthropologist* 71, (1969): 828–856.

SECTION III: INTERCULTURAL COMPETENCE: INTERNATIONAL AND DOMESTIC

[1] U.S. Census Bureau, 2004, "U.S. Interim Projections by Age, Sex, Race, and Hispanic Origin," http://www.census.gov/ipc/www/usinterimproj/

[2] The benchmark events and programs mentioned in this section are adapted from lists developed by various scholars including Mitchell Hammer, Robert Kohls and David Bachner.

[3] See Gary R. Weaver, "The evolution of international communication as a field of study: a personal reflection," *The Aoyama Journal of International Politics, Economics and Communication,* No. 72, May 2007, 139–168.

[4] The training focused on how to do business in the destination culture as well as understanding the dynamics of cross–cultural communication, adaptation, negotiation and conflict. Most courses also provided some basic language training. There was also extensive discussion of the political and economic climate of the destination cultures and the concerns of families adjusting overseas. Much of the culture specific and area studies expertise was provided by American University scholars who were employed to continually update the *Army Area Handbooks* on almost every country in the world. Today they are published by the Library of Congress in their Country Studies/Area Studies Handbooks program and can be accesses via the Internet at http://lcweb2.loc.gov/frd/cs/about.html.

[5] Albert R. Wright, "Where It All Began" unpublished paper presented at the SIETAR conference in Japan in 1998.

[6] Chapters of SIETAR now exist on almost every continent and there are many other organizations that promote the field such as the Intercultural Management Institute at American University, the Intercultural Communication Institute at Portland State University, and the Institute for Research on Intercultural Co-operation (IRIC) in Amsterdam. In addition to the *International Journal of Intercultural Relations* (IJIR), there are dozens of publications for both scholars and practitioners such as the *Intercultural Management Quarterly* (IMQ) and *Mobility*.

[7] Milton J. Bennett, "A Short Conceptual History of Intercultural Learning in Study Abroad," in W. Hoffa and S. Depaul (eds.) *A History of U.S. Study Abroad: 1965–present.* Special publication of *Frontier: The Interdisciplinary Journal of Study Abroad,* (2010), 419–449.

[8] *Ibid.,* 422.

[9] Much of this section is a modification of the article "American Identity Movements: A Cross-Cultural Confrontation," by Gary R. Weaver, *Intellect Magazine,* March 1975, 377–380.

[10] This discussion of American identity movements is based upon the article "American Identity Movements: A Cross-Cultural Confrontation," in *Intellect Magazine,* March 1975, 377–380 and

"All Is Not Quiet on the Academic Front," in the *Connecticut Law Review*, Spring, 1971, Vol. 3, No. 3, 466–479, by Gary Weaver.

[11] Robert F. Worth, "Twitter Gives Saudi Arabia a Revolution Of Its Own," *New York Times*, October 21, 2012, 5, 11.

[12] Lawrence E. Harrison and Samuel P. Huntington, eds. *Culture Matters: How Values Shape Human Progress* (Basic Books, 2000). Also see "Hearts, Minds and Schools," *Intercultural Management Quarterly*, Vol. 8, No. 1, 3–5.

[13] Lawrence E. Harrison, *"Culture Matters," Intercultural Management Quarterly*, Vol. 10, No. 1, Spring 2009, 6.

[14] Seymour Martin Lipset, "Some Social Requisites of Democracy: Economic Development and Political Legitimacy," *The American Political Science Review*, Vol. 53, Issue 1, (March, 1959), 69–105.

[15] A.H. Maslow, "A Theory of Human Motivation," *Psychological Review*, Vol. 50(4) (1943), 370–96.

[16] Many were also avoiding the wars taking place in Europe and some were criminals who were sent to America by the British. The state of Georgia was originally a British penal colony.

[17] The largest is the Department of Defense followed by Veterans Affairs.

[18] The phrase the "melting pot" was first used in a play produced in New York in 1907 when there was a wave of immigrants coming to the U.S. primarily from central, southern and eastern Europe. See Gary R. Weaver and Adam Mendelson, *America's Midlife Crisis: The Future of a Troubled Superpower*, (Boston and London: Intercultural Press, A Nicholas Brealey Publishing Company, 2008). Chapter 3, "Melting Pots to Mosaics: Race and Immigration," 47–78. Also see, Gary R. Weaver, "The American Cultural Tapestry," *eJournal USA: Society & Values*, vol. 11, no. 2 (June 2006): 18–20. U.S. Department of State Bureau of International Information Programs at http://usinfo.state.gov/journals/itsv/0696/ijse0606.htm.

[19] Data from U.S. Census Bureau, 2007. Derived from number of people who "spoke a language other than English at home" and whose English-speaking ability was reported as "not at all." Information accessible online at http://www.census.gov/hhes/socdemo/language/data/acs/ACS-12.pdf.

[20] The power to assimilate is controlled by the dominant culture. See Rich and Ogawa's "Intercultural and Interracial Communication: An Analytic Approach" in Gary R. Weaver, *Culture, Communication and Conflict: Readings in Intercultural Relations, revised 2nd edition* (Boston: Intercultural Press, 2000) Section I, 54–59 and Benjamin Schwarz, "The Diversity Myth: America's Leading Export" in Ibid, Section VI, 471–479.

[21] The Mexican *Quinceañera* tradition is a coming out party of a girl entering adulthood as she celebrated her 15th birthday. *Quinceañera* comes from the Spanish words *quince* (15) and *años* (years). The preparation for this celebration may take months and it is a very significant event for parents. It is as important as a wedding.

[22] Nancy Adler, *International Dimensions of Organizational Behavior, 3rd edition* (Cincinnati: South-Western College Publishing, 1997), 101–104.

[23] R.T. Moran and P.R. Harris, *Managing Cultural Synergy* (Houston: Gulf Publishing Company, 1981).

[24] Gerald Jackson, "The Roots of the Backlash Theory in Mental Health," *The Journal of Black Psychology 6,* no. 1 (August, 1979): 17–45.

[25] A discussion of the impact of diversity on law enforcement can be found in Gary R. Weaver, "Law Enforcement in a Culturally Diverse Society," *FBI Law Enforcement Bulletin* (September, 1992): 1–7.

[26] All academic areas are somewhat amoral in that it is ultimately up to the individual and his or her society as to how knowledge is used.

[27] In its early history, the International Society for Intercultural Education, Training and Research (SIETAR) had a committee that examined ethical issues in the field and had the authority to "sanction" members who violated ethical standards. Today, there are universities and professional organizations that provide some kind of "certification" in the field of intercultural relations or cross-cultural communications. For example, the Intercultural Communication Institute (ICI) in Portland, Oregon and the Intercultural Management Institute (IMI) in the School of International Service (SIS) at American University in Washington, DC offer certification based upon attending classes, institutes or workshops. The Worldwide Employee Relocation Center (ERC) certifies Global Mobility Specialists based upon completion of specific courses and attendance at conferences. Fellows in the International Academy for Intercultural Research (IAIR) are nominated by other members and must meet certain requirements regarding research and publication.

[28] In the fall of 2012, SIETAR-USA published *Eye of Ethics: A conversation for Intercultural Professionals,* Maria Thacker, editor, (Society for Intercultural Education Training and Research, SIETAR-USA: 2012).

[29] William H. Blanchard, "Ecstasy without Agony in Baloney," *Psychology Today* 3, no. 8 (January 1970), 8, 10, 64.

[30] R.D. Laing, *The Divided Self* (London: Tavistock Publications: New York: Pantheon, 1960).

SECTION IV: CROSS-CULTURAL ADAPTATION

[1] Much of this discussion of culture shock is a modification and elaboration of Gary R. Weaver, "Understanding and Coping with Cross-Cultural Adjustment Stress," in *Education for the Intercultural Experience*, ed. R. Michael Paige (Yarmouth, ME: Intercultural Press, 1993), 137–167.

[2] Kalervo Oberg, "Cultural Shock: Adjustment to New Cultural Environments," *Practical Anthropology* 7 (1960), 177–182.

[3] Richard W. Brislin, *Cross-Cultural Encounters: Face-to-Face Interaction* (Elmsford, NY: Pergamon, 1981), 40–71.

[4] Oberg, *op.cit.*

[5] The U-Curve and W-Curve hypothesis was first developed by John Gullahorn & Jeanne Gullahorn, "An Extension of the U-Curve Hypothesis," *Journal of social Issues*, 1963, Vol. 19, No 3, 33–47. There have been many articles written which both support and refute the hypothesis.

[6] Nancy J. Adler and Mariann Jelinek, "Is 'Organization Culture' Culture Bound," *Human Resource Management* 25, no. 1 (April 1986), 73–90.

[7] A fascinating example of the collision of organization cultures is described in the essay "Defense is from Mars, State is from Venus." Col. Rickey L. Rife, Army War College, 1998, *Improving Communications and Promoting National Security.* Col. Rife described the clash of organization cultures of the U.S. Department of Defense and the U.S. Department of State.

[8] This explanation of culture shock draws together behavioral, psychoanalytic, and existential or humanistic psychological approaches with an overlay of cognitive theory.

[9] William H. Blanchard, "Ecstasy without Agony Is Baloney," *Psychology Today* 3(8), 1970, 8, 10, 64.

[10] There "is mounting evidence that some of the most profound schizophrenic disorganizations are preludes to impressive reorganization and personality growth—not so much a breakdown as breakthrough. Kazimierz Dabrowski has called it 'positive disintegration.'" Julian Silverman, "When Schizophrenia Helps," in Gary Weaver, *Culture, Communication and Conflict: Readings in Intercultural Relations, 2nd edition, revised* (Boston: Pearson, 2000), 202.

[11] The language of acute schizophrenics is often highly "associative" or "relational." See Brendan A. Maher, "The Shattered Language of Schizophrenia" in Gary Weaver, *Culture, Communication and Conflict: Readings in Intercultural Relations, 2nd edition, revised* (Boston: Pearson, 2000), 195–201.

[12] Gail Sheehy, *Passages: Predictable crisis of Adult Life* (New York: Bantam, 1977), 29.

[13] Passive-aggressive individuals are especially effective at cutting off communication with others to indirectly induce pain and frustration. Victims of this type of aggression often have no conscious awareness of why and how the passive-aggressive behavior causes them so much anguish. In these types of relationships, the victim often feels "out of control" and helpless because the situation is controlling him or her.

[14] Nathan Azrin, "Pain and Aggression," in N. T. Adler, ed., *Readings in Experimental Psychology Today* (Del Mar, CA: CRM Books, 1970), 103–107.

[15] See Theodore Isaac Rubin, *The Angry Book* (New York: Collier Books, 1969). He believes that in the United States anger is equated with irrationality and is therefore denied and internalized. This, in turn, can lead to depression or the feelings build up until they explode with rage.

[16] The flight, fight and filter reactions of culture shock are much akin to what Sigmund Freud described as neurotic defense mechanisms—unconscious steps we take to protect our ego or self from a painful reality.

[17] Gary Weaver and Philip Uncapher, "The Nigerian Experience: Overseas Living and Value Change." Paper and workshop presented at Seventh Annual SIETAR Conference, Vancouver, BC, Canada, March 11, 1981.

[18] Kenneth H. David, "The Use of Social-Learning Theory in Preventing Intercultural Adjustment Problems," in Paul Pedersen, W. J. Lonner, and J.G. Draguns, eds., *Counseling Across Cultures.* (Honolulu: University of Hawaii Press, 1976), 123–138.

[19] Elisabeth Kübler-Ross, *On Death and Dying* (New York: Macmillan, 1969).

[20] Much of this discussion of reverse culture shock is a modification and elaboration of Gary R. Weaver, "The Process of Reentry," *The Advising Quarterly*, 27 (Winter 1994), 1–8, AMIDEAST, 1730 M Street,

NW, Suite 1100, Washington, DC, 20036–4505. An earlier version was published in the same publication in the Fall of 1987.

[21] The award-winning Broadway musical *Fela!* is based upon the life of this jazz artist.

[22] Nan M. Sussman, "Re-entry Research and Training: Methods and Implications," *International Journal of Intercultural Relations,* Vol. 10, 1986, 241–242.

[23] Survey developed by Gary Weaver, Philip Uncapher and Fran Pruitt, and Nan Sussman, Washington International Center, 1979. This was part of a re-entry program designed for all 1500 Nigerians who were returning to Nigeria after studying in the U.S. for two or more years. See Gary R. Weaver and Philip Uncapher, "The Nigerian Experience: Overseas Living and Value Change," a workshop presented at the Seventh Annual SIETAR Conference in Vancouver, B.C., Canada, March 11, 1981.

[24] Most scholars would rate religion as a very significant value for Americans and yet it is ranked very low by these students. The explanations for this misperception are that the majority of students came from northern Nigeria which has a large Muslim population. Religion is much more overtly practiced there than in the U.S. In addition, almost all of these students lived in college dormitories rather than with families where they would likely see Americans practicing their religion, especially if they were in the southern part of the country.

[25] This is what Edward Hall describes as a social action chain. "An action chain is a set sequence of events in which two or more individuals participate. It is reminiscent of a dance that is used as a means of reaching a common goal that can be reached only after, and not before, each link in the chain has been forged." High-context people are more committed to completing action chains. Edward Hall, *Beyond Culture* (Garden City, New York: Anchor Press/Doubleday, 1977), 141.

[26] H. Cleveland, G. Mangone and J. Adams, *The Overseas Americans.* (New York, McGraw-Hill, 1960), 25.

[27] Nancy J. Adler, *International Dimensions of Organizational Behavior, 4th edn.,* US: South-Western/ Thompson Learning, 2002, p. 272.

[28] Barbara Bodine, "Saddam's Siege of Embassy Kuwait: A Personal Journal, 1990." In *Embassies under Siege: Personal Accounts by Diplomats on the Front Line,* Joseph G. Sullivan, ed. Washington: Institute for the Study of Diplomacy, 1995, pp. 130–1.

[29] Mitchell R. Hammer, "The Importance of Cross-Cultural Training in International Business, *SIETAR Communiqué,* 21, no. 2 (February/March 1991), 5–6. Also see, J.S. Black and M. Mendenhall, "Cross-cultural Training and Effectiveness: A Review and a Theoretical Framework for Future Research," *The Academy of Management Review,* Vol. 15, no. 1, January, 1990, 113–136.

[30] Eric Pace, "Oil Boom Spawns Disorder in Isfahan." *New York Times,* September 8, 1974, 43.

[31] Tsila Zalcman, "A Strategic Role for IHR Professions," *Intercultural Management Quarterly,* Vol 2, no. 2, Spring 2001, 4. You can obtain copies of the full report through the Employee Relocation Council at: www.erc.org.

[32] During pre-departure and arrival training programs, when sojourners are asked to list their concerns 3–6 months prior to departure, they list mostly cross-cultural issues and few survival concerns, whereas

immediately upon arrival they list mostly survival concerns. This is also supported by William B. Gudykunst and Mitchell R. Hammer, "Basic Training Design: Approached to Intercultural Training," in the *Handbook of Intercultural Training, Vol. 1,* eds. Dan Landis and Richard W. Brislin (New York: Pergamon Press, 1983), 145.

[33] An excellent paperback book is R.W. Leki, *Travel Wise: How to Be Safe, Savvy and Secure Abroad.* (Boston: Nicholas Brealey/Intercultural Press, 2008). The National Association of Foreign Student Affairs (NAFSA) has a number of on-line articles on health, safety, and security overseas. NAFSA, Interorganizational Task Force on Safety and Responsibility in Study Abroad (2002). *Health, Safety & Security: Sample Web sites of Programs & Institutions* : http://www.nafsa.org/resourcelibrary/default.aspx?id=8295. Also, NAFSA, (2002), *Responsible Study Abroad: Good Practices for Health & Safety:* http://www.nafsa.org/knowledge_community_network.sec/education_abroad_1/developing_and_managing/practice_resources_36/policies/guidelines_for_health/.

[34] David Sarefinas, International SOS, remarks at conference on "Travel Security Programs and Cultural Considerations," organized by Long Island InfraGard, CS Technologies, International SOS, and U.S. Customs and Border Protection, May 15, 2012.

[35] Canadian researcher Hans Selye wrote over 1,000 articles on stress and much of his research focused on the military. He found that sailors who had undergone too many change events in their lives shortly before embarking overseas often ended up in sickbay before their return. It may no difference if the change events were positive or negative.

[36] Richard W. Brislin, *Cross-Cultural Encounters: Face-to-Face Interaction* (NY: Pergamon Press, 1981), 54–63.

[37] Geert Hofstede has identified five "dimensions" which he believes are shared by people in particular cultures. These are similar to what Brislin refers to as "traits." Hofstede, G. (2011). Dimensionalizing Cultures: The Hofstede Model in Context. *Online Readings in Psychology and Culture, Unit 2.* Retrieved from http://scholarworks.gvsu.edu/orpc/vol2/iss1/8.

[38] A high need for individual achievement (N Ach) is inversely related to a high need for affiliation (N Afil), according to David McClelland. As one goes up in a culture, the other goes down. Those with a high N Ach tend to be motivated to work harder if they are rewarded for their individual efforts with greater money or praise. Evidence of what they do is provided by their financial rewards. Those with a high N Afil are more likely to work hard because they value being part of a team and their primary source of gratification comes from their relationships with others. The cultures where McClelland found the highest N Ach included the U.S. and Protestant countries in northern Europe. Those with high N Afil were what Hall would refer to as high-context cultures such as those of Latin American, Africa and Asia. David McClelland, *The Achieving Society* (New York: Free Press, 1961).

[39] Nancy Adler, *International Dimensions of Organizational Behavior: 3rd ed.* (Cincinnati: South-Western College Publishing, 1997), 107, 157.

[40] *Ibid.,* 263.

[41] Mariam Jordan, "Small Group of Husbands Crashes What Was Once Global Wives' Club," *Wall Street Journal,* February 13, 2001.

SECTION V: CULTURE AND IDENTITY

[1] Marshall Singer, *Intercultural Communication: A Perceptual Approach* (Englewood Cliffs, NJ: Prentice-Hall, 1987) and Geert Hofstede and Gert-Jan Hofstede, *Cultures and Organizations: Software of the Mind.* New York: McGraw-Hill U.S.A., 2004.

[2] A handful of psychiatrists have noted this "positive disintegration" with acute schizophrenics or those who go through want is often called a "nervous breakdown." These include Karl Menninger, Harry Stack Sullivan, R.D. Laing and others. See Julian Silverman, "When Schizophrenia Helps," *Psychology Today,* Vol 4, no. 4 (September 1970), 63–65.

[3] For example, a boy who is exceedingly close to his mother during these early years may view his distant father as a rival for her attention. The father may be very rigid and authoritarian and therefore he cannot bond or identify with him. The boy intuitively knows he should not hate his father and feels guilty. According to Freudian theory, he buries or represses his feelings but they control him later in life when he finds that he views all men of authority as a threat because they are representative of his father. Although he is attracted to women who resemble his mother, he has numerous failed relationships with them because none could really replace his mother. This conflict is often referred to as the Oedipal conflict in psychoanalytic literature.

[4] Gail Sheehy believes that they happen about every 7 years when we redefine who we are because of changing roles such as graduating from college, getting married, having a child, and so on. Gail Sheehy, *Passages: Predictable Crises of Adult Life* (New York: E.P. Dutton, 1976).

[5] Erik H. Erikson, *Identity, Youth and Crisis* (New York: Norton, 1968).

[6] There are dozens of books, monographs and articles that have been written about TCKs and the topic is usually featured at professional conferences such as those sponsored by the Intercultural Management Institute (IMI), the Society for International Education, Training and Research (SIETAR), the National Association of Foreign Student Affairs (NAFSA), and Families in Global Transition (FIGT). The Department of State's Overseas Briefing Center (OBC) and the web site TCKWorld.com provide training and information on the TCK phenomenon.

[7] In psychoanalytic theory, this is the time when the struggle between the urges of the *id*, which operates on the pleasure principle, and the restrictions of the *superego*, which operates on the reality principle that there are limits to when and how we receive pleasure. Infants want immediate and unrestricted gratification of their needs and yet when they reach the age of 5 or 6 they find that pleasure if often delayed. The father or authority figure represents the society in terms of what the child "ought" to do (ego ideal) and what happens if the child doesn't behave appropriately (conscience). This struggle may last for many years and is usually resolved when the male child identifies with the father by imitating him and, in turn, develops a conscience.

[8] Double bind theory was first described by Gregory Bateson and his colleagues in the 1960s as an explanation for schizophrenia. An individual must respond to two messages or demands that are in opposition. For example, a child is told to be open and honest and yet when the child expresses his or her anger toward a parent, the parent punishes the child. The child learns to withdraw from the loved ones who create the double bind and eventually develops a pathological or fantasy world. G. Bateson, D.D. Jackson, J. Haley, and J. Weakland, "Towards a Theory of Schizophrenia" in *Behavioral Science,* Vol 1, 1956, 251–264.

[9] Before she died in 2003, Ruth Useem was conducting a study of Adult TCKs (ATCKs) with her husband, John Useem, Ann Baker Cottrell and Kathleen Ann Finn Jordan. This project involved the analysis of nearly 700 responses to a twenty-four page self-administered questionnaire. Respondents ranged in age from 25 to 90 and included men and women. See Kathleen Ann Finn Jordan, "Third Culture Persons," in Gary R. Weaver, ed., *Culture, Communication and Conflict: Readings in Intercultural Relations, revised 2nd edition* (Boston: Pearson, 2000), 232–239. Also see a summary of their research in Carolyn D. Smith, *Strangers at Home: Essays on the Effects of Living Overseas and Coming "Home" to a Strange Land*, (Putnam Valley, NY: Aletheia Publications, 1996).

[10] David Pollock and Ruth Van Reken, *Third Culture Kids: The Experience of Growing up Among Worlds* (Boston: Nicholas Brealey/ Intercultural Press, 1999), 19.

[11] Marshall Singer, *Perception and Identity in Intercultural Communication* (An abridged and revised edition of *International Communication: A Perceptual Approach*) (Boston: Nicholas Brealey/Intercultural Press, 1998).

[12] Kathleen A. Finn Jordan would certainly be one of the most comprehensive scholars to identify common characteristics. Her research spanned many decades.

[13] Momo Kano Podolsky, "Internationally Mobile Children: the Japanese Kikoku-shijo Experience Reconsidered," *Contemporary Society Bulletin* (Kyoto Women's University, 2008), 49–69.

[14] *Ibid.*, 50.

[15] Yasuko Kanno describes the *kikoku-shijo* as a bicultural person who is Japanese on the outside, yet foreign on the inside and speaks better English than Japanese. However she found that the level of English among more recent returnees is steadily decreasing and they have less in-depth understanding of the overseas host culture. Nevertheless, they are bicultural and do feel that they do not fit into any one culture. Yasuko Kanno, "Kikokushijo as Bicultural," *International Journal of Intercultural Relations*, 24 (2000). 362–82.

[16] "The [Korean] government said it will open 26 'preliminary schools' across the country for multi-racial children to teach them the Korean language and culture for six months, before they start regular schooling. This move comes as more Korean men are marrying foreign wives and as more migrant workers live in Korea with their children. According to government statistics, in Seoul alone, more than 68-hundred multicultural students were enrolled in primary and secondary schools last year." Reporter: connie@arirang.co.kr. "Korean Government to Set Up Schools for Multi-Racial Students." *Arirang: Korea for the World,* March 12, 2012.

[17] Many of these findings are found in Kathleen A. Finn Jordan's research. But they are also listed by many other scholars in who have studied the TCK phenomenon such as Ann Baker Cottrell, David Pollock, Ruth E. Van Reken, Ruth Useem, et al. See Ruth E. Van Reken and Paulette M. Bethel, "Third Culture Kids: Prototypes for Understanding Other Cross-Cultural Kids," *Dynamics of Living Among Cultures*, (29 July 2007), 2–3.

[18] Jordan, 234.

[19] According to TCKID, "80% believe they can get along with anybody," but "90% feel 'out of sync' with their peers." "What is a Third Culture Kid? (TCKs)," TCKid.com, 2008. The website TCKID.com provides an opportunity for TCKs to connect with others around the world. It has over 21,000 members.

[20] Nancy J. Adler, "Domestic Multiculturalism: Cross-Cultural Management in the Public Sector," in *Culture, Communication and Conflict: Readings in Intercultural Relations, revised 2nd edition.* ed. Gary R. Weaver, (Boston: Pearson Publishing, 2000), 114–15.

[21] See Ruth E. Van Reken and Paulette Mr. Bethel, "Third Culture Kids: Prototypes for Understanding Other Cross-Cultural Kids," *Dynamics of Living Among Cultures*, (29 July 2007), 2–3.

[22] Arsalan Barmand, "TCKs, MCKS, and the American Phenomenon," (Unpublished Paper), American University, Washington, DC, November 24, 2008, 7.

[23] *Ibid.*, 8.

[24] Gary R. Weaver, with Cord Hart, Mary Nye, Mary Finch and John Picarelli, *Home Invasions & Identity Theft: the Role of Asian Gangs (Monograph)* prepared for The Center for Asian Crime Studies, International Association of Asian Crime Investigators for The County of Orange, California, April 22, 2004.

[25] Peter S. Adler, "Beyond Cultural Identity: Reflections on Cultural and Multicultural Man," in *Culture, Communication and Conflict: Readings in Intercultural Relations, revised 2nd edition*, ed. Gary R. Weaver (Boston: Pearson, 2000), 240–255. Originally published in *Topics in Cultural Learning, vol. 2,* ed. Richard W. Brislin (Honolulu: East-West Center), August 1974, 23–40, Institute of Cultural Learning.

[26] *Ibid.*, 241.

[27] Kazimierz Dabrowski, *Positive Disintegration*, (Boston: Little, Brown, 1964).

[28] Adler, 253.

[29] *Ibid.*, 251.

[30] See Malcolm Gladwell, *Outliers* (New York; Back Bay Books, 2008).

[31] Frederick Nietzsche is often considered a pre-existentialist. He is credited with first using the phrase "becoming" and "unbecoming" was well as developing the contrast between Apollonian and Dionysian thinkers which became central to the writing of anthropologist Ruth Benedict in her famous book *Chrysanthemum and the Sword: Patterns of Japanese Culture*. It was a seminal 1946 study of Japan and America.

[32] The theme of invisibility of black Americans was also basis for the 1952 novel *Invisible Man* by Ralph Ellison. However, Wright's book *The Outsider*, published the following year, is usually considered the first existentialist novel. Wright, who was accused by black novelist James Baldwin of being an "Uncle Tom," actually a superman theory of black Americans which was based upon Nietzsche's superman— one who is aware of the absurdity of the dominant society and its contradictions. This awareness gives him super powers because he can transcend that culture.

[33] See Gary R. Weaver, "Police and the Enemy Image in Black Literature," in *The Police and Society*, Emilio C. Viano and Jeffrey H. Reiman, eds. (Lexington: D.C. Heath and Company, 1975), 139–147.

[34] Obama, Barack, *Dreams From My Father: A Story of Race and Inheritance* (New York: Three Rivers Press, 2004), 51–52.

[35] See Ruth E. Van Reken, "Obama's 'Third Culture' Team," *The Daily Beast*, November 26, 2008.

[36] Jordan notes that TCKs are "perceptive observers" who are "slow to jump in, mapping the territory, collecting information and processing it, and, while doing all that, feeling marginal at the outset of their expose to any new environment, though constructively so." Kathleen A. Finn Jordan, "Third Culture Persons" in *Culture, Communication and Conflict: Readings in Intercultural Relations, revised 2nd edn.*, ed. Gary R. Weaver (Boston: Pearson Publishing, 2000), 233.

[37] Some physical anthropologists have argued that skin color and even body type may be a matter of autoplastic adaptation. For example, it is possible that darker skins protected humans from skin cancer in tropical climates while a body type with greater fat allowed those in northern climates to survive harsh winters.

[38] Edward T. Hall, *Beyond Culture* (Garden City, NY: Anchor Press/Doubleday, 1977), 38.

[39] Margaret Mead, *Culture and Commitment: A study of the Generation Gap* (Garden City, NY: Natural History Press/Doubleday & Company, Inc., 1970),

[40] Jack Newfield, *The Prophetic Minority* (NY: The New American Library, 1966).

[41] Gary R. Weaver, "American Identity Movements: A Cross-Cultural Confrontation," *Intellect* (March 1975), 377–380.

[42] The idea of a people purifying their religious beliefs and beginning anew is often viewed as something found in the New Testament. However this theme is actually found in Jeremiah in the Old Testament.

[43] Robert Wright, "Islamophobia and Homophobia," *New York Times*, October 26, 2010.

SECTION VI: INTERNATIONAL CONFLICT AND INTERCULTURAL RELATIONS

[1] Much of this scholarship focused on the Cold War to explain both American and Soviet foreign policy. Examples of this scholarship includes the writings of Ole R. Holsti and Robert C. Tucker. Ole R. Holsti, "The Belief System and National Images: John Foster Dulles," *Conflict Resolution*, Vol. 6, No. 3 (September 1982), 244–52. Robert C. Tucker, *The Soviet Political Mind: Stalinism and Post-Stalin Change,* (New York: Norton, 1971).

[2] Jerrold M. Post, *Political Paranoia: The Psycho-politics of Hatred,* (Yale, 1997) and *The Psychological Evaluation of Political Leaders, With profiles of Saddam Hussein and Bill Clinton* (University of Michigan Press, 2003).

[3] Marshall Singer, *Intercultural Communication: A Perceptual Approach* (Englewood Cliffs, NJ: Prentice-Hall, 1987).

[4] Boulding was one of the earliest scholars to write about national images and his PhD dissertation was entitled "The Image." His approach is often described as a systems approach or historical sociology. Kenneth E. Boulding, "National Images and International Systems," *Journal of Conflict Resolution* 3, no. 2 (June 1959), 120–131.

[5] Martin Gilens, a Yale political scientist, analyzed the race of people pictured as poor in TV news stories and in photos in *Time*, *Newsweek* and *U.S. News & World Report* between 1988 and 1992 and reported his findings in the spring 1997 issue of *Public Opinion Quarterly*. Blacks comprised about 29 percent

of the nation's poor during this period, but made up 62 percent of the people pictured in news magazine stories about poverty. He found the same pattern on the three major television networks, where 65 percent of the people featured in stories about poverty were black. (Proportionately, poverty affects a higher percentage of the black population. About 29 percent of all blacks live in poverty, compared with about 11 percent of all whites.) Reported in "Unconventional Wisdom: Poverty in Black and White" by Richard Morin, *The Washington Post*, 18 May 1997: (C5).

6 Based upon a study written by sociologists Gary Foster and Richard Hummel in the spring 1997 issue of *Sociological Spectrum* and reported in "Needed: A Hillbilly Anti-Defamation League," by Richard Moring, *The Washington Post*, 4 May 1997, p. C5. Examples of television shows featuring stereotypical hillbillies are "Dukes of Hazzard," "The Beverly Hillbillies," "Green Acres," "Hee-Haw," or more recently, animated cartoons such as "The Simpsons" and "King of the Hill."

7 A brilliant argument for the importance of understanding the intentions of the adversary is given by Robert Jervis, *Perception and Misperception in International Politics*, (Princeton University Press, 1978).

8 *Ibid.*

9 Erich Fromm, *May Man Prevail?* (Garden City, NY: Doubleday & Company, Inc./Anchor, 1961), 19–21.

10 See Adorno, et al., *The Authoritarian Personality*.

11 Greg Braxton and Jane Hall, "Simpson Trial Lifts Ratings of TV Stations," *Los Angeles Times*, February 11, 1995. Retrieved from: http://articles.latimes.com/1995-02-11/news/mn-30652_1_simpson-trial.

12 Meg Greenfield suggested that real-life sagas often replace fictionalized dramas on television. In the past fifty years, the O.J. Simpson and Menendez brothers' trials, the prolonged Clarence Thomas–Anita Hill confrontation in the Senate hearing, and the case of the Air Force Lieutenant Kelly Flinn's adultery and insubordination, the Michael Jackson trial and the trial of his doctor who was accused of medical malpractice and contributing to his death—all are preferred forms of national entertainment. Many of the characters in these incidents, such as lawyers and expert witnesses, have become celebrities in their own right and have made fortunes writing books and appearing in the mass media. "Real-Life Miniseries," *The Washington Post*, 26 May 1997: 19 (A).

13 Jerome D. Frank, "Profile: The Face of the Enemy," *Psychology Today*, November (1968). Also see Sam Keen, "Faces of the Enemy," *Esquire,* February 1984.

14 Urie Bronfenbrenner, "The Mirror Image in Soviet-American Relations: A Social Psychologist's Report," *Journal of Social Issues* 16, no. 3, 1961, 45–56. Also see Ralph R. White, "Empathizing with the Rulers of the USSR," *Political Psychology* 4, no. 1, 1983.

15 Robert Jervis, "Cognitive Dissonance and International Relations," in Gary Weaver, ed., *Culture, Communication and Conflict*, 442–443. Excerpted from Robert Jervis, *Perception and Misperception in International Politics*, Chapter 11, 382–406.

16 Samuel P. Huntington, "The Clash of Civilizations?" *Foreign Affairs*, 72, no. 3 (Summer 1993), 22–49. The title of his books was *The Clash of Civilizations: The Remaking of the New World Order* (NY: Simon and Schuster, 1996).

[17] Joshua S. Goldstein, *Winning the War on War: The Decline of Armed Conflict Worldwide* (NY: Dutton, 2011). Also see Steven Pinker, *The Better Angels of Our Nature: Why Violence Has Declined* (NY: Viking, 2011).

[18] Much of this discussion of intercultural conflict in groups is a modification and excerpt from "The Multicultural Child Care Staff," by Gary R. Weaver, *Child and Youth Care Administrator* (CYCA) (Fall 1988): 49–55.

[19] Edmund Glenn, D. Witmeyer, and K. Stevenson, "The Cultural Styles of Persuasion," *International Journal of Intercultural Relations* 1, (3), 1977: 52–66.

[20] Juan Williams, "Missing the Message," *The Washington Post.* 9 February 1985, 1, 8 (B).

[21] See Thomas Kochman, *Black and White Styles in Conflict* (Chicago: University of Chicago Press, 1981).

[22] R. Dias-Guerrero, *Psychology of the Mexican Culture and Personality* (Austin: University of Texas Press, 1975).

[23] See Gary Weaver, "Law Enforcement in a Culturally Diverse Society," *FBI Law Enforcement Bulletin* 61, (9) (September 1992): 1–7 and "Psychological and Cultural Dimensions of Hostage Negotiation," in *Dynamic Processes of Crisis Negotiation: Theory, Research and Practice*, Randal G. Rogan, Mitchell R. Hammer, and Clinton R. Van Zandt, eds. (Westport, CT: Praeger, 1997), 115–127.

[24] V. Deloria, Jr., and C. M. Lytle, *American Indians, American Justice* (Austin: University of Texas Press, 1983), 111. See also Carol Chiago Lujan, "American Indians, Criminal Justice and Stereotyping," in *Understanding Cultural Diversity*, Elliott Caggins, ed. (Laurel, MD: American Correctional Association, 1993), 56–71.

Copyright Acknowledgments

Grateful acknowledgment is made to the following sources for permission to reprint material copyrighted or controlled by them:

"How Cultures Collide," by Edward and Elizabeth Hall, reprinted from *Psychology Today* (July 1976), by permission of Sussex Publishers.

"The Role of Culture and Perception in Communication," by Marshall R. Singer, reprinted from *Perception & Identity in Intercultural Communication* (1998), by permission of Paul Singer.

Excerpt from *Gemeinschaft and Gesellschaft*, by Ferdinand Tönnies, edited by Marcello Truzzi (1971), by permission of Michigan State University Press.

"Think American, Japanese are Advised," by Doug Struck, reprinted by permission from the *Washington Post*, January 20, 2000.

"Communication Without Words," by Albert Mehrabian, reprinted from *Psychology Today* (September 1968), by permission of Sussex Publishers.

"The Intercultural Meeting," by Gary Althen, reprinted from *National Association of Foreign Students Affairs Newsletter* (November 1981), by permission of NAFSA: Association of International Educators.

"Culture Matters," by Lawrence E. Harrison, reprinted by permission from the *National Interest*, no. 60 (Summer 2000).

"Islamophobia and Homophobia," by Robert Wright, reprinted by permission from the *New York Times*, October 26, 2012.

"Dimensionalizing Cultures: The Hofstede Model in Context," by Geert Hofstede, reprinted from *Online Readings in Psychology and Culture*, edited by Larry Samovar, Richard E. Porter, and Edwin R. McDaniel (2009), by permission of the author.

"Building a 'Cultural Index' to World Airline Safety," by Don Phillips, reprinted by permission from the *Washington Post*, August 21, 1994.

"Why Johnny Can't Disobey," by Sarah J. McCarthy, reprinted from *The Humanist* 5 (September/October 1979), by permission of the author.

"The Obama of 'Dreams,'" by David Ignatius, reprinted by permission from the *Washington Post*, January 17, 2008.

"Foul Shots," by Rogelio R. Gomez, reprinted from the *New York Times Magazine*, October 13, 1991.

"The Face of the Enemy," by Jerome D. Frank, reprinted from *Psychology Today* (November 1968), by permission of Sussex Publishers.

"Faces of the Enemy," by Sam Keen, reprinted from *Esquire* 101 (February 1984), by permission of the author.

"Cognitive Dissonance and International Relations," by Robert Jervis, reprinted from *Perception and Misperception in International Politics* (1976), by permission of Princeton University Press.

"International Negotiation: Cross-Cultural Perception," by Glen Fisher, reprinted from *The Humanist* (November/December 1983), by permission of Lorita Fisher.

Index